An International History of the Recording Industry

An International History of the Recording Industry

Pekka Gronow and Ilpo Saunio

Translated from the Finnish by Christopher Moseley

CASSELL

London and New York

Cassell

Wellington House, 125 Strand, London WC2R 0BB, England
370 Lexington Avenue, New York, NY 10017-6550

First published 1998. Reprinted in paperback 1999

British Library Cataloguing-in-Publication Data

A catalogue record for this book is available from the British Library.

ISBN 0-304-70173-4 (hardback)
      0-304-70590-X (paperback)

Designed and typeset by Ben Cracknell Studios
Printed and bound in Great Britain by Biddles Ltd, Guildford and King's Lynn

Contents

Illustrations

Acknowledgements

While every effort has been made to contact all the holders of copyright in the illustrations and of other material used in this book, it has not always been possible to obtain permission. If an unacknowledged copyright holder wishes to write to the publishers, the publishers will be happy to make acknowledgement in any future edition of this book.

Introduction

This book is basically a translation of *Äänilevyn historia*, published in Finnish in 1990. Actually it has its beginnings in 1970, when we published an earlier version of this book entitled *Äänilevytieto* (The Record Book). During the two decades that passed between these two publications, our knowledge of the history of the gramophone increased tremendously. Yet there is still, to our knowledge, no book in any other language which attempts to cover the world history of the gramophone record in a similar fashion, and we feel justified in presenting this volume for a larger, English-speaking audience. In the process of translation, we have omitted some chapters dealing largely with developments in Finland. We have also added material on developments since 1990, and corrected a few details.

A true international history of the gramophone record would, of course, be a series of books in many volumes. Guy Marco, who published the admirable 910-page *Encyclopedia of Recorded Sound in the United States* in 1993, admits in his preface that he originally set out to write a world encyclopedia of recorded sound, but discovered that it could not be written. One of the problems is that the history of the gramophone in many parts of the world is still not adequately covered.

In your hands, then, is a book that tells the history of the gramophone record in a global perspective. Certainly not every reader's favourite recordings are to be found in this book. Nor have we attempted to write the history of the technology of sound reproduction, even though there is a need for such a book. *An International History of the Recording Industry* is primarily written from the standpoint of cultural history. We are attempting to show how the development of music and technology have together created a new medium, the gramophone record, which has gradually become a leading force in the development of twentieth-century music.

Naturally, we have included those artists who have had a major influence, artistic or commercial, on the development of recordings. To write the history of the gramophone record without mentioning Caruso or Karajan, Louis Armstrong and Elvis Presley, would not be possible. The history of Finnish gramophone recordings is a sub-plot running through the book, generally an insignificant one from the point of view of international developments, but we hope the reader will excuse us for choosing Finland as an example of developments in the smaller European countries. We have tried to broaden our perspective by bringing into this history some of the more exotic countries' recordings. The choice may be just a sample, but we hope that it will indicate, as in the case of Carlos Gardel, for example, how an artist of, originally, purely local influence may take on an international significance.

Artists from the early years of recording are treated in a relatively detailed way. The closer we come to the present day, the more selective we have had to be, and, generally, we have included those artists whose recordings have in some way constituted landmarks in the development of recordings. We believe that there is enough information available elsewhere about record production in recent years. Nevertheless, the history of the gramophone record is not merely the history of a performing art, just as the history of the cinema is not written merely by reference to the actors. The development of recordings has, ultimately, been guided by those who, invisible to the public eye, are responsible for the choice of repertoire and who reconcile the sometimes conflicting claims of art and commerce. The first great figure in the history of recording was Fred Gaisberg, the man who discovered Caruso. An undeniable place in the history of recordings belongs to John Hammond, whose finds included Billie Holiday, Count Basie and Bob Dylan; and to Walter Legge, before whose authority in the studio both Wilhelm Furtwängler and Herbert von Karajan gave way. George Martin was the fifth Beatle.

In writing this book, we have naturally used a large number of sources. We acknowledge a debt of gratitude to Roland Gelatt: *The Fabulous Phonograph*, which appeared in the 1950s, is a book that gets better with age. Friends and colleagues in various archives have generously given of their knowledge. Of special importance were the Library of Congress (Washington), National Sound Archive (London), Arkivet för ljud och bild (Stockholm), the New York Public Library (the Rodgers and Hammerstein archive), and the Finnish Broadcasting Company's gramophone library. Over the years we have been pestering many former and present figures in the Finnish recording industry with questions, and we are especially grateful to Professor Kim Borg, who shared with us his recollections of his years with DGG. Jukka Isopuro and Martti Lahtinen suggested various additions to our text, and Jarmo Santavuori helped us to prepare the translation into print. We cannot list everyone who has assisted us by name, but we thank them all very much.

Pekka Gronow
Ilpo Saunio
Helsinki, March 1997

CHAPTER ONE

The Song of the Future

The Inventor

In 1877 Thomas Alva Edison (1847–1931) discovered how sound could be stored. On 6 December, his assistant, John Kruesi, completed the construction of a 'phonograph', built from plans drawn by Edison. Edison attached a piece of tinfoil around a brass cylinder. Then he spoke into a mouthpiece the immortal words 'Mary had a little lamb', turning the cylinder as he did so. The diaphragm at the end of the mouthpiece began to vibrate from the effect of his voice. A stylus attached to the diaphragm produced indentations in the tinfoil corresponding to the vibrations of the voice. When Edison put the stylus back to its starting point and turned the cylinder, what he had said could be heard, indistinctly, but nevertheless comprehensibly. The new invention was patented immediately, and Edison issued a statement to the North American Review in which he predicted the following applications for his new invention:

1. Letter writing and all kinds of dictation without the aid of a stenographer.
2. Phonographic books, which will speak to blind people without effort on their part.
3. The teaching of elocution.
4. Reproduction of music.
5. The Family Record – a registry of sayings, reminiscences, etc., by members of the family in their own voices, and of the last words of dying persons.
6. Music boxes and toys.
7. Clocks that should announce in articulate speech the time for going home, going to meals, etc.
8. The preservation of languages by exact reproduction of the manner of pronouncing.
9. Educational purposes, such as preserving the explanations made by a teacher . . .
10. Connection with the telephone . . .

Although speaking clocks have remained a rarity, speak-your-weight machines are an everyday phenomenon. Edison predicted with surprising accuracy the possible applications of his invention. But Edison, who was rather unmusical, guessed the possibilities wrongly in some respects. The phonograph, and its successor, the gramophone, became primarily a music box, whereas the other applications of sound recording were eventually transferred to a competing invention, the tape recorder.

At first, the miracle of sound recording itself was enough. In April 1878, in order to exploit the new invention, the Edison Speaking Phonograph Company was founded, a company whose purpose was to demonstrate the phonograph to the public for a fee. Each of the company's agents was given a territory. Their activities were by no means limited to the United States. The phonograph had already been presented in London at a meeting of the Royal Institution in February 1878. In Finland, the first demonstration of the phonograph was given in February 1879. By June of the same year, the invention was being exhibited in Australia.

The demonstration in Finland must have been fairly typical. The man behind it was Edison's Danish agent Louis C. Samson. On 10 February the public could hear and see the phonograph in the auditorium of Helsinki University for a fee of one *markka*. Advertisements promised that the wonderful speaking machine would repeat complete sentences, sing, and play musical instruments. On Sunday, the 16th, the entrance fee was reduced by half, and Samson left Helsinki for a tour of provincial towns.

The Helsinki papers were cautiously favourable. *Uusi Suometar* reported that the sounds heard were somewhat indistinct. But in *Helsingfors Morgonblad*, the popular author Zachris Topelius published a poem in honour of the first phonograph:

> *Ekots rival, ljudets spökande,*
> *härmande, sökande spegeltal!*
> *Du skall sjunga en framtids visa...*

> Rival of echo, a haunting, tempting,
> searching mirror-image of speech!
> You will sing a song of the future...

Sources: Gelatt (1956:10–11); Hirn (1981); Koenigsberg (1969); Read and Welch (1976)

A French Interlude

If Edison had not invented sound recording, someone else would have. The basic knowledge of physics and the mechanical skills necessary for its invention were widespread by the end of the nineteenth century. In 1857 a French scientist named Leon Scott de Martinville had constructed a device called a 'phonautograph', which was used in teaching physics. The machine traced a 'picture' of sound vibrations on smoked glass, but it could not reproduce sound. In April 1877, a few months before Edison, the French poet and amateur scientist Charles Cros (1842–88) deposited with the French Academy of Sciences a description of a device he had designed, which would also record sound. In October the abbé Lenoir published an article in the journal *La Semaine du Clerge*, in which the first known use of the word 'phonograph' occurred as a name for a machine for reproducing sound (the word had previously been used for stenography, among other things).

Cros was a bohemian who preferred Aristide Bruant's cabaret to the research laboratory – unlike Edison, who thought that genius was '99 per cent perspiration and one per cent inspiration'. His imagination flew quickly from one subject to another. In 1869 he had published a study of the theory of colour photography, and in 1874 a volume of poetry. The phonograph took Martinville's idea of the 'phonautograph' one step further. The sound would first be recorded on smoke-blackened glass. 'The wavy and transparent spiral thus obtained is translated by accepted photographic means into a line of similar dimensions traced in relief upon, or carved into, a durable material such as hardened steel,' wrote Cros in the account he submitted to the Academy of Sciences. Although possible in theory, in the 1870s there was no practicable way to make the invention a reality on an industrial scale.

Cros waited in vain for a practical man who would construct a functioning machine based on his idea. Meanwhile the ever-realistic Edison (who is not known to have been aware of Cros's ideas) solved the problem by completely abandoning the pane of smoked glass and indenting the sound vibrations straight onto tinfoil. As the years passed, Cros was enjoying more and more the company of his artistic friends, and died in 1888 from an excess of absinthe. In 1977, when the world was celebrating the centenary of recorded sound, the patriotic French raised their countryman to prominence alongside Edison as the father of the invention. A distinguished French prize for recording bears his name. Nevertheless, it is doubtful that Cros had any practical influence on the development of sound recording.

Source: Marty (1977:14)

Oblivion and Resurgence

Once the initial excitement died down, it became apparent that the phonograph was not of much use. True, it did reproduce sound, but it was difficult to make out speech. When the tinfoil was removed from the machine, it could not be played again, so recordings could not be preserved. The travelling phonograph salesmen moved on to other, more profitable fields. 'It's useless to invent something that can't be sold,' was one of Edison's famous maxims. He soon turned his attention to other things, though he always remembered to tell the press that the phonograph was his favourite invention.

In 1877 Edison was a 30-year-old, self-taught inventor, who had become famous for making improvements in telegraphic equipment. The phonograph was a by-product of this development work. In July 1878 Edison travelled to Wyoming to observe a full solar eclipse, and during the trip he was persuaded to devote all his energy to developing the electric light. The world gained the electric lamp, but, as the recording historian Roland Gelatt remarked, it lost for all time the piano playing of Franz Liszt and the singing of Jenny Lind. Liszt died in 1886 and Lind in 1887, the same year that Edison resumed work on the development of sound recording. In the intervening years, Edison had become a major industrialist. In 1882 alone, he was granted 75 different patents. He contributed to the development of electric lighting, railways, moving pictures and the cement industry.

In 1885 Charles Sumner Tainter and Chichester Bell, the cousin of the inventor of the telephone, Alexander Bell, had patented the 'graphophone'. It was, in fact, Edison's phonograph, with the tinfoil exchanged for a wax cylinder, so that sound could be permanently recorded. The jealous Edison again recalled his own invention, and in 1888 constructed his 'improved phonograph', which was very reminiscent of the 'graphophone'. Patent lawyers were expecting a lively court case, but the Pittsburgh businessman, Jesse Lippincott, solved the dispute by buying both patents and investing more than a million dollars in a company called the North American Phonograph Company, whose purpose was to exploit the invention commercially.

At the end of the nineteenth century huge industrial enterprises were being created on the basis of new inventions. The Singer sewing machine, the Kodak camera, the telephone, wireless telegraphy, the electric light and moving pictures encouraged industrialists to invest their funds in inventions whose future was still uncertain. Lippincott lost a fortune by making a completely wrong assessment of the possibilities of sound recording. He started marketing the device on a large scale to offices and businesses as a dictating machine which would render stenographers redundant. The machine was not yet ready for such a demanding task, and secretaries who were worried about their jobs did their best to emphasize its unreliability. Lippincott was soon on the verge of bankruptcy, and he died a broken man in 1891. Lippincott had paid Edison $435,000 for the patent rights to the phonograph. The ruthless Edison bought the rights back, through brokers, from the bankrupt estate for $135,00. Later, though, he did agree to pay a pension of $250 to Lippincott's widow.

The district representatives, who had been lured by great promises, began to desperately seek new markets for their devices. Phonographs were sold to universities and wealthy private homes. They were placed inside talking dolls. Then someone thought of recording music on a wax cylinder and placing a phonograph in a coin-operated machine. Surprisingly, these first 'jukeboxes', installed in amusement parlours, produced more profit than the equipment hired to offices. From 1889 onwards, both Edison and the Columbia Phonograph Company, Lippincott's agent in Washington, District of Columbia, began regularly producing recorded music cylinders. The recording industry was born.

At that time it was not yet possible to mass-produce cylinders, and the sound reproduction also left much to be desired. Recordings virtually had to be made by hand. Ten phonographs would be placed in front of a loud-voiced singer or a small brass band, and in this way ten recordings would be made of one performance. If there was more demand, the performance would be repeated. Gradually, ways were found of copying the cylinders in small batches, but it was not until the turn of the century that they could be copied industrially. When the Irish-American comedian, Dan Quinn, told *Phonoscope* in 1896 that he had made 15,000

4

recordings in the past month, he had, in fact, had to sing his favourite songs hundreds of times to put them onto wax.

In the mid-1890s, Edison and other people in the business had to admit that the phonograph was just a music box. In 1896 Edison brought onto the market an improved model, the 'Home Phonograph', which cost just $40. Soon Columbia was putting out its own competing model. Edison was offering his machine to 'millions of homes' in his newspaper advertisements, but $40 was still a lot of money. In an America that was becoming prosperous, however, the phonograph soon became widespread, and in 1899 over 150,000 of them were manufactured. In the spring of that year, even in newspapers in Finland, advertisements were appearing that said 'Take an Edison concert machine to the countryside', and by the end of the century phonograph shops had been set up all over the world, as far afield as Egypt and India.

Source: Gelatt (1956); Koenigsberg (1969); Read and Welch (1976)

Herr Doktor Brahms Plays the Piano

In the 1890s the owners of a phonograph could choose from a wide range of recordings including banjo and cornet solos, humorous and sentimental songs and brass band selections. The 'American Symphony Orchestra' had recorded *Yankiana Rag* and *Chiribiribin Waltz*.

However, it was not necessary to purchase recorded music. On the phonograph it was easy to make recordings oneself. It worked like a cassette tape recorder. One could even record on the same cylinders many times. For this reason many recordings never intended for sale have been preserved from the last century. When the 'improved phonograph' came on the market in 1888, Edison's agents rushed to demonstrate the machine to prominent statesmen and artists, whose opinions were then quoted in newspaper advertisements. At the same time, trial recordings were made. In this way such famous people as the German Kaiser, Pope Leo, Florence Nightingale, Gladstone and Bismarck had their voices immortalized. Many of these recordings still exist. The earliest voice recording known to exist is the speech by the Governor-General of Canada, Lord Stanley, opening the Toronto industrial exhibition in September 1888. There are rumours that even older recordings are preserved in the Edison company's archives in New Jersey, but no one has had access to them since the turn of the century.

In December 1889, Edison's agent Theo Wangemann had the opportunity to demonstrate the machine to Johannes Brahms at the latter's home in Vienna. The elderly composer agreed to play his Hungarian dance no. 1. Recently the Austrian Academy of Sciences decided to restore this recording, using the latest digital technology. The original wax cylinder was completely ruined, but from a copy of it made in the 1930s a faint sound of a piano could be heard in addition to the hissing. When the hiss was removed there was not much left; one might imagine oneself eavesdropping on Brahms's playing from behind a closed door. At the beginning one can clearly hear the eager agent introducing 'Herr Doktor

Brahms', and the recording is the only audible relic of the composer, who died in 1897.

Dr Jesse Fewkes, of Harvard University, had more success in 1890. On his new Edison phonograph he recorded the songs and stories of the Passamaquoddy Indians of Maine. In 1977 the Library of Congress reissued one of these recordings, of a snake dance performed by an Indian named Noel Josephs. It is a remarkably well preserved relic of the culture of an extinct people. Fewkes gained plenty of followers among anthropologists and ethnomusicologists, and many folk music archives still have important early collections of cylinder recordings. One of the most famous users of the Edison phonograph was the composer Béla Bartók, who, in 1906, began systematically collecting the folk music of Hungary and neighbouring countries.

The most famous 'home recordings' preserved on wax cylinders are the work of the music librarian at the New York Metropolitan Opera, Lionel Mapleson, who acquired a phonograph for $30 in 1900 for his own amusement. His position offered good opportunities for recording live music, and from 1900 to 1903 he recorded, from the wings of the Metropolitan, performances by Nellie Melba, Emma Calvé, Lillian Nordica, Pol Plançon and Jean de Reszke, to name but a few. De Reszke was one of those legendary operatic stars of the nineteenth century who did not leave his mark on record at all, but from Mapleson's amateur recordings we get at least some aural impression of this tenor of the old school. Mapleson's cylinders are preserved in the collection of the Rodgers and Hammerstein Archives of Recorded Sound at the New York Public Library collection, and in 1985 the library reissued them as a boxed set of six long-playing records.

Twilight of the Phonograph

In 1900 the position of the phonograph was being seriously threatened by Berliner's gramophone, which will be examined in detail in the next chapter. Within a few years most of the producers of recordings had given up cylinders in favour of flat discs. Nonetheless, Edison continued manufacturing cylinders. At the turn of the century he had developed a process whereby unlimited numbers of cylinders could be moulded. However, Edison cylinders were fragile. Their sound reproduction was of good quality, but the volume was lower than on a disc. Edison's blue 'Amberol' cylinders, developed in the second decade of the century, with a playing time of four minutes, represented the acme of sound reproduction in their time. Edison's factories continued making cylinders until the 1920s.

By this time, however, the general public – and the most prominent artists – had already gone over to disc. In the United States the phonograph still had its adherents, but in Europe the cylinders were no longer selling. Fortunately, the company's stores in Antwerp burned down, saving the company heavy losses. Things were not helped by Edison – whose favourite tune was 'I'll take you home, Kathleen' – insisting on having a say in the published repertoire. Edison's cylinders tended to contain performances by less well known artists, and therefore most cylinders made after 1910 are of no particular interest, even to keen collectors.

The old wax cylinder did not disappear completely, however. In the 1920s it was finally ready to fulfil Lippincott's old idea. Phonographs began to be used as dictating machines, and they continued to be used until the 1950s, when they were replaced by tape recorders.

CHAPTER TWO

The Gramophone Conquers the World

The Infancy of the Gramophone

While Edison was developing his improved phonograph, Emile Berliner (1851–1929) was experimenting with the problems of sound recording in Washington. In 1877 he had invented a new telephone transmitter. Now he wanted to invent a better way to capture sound. In 1887 Berliner patented the gramophone.

The basic principle of the gramophone was the same as Edison's phonograph: recording sound mechanically by means of the vibrations of a needle. Berliner's invention, however, differed fundamentally from Edison's idea in two respects. First, the sound vibrations were recorded not on a cylinder but on a flat disc, in the grooves of which the needle vibrated laterally (not vertically as on the phonograph). Secondly, Berliner's intention from the start was to reproduce records industrially, and not be limited to single copies.

Many years passed, however, before the gramophone was ready for operation. Initially Berliner etched sound on a zinc disc, with which he then tried to press the record onto hard rubber, sealing wax and even glass, until finally, in the 1890s, he thought of using shellac, a substance used in making telephone parts. The gramophones themselves left much to be desired. In the first models, the disc was revolved manually by turning a handle, so speeds were unstable. Only when Eldridge Johnson, who managed a machine shop in Camden, New Jersey, designed a reliable motor operated by a spring, for Berliner in 1896, did the gramophone become a viable instrument.

The first records were made in 1889 under licence from Berliner by the toy manufacturers Kämmerer & Reinhardt of Waltershausen, Germany. These 5-inch discs, pressed from rubber or celluloid, and the players designed for them, were on sale for a few years. The most popular discs were The Lord's Prayer and 'Twinkle, twinkle, little star'. In the mid-1890s, at the same time as Edison and Columbia were bringing their new phonographs onto the market, Berliner himself was ready to offer his gramophone records to the American public. The Berliner Gramophone Company's operations had meanwhile moved to Philadelphia. Berliner himself was the company's managing director; the company's first record sales were administered by Alfred Clark, and the recording studio was under the charge of Fred Gaisberg, who, as a schoolboy in Washington, had played the piano on Berliner's first experimental discs. Both of these men came to leave a prominent mark on the history of recording.

At this stage Berliner used 7-inch discs, the same as present-day singles. They had no labels; instead, the name of the piece was etched in the middle of the record, and often it was announced at the beginning of the record also. The sound reproduction was poor, as on the cylinders of the period, but it was possible to copy records more quickly. The Berliner company's annual report for the accounting year 1897/98 states proudly that the company had manufactured 11,211 gramophones and 408,195 records, and was expecting big orders from Europe.

Records from the Berliner era are almost as rare as printed material from the Gutenberg era. There are hardly any great artistic moments to be found on them, but there are attractive examples of popular music from the turn of the century: cornet virtuosi or banjo players, sentimental ballads and dialect comedians. Traces of ragtime influence can be heard in the playing of brass bands. Also on record is Berliner's own composition of a proposed national anthem for the United States.

Sources: Charosh (1995); Gelatt (1956); Read and Welch (1976)

Johnson, Owen and Nipper

Berliner grew up in Germany and lived there until the age of 19. When his first agents, Kämmerer & Reinhardt, had given up marketing records, he started seeking a suitable representative in the Old World. In 1897 he sent the rights to the patent of his gramophone to a lawyer in London named William Barry Owen. At first there seemed to be no buyers, but in May 1898 Owen, together with a local businessman, Trevor Williams, established the Gramophone Company, to which Berliner gave exclusive rights to sell gramophones and records in Europe. Berliner's brother Joseph, who had a telephone factory in Hanover, promised to take care of pressing the records. The record factory was named Deutsche Grammophon. To get the business started on a sound footing, Berliner sent his nephew, Joseph Sanders, and Fred Gaisberg to London as Owen's assistants. Alfred Clark was despatched to Paris to set up a branch there.

Soon Europe turned out to be vital to Berliner, when a series of lawsuits over patents, beginning in 1898, forced him to abandon his business in the United States for two years. The parties in the case were Berliner, Eldridge Johnson, the Columbia company, which made graphophones, and a former sales representative of Berliner's, Frank Seaman. Columbia claimed that Berliner's gramophone infringed a patent granted to Tainter and Bell, which had been taken over by Columbia. Seaman was trying to get possession of the whole Berliner enterprise. When the court reached its verdict in the spring of 1901 and the dust of the great patent battle had settled, both Columbia and Berliner had the right to make records in the United States. The third veteran in the field, Edison, was content to go on making phonograph cylinders and soon after the turn of the century he developed a method of mass-producing cylinders on the same scale as records. On the face of it, Berliner was the victor, but when, on 3 October 1901, a company named the Victor Talking Machine Company was formed in celebration of this victory to carry on the Berliner company's work, it was Eldridge Johnson who became the company's managing director and chief shareholder. Berliner had to be content with a minority holding, but his son Herbert carried on in his father's footsteps by setting up a new record company in Canada.

Eldridge Johnson, who had already been responsible for the manufacture of the Berliner company's gramophones for some years, turned out to be both a better businessman than Berliner and his equal as an inventor. In 1900 he had invented a process whereby the scratchy zinc discs Berliner had used were replaced in recording by wax plates, so-call 'matrices'. The quality of recording improved considerably, and furthermore, from the same original recording one could now make several matrices. As the record industry was internationalized, the significance of this invention became apparent. If copies could be made of matrices, it was possible to press the same records at record factories in different countries simultaneously. Over the years Johnson invented several improvements in recording technology, and under his management the Victor company soon became the United States' leading record company.

In the meantime the Gramophone company had also made a promising start in Europe. The technicians sent by Berliner were making new recordings, and the discs were manufactured in Hanover. William Barry Owen, however, feared that the gramophone record was just a passing fad, and he started looking around for new items to sell. The typewriter seemed more promising to Owen than the gramophone record, and in 1900 the company's name was changed to the Gramophone & Typewriter Co. The kind of typewriter chosen by Owen, however, was a slow, clumsy contraption, on which the letters were selected by revolving a disc, as on some present-day children's typewriters. Financially it was a disaster and Owen was dismissed. He went back to the United States and became a gentleman farmer. The word 'Typewriter' was dropped from the company's name in 1907, and Alfred Clark was invited from Paris to become the new managing director. Owen did, however, leave an indelible stamp on recording history. In 1899 he had seen a painting by the London artist, Francis Barraud, showing a dog listening to an Edison phonograph.

Owen became interested in the picture and promised to buy it if Barraud painted a gramophone in place of the phonograph. This was agreed, and for the price of £50 the painting 'His Master's Voice' became the property of the company. It was typical of Owen's way of doing things that he was content to hang the painting on his office wall. When the far-sighted Eldridge Johnson saw it the following year on his trip to England, he immediately decided to register it as his trademark in the United States. His Master's Voice was an image that appealed to the emotions, and it soon became the symbol for all Victor products. Advertising of consumer goods was burgeoning at that time in the United States, and Johnson believed strongly in the power of publicity. The dog and the gramophone were displayed on an unprecedented scale in full-page advertisements in the *Saturday Evening Post* and other journals with big circulations, and soon they were also on giant illuminated billboards on Broadway in New York. In England the dog and the gramophone did not become a part of the Gramophone company's advertising until 1909. Since the 1920s the company's trademark throughout Europe has been

His Master's Voice, adapted into various languages. The dog's name was Nipper, and he was originally owned by Barraud's brother Mark. Nipper had already died in 1895, so the picture was painted from memory. In 1950 the record company tried to locate Nipper's grave in order to erect a memorial to the dog that had earned them millions, but the spot could no longer be traced with any certainty.

Sources: Chew (1981); Fagan and Moran (1983); Gelatt (1956); Johnson (1975); Read and Welch (1976)

Birth of the International Recording Industry

At the turn of the century colonial power and international trade were flourishing. The newly established record companies were starting their competition to distribute their products throughout the world. Victor had handed over the representation of its products in Europe to the Gramophone Company, and soon the agreement was made more specific, so that the partners shared out territories around the world. Victor got Eastern Asia in addition to North and South America, while the Gramophone Company had the rest of Asia, Africa and Australia, as well as Europe. Local subsidiaries were established in the more important countries, while smaller countries were served by agents.

The ambitious plans for the conquest of the world began to be implemented immediately. Berliner and Johnson sent a group of technicians they had trained to Europe, including the legendary Gaisberg brothers, Fred and Will. Fred Gaisberg (1873–1951) had made his first recordings as a schoolboy in the 1880s in Washington, accompanying singers on Columbia wax cylinders under the name 'Professor Fred Gaisberg', and later he had studied recording technique in Philadelphia under Berliner's tuition. At that time the division of labour in the recording studio was not very highly developed, with the same man often having to do the work of sound recordist, producer and sales representative. The brothers were given the task of conquering new markets for records in the Old World, as well as recording the best-known artists in each country, whose performances would persuade the public to buy gramophones.

The Gaisberg brothers' recording trips at the beginning of the century would seem almost incredible if details of them were not preserved both in the archives of the Gramophone Company (now EMI) and in Fred's memoirs. Within a few years their journeys took them to London, Paris, Milan, Zurich, The Hague, Vienna, Budapest, Brussels, Lvov, Breslau, Königsberg, St Petersburg, Stockholm and Helsinki. Recording equipment was set up in reserved hotel rooms in each case, and singers and players selected by the local agent were each invited to perform in turn. The matrices were sent to the factory on completion, and the recording team would move on to the next city. When the musical centres of Europe had been exhausted, the Gaisbergs were sent to more exotic places. In Kazan, Russia, Fred Gaisberg recorded the music of the Tatars, for the local market. While he was setting up the recording equipment in his room at the Hotel de France in Kazan, the local record dealer Malakapff set off to find performers. The first performer was an accordionist. 'His music haunts me still ... We asked the accordion player if that was the best he could do, and he said it was,' wrote Fred Gaisberg in his diary on 24 June 1901. In Vilnius, famous Jewish cantors were recorded; in Tbilisi, magnificent Georgian choirs. The following autumn he toured India, Burma, Thailand, China and Japan. In Shanghai he had to curtail his recordings on the very first day, as the sound of the Chinese orchestra was too hard on the ears. With the help of a local representative, however, he resumed the next day, and the orchestra was paid a dollar for each piece.

Small streams grew into great rivers. Between 1898 and 1921 the Gramophone Company made about 200,000 different recordings in its hemisphere. The Hanover factory no longer had sufficient capacity, and new factories were built in England, France, Russia, Austria-Hungary, Spain and India. At the same time the Victor company was spreading its activities into the western hemisphere. Few precise figures of record sales have survived from this period. We know that the sales of the Victor Talking Machine Company, representing at least one-third of US sales, increased from 2 million records in 1903 to 18.6 million in 1915. According to official statistics, in 1913 2.7 million records were sold in Argentina and 300,000 in Sweden. It can be estimated that in the early-1910s, world record sales were at least 50 million copies, with Germany, Russia and Great Britain each selling about 10 million records.

Sources: Farrell (1993); Gaisberg (1942); Jones (1985); Kinnear (1994); Moore (1976)

Commercial Wars and Competitors

The flourishing new field was attracting entrepreneurs. In the United States, Victor and Columbia were able, thanks to their patents, to prevent encroachment by competitors until after 1910, but in Europe there were no such obstacles, and soon after the turn of the century local record industries were set up in England, Germany, France and Russia. The more important German companies were soon grouped under the Carl Lindström concern, which made records on such labels as Odeon, Beka, Parlophon, Fonotipia and Jumbo. From a Berlin workshop set up by a Swedish born engineer, Carl Lindström, the company grew into a large concern under the management of Max Strauss. The Lindström conglomerate became a serious competitor for Victor and Gramophone, spreading as far as South America, and on the eve of the First World War it was even establishing a factory in the United States.

In France, the Pathé brothers were becoming prominent figures in the record industry, with interests in the cinema as well. The Frenchmen developed their own competing method of recording, which was a sort of compromise between the Edison and Berliner methods. Pathé records could not be played on an ordinary gramophone, so the owner of a Pathé machine had to remain loyal to the records made by the same firm. These so-called 'vertical-cut' Pathé records were manufactured until the 1920s. The company was especially successful in Russia right up to the revolution, making recordings in all parts of the empire.

After 1910 record production grew so much that the industry suffered from overproduction, and in Germany many of the smaller companies went bankrupt.

The English, French and Germans competed keenly, even for distant markets. When, in 1910, the Gramophone Company issued their first Afghan records, the singer on the records, named Mirabon, was soon gracing the Pathé catalogue as well. There was competition even in the bazaars of Kabul. The gramophone record had become such a cultural factor that the officials were also beginning to turn an eye to the industry. The *Phonographische Zeitschrift* reported from Germany that the police had confiscated cabaret records, because of their unsuitable lyrics. The Russian trade journal *Grammofonnyi Mir* announced that the Holy Synod of the Orthodox Church had forbidden Jews to sell records containing liturgical music. When it came to light that Russian emigrants to the United States had been singing revolutionary songs on record there, the Tsar's police had to step in to censor recordings. In Odessa, a factory owner named Josele Grinschpur began pressing illegal copies of 'Danube Waves' and other popular records, and the record industry demanded stricter measures to punish pirates.

The Angel of Rome

In the early years of recording, virtually anyone could make a record. Emile Berliner himself had sung on them. When, in 1898, Fred Gaisberg arrived in London to set up his recording operations, the first singer he recorded was a barmaid from a nearby public house. Soon, however, record producers realized that to improve the image of records it was necessary to have renowned performers. In early 1902, the Milan agent of the Gramophone Company, William Michaelis, got a tip from a friend serving in the Swiss Guard that Pope Leo XIII would be prepared to commit his voice to disc. Michaelis quickly alerted the Gaisberg brothers, and at the beginning of April a party arrived at the Vatican, where a studio was immediately set up in the Sistine Chapel.

The Father of the Church, who was over 90, cancelled his recording engagement at the last minute, owing to failing health. Nevertheless, the Gaisbergs' journey was not in vain. As a result of it, the Gramophone Company issued a fine series of performances by the choir of the Sistine Chapel. At the same time the last male soprano in the Vatican was preserved on record: Alessandro Moreschi, known as 'The Angel of Rome'.

At one time, male sopranos had an important place in musical history. Singing eunuchs had been admired even in Byzantium. Since the medieval Church had not tolerated female singers, promising choirboys underwent a small operation whereby their voices retained a soft soprano or alto quality to the end of their days. In the early days of opera it was customary for composers to write decorative soprano parts for these *castrati*. In the nineteenth century, women were gradually taking over the soprano roles in opera. The Catholic Church forbade the castrating of singers, but since there was still a demand for male sopranos, new talents were constantly appearing on the scene, all of whom had allegedly been bitten by wild boars when they were little boys. It was not until the end of the last century that public opinion turned against the practice.

Alessandro Moreschi (1858–1922) was the last of the famous *castrati*. He appeared both in the concert hall and as a soloist with the choir of the Sistine

Chapel. His seventeen recordings encompass both religious and secular music. Heard for the first time, Moreschi's renderings of Gounod's *Ave Maria* or Tosti's *Ideale* are amazing experiences. Moreschi sings the *Ave Maria* to violin and piano accompaniment, and his interpretation is not very different from Maria Michailowa's or Nellie Melba's contemporary recordings, which were very popular in their day, but his tone is ethereal, almost angelic.

Leo XIII died in 1903. His voice was recorded on wax cylinder that same year. His successor, Pius X, made it his first task to bring about a great reform in church singing. The Motu Propriu, published on 22 November 1903, brought Gregorian chant back into favour, and purged liturgical music of its romantic influences. The use of *castrati* in church music was finally abolished, though Moreschi was allowed to continue his career until he retired in 1911. His records are the only preserved documents of a singing style that once occupied a central place in the development of opera.

Sources: Gaisberg (1942); Scott (1977)

The Immortal Caruso

It would hardly have occurred to the Gaisbergs that they had rescued for posterity a singing tradition that was vanishing. In recent years it has again become fashionable to play Beethoven on authentic 19th-century instruments, but we are hardly likely to ever hear a real *castrato* on the operatic stage again. But what was of more concern to the Gaisberg brothers as they left the Vatican was that a short circuit in the recording equipment had threatened to set fire to the whole Sistine Chapel. Fortunately the fire was put out without the help of the brigade, and in 1904 the recording team was welcomed back to the Vatican to record the revived Gregorian chant. In April 1902 the Gaisbergs and Michaelis hurried straight to Milan, where the opera season was at its height. Franchetti's brand new opera *Germania* was playing at La Scala, and there was much talk in musical circles of a promising tenor named Enrico Caruso. Caruso (1873–1921) did indeed live up to his prior reputation on the stage in every way, and the recording men rushed to offer him a contract. In 1902 records were hardly more than exclusive toys, whereas successful opera singers were great stars. Caruso could afford to dictate his terms: an unheard-of fee of £100, for an afternoon's work. Gaisberg telegraphed the offer to the head office in London, whence came the immediate reply: 'Fee exorbitant, forbid you to record'. Gaisberg's own weekly wage in 1902 was £12. However, he was so convinced of his find that he decided to defy the decree from head office. Besides, he knew that sales of 2000 records would be enough to recoup the company's investment. On Friday, 11 April, he recorded ten performances by Caruso in his room at the Grand Hotel, Milan, including the aria 'Studenti, udite' from the opera *Germania*. The records sold well, and Caruso became one of the company's most successful singers. The meeting was an important step in Caruso's career. On the strength of the recordings he gained a contract with the Metropolitan Opera, New York, and moved to the United States. There he continued to record for Victor, Gramophone's associate company.

The turn of the century may well be regarded as the golden age of opera. Although comic songs and brass bands sold many more copies than arias, opera was of vital importance to the prestige of the gramophone record. Opera was the art form of the moment; opera singers were admired celebrities. Opera tunes were borrowed into the repertoires of brass bands and street organs. Verdi's *Otello* had had its first night in 1887, Leoncavallo's *Pagliacci* in 1892, Puccini's *La Bohème* was premiered in 1896, *Tosca* in 1900 and *Madama Butterfly* in 1904. With the arrival of the gramophone record they were quite new, and many of the singers who had created the main roles on their first nights were at their peak.

Fred Gaisberg realized that an opera singer's voice, which was trained to carry in large halls without amplification, was ideally suited to the acoustic recording methods of the times. Recording technology from the turn of the century gives only a vague impression of the sound of the violin or the piano, and the recording of large symphony orchestras was only mastered to any tolerable degree over a decade later. The tone of an operatic tenor, on the other hand, was ideal for the capacities of recording technology at that time, and for some reason Caruso's tone in particular was the best possible from the point of view of recording. When Caruso had demonstrated that the gramophone record was able to convey singing in a way that could be taken seriously, opera singers, gramophone records and the buying public soon found each other. By the First World War, practically all the renowned opera singers had made records.

Source: Bolig (1973)

The Age of the Golden Voices

In 1902 Caruso was one of the young lions of Italian opera, whose singing style was viewed with some suspicion by the older cognoscenti. The queen of the sopranos was Adelina Patti (1843–1919) – 30 years older than Caruso – whose performance in *Rigoletto* Verdi himself had thought inexpressibly beautiful. Representing a slightly younger generation, Nellie Melba (1861–1931), a pupil of the famous singing teacher Marchesi, had sung in first performances of works by Verdi, Massenet and Gounod. Both of them made numerous recordings. The leading Italian baritone of the same generation, Mattia Battistini (1856–1928), was also prolifically recorded. This singer, known as the world's best Don Giovanni, was first committed to record in Warsaw in 1902, when he was 46 years old. He was a regular visitor to the studio until 1924.

The most famous tenor of the late nineteenth century, Jean de Reszke (1850–1925), on the other hand, made only two records for the Fonotipia company which have never been found. All that is known is that on 22 April 1905, in Paris, he sang the burial scene from Gounod's *Romeo and Juliet* and the aria 'O souverain' from Massenet's opera *El Cid*, and that the company gave the records the serial numbers 69000 and 69001. De Reszke, who had retired from the opera stage three years before, might not have been satisfied with his ageing voice and may have forbidden them to be issued. Another possible explanation for the disappearance of the records is that they were in the new 14-inch (35-cm) size, which never gained public acceptance despite the efforts of record companies. Among collectors there have been rumours at regular intervals that the records have been located in Paris, or Havana, but so far they have proved to be false. We can, however, hear a snatch of de Reszke's voice on the cylinders recorded by Mapleson at the Metropolitan.

The recordings of these singers of the old school give us an opportunity to get to know the vanished singing ideals of the last century. Singers of the order of Patti and Melba were great stars. Patti, whose real name was Baroness Cederström, was, in a way, a predecessor of Maria Callas. Apart from having an exceptionally wide soprano range and great technical skill – she was called the 'Paganini of Song' – she was a society figure and a diva, about whom countless stories have been told. Patti's debut had been in New York in 1859 as Lucia di Lammermoor, and for about 50 years she was the empress of the concert halls, alongside Jenny Lind. In America her concert fee was $5000 a night, a colossal sum for those days.

It was quite a coup for the Gramophone Company to persuade Patti to record. Patti's main condition for making a recording was that Fred Gaisberg himself be the sound recordist (later singers too, including Beniamino Gigli, would refuse to sing unless Gaisberg was present). Landon Ronald was the accompanist. When the first of fourteen recordings, the aria 'Voi che sapete' from *The Marriage of Figaro*, was recorded at Patti's castle, Craig-y-nos, in Wales, the diva was beside herself with enthusiasm, and when he returned to London, Ronald found a princely gift waiting at his home: a tiepin and cuff links decorated with sapphires and diamonds. The records were released in February 1906 with a great advertising campaign. Advertisements appeared in a total of 200 newspapers. It goes without saying that the records had special 'Patti' labels and were sold at the special price of one guinea. That same year Patti gave her farewell concert.

The recordings by Patti, Melba, Marcella Sembrich, Blanche Marchesi and other singers of the old school, take us back to a time when the stars travelled around the world with twenty or so chests of costumes, when opera was the art of *bel canto* and singers were expected to take considerable liberties in interpreting the composer's score. New trends were already coming to the fore. In Italy, Mascagni's *Cavalleria rusticana* had brought realism to opera. Opera was changing, and much of this change was captured on record as it happened.

Sources: Scott (1977); Steane (1974)

The '*Verismo*' Revolution

'*Verismo*' was a trend that appeared in Italian opera in the 1890s, and its rise coincided more or less with the arrival of the gramophone record. Mascagni's *Cavalleria rusticana* had its premiere in 1890, Leoncavallo's *Pagliacci*, another *verismo* opera, two years later. We can hear Mascagni's first Santuzza, on a recording made in 1903 by Gemma Bellincioni, and a good selection by Puccini's favourite soprano, Gilda dalla Rizza, is also available. There is even an almost complete recording of *Pagliacci* from 1907, conducted by Carlo Sabajno together with the composer.

Verismo was both a philosophical and a musical movement. *Cavalleria* is set in a rural Sicilian village. Santuzza is a pregnant country girl whose boyfriend has abandoned her. The *veristi* were trying to bring ordinary people and everyday life to opera. In their music they aspired to realism by encouraging the singers to use theatrical expression: instead of beautiful singing there were sobbing, spoken lyrics and outbursts of rage.

The most usual objection from its opponents was that *verismo* ruined the singers' voices. Records do indeed lend some support to this claim. These early recordings are often overdramatized, with more acting than music. On her last records, made when she was 39 years old, dalla Rizza's voice had already given out. Like many other new currents in art, *verismo*, in its early stages, was guilty of exaggeration. Thesis and antithesis have led to synthesis. The music of Leoncavallo, Mascagni and their followers has merged into the main current of opera, and the tamed '*verismo*' singing style has become part of the expressive vocabulary of 20th-century opera singers. But without these historic recordings we would not have a perspective on Callas's, Carreras's, or Pavarotti's interpretations of *Cavalleria*.

Source: Scott (1977)

Caruso in New York

Enrico Caruso is the model of a singer who was able to combine the best features of the old and the new styles. One of the consequences of Caruso's first recordings was a contract with the Metropolitan Opera in New York. In 1903 Caruso became an American, like millions of other Italians. He sang at the Metropolitan for 17 seasons, in 622 performances and, in 37 different roles. At the same time he signed a recording contract with the Victor company, and by 1920 he had made over 400 recordings for that company (some of them unissued takes). In the United States Caruso became known as 'the world's greatest singer' and he was also probably the best-selling singer in the early years of recording.

When we look at the growth of Caruso's reputation, it is difficult to distinguish cause and effect. When he came to America Caruso already had an exceptional voice and a superb technique. A contract with the Metropolitan Opera would make a celebrity out of anyone, and in the early years Victor was aiming his records consciously at the wealthy connoisseurs who frequented the 'Met'. Whereas ordinary records cost 85c., Caruso's 'Red Seal' records cost $3. If he sang duets, the price was $4, and if the duet was with Melba it was $5. For the quartet in *Rigoletto*, where Antonio Scotti, Bessie Abbot and Louise Homer were singing with Caruso, the charge was $6, and $7 was charged for the famous sextet in *Lucia di Lammermoor*. That was a week's wages for many Americans at the time. Caruso committed to record many central roles in the operatic repertoire: from *Aida*, *La Bohème*, *Faust*, *Pagliacci*, *Rigoletto* and *Tosca*. His voice was unique, immediately recognizable, and many of his interpretations stand comparison with any present-day recording. Unfortunately, Victor did not have the ambition at the time to put whole operas on record, although several had already been made in Europe. Victor could have recorded *Madama Butterfly* in its entirety with the cast of the sensational production at the Metropolitan Opera, with such singers as Caruso, Farrar, Homer and Scotti. All of them were recording for Victor. Instead we must be satisfied with a few arias.

After 1910, when record sales in the United States were reaching tens of millions, prices dropped. By 1920, however, Caruso's records were still being issued as precious one-sided discs, even though double-sided ones had been the norm since 1908. Caruso's greatest success on record was the famous aria 'Vesti la giubba' from *Pagliacci*, which appears to have sold hundreds of thousands of copies. In addition to operatic arias and classical songs he recorded Neapolitan folk songs, and in 1918 he even recorded the fiercely patriotic American battle song 'Over There'. He died on 1 August 1921 in Naples, his native city. At the time of his last recordings he was already seriously ill, and one can hear from the records how bad his breathing was. Caruso is probably the only singer of the acoustic period whose records have been continuously available to this day, first reissued as 78 r.p.m. pressings, then on LPs in various compilations, and now on CD. In the 1930s there were attempts to improve them by adding a modern orchestra to his voice. Although this was sacrilege to the purists the results were surprisingly good. It is fitting that Caruso's recordings were among the first to be restored with the aid of new digital technology. This technology has provided a rebuttal to his critics, since they have had to concede, having heard the new pressings enhanced by computer, that what was regarded as Caruso's weakness in his day – the shift in his voice in the upper register – was due to resonance in the recording horn and not to any flaw in his singing technique.

Shalyapin

In his book, *The Record of Singing*, Michael Scott has assembled the basic information about the most important singers who made records in the so-called acoustic period before the arrival of the microphone – that is, up to 1925. The book discusses the recordings of about 500 singers. It makes no claims of completeness. For example, only two Finnish singers are mentioned: Aino Ackté, who sang at the Paris Opera, and Alma Fohström, who sang at the Metropolitan, Covent Garden, and the Moscow opera. But a dozen less prominent singers of the Helsinki opera, who also made recordings for the Finnish market, are not included – Ida Ekman, for instance, to whom Sibelius dedicated many of his songs.

Many recordings of the 'golden era' have, over the years, been reissued on CD, although some of them can still only be heard on the original discs or cylinders. Some of the original recordings are extremely expensive rarities, while some were so popular in their day that they can still be had in their original pressings from collectors' auctions for modest sums.

Most of the historically significant vocal recordings, of course, appeared on the major labels. The Gramophone, Victor, Columbia, Pathé and Lindström companies were in prime position when it came to signing up singers of renown. They were able to offer their artists worldwide distribution, so that, for example, the recordings made in Europe for the Gramophone company would be issued in the United States on the Victor label and *vice versa*. Gradually, there appeared on the market small local companies, some of them short-lived, which managed to make significant recordings. In Naples in 1917, the famous tenor, Fernando de Lucia, joined forces with a family friend, a local record dealer who had set up his own label, Phonotype. The main Phonotype artist was de Lucia, and in the course of five years, the company recorded virtually his entire repertoire. These records are extremely rare in their original pressings, but their matrices were found recently in a warehouse in Italy, and a limited edition was pressed from these on vinyl, at 78 r.p.m.

In this case the number of revolutions per minute is purely notional, as Phonotype was even more careless about speeds than some of its contemporaries, and since de Lucia was in the habit of transposing well-known arias according to whim (or the condition of his voice), the listener could be in some difficulty in finding the right speed. This problem applies to some extent to all recordings of this era, and long articles have been devoted to the correct speeds of Caruso's recordings.

Among the vocal recordings of the early years of the century there are even several attempts at recording entire operas. In 1903 Gramophone's Italian branch had begun to assemble abbreviated sets of well-known operas, usually with performers from La Scala. In 1907 an almost complete *Pagliacci* was recorded under the composer's supervision. Handel's *Messiah* was issued in London in 1906 on 25 single-sided discs. In France, in the 1910s, the Pathé company issued the original French version of Donizetti's *Favorite*, a version of *Il trovatore*, which Verdi had arranged for the Paris Opéra, and other similar documents of 19th-century French performance style. The time was not yet ripe for an entire recording of one of Wagner's gigantic operas, but the second act of *Tannhäuser* was recorded in 1909 in the Dresden version, with a cast including Walter Kirchhoff and Anny Krull (who created the role of Elektra in the same year).

There is one name that cannot be omitted from a general presentation of the history of recording and that is the Russian bass, Feodor Shalyapin, who is regarded, along with Caruso and Callas, as one of the three greatest singers of the century. When the gramophone record reached Russia, opera was already flourishing there. This art form, which originated with visiting Italian companies – Tolstoy's *Anna Karenina* contains a delicious description of one of these visits – had taken on a uniquely Slavonic form in the hands of Russian composers and singers. Foreign visitors used to complain that the Russian nobility were spoiling their opera singers with too much applause, excessive appearance fees and over-generous gifts.

As with many other countries, it was the British Gramophone Company that brought the gramophone record to Russia at the end of the last century. Soon there were German, French and domestic competitors. Sales were considerable; the Soviet recording historian, Volkov-Lannit, estimates that in the years after 1910 there were annual record sales of 15,000,000 in Russia. Gypsy choirs, balalaika players and comic singers appeared on record, but here, too, it was the opera singers who gave the record companies an opportunity to increase their prestige.

In 1900, a businessman named Rappaport, who had acted as the Gramophone Company's agent in St Petersburg, set up a luxurious gramophone salon on Nevsky Prospekt, aimed at the very wealthiest customers. Rappaport suggested to Fred Gaisberg, who had come on a recording expedition, that he should record famous opera singers and put a special label on their records. Thus the Gramophone's famous Red Label series was created, on which only the finest – and the most expensive – music appeared. Their partners, Victor, soon borrowed the idea for their Red Seal records. Gaisberg did indeed manage to contract Sobinov, Davidov and other illustrious singers for recording, but a 28-year-old bass from Kazan, a singer in the Imperial Opera who looked like a young Hercules, Feodor Shalyapin, turned down offers to record on two occasions. To this rising star the recording fees being offered at the time meant nothing, but the third time, after protracted, champagne-soaked negotiations, he graciously agreed to record. For his first session, in 1901, Shalyapin recorded, among other items, an aria from *Faust*, two songs by Tchaikovsky and the folk song 'Rise, Red Sun'.

Until then the bass had mainly been offered minor roles in opera. Basses were not expected to have the same artistic skills as tenors. Shalyapin raised the profile of the bass to that of other voices. He was a brilliant singer and a first-class actor – glimpses of this can be seen in Pabst's film, *Don Quijote*, for example. But he had another crucial advantage: he had Russian opera, in which the bass has an imporant role, as his springboard. Shalyapin and Mussorgsky's *Boris Godunov* belong together, and he was a sensational Boris in London in 1913.

Over the years Shalyapin recorded all the important arias for bass from this opera, many of them several times. Shalyapin started his recording career in Russia before the revolution. The recordings he made then were given worldwide distribution by the Gramophone Company and made him just as well known around the world as did his tours. After the revolution Shalyapin stayed for some years in Soviet Russia and gained the title of 'People's Artist', but the financial opportunities offered to him by the Soviet state did not satisfy him. In 1921 he moved first to England and then to the United States, taking with him eight priceless tapestries, which he declared to customs as part of the set for his performances of *Boris Godunov*. He never ceased to be a Russian. He made his favourite recording, 'Song of the Volga Boatmen', as an emigrant in London in 1927, when electrical recording had already begun. He made his last recording of the 'Boatmen' on tour in Japan in 1936, his accompanist being the young Finnish pianist George de Godzinsky.

Source: Borovsky (1988)

Early Instrumental Recordings

The nineteenth century had seen many changes of emphasis within western music. The stress on expressiveness that was so typical of Romanticism elevated the soloist to a star, worshipped by the concert audience. Virtuosi of the calibre of Paganini and Liszt created schools of music whose influence can be felt down to our own day. Paganini, who died in 1840, did not leave any audible documents behind him. The next generation of violinists, however, can be heard on records which, despite their faults, give us a picture of playing styles and musical ideals of the nineteenth century.

The leading violinists of the second half of the nineteenth century were the German Joseph Joachim (1831–1907), and the Spaniard Pablo Sarasate

(1844–1908), a virtuoso of the Paganini school. Carl Flesch, a famous violin teacher, described them as two extremes, between whom can be placed all the violinists in the world. To Flesch, Joachim was the serious, sensitive and profound artist, for whom violin technique was secondary to artistic integrity. The elegant Sarasate, on the other hand, was a perfectionist whose playing was refined down to the last technical detail. We can hear both of them today. Joachim recorded five pieces in 1903, and Sarasate nine sides the following year.

Both masters were already aged when they made records, Joachim being over 70; and the recording technology of the time could not reproduce the sound of the violin in all its richness. Nevertheless, a sympathetic listener can easily detect, behind the surface noise, Sarasate's masterful interpretations of Spanish dances. Joachim's playing, on the other hand, sounds strange on first hearing, in places even faulty and out-of-tune, especially in two of Bach's pieces for solo violin. However, even George Bernard Shaw, who heard Joachim in London in the nineteenth century, was initially surprised by his intonation, which was closer to the old natural scales than the modern, tempered ones. Joachim's playing harks back to the ideals of early nineteenth-century violin playing.

The gramophone record arrived just in time to document the old generation of violin players which was still reigning during the early years of the twentieth century. Eugène Ysaÿe, who had to abandon performing early owing to a serious illness, made a few recordings for Columbia in 1912. Another luminary of the romantic generation of violinists, Leopold Auer, left some recordings behind him as well. Auer was not only a renowned teacher but also a considerable soloist whose interpretation of Tchaikovsky's violin concerto was regarded as unparalleled in its time. Auer's grandiosity and verve are hardly evident in the smaller pieces by Tchaikovsky and Brahms.

However, a new generation of violinists was evolving, some of whose members continued recording even into the LP era. Joseph Szigeti made his debut on record in 1908 for the Gramophone Company, with Bach's prelude in E major from the sixth solo sonata, which Sarasate had also recorded somewhat earlier. This was followed by the variations from Beethoven's *Kreutzer* sonata, the Romance by Rubinstein and Sibelius's *Valse triste*.

Two other names were starting to rise to the fore alongside Szigeti's: those of Mischa Elman and Fritz Kreisler. Both their reputations are largely based on recordings. Elman was famous for his 'golden' violin tone, and Kreisler, who made more records than any other violinist, was the central figure in violin playing for the first four decades of the century, not least because he was as talented a publicist as he was a musician. Their recordings were initially typical of the violin repertoire of the acoustic period: small, sensitive pieces and demonstrative *bravura* numbers, but with the advent of electric recording they came to record the great works of the violin literature as well.

Recording the piano at the beginning of the century was technically even more difficult than recording the violin. Even at their best the results demand a lot of empathy from the listener. Yet the outcome was by no means always bad, and there is much that is worth studying from the early days of piano recording. The earliest important pianist whose playing can be heard on record is Camille Saint-Saëns, who was born in 1835, making him 25 years younger than Chopin. Dozens of renowned pianists who made their debuts in the last century can be heard on record today, giving us a picture of the major currents in 19th-century piano playing and the advent of the modern piano style.

The most famous pianist of the last century was Franz Liszt, whose performances provoked hysteria akin to modern-day pop artists. Women fainted at his concerts, aristocratic ladies would throw him their jewellery and his cigar stubs were collected like holy relics. Liszt was the archetypal Romantic pianist, from whom brilliant technique, dramatic performance and great liberties in interpretation were expected. Piano strings would break when he played his arrangements from Beethoven's and Berlioz's symphonies. Liszt died in 1886 without making any of the kind of wax cylinder recordings that Brahms was to make in 1889. However, his legacy lived on through his students.

Among Liszt's students who made recordings were Arthur Friedheim, Joseph Weiss, Eugen d'Albert and Moriz Rosenthal. Some of these were made after electrical recording came into use, when the sound of the piano could be captured quite satisfactorily. Although no attempts were yet being made to record entire piano concertos, we are able to hear a considerable number of Liszt's smaller works as interpreted by his pupils. One cannot detect a common 'Liszt style' from these records, nor was Liszt a systematic teacher. Perhaps the best picture of him, as interpreted by his students, can be gained from the records made in the 1920s by Emil Sauer, which represent the best aspects of the 19th-century Romantic piano style.

Also important in the history of piano playing is Vladimir de Pachmann, the virtuoso from Odessa who made his debut in 1869. A typical eccentric of the old school, he was christened 'Chopinzee' by one American critic who grew tired of his antics on stage. On record, at least, he was a shameless cheat, skipping over the hard passages and running false notes together. It is hard to believe, on the strength of the records, that he was once regarded as one of the best interpreters of Chopin in his day. Had he already seen his best days when he made his recordings, or has the standard demanded of pianists risen since those days? The first alternative is probably the true one; nevertheless, Pachmann's mazurkas are elegant.

The young and technically brilliant Mark Hambourg began in 1910 by recording a considerably abridged version of Beethoven's *Moonlight* sonata. The Polish pianist, Paderewski, who later became equally famous as a statesman, began his recording career in 1911; it lasted until 1930. Another Pole, Josef Hofmann, whom Harold Schonberg called 'the first great modern pianist', started as early as 1904, but attained perfection only with his famous recordings in the 1930s.

Sources: Creighton (1974); Gelatt (1956); Methuen-Campbell (1984); Schonberg (1987)

Symphonies from Europe

The 1915 Victor catalogue was an imposing volume listing thousands of records. American opera lovers were offered 1200 different selections from 100 operas. The potential buyer interested in symphonic music had much less to choose from.

Under the listing 'Symphonies – excerpts from', only fifteen records were listed. Beethoven was represented by the *andante* from the fifth symphony and *andante molto* from the *Pastoral* symphony, performed by the Victor Concert Orchestra. Tchaikovsky had one record, the *adagio lamentoso* from the sixth symphony, played by Pryors's Band. The only orchestral recording in the catalogue which has lived to this day is an abbreviated version of Bach's double violin concerto, played by Kreisler and Zimbalist. Obviously, the era of orchestral recordings had not yet begun in America.

In planning their repertoire, record producers at the beginning of the century always had to bear in mind the limitations of acoustic recording. Very high or very low sounds could not be captured at all, and soft and loud sounds also caused problems. Brass instruments were desirable, whereas the double bass was completely unviable. Attempts were made to overcome the problems caused by the sensitive sound of the violin by using the so-called 'Stroh violin'. Developed by the London instrument maker Charles Stroh for recording purposes, it was a violin with the soundbox replaced by a diaphragm and a metal trumpet. In the hands of a skilled violinist it could record surprisingly well. The result was, however, that record producers approached orchestral music cautiously, and the first attempts sound unsatisfactory.

The recording of orchestral music began in Europe. In 1905, the La Scala orchestra, conducted by Carlo Sabajno, recorded a number of opera overtures for Gramophone. In 1909 Odeon made history by issuing Tchaikovsky's *Nutcracker Suite* on four double-sided discs, the first recording of an extented work. The following year Gramophone presented an abbreviated version of Grieg's piano concerto, conducted by Landon Ronald. The soloist was Wilhelm Backhaus, and the players were the New Symphony Orchestra. In 1911 Columbia produced Schubert's 'Unfinished' Symphony under the title 'The Finest Orchestral Record Ever Issued'. The symphony was more unfinished than usual, as only about a third of it could be fitted onto the record. Nevertheless, it was the first recording of a symphony, and thousands of copies were sold.

Encouraged by Columbia's success, in 1911 Gramophone issued more orchestral works, such as an abridgement of Sibelius's *Finlandia*, conducted by Landon Ronald. For some reason the English record companies did not take the trouble to sign up Hans Richter, who had been driven from Vienna to Manchester in the years 1900–10 by his bitter competition with Gustav Mahler, and thus the work of this great Wagnerian conductor, who died shortly afterwards, remains unheard. Meanwhile, Odeon was already recording complete Beethoven symphonies in Germany. The fifth appeared anonymously in 1911; the sixth in the following year. But the real breakthrough came in February 1914, when Gramophone released Beethoven's fifth symphony, performed by the Berlin Philharmonic conducted by Arthur Nikisch.

This was a sensation, as Nikisch was, at the time, undoubtedly the world's most outstanding conductor, with a reputation to rival Caruso's or Melba's. At the foundation of the Bayreuth Opera House he played violin under Wagner himself; he had then spent four years in Boston and was now the permanent conductor of the Leipzig Gewandhaus Orchestra and the Berlin Philharmonic. Nikisch had the standing before the First World War that Toscanini and Furtwängler had between the wars. He was said to be mesmeric; able to hypnotize any orchestra into submitting to his will. He was, above all, a magician with tone, to whom emotion and intuition meant most, and he hardly ever conducted the same work twice in the same way.

Unfortunately, the records do not do justice to Nikisch's great skill as a conductor. His Beethoven is spirited and Furtwängler-like, but on the record the sound is dominated by wind instruments, and there are other compromises in the orchestral sound. Toscanini, who heard the recording in 1943, criticized it as a distortion of Nikisch's art, and complained that neither the tempo nor the phrasing corresponded to his memory of Nikisch's concert performance.

It was about 1915 that a conductor became a recording star for the first time, when the English papers began printing pictures of Mr Thomas Beecham and Sir Henry Wood everywhere, with accounts of their latest recordings. The energetic director of Columbia in England, Louis Sterling, had found it a hopeless task to compete with Victor for singing stars, but in the field of orchestral music the curtain had barely gone up. Sterling engaged the young Beecham and Sir Henry Wood, who had become popular through his Promenade Concerts at the Queen's Hall. When *Till Eulenspiegel*, conducted by Wood, appeared in 1916, the advertising men thought up an impressive headline: 'THE APOTHEOSIS OF GENIUS AND ART IN ORCHESTRAL PERFORMANCE AND RECORDING'. The trade press reported that the record achieved a 'phenomenal popularity'.

The Gramophone Company now entered the fray, and the old veteran Sir Landon Ronald returned to the studio, this time with the orchestra of the Royal Albert Hall. Between 1915 and 1925 most major orchestras and conductors active in Germany and in the United Kingdom made recordings. By the mid-1920s, an impressive range of orchestral music was available on recordings, although often in abbreviated form and recorded with relatively primitive technology. Schubert's 'Unfinished' had been recorded seventeen times.

Inspired by the success of their European affiliates, American record companies now became interested. Victor recorded an abbreviated version of Beethoven's fifth symphony played on four double-sided discs. It was released in instalments, so that buyers who had bought the first disc in October 1916 had to wait until October the following year to hear the finale. Willem Mengelberg and the New York Philharmonic recorded Liszt's *Les préludes* in 1923. Leopold Stokowski and the Philadelphia Orchestra recorded Stravinsky's *The Firebird*. But the most ambitious recordings continued to emanate from Germany.

Deutsche Grammophon, which had started as the German subsidiary of the UK Gramophone Company, had got into German hands in the turmoil of the war. It began the 1920s by issuing pirate editions of Caruso's, Scotti's and Melba's Red Seal records, but it was soon brought to account. They no longer had the rights to the English parent company's repertoire or trade marks. On the Polydor label, they now began to issue Wagner records in particular, and on the labels was the guarantee 'Partiturgetreu – Ungekürzt'.

As the culmination of acoustic recording in the twenties, Polydor issued such colossal works as Mahler's second and Bruckner's seventh symphonies, demonstrating how far recording technology had progressed in a quarter of a century, even without the aid of the microphone. The former was conducted on eleven records by Oskar Fried, who later fled to the Soviet Union, driven by the political situation in fact, to the same Tbilisi opera house where Shalyapin's triumphal passage had begun.

Sources: Gelatt (1956); Holmes (1982); Hunt (1995)

The Waltz Dream and the Black Cat

On 30 December 1905 there was a premiere at the Theater an der Wien which went largely unnoticed. The theatre, which had stood empty for a long time, had been hired by the Hungarian Wilhelm Karczag, who had taken the risk of presenting an operetta, *Die lustige Witwe* ('The Merry Widow'), by an unknown young conductor named Franz Lehár. It turned out to be a great success, and on 22 June 1906, Mizzi Günther, the first to play Hanna Glawari, and Louis Treumann, who played Danilo, recorded a number of songs from the operetta for the Gramophone Company, including the famous 'Vilja-Lied'.

Lehár did not, of course, invent operetta; that had been done by Offenbach in Paris half a century earlier. In the 1870s Johann Strauss had developed the Viennese form of operetta, based on a combination of romantic plots, sentimental melodies and waltz rhythms. *Die Fledermaus* (1874) had been a great success, but by the turn of the century audiences were turning to other types of music. With *The Merry Widow*, however, operetta enjoyed a worldwide resurgence. Merry Widow handbags, powders, shoes and so on began to appear for women. Lehár became famous. A month after his next operetta, *Der Graf von Luxemburg* ('The Count of Luxembourg') had its premiere at the same theatre (12 November 1909), the composer himself was asked to conduct the orchestra, while Louise Kartousch and Bernhard Bötel recorded popular duets from the operetta. Viennese operetta had begun its path of conquest, although strictly speaking it was not Viennese at all: the events were usually set in Paris, and the music was Hungarian.

Lehár was followed by Oscar Straus, the composer of the *Waltz Dream* (Ein Walzertraum), and the inventor of the 'rustic operetta', Leo Fall. Paul Lincke conquered Berlin with *Frau Luna*, *Lysistrata* and *Berliner Luft*. The darling of the audiences at Berlin's Metropol theatre was the Viennese actress Fritzi Massary, whose schlagers were also great hits for her record company. The flood of Viennese waltzes which coincided with an increasing demand for recorded music, encouraged Deutsche Grammophon, as early as 1906, to reduce its 7-inch one-sided discs to a price of one German mark, and the larger, 12-inch, double-sided discs to four marks.

The world of Viennese operetta was one of escapism. It became highly popular for at least half a century in theatres of central and eastern Europe and was quite successfully transferred to the medium of sound film. Its influence can be felt on a large proportion 20th-century popular music, in all the hundreds of thousands of songs whose theme is romantic love.

Another form of musical theatre from the same era, which once was hugely popular with audiences and record buyers alike, has not withstood the test of time as well. Towards the end of the nineteenth century there were numerous variety theatres and similar places of amusement in all large European and American cities. In Britain, where they were known as Music Halls, there were, in 1899, 39 such halls in London and 226 in the provinces. Unlike the operetta, the music halls and variety theatres did not present complete musical plays. Instead they mixed musical numbers with other types of entertainment ranging from acrobats to trained animals.

Although many types of music could be included in such programmes, the halls favoured performers who specialized in comic songs. Music-hall songs were often topical, frequently featuring spoken parts. Dialect comedians were popular, and audiences in the provinces laughed at Cockney characters. The accompaniment was usually provided by a pianist or a small orchestra, and the manner of delivery was far more important than sweetness of voice. Many of the songs were in fact brief comic sketches, and the performers were dressed for the part.

Hundreds of music-hall records were issued in Britain before the First World War. They featured well-known performers of the day such as the archetypal Cockney, Albert Chevalier; the Scottish comedian Harry Lauder; the male impersonator, Vesta Tilley; G.H. Elliot, 'The Chocolate-Coloured Coon'; and numerous others. When we browse through old record catalogues, we find similar characters in all European countries. New ideas were gradually disseminated from London, Berlin and Paris to more remote localities such as St Petersburg, Stockholm and Helsinki. In Russia, record buyers laughed at the antics of the comedy team Bim and Bom, while the Swedes loved the dialect songs of *bondekomiker* ('rustic comedians'). Although the songs are written in local languages and dialects and feature references to local happenings, the manner of execution is remarkably similar, and sometimes even the melodies migrate across borders – frequently without any credit to the original composer. Copyright was still in its infancy, and the inventive comedian, J. Alfred Tanner, the best-selling Finnish recording artist of the 1910s, was able to quote freely from such diverse sources as Lincke's 'Berliner Luft' and Berlin's 'Alexander's Ragtime Band'.

Yet another form of turn-of-the-century entertainment deserves mention because of its connection with one of the inventors of sound recording. The father of all the cabarets of Europe was the Chat Noir in Paris, which functioned in Montmartre from 1881 to 1897. The 'Black Cat' was originally a little artists' café on the Boulevard Rochechouart, where poets, painters and singers used to gather and present a programme for their own entertainment. Among its habitués was Charles Cros, whose poem 'Salted herring' was a great success among this coterie. Verlaine praised its 'angelic childishness'. Unlike Edison, Cros did not think to commit his work to record, but we can hear it on record, performed by Cros's good friend, Coquelin the younger, the legendary actor, and recorded in 1903 for the Gramophone Company.

The Chat Noir became the cradle of the modern French *chanson*. Among the regular singers at the Chat were Jules Jouy, Maurice Mac-Nab and Aristide Bruant. Whereas operetta represented escapism, the world-view of the chanson was anarchical and satirical, akin to Dadaism. In the background of most of Bruant's chansons are the slum streets of Paris, and often the hero of the song loses his head on the guillotine at La Roquette prison, which was still in regular use in those days. Jouy and Mac-Nab died before the turn of the century, but Bruant made several records. His voice is just as gloomy as his appearance in the famous poster by Toulouse-Lautrec.

Cabaret never became a form of mass entertainment like the music hall. It was too exclusive, akin in spirit to the forms of modern art that were evolving at the same time. But during its brief existence the Chat Noir became so well known that similar cabarets sprang up all over Europe. In Barcelona the young Pablo Picasso frequented Els Quatre Gats, while Oskar Kokoschka was enjoying himself at the Fledermaus in Vienna. When the first cabaret was founded in Kristiania (Oslo), Norway, in 1912, it was not suprising that it was called the Chat Noir. But it was not until the 1920s that cabaret music began to appear more frequently on records.

Sources: Leimbach (1991); Riess (1966); Rust (1979); Segel (1987)

From Ragtime to Jazz

In New Orleans, in 1907, a cornet player by the name of Buddy Bolden was committed to an asylum, where he died, forgotten, in 1931. In the memoirs of New Orleans musicians, Bolden is a legendary figure, whose band was the first, in the 1890s, to play a new kind of music – jazz – which younger players like King Oliver, Freddie Keppard and Bunk Johnson subsequently developed.

Sadly, we will never be able to hear Bolden playing, although the story goes that his playing was once captured on a wax cylinder. The idea does not seem impossible, because phonographs suitable for the purpose had been sold in their hundreds of thousands in the United States by 1907. However, the recording has never been found. At the beginning of the century, the American record industry was concentrated in New York, and no-one was interested in what was being played in New Orleans. It was not until 1917 that a New Orleans band named the Original Dixieland Jass Band was signed up to play at Reisenweber's restaurant in New York. They had the distinction of making the first jazz records. The 'Dixie Jass Band One-Step', made for the Victor company, sold hundreds of thousands of copies, and it made the new music widely known.

Between 1900 and 1917 a great deal happened in American popular music, and glimpses of this great breakthrough can be gleaned on record. As the century changed, the romantic ballads and European dance tunes had to make way for new trends. In the place of the waltz and the polka came a wave of new dance crazes, whose animal names give some clue to their character: the turkey-trot, the bunny-hug, the foxtrot. Variety artists would paint their faces black and start imitating the vocal characteristics of black singers. Pianists began to develop a new rhythmical style that was given the name 'ragtime'.

At that time it was difficult to record piano solos, and thus the best performances of ragtime are preserved on automatic piano rolls, which, at their best, were able to reproduce even the touch of the original performer. Thus we have a chance to hear Scott Joplin, who died in 1917, performing his own compositions, *Original Rags* and *Maple Leaf Rag* (later transferred onto record). Echoes of ragtime can also be heard in the popular banjo recordings from early in the century. After 1910 the new music was so popular that even European military bands were recording their arrangements of ragtime tunes.

By 1917 ragtime had turned into jazz. Unfortunately, only occasional solitary examples of this development are captured on record, such as (Jim) 'Europe's Society Orchestra' from New York playing a mixture of rags, tangos and waltzes in 1913. We are in the same position as if we were to interpret some great course of historical events in retrospect on the basis of a few faded photographs. Some people argue that the records made by the Original Dixieland Jass Band in 1917 represent some primitive precursor of jazz, while others see it as the flowering of its mature phase. Jazz historians will probably go on disputing forever whether there was any jazz at all before 1917. Hopes of finding Buddy Bolden's cylinder are waning, and even if it were to be found, the natural chemical decomposition of the wax solution in the cylinder would probably render it useless.

Sources: Jasen (1973); Laird (1995); Rust (1978a)

The First World War and its Consequences

When the German authorities threatened to melt down the valuable record matrices of the English-owned Deutsche Grammophon for scrap metal, directors of the company consulted with representatives of the parent company in neutral Holland, and most of them were saved. However, the war broke old trade contacts, and record factories were turned over to munitions work. When the Germans confiscated the Pathé factory in Belgium, a mob burned down the Lindström factory in Paris in revenge. The record industry suffered in other ways too. Will Gaisberg died, in France, on 5 November 1918 as a result of gas poisoning. He had been trying to record, from the trenches, the authentic sound of the front.

The United States, by contrast, had become rich from trade with Europe. She finally joined the war in 1916 and survived with little damage. Wartime rationing prevented enough gramophones and records being made to meet the demand, but production of new records continued. In 1921 the Victor company bought half the shares in its European partner, the Gramophone Company, boosting the impoverished company with new capital.

In 1913 an unprecented dance fever had taken hold of the United States, and everyone wanted to learn new dances. Victor and Columbia turned out huge amounts of dance music: one-steps, two-steps, foxtrots, Boston waltzes and tangos, which had just come into vogue. Columbia advertised its records with the claim that a certain Hepburn Wilson had been dancing to the records in the studio. Victor used the society dance stars Irene and Vernon Castle for the same purpose; they danced without prejudice to the black salon orchestra of James Reese Europe. Castle died in the Air Force in 1918, and in 1939 Fred Astaire and Ginger Rogers filmed the couple's story. For the first time, ordinary people could buy dozens of records at a time.

When rationing ended, with the advent of peace, record sales rose dramatically. Over 100 million records were sold in the United States in 1920. The previous year, the Supreme Court had declared the Victor and Columbia cartel illegal, and dozens of new contenders came onto the scene – so many that in 1922 the industry experienced a wave of bankruptcies that threatened to topple even Columbia. Despite the consequent drop in sales, however, in the mid-1920s, tens of millions of records were sold in the United States, and the record companies were eagerly pursuing the new trends in dance music.

The Original Dixieland Jass Band set in motion the decade which Scott Fitzgerald called the 'jazz age'. It was the age of short skirts, the Charleston, bootleggers and Ford cars. It had very little to do with real jazz, but it was eager to dance to the rhythms of new kinds of dance bands. Popular dance records sold in unprecedented numbers. Ben Selvin's *Dardanella* (1920) sold over 900,000 copies, Paul Whiteman's *Whispering* (1920) over a million. Whiteman's *Three O'clock in the Morning* (1923) eventually sold 1,723,034 copies in five years and became Victor's best-selling record to date.

The First World War revolutionized popular music. In its search for modernity, Europe needed something other than Viennese operettas and music-hall comedians to complement its cult of nudity and its neon-lit realism. Ragtime had created a basis for the new dance music in Europe. In 1918, Paris was full of black army musicians, who were glad to stay on and perform in the city's many nightspots. The Original Dixieland Jazz Band (note the change in spelling!) was invited to England in 1919, and soon there were jazz bands in all major European cities. The famous American evangelist, Billy Sunday, declared that jazz had already caused the fall of half a million girls and would soon bring about the downfall of the nation.

The Creole Jazz Band

There is little disagreement among jazz historians about the claim that jazz was originally created by black American musicians. Yet the first jazz records were made by white musicians. Although some black performers had appeared on records soon after the turn of the century (the first known case seems to be George W. Johnson, who recorded coon songs on cylinders from 1891 to his death in 1903), American record companies were reluctant to record black bands. The first recordings by a black jazz group were made in 1922 for an obscure Los Angeles company, Nordskog, by Kid Ory's band.

It was in Chicago that black musicians were first recorded on a large scale. By the beginning of the 1920s, Chicago had become an important musical centre. Dozens of musicians from New Orleans had moved to the city. The big variety theatres and restaurants were employing both black and white musicians. The places of entertainment in the city's black quarter, the South Side, offered opportunities for jazz musicians and blues singers to perform. In 1923 King Oliver's Creole Jazz Band was the most famous jazz band in the city. Nearly all the members of the band were recent arrivals from New Orleans. The leader himself played the cornet, and the second cornet was blown by the young Louis Armstrong; on clarinet and drums were the famous Dodds brothers, Johnny and Baby.

The recording industry had already discovered Chicago, and major labels had held sessions there. In 1923 the Creole Jazz Band made recordings for as many as four companies. The first were made on 6 April in nearby Richmond, at the Gennett studios. Gennett was owned by the Starr piano factory. It was one of the many new labels that had been set up when demand for records had reached explosive proportions after the end of the war. Since the big names were already on Victor or Columbia, Gennett trawled for its performers among the local talent. The numbers they recorded included *Dippermouth Blues, Canal Street Blues* and *Snake Rag*. They may be seen as a turning point in the development of jazz. The records were made acoustically, and the piano, for instance, can hardly be heard at all. There is still a trace of the jagged rhythms of the Original Dixieland Jazz Band, but the solos of the two cornetists and clarinettist Johnny Dodds take flight in a way that had never before been heard on record, and King Oliver's and Louis Armstrong's shared breaks reveal why the city's young musicians would flock every night to wherever the Creole Jazz Band was playing. The band recorded some numbers several times in the course of the year, and the three versions of *Mabel's Dream* give us an idea of King Oliver's inventiveness.

At the time the records appeared, their sales were only moderate. Today the original pressings of the Creole Jazz Band's records are pearls in any jazz collection. Gennett's marketing was not particularly effective. Only one copy is known to exist of Gennett 5275, *Zulu's Ball*, in its original pressing, and it may well be regarded as the Mona Lisa of the jazz discography. Since the 1940s, King Oliver's records have been repeatedly reissued, and even today one can hear trumpeters who are trying to restore the original sounds of jazz, using King Oliver's records as a model.

Source: Allen and Rust (1958)

Tangos from the Mouth of La Plata

While the first recording technicians were touring the musical centres of Europe, their American counterparts were travelling through South America by ship, train and sometimes even by mule train. In Mexico in 1904, contemporary *corrido* songs were recorded, with guitar accompaniment. Early forms of calypso were recorded in Trinidad. In Cuba, in 1904, the Zonophone company recorded the black cornet player, Pablo Valenzuela's rumba band. Valenzuela was eighteen years older than Buddy Bolden, and in the sound of his cornet there are traces of the lost Afro-American musical sound of the last century.

At the turn of the century, Argentina and Uruguay were rapidly expanding and flourishing countries. Both of them still had a black population originating from the slave era, but a big new wave of immigrants was arriving from Europe, particularly from Italy. Conditions in Buenos Aires and Montevideo at the turn of the century were in many ways similar to those in New Orleans or New York – old money side-by-side with great poverty; famous guest artists from Europe appearing at the opera houses – while in the harbourside taverns and the dance halls of the shanty towns, new musical forms were being born out of the meeting of nationalities.

In the last quarter of the nineteenth century a new form of song and dance developed in Buenos Aires and Montevideo, one whose roots evidently lay among the cities' black populations. The *tango* was also sung to guitar accompaniment, but in the dance halls the tango orchestras came to consist of bandoneon, violin, piano and double bass. The unique sound of the bandoneon gave the tango its special stamp; it differs considerably from its relative, the accordion. The little bandoneon lacks the accordion's strong upper register; on the other hand, its supple bellows provide its capacity for extremely varied rhythms.

The oldest preserved tango compositions date back to the turn of the century, the same period that saw the birth of ragtime in the United States. *El enterriano*, by the black pianist Rosendo Mendizabal, appeared in printed form in 1897; the cabaret singer, Angel Villoldo, recorded his tango *El choclo* in 1906. In 1911, six years before the first jazz record, the first tango orchestras, 'orquestas tipicas', were captured on record. These contemporaries of King Oliver and the Original Dixieland Jass Band are known as 'the old guard' (*la guardia vieja*) in the history of tango. On the records made after about 1910 in Buenos Aires we can hear such legendary bandoneon players as Eduardo Arolas, Juan Bautista Deambroggia and Vicente Greco.

As early as 1907, Villoldo had been performing his exotic songs in the revue theatres of Paris. In 1913 two *tipica* orchestras, complete with dancers, arrived in Paris. Instantly the tango became the fashionable dance of the Parisian salons, and it spread through Europe so quickly that in a few years' time European composers and musicians were producing tangos regularly. Initially the multinational record companies sent their recording technicians to Buenos Aires, or an Argentine artist, such as Villoldo, would perform on one of his tours abroad. The finished records would then be sent to Argentina for sale. In 1909, 880,000 records were sold in Argentina; by the following year the figure was 1,750,000. European and American companies competed with each other for recording trips to Argentina. In 1913, when sales were approaching three million, the German Lindström concern resolved to knock out its American competitors at a stroke and set up its own factory in Buenos Aires to manufacture records for the South American market, thereby speeding up production and lowering costs. Many of the classic tango records of the decade appeared on the *Discos Nacional* label, which Lindström set up together with a local businessman, Max Glucksmann. The best were also issued in Europe on the Beka, Odeon, or some other of Lindström's numerous labels.

The World War briefly cut short the tango's triumphal progress through Europe, but in Argentina the tango continued to develop. In 1920 a young bandoneon player named Osvaldo Fresedo, the Louis Armstrong of the tango, appeared, bringing improvised solos and a freer treatment of rhythm to the tango. The 'new guard' (*la guardia nueva*) came to the fore, bringing with it more complex rhythms and larger orchestras. Soon Argentine musicians were once again finding their way to Europe. In 1925 the violinist Francisco Canaro brought his eight-man *tipica* orchestra to the Florida cabaret in Paris. At the owner's request, they dressed in gaucho clothes. Among the regular customers was a young man named Rudolf Valentino, whose simplified version of the tango soon became the hit of Paris. What followed belongs more to the history of the cinema than of recording.

Source: Åhlén (1984; 1987)

Honolulu Moon

In 1915 a great Panama Pacific Exhibition was held in San Franscico in honour of the recently opened Panama Canal. Among the most popular performers at the exhibition were the hula dancers from Hawaii and the musicians accompanying them; in particular, the guitarists, plucking on instruments laid across their knees, left a lasting impression on the public. Organizers of touring revues rushed to offer tours to the Hawaiian groups, and soon everything Hawaiian was so popular that the tunesmiths of New York were vying with one another to write songs about palm trees, hula girls and the Honolulu moon.

When the old kingdom of Hawaii was annexed to the United States in 1898, the islands' Polynesian culture was already giving way to a new hybrid culture under European influence. The Hawaiians, however, made creative use of the new influences: and so they used a steel bar held in the left hand to produce the distinctive sliding sound characteristic of Hawaiian guitar playing, using a technique possibly learned from Indian farm labourers. They began playing the old hula tunes, European waltzes and new ragtime numbers in this way.

In 1905 the Victor company had been in Hawaii, recording indigenous music for the local market. When the craze for Hawaiian music struck in the 1910s, the Hawaiian guitarists touring the United States began to find themselves in demand in the studios. The most prolific of these was Frank Ferera, a Portuguese-Hawaiian musician who probably recorded for every single American record company in the 1910s and 1920s, under different pseudonyms when necessary. Many of these records are syrupy waltzes, on which the gliding sound of the Hawaiian guitar gives a little extra touch, but the records do also contain some virtuoso guitar duets, the players managing to keep up a hectic ragtime tempo by dexterously moving the steel bar in the left hand from one note to another. The technique of Hawaiian guitar playing was brought to perfection on records made by Sol Hoopii and King Benny Nawahi in the 1920s.

The carefree and adventurous Hawaiian musicians travelled across the United States to its remotest corners, taking in revue theatres and circus companies on the way, leaving waves of admiring young beginners in their wake. The mail-order shops of New York did a brisk business in Hawaiian guitars and textbooks. The results began to appear ten years later, when the first country singers started taking up Hawaiian guitarists as accompanists, and bottleneck guitarists began to appear on blues records.

Meanwhile the bold Hawaiians were touring the Far East and Europe. In 1920 a guitarist named Segis Luavan visited Denmark and Sweden. To judge from the records he made in Sweden on the Ekophon label he was not one of the best. But this visit was not in vain. By the end of the thirties, there were Hawaiian guitarists in most European countries. Yngve Stoor's Hawaiian group was one of Sweden's most popular dance orchestras. In Holland, Bill Buysman led the Kilima Hawaiians. In England, Alfred Randell took the stage name Kealoha Life and became a highly successful steel guitarist with Felix Mendelssohn's Hawaiian Serenaders.

Source: Kanahele (1979)

The Gramophone is Established

The hi-fi buff of today, intent on ensuring perfect sound reproduction, might not be very interested in records made in 1923. All records in those days were made by the acoustic method, and although Columbia did in that year develop a new substance for records that reduced hiss, the records of that era have inevitable shortcomings when heard through modern ears.

In 1923, though, the record industry was optimistic. All of Beethoven's symphonies were available, recorded in full. Wanda Landowska had already begun her series of recordings on the harpsichord. Modern music was now being regularly recorded: Stokowski conducted Stravinsky; Gustav Holst put *The Planets* onto record. Louis Armstrong had just made his first record. Records had been made in just about every country, although most of the more exotic recordings had been rushed back from the factory to their countries of origin. In 1924 the Oxford University Press published *The First Book of the Gramophone Record* by Percy Scholes, in which the critic presented the world's 50 best recordings.

In all the big manufacturing countries there were specialist magazines for the record trade. In Germany the *Phonographische Zeitschrift* had been established in 1900. The leading publication in the field in the United States was *Talking Machine World*; in England, *Talking Machine News*, which had no less than three competitors. The Russian *Grammofonnyi Mir* had published its last issue in 1917, shortly before the revolution.

However, there was no periodical available to the ordinary listener. Compton Mackenzie was an English amateur actor and writer who had become fascinated with recorded music in 1922, when he purchased a new gramophone and an abridged recording of Schumann's piano quintet. In his enthusiasm he bought 1200 records in the space of two months (the bill came to £400), and then decided to set about publishing a journal for like-minded enthusiasts. The first issue of the magazine, *The Gramophone*, appeared in April 1923, with Mackenzie as Editor-in-Chief and his brother-in-law, Christopher Stone, as editor. Its offices were initially at Mackenzie's home in the Channel Islands, but they soon moved to London. The first issue had a print run of 6000. The journal had nothing to do with the English record company of the same name; in a legal case involving the Gramophone Company and the International Talking Machine Company in 1909, the British High Court of Justice had declared the word 'gramophone' a generic term.

The Gramophone is still appearing; it is the world's oldest record magazine still in existence, having warded off competition from many other similar journals, aimed particularly at those interested in classical music and sound recording technology. The establishment of *The Gramophone* was a turning point in the changing relationship between music and sound recording.

Sources: Mackenzie (1955); Wimbush (1973)

A Musical Instrument or Decorative Furniture?

The first record players were extremely primitive in construction. The revolving of the disc was done by a mechanism of springs, the same kind as used in clocks, musical boxes and many toys. The spring was wound by hand. Sound was reproduced by a soundbox, which consisted of a needle attached to a vibrating diaphragm. The needles were usually made of steel, and needed replacing for every playing. The sound created in the soundbox was amplified by a wooden or a metal horn.

There were many advantages in such simplicity. The gramophone did not need electricity or any other external source of power. Since the construction was simple, any faults could easily be rectified. In 1909 the explorer, Ernest Shackleton, took a gramophone with him to the South Pole, and when the horn dropped into a fissure in the polar ice, he improvised a new one out of a used tin can. As a reward he later had the opportunity to record the tale of his adventures for the Gramophone Company. Scott's ill-fated expedition also took a record player with it to the ice caps.

Although the big companies that had developed the record player did try to keep production in their own hands with the aid of patents, soon after the turn of the century numerous factories sprang up, especially in Germany and Switzerland, which made large numbers of cheap gramophones and thus promoted the spread of the invention. Even though the principle of the acoustic record player was simple, many of its details were of great significance for the quality of sound reproduction. The invention of a tone-arm equipped with a joint was a great step forward, as the whole weight of the horn no longer affected the needle. Dozens of different brands of gramophones were available, and the most discerning music lovers would play their records with bamboo needles, which were believed to wear out records less than steel ones. In the early years the inventors' attention was mainly concentrated on the soundbox and the horn, and in the first decade of the century manufacturers were bringing out players equipped with ever-grander horns.

In August 1906 the Victor company presented its new model of gramophone, designed by Eldridge Johnson and differing in appearance from earlier models, called the 'Victrola'. This cabinet model lacked a horn altogether, or rather, it was hidden inside. The cheaper models were simple boxes, in which the turntable was concealed under a cover when the device was not in use. Around 1910 the cheapest Victrola cost only $15 US. A customer who was prepared to pay from $500 to $900 could choose between the Louis XV, Louis XVI, Chippendale, Queen Anne and Gothic styles.

The differences between the cabinet gramophone and the old outside-horn type were not merely aesthetic. The internal horn hidden inside the cabinet offered new acoustic solutions which appreciably improved sound reproduction, although experts claim that they did not surpass the sound of the best outside horns. The more expensive models were equipped with electric motors, so that the music lover no longer needed to resort to muscle power. The Victrola soon found imitators in Europe. The Gramophone Company's 'Grand Sheraton' model came on the market in 1907, and was followed by numerous cabinet models from England, France and Germany. In their operating principles, however, the Victrola and the other cabinet models did not differ essentially from the first record players. Sound reproduction was entirely acoustic, which set limits on volume. This problem was finally solved in the 1920s, when new soundboxes and electric amplifiers were developed.

Before this, however, inventors were offering the public many strange – though mostly short-lived – solutions. In the 'Auxetophone', developed by C.A. Parsons in 1904, compressed air was used to amplify sound. The device was too expensive for domestic use, but some were sold to public venues. The 'Flamephone', which appeared in England at the beginning of the 1920s, used a column of air heated by a gas flame to enhance sound. The record player had to be connected to the gas mains when in use. The German Stollwerck factory, on the other hand, manufactured miniature record players intended for children's rooms; they played records pressed out of chocolate. One of these was, for a long time, in the EMI collection, until it was sold to a private collector in the early 1980s.

By the First World War, tens of millions of record players had been manufactured, from cheap popular players to magnificent salon models. Old record players are collectors' items today. But the modern collector should exercise caution when playing old records; with an arm weight of as much as 100g, an old record player will eat mercilessly into a record, so it is better to use a modern player equipped with a 78 r.p.m. function and a diamond stylus intended for playing old records.

Sources: Baumbach (1981); Chew (1981); Marty (1977)

CHAPTER THREE

The Microphone and Gramophone Fever

The Microphone Rescues the Gramophone Record

Shortly after the turn of the century, practically all manufacturers of recordings had given up the wax cylinder in favour of the disc. Only Edison remained faithful to his own invention. In 1913 he was finally convinced that the phonograph was obsolete, but his reaction was typical: he brought his own 'Edison Diamond Discs' onto the market, which differed in every way from Berliner's. They were a centimetre thick and weighed nearly half a kilogram. They were not made of shellac in the usual way, but of Bakelite, and revolved at 80 r.p.m. The most important difference, though, was that they were not etched horizontally like Berliner's records, but vertically, as on Edison's phonograph cylinders. Of course, a special Edison record player was needed to play them.

The critics were unanimous that the sound reproduction on Edison records was second to none. The Edison company organized 'tone tests' all over America, at which the well-known opera singer, Anna Case, sang behind a curtain, alternately 'live' and from an Edison record. The critics could not detect any difference in the performances. The entire Edison organization was set to work collecting repertoire for the records. Edison signed Alessandro Bonci, Emmy Destinn, Aino Ackté and other famous singers. At a later stage, Rakhmaninov himself was signed up for Edison recordings, and his Edison piano recordings are undeniably among the best of their era from a technical point of view. The Edison record arrived far too late, however. The ordinary American family, which had already acquired an elegant hardwood Victrola for its living room, saw no reason to buy new equipment simply to improve the sound reproduction. All the foremost artists' performances were already available on other companies' records. Besides, the technical quality of Edison records declined during the war years, so that the most important competitive advantage of the new technology was lost. Edison records were still being made long into the 1920s, but their share of the United States market was insignificant, and they never spread to Europe. Nowadays, Edison records are curiosities, and not particularly rare, since many dealers were left with large stocks.

Initially the other record companies paid no attention to old Edison's efforts. With the end of the First World War, record sales in the United States had enjoyed an explosive growth. In 1920, nearly 150 million records were sold there, and dozens of new companies had come onto the market. Victor was still the undisputed market leader, with Columbia a good second.

With the arrival of radio, records found a serious competitor. Record sales experienced a slump, and in 1923 the country's second biggest record company, Columbia, was on the verge of bankruptcy. In Europe, radio made slower inroads, but the record industry was already in a slump as a result of the war. In 1920 Victor had to buy 50 per cent of the shares of its English partner, the Gramophone Company, to put it back on its feet (the shares only returned to British hands in the 1930s). Columbia's British subsidiary became an independent company when a group of English businessmen bought it from its American parent company. In Germany a great redistribution of the record industry was going on as a result of the war. During the war, Deutsche Grammophon had cut its ties with its English parent, and after the war the Gramophone Company could not manage to get it back.

Nipper, the dog, had remained faithful to his master, though, so Deutsche Grammophon had to issue its records on the Polydor and Polyphon labels. To retain its position in central Europe, the Gramophone Company established a new subsidiary in Germany: Electrola. The biggest German record company, Lindström, could not get back on its feet after the war, and eventually the English Columbia company bought it. Things were just as bad elsewhere in Europe. Few records other than the speeches of Lenin and his comrades were made in Soviet Russia after the revolution. Not a single record was made in Finland between 1920 and 1924. Threatened with crisis, the record companies were forced to admit what Edison had said a decade earlier; that sound reproduction on records left a lot to be desired.

Hitherto, records had been recorded acoustically, that is, without a microphone. The singers' and players' sonic energy collected in the recording horn was enough to cut the grooves in a blank wax disc. In the hands of skilled technicians, sometimes unbelievably good results were achieved with this primitive technology, but the method did have its limitations. In 1918, when Victor was advertising records of the Philadelphia Orchestra conducted by Stokowski, the experts noted scornfully that, at most, a third of the members of the orchestra would get close enough to the recording horn for their playing to be captured on record.

The sound quality on the first radio sets, too, was deficient by modern standards, but radio technology did offer new opportunities for recording and reproducing sound. With the aid of microphones and electric amplifiers, the chain of reproduction was dramatically improved, so that the frequency range was considerably expanded, and the dynamics were enhanced. Experiments were done in various parts of the world with making records using microphones; the first known instance was in England in 1919. In 1924 the American company Western Electric, a large manufacturer of electrical goods, demonstrated its new electric recording method to the leaders of the record industry. The real fathers of the invention were two engineers at the company, Joseph Maxfield and H.C. Harrison. Victor, the market leader, immediately bought the rights to the process, but Columbia, which was on the brink of bankruptcy, was not interested. Western Electric was not willing to sell the rights to the Europeans. The company had, however, had some experimental records made using the new process at the Pathé factory in Brooklyn. The manager of the factory, Frank Capps, sent samples of them to his old friend, Louis Sterling, who was the managing director of Columbia's English subsidiary.

The far-sighted Sterling instantly perceived the possibilities for microphone recording. On Boxing Day, 1924, he bought a first-class ticket on a ship to New York; and as soon as he got there he bought the American Columbia company,

Table 3.1 *World Record Sales, 1921–45 (Selected Countries).* (Millions of units sold. For USA, $ value, in millions.)

	USA	UK	Germany	Sweden	South Africa	Colombia
1921	106			0.3	0.2	..
1922	92			0.2	0.2	0.1
1923	79	..		0.2	0.5	0.1
1924	68	24	..	0.3	0.8	0.2
1925	59	..	18	0.3	1.2	0.4
1926	70	..	..	0.5	1.7	0.6
1927	70	..	19	1.0	2.0	0.8
1928	73	33	20	2.1	2.0	1.2
1929	75	..	27	3.0	2.3	1.0
1930	46	59	19	2.4	1.6	0.4
1931	18	..	11	1.6	1.1	0.1
1932	11		10	1.8	0.7	0.1
1933	6		7	1.2	0.8	0.0
1934	7		6	0.9	1.2	0.1
1935	9		3	0.8	1.5	..
1936	11		5	0.9	1.9	
1937	13		8	1.2	2.4	
1938	26		9	1.4	1.9	
1939	44		..	1.3	..	
1940	48		..	..	..	
1941	51					
1942	55					
1943	66					
1944	66					
1945	109					

Source: Gronow, 1996

Note: On the basis of average retail prices, it can be estimated that the number of records sold in the USA was about 140 million copies in 1921, 100 million in 1925, 150 million in 1929 and 25 million in 1935. Other countries from which sales figures are available for this period include Denmark, Norway, Finland, Ireland, Switzerland and Dutch East Indies.

which thus became the subsidiary of its former subsidiary. At the same time he made a deal with Western Electric for the application of the new recording technique.

On the surface, the new microphone-recorded records were no different from their predecessors. Indeed, initially the record companies tried to keep the new invention a secret, because they still had hundreds of thousands of old acoustic records in their warehouses. Playing them on a cheap gramophone, one could hardly detect a difference between them.

Soon, though, sharp-eared music lovers could hear that something crucial had happened – at least by the time Columbia issued its recording of a 5000-strong choir singing *Adeste Fideles*, in June 1925. Recording a huge choir like this by the old method would have been impossible.

Source: Gelatt (1956)

The Boom Period

The new technology brought about a growth in the record industry which was accelerated by the general economic boom. Between 1925 and 1929 record sales increased annually. In 1929 about 150 million records were sold in the United States, and in England and Germany about 30 million each. Even in Finland, annual sales figures of one million were exceeded for the first time.

Statistics for international record sales from these years are scarce, but it is known, for instance, that a million records were sold in Cuba and Colombia in 1929. In Indonesia, then the Dutch East Indies, as many as two million were sold. The end of the 1920s was the period of international gramophone fever, when records were being made at a furious pace. That is why we should look at this period, short though it was, as a separate phase in the history of records.

Electrical recording was quickly adopted all over the world. The last place to adopt it was the Soviet Union, in the mid-thirties; the record industry there had not yet really recovered from the revolution. The change brought with it a 'change of generations' in the industry. Some of the companies established in the early 1920s which did not have the resources to adapt to the new technology now quietly faded from the market. There was speculation in gramophone companies' shares. In 1926 two American banking consortia made Eldridge Johnson a tempting offer: they would buy from Johnson a majority shareholding in Victor for $28 million. In December, Johnson finally concluded the deal and withdrew to retirement. In January 1929, having made a profit the previous year of $7 million, the bankers sold the company to Johnson's arch-foe, RCA, a company which was growing fast thanks to the popularity of radio. Victor now became RCA Victor. Eldridge Johnson suffered from deep depression toward the end of his days.

For the far-sighted director of RCA, David Sarnoff, the purchase of the Victor company was the first step on a road which eventually was to make RCA one of the biggest communications companies in the world. But even though Victor was the undisputed market leader in records, it had many serious competitors in the United States. Apart from its old rival Columbia, there was Brunswick, set up in the 1920s and aiming at the international market; it was signing up famous artists from all spheres of music. In 1924 Brunswick had snapped up Al Jolson from Columbia; for several years he had been one of the company's most popular singers. Brunswick offered Jolson an unprecedented $10,000 per record. The investment paid off; within a couple of years Jolson had become the first singing star of the talking pictures.

Among the medium-sized American record labels there were Gennett, Paramount, Banner, Cameo, Perfect and Grey Gull. They produced hit songs, dance music, hillbilly music, blues, and anything else that was in demand. There were dozens of smaller companies, using the larger ones' studios and presses. Millions of records were sold through discount stores and mail order.

In Europe, the British record industry had already recovered from the damage wrought by the war. In the latter half of the 1920s it dominated a considerable part of the record market of the Old World, as the German record industry continued to struggle with the slump and hyperinflation. The Gramophone Company's trademark 'His Master's Voice', with Nipper the dog, was known everywhere, but Columbia was providing stiff competition. When the Gramophone Company, having lost Deutsche Grammophon in the war, set up the Electrola company in its place to produce 'electric recordings' for the German market, Louis Sterling of Columbia responded by buying a majority shareholding in both the German Lindström concern and the French Pathé company. Both of them also had strong American links. Columbia not only owned the American Columbia company, but it also had the subsidiaries of the Lindström concern in various parts of the world under its control. Again, Victor held 50 per cent of Gramophone shares. Such economic facts as these explain why an artist who recorded for a certain record company in America would appear in Europe on a particular label.

Columbia and His Master's Voice were thus the leading labels in Europe, but by the end of the 1920s they had dozens of larger and smaller competitors. Investors were literally fighting for shares in record companies, and new companies were springing up virtually every month. Some specialized in producing cheap popular records for sale in discount stores. Others were trying to develop new kinds of records. Half a dozen companies – Durium, Filmophone, Phonycord and others – were making paper-thin, transparent flexible discs, which were sold at kiosks and tobacconists. But although these interesting curiosities – from a collector's point of view – were being made, the important artists of the era were still to be found almost exclusively in the catalogues of the big, established companies.

The dance fever that had started in the previous decade was still hot in both the United States and Europe. The record companies responded by producing thousands of dance records – foxtrots, tangos and waltzes. The famous orchestras of the big city hotels and dance halls could be sure of a recording contract, especially if they had performed on the radio as well. But the need for dance music was so great that every record company also had its own studio orchestra, a temporary ensemble which, under the supervision of the company's 'artistic director', would record more dance music, usually in the mornings, when the musicians were free from their regular commitments.

The Finnish-American trumpeter, Sylvester Ahola, was in London at the end of the 1920s, like so many other American musicians swelling the ranks of the city's finer hotel dance bands. Ahola kept notebooks of all his engagements, which give us a unique glimpse of life in London's recording studios at the time. In 1929 he was paying weekly visits to the studio as a member of Bert Ambrose's May Fair Hotel Orchestra. But in June 1929 alone, he was called in for fifteen additional sessions with studio groups such as the Rhythmic Eight, Zonophone Salon Orchestra, the London Orchestra, and Arcadians Dance Orchestra. In the course of one year, he played as a sideman on nearly 1000 recordings, including 'Sweet Sue', 'Softly as in a Morning Sunrise', 'I Kiss Your Hand Madame', 'Vilia' (from *The Merry Widow*), 'I'm Thirsty For Kisses', 'A Dicky Bird Told Me', and 'Sax-appeal Sarah'.

Most of the dance records made in the 1920s were run-of-the-mill, and are not particularly sought-after by collectors nowadays. Yet, compared with the music of the previous decade, the dance records of the twenties are notable for two interesting features. Firstly, as we approach the end of the decade, more and more jazz influences are found on the records. The waltzes and the other older dances are on the wane, the foxtrots take on a new beat, and occasionally there are improvised solos on record. Dance music acted as a stimulus to the spread of jazz, initially in the United States, but soon in Europe as well, where the younger generation of dance musicians, from the mid-twenties onwards, was keen to adopt new influences from America.

Secondly, more and more solo singers were appearing on dance records. In the acoustic period dance music was generally instrumental, because it would have been difficult to record singing with a loud orchestra. Songs were usually recorded with the accompaniment of just a piano or a small group. The microphone changed all that. A soloist singing in a soft, sensitive voice could be recorded just as effectively as a whole dance band. The basic form of the modern pop song – a song performed with dance band accompaniment – had been created. However, some years were to pass before artistic ambition was brought to bear in using the new form.

Exact figures are not available, but it would not be going too far to say that at least three-quarters of the records sold in the second half of the 1920s contained popular songs and dance music. Yet there was room for much else on the records produced in this era. With the boom in the record industry, it re-established the links with distant markets that had been broken by the World War. The first recordings were made in sub-Saharan Africa, and in Australia a local record industry was set up. Production of classical music was also given a new impetus.

Sources: Gelatt (1956); Hill (1993); Jones (1985); Rust and Walker (1973)

The Rise of the Great Conductors

It was natural that microphone recording caused a veritable flood of orchestral recordings, for now, for the first time, a symphony orchestra could really be captured faithfully on record. The first electrical orchestral recording, Saint-Saëns's *Danse macabre*, played by the Philadelphia Orchestra under Stokowski, was issued in the United States in June. This tone poem, which is an acrobatic work full of xylophones and dynamic percussion effects, showed off the possibilities of microphone recording to the full.

Europe followed with only a few months' delay. By the end of the year, Gramophone had issued a complete electrical recording of Tchaikovsky's fourth symphony (on the His Master's Voice label, which had now become the company's main trade mark). But the major companies still had a backlog of earlier material awaiting publication, and, for a time, acoustic and electrical recordings continued to be issued side by side. The centenary of Beethoven's death in 1927 provided record companies with an ideal opportunity to demonstrate the new technology. English Columbia issued all Beethoven's symphonies, the last five conducted by Felix Weingartner, and Columbia issued 29 of Beethoven's works in honour of the occasion, for which 100 records were required. Its competitor, His Master's Voice, only produced 52 Beethoven records.

A year earlier, in Germany, Wilhelm Furtwängler's first record had appeared: Beethoven's fifth symphony. Furtwängler was a subjective artist, who preserved the romantic tradition right into the 1950s. He did not wish to submit to the time limitations that then prevailed, and his artistic ambition drove the directors and technicians of Deutsche Grammophon to their wits' end. It was the practice in those days for large orchestral works to be recorded in sections of three to five minutes, suitable for one side of a 78 r.p.m. record. Furtwängler's first rendering of Beethoven was recorded by the optical (film) method, which was also being tried out in recording studios at the time, but the result was technically meagre. However, by the time he died in 1954, the great Kapellmeister managed to record the 'Fate' symphony a further eight times.

The greatest German composer of the period, Richard Strauss, made a somewhat mechanical-sounding recording of Beethoven's seventh symphony at the same time. Strauss was generally not successful at making recordings, not taking them seriously. Even where he was at his strongest, as a Mozart conductor, he did not manage to leave a convincing impression for posterity.

In the most German sphere of all, however, the first significant inroads were made by English Columbia. In 1927 Sterling sent a party to Bayreuth to record excerpts from Wagner's *Parsifal* and *The Ring of the Nibelung*. The conductors were Karl Munck and Siegfried Wagner. A year later, Columbia engineers travelled to Bayreuth to record almost an entire *Tristan and Isolde*, conducted by Karl Elmendorff. These records, many times reissued, are still highly regarded.

The new technology encouraged the record companies to issue other entire operas. In 1928 Columbia and HMV converged on Milan, where both recorded performances at La Scala. The conductor for Columbia was Molajoli, for HMV Sabajno. Eventually, however, they were forced to give up recording 'live' performances, because there were too many risks involved in recording them before the advent of recording tape. An entire *Tristan and Isolde* went to waste because of coughing in the audience, and a concert recording of the symphony by César Franck had to be aborted when, during a quiet passage, a woman in the front row could clearly be heard whispering to her neighbour, 'A lovely camisole for 11 shillings and sixpence.'

In 1928 Sterling, now the leading figure in the record world, celebrated his fiftieth birthday, and in honour of the occasion he distributed two million dollars among his employees. At the same time he decided to announce a competition to mark the centenary of Schubert's death, the purpose of which was to finish Schubert's 'Unfinished' Symphony. Subsequently, the rules were watered down so that it sufficed to write a symphony in the spirit of Schubert. The first prize was £2000, and it was won by the Swedish composer, Kurt Atterberg. It has been alleged that Atterberg won because he used themes from compositions by members of the jury in his work. The critic, Ernest Newman, later demonstrated that Atterberg had at least quoted from the musical language of each member's homeland: for example, for Aleksandr Glazunov's benefit he borrowed a passage from Stravinsky's *Petrushka*. Atterberg's winning sixth symphony appeared the same year on record, conducted by Sir Thomas Beecham. Later, Atterberg recorded his symphony with the Berlin Philharmonic. Critics called the work a pleasant counterweight to some of the extreme trends of modern music, but later generations have not held the work in very high esteem. Both recordings, however, have been available as LPs. From the record company's point of view the competition served its purpose. It also had other consequences: the Soviet government, for example, had given Glazunov an exit permit. However, he did not make the return journey.

Victor now began its new 'M series' catalogue, the first issue of which was Dvořák's 'New World' symphony, conducted by Stokowski. Before the 78 r.p.m. record lost its importance, over 1000 orchestral recordings had appeared in this series, planned by the head of Victor's classical department, Charles O'Connell; in terms of sound quality they are among the best achievements of the electrically-recorded 78 r.p.m. record. The most impressive record of the early period must surely be Stokowski's orchestral arrangement of Bach's toccata and fugue in D minor, from 1928. This was microphone recording at its best and most attractive. Credit is due not only to Victor's engineers, but also to the excellent recording venue, the Philadelphia Academy of Music; to the orchestra, whose playing at the time could hardly be surpassed in warmth and brilliance; and to the conductor, who was interested in the problems of sound reproduction. Stokowski became the first recording conductor to have a broad popular appeal, and with the advent of the film soundtrack he also became its great star. Stokowski did not even hesitate to conduct an orchestra with Mickey Mouse in an animated film by Walt Disney. In advertisements in the 1920s he was described as 'the man with the brow of a dreamer, the gaze of a genius and the commanding mouth of a dictator'. However, the myth that took shape around Stokowski was bigger than the man himself. Stokowski left the Philadelphia Orchestra in 1941. Later, when the entire recorded repertoire was being reissued on LP, the big companies hardly even noticed Stokowski.

Stokowski represented an American ideal of beauty; a certain new, many-layered aesthetic ideal, the lower layers of which consisted of cars and chrome, Coca-Cola and the toothpaste smile, along with the Cubism of the skyscraper. On its upper echelons were Horowitz, Heifetz, Stokowski and Toscanini.

Arturo Toscanini did have reason to lay claim to the mantle of Greatest Conductor in the New World. After Nikisch's death, only Furtwängler, and perhaps later Koussevitzky, could compete with him for the crown among orchestral conductors. Toscanini had begun his recording career in 1920 in New York with the orchestra of La Scala. In the 1920s he recorded three times with the New York Philharmonic, but was never satisfied with the results, and withdrew into silence for years. It was only in the 1930s that he really made his mark on recording history.

The rival to Stokowski's Philadelphia Orchestra at the time was the Boston Symphony Orchestra, which was conducted by Serge Koussevitzky from 1924 right up to his death in 1951. Koussevitzky was above all a colourist and a wizard of the orchestra, a sensual and dramatic conductor who was especially suited to the works of French and Russian composers. In fact, his recording career began in 1928 with *Petrushka*. Koussevitzky had also known Sibelius since 1905, when they had met in Finland. He introduced the music of Sibelius to America and subsequently recorded his second and fifth symphonies.

Sources: Gelatt (1956); Holmes (1982); Miller, Boar and Lowe (1982)

Instrumental Soloists

Whereas, thanks to microphone recording, orchestral music could now be heard on record in all its magnificence, the effect of electric recording on vocal music was nowhere near as dramatic. In the first place, the old recording method had captured singing quite satisfactorily. In the second, the art of singing was at a low point in the 1920s. There were plenty of good singers in the world, and they were making records, but in the twenties there were few really great singing personalities. Not until the following decade would this situation alter.

On the other hand, there was a surfeit of instrumental soloists in the twenties. In this field the new recording technology quickly proved its worth. Rakhmaninov's and Kreisler's playing could now be captured in its full brilliance, and even as delicate an instrument as the flute could be committed to record successfully. The record companies, which in the acoustic period had contented themselves with recording mostly the pianists' and violinists' favourite little pieces, now dared to put out great concertos and sonatas as interpreted by the foremost artists of the age.

By the end of the decade, Berlin had become the real Mecca of the musical world, and its artists were competed for not only by the Germans but by both of the leading English record companies. Bronisław Hubermann recorded Tchaikovsky's violin concerto for Columbia; it is regarded not only as technically one the best-recorded orchestral works in Europe in the twenties, but also as one of the best recordings of Tchaikovsky's violin concerto ever made.

Hubermann was a charismatic interpreter, and in the firmness of his artistic convictions was comparable to the masters of the piano, Rakhmaninov and Hofmann. Hubermann was a child prodigy, who began his concert career at the age of seven. Brahms greatly admired the performance of his violin concerto by Hubermann. Many of those who heard Hubermann's concerts called him a superman, who had both a staggering interpretative ability and faultless technique.

In 1927 Hubermann, Casals and Ignaz Friedman gave several concerts in Vienna, at which they played all Beethoven's piano trios, among other pieces. Resulting from this period is Hubermann's and Friedman's recording for Odeon of Beethoven's *Kreutzer* sonata, which may, even today, be regarded as exemplary.

Their interpretation of the *Kreutzer* sonata is marked by fiery temperament, bold emphasis, rapid tempos and a Gypsy-like sense of rhythm.

Fritz Kreisler had made dozens of records of small pieces during the acoustic era, but of the great works of the violin literature he had only recorded Bach's concerto in D minor for two violins, on which the second violin part was played by Efrem Zimbalist, a pupil of Auer. When, in 1926, HMV recorded Beethoven's violin concerto with Kreisler, Columbia rushed to put out Joseph Szigeti's interpretation of the same work. Kreisler's performance, though, with its elegant Viennese lyricism, became the definitive reading of the work.

Kreisler made many more recordings in the 1920s and 1930s, the most significant of which may be Mendelssohn's violin concerto (1935) and Brahms's violin concerto (1936). In 1936 he made another recording of Beethoven's violin concerto with Barbirolli (the conductor on the previous version had been Leo Blech). With Franz Rupp, Kreisler recorded all of Beethoven's violin sonatas in the mid-1930s.

It was in the 1920s, in Berlin, that the career of the child prodigy Yehudi Menuhin took off. When, in 1929, he performed Beethoven's and Brahms's violin concertos at a concert by the Berlin Philharmonic under the direction of Bruno Walter, it is said that Albert Einstein, then a professor in Germany, came to meet the 13-year-old virtuoso and said the famous words: 'Today you have demonstrated that Jehovah exists.' Menuhin's first record appeared in 1928, and in 1929 he was already recording Bach's solo violin sonata in C major.

Among the masters of the piano, Moriz Rosenthal and Leopold Godowsky made some notable recordings around 1930. Of all Liszt's pupils, Rosenthal's playing is said to have been most reminiscent of his teacher's style. Rosenthal recorded Chopin's mazurkas, waltzes and études, as well as a splendid rendering of Liszt's second Hungarian rhapsody. His masterpiece was Chopin's E minor piano concerto, recorded in Berlin in 1930.

Godowsky developed a technique which is regarded as supreme. Few pianists have been able to play all his arrangements of Chopin's études – it is a pity that Godowsky himself never recorded them. The degree of difficulty in the arrangements is shown by the fact that in the last, unpublished (53rd) étude the pianist must play all three of Chopin's études in A minor at once.

The arrival of the microphone also brought recordings of chamber music to the catalogue, notably those by Alfred Cortot, Jacques Thibaud and Pablo Casals, each acknowledged artists in their own right. Jacques Thibaud was a Gallic man of the world and the most French of French violinists. With Cortot he made several significant recordings, including Debussy's violin sonata and Franck's sonata in A major. In 1928 Cortot made a remarkable recording with Landon Ronald of Schumann's piano concerto. Later, in the 1930s, he recorded nearly all of Chopin's piano works, Schumann's major pieces, Liszt's sonata in B minor as well as some Debussy and Ravel.

Casals was one of the most remarkable cellists of all time, whose recordings of Bach's series of works for solo cello became famous. He was also a distinguished orchestral conductor. Casals conducted his own orchestra in Barcelona for almost twenty years, performing such great works as Haydn's *The Creation*, Beethoven's *Christ on the Mount of Olives*, Schubert's E major mass and Liszt's *Faust* symphony. However, of the performances by the Pau Casals Orquesta of Barcelona, only Thibaud's and Casals's performance of the Brahms's double concerto in 1929, conducted by Cortot, has been preserved on record.

Even before the First World War these three masters were performing chamber music together, but it was difficult to record it using the technology of the time. By the advent of electric recording, their playing having been perfected, they played Schubert's B flat major piano trio, in October 1926, at the Gramophone studio in Hayes, and, in 1928, they made their famous recording of Beethoven's *Archduke* trio, which is still unparalleled in some respects. They also recorded works by Haydn, Mendelssohn and Schumann before disbanding in the 1930s.

Source: Hamilton (1982)

A Ukrainian Wedding in America

At the beginning of the century, 13.5 per cent of the people of the United States were émigré. There were over 700 foreign-language dailies or weeklies in the nation with a total circulation exceeding five million. While the Gramophone Company's agents were busy touring Europe and Asia seeking local artists, the talent scouts of Victor and Columbia were rounding up immigrant artists in New York to provide recordings for their 'foreign-speaking' customers, as they were called.

At first, the companies were satisfied with national anthems and other well-known songs from various European countries, accompanied by studio orchestras. Gradually, their repertoire grew to include Finnish accordionists, Italian bagpipe players, Jewish *klezmer* bands, Chinese theatrical troupes and many other types of musicians. In many cases the companies were able to sell these recordings to their European affiliates in exchange for European recordings which were in demand in the US.

In 1925, Myron Surmach, the owner of a Ukrainian book and music store on New York's 11th Street, complained to OKeh's sales representatives that their Ukrainian records did not satisfy his customers. Surmach recommended them Pawlo (Paul) Humeniuk, a Galician fiddler who had become popular among New York's Ukrainian community, and promised to place an order for his records. Humeniuk's first record, featuring two *kolomyjkas* (instrumental dance numbers), was reasonably successful. His next record, made in April 1926 for Columbia, was 'Ukrainske Wesilia' (Ukrainian Wedding). Recorded on two sides of a 12-inch disc, it played for nearly ten minutes. It consisted of songs, dances and brief skits describing a typical Ukrainian country wedding. The group consisted of two singers, violin, guitar, tambourine and drum. Humeniuk played in a traditional style which appealed to Ukrainian-Americans, many of whom had only recently left their native villages. The record was surprisingly successful, and sold tens of thousands of copies not only to Ukrainians, but to Poles and Slovaks as well.

Humeniuk made more than a hundred recordings for Columbia. In addition to dozens of *kolomyjkas*, polkas and comic songs, he repeated his original success with *A Ukrainian Wedding in America*, and other similar descriptive records. He continued recording regularly until 1940. His success apparently encouraged record companies to issue more traditional-sounding music in their 'foreign' catalogues.

During the first quarter of the century, the companies had offered Irish-American buyers mainly sentimental ballads about the mother left in old Ireland. In 1925 Columbia inaugurated a new Irish 33000–F series with the traditional fiddling of Frank Quinn, a New York policeman who was well known in Irish-American circles. During the next decade, while relatively few recordings were being made in Ireland, Columbia and other American companies issued several hundred recordings of traditional Irish music. The most influential of them were probably the recordings made by three fiddlers from County Sligo: Michael Coleman, James Morrison and Paddy Killoran. Through their recordings, the Sligo style came to dominate Irish traditional music both in America and in the old country.

During the 78 r.p.m. era, American record companies issued thousands of records for the immigrant market. Some of them are just conventional renditions of well-known popular songs and semi-classical numbers, but there is a surprising amount of traditional music from Europe and the Near East. At a time when little traditional folk music was being recorded in Europe, recent immigrants from the rural parts of Europe had acquired enough wealth to buy a Victrola, and recordings of their favourite music. Even types of traditional music which were hardly ever recorded commercially in Europe can be found on these 'foreign-language' records. Until very recently, these recordings have been almost completely unknown outside a small circle of collectors, but good examples of them are now available on CD reissues.

Sources: Gronow (1976, 1979, 1982); Spottswood (1990)

Race Records

By the 1920s, American record companies had made records for every immigrant group, from Albanians to Icelanders. Yet, although there were millions of Negroes in the United States, black music had not been recorded more than occasionally, and when it had, it was mostly in 'refined' versions for a white audience. There were several reasons for this. The Negroes, mostly poor, did not constitute a significant market, and doing business with blacks was not thought proper, due to the long tradition of racial segregation. In 1916, the *Chicago Defender*, a weekly newspaper that had a quarter of a million readers in black communities, appealed to record companies to have 'records of the race's great artists placed on the market', but at the time nothing came of it.

The manager of the OKeh company in New York, Otto Heineman, was a German immigrant who had begun his career with the Lindström concern. He suspected that the large black minority in the city was a potential source of custom. Harlem, in New York, was becoming a popular entertainment centre, with people coming from far and wide to its nightclubs and restaurants. In February 1920, OKeh invited the popular black singer, Mamie Smith, to its studio, and 'That Thing Called Love' was a moderate hit. 'Crazy Blues', recorded in August of the same year, was a great success. Fired with enthusiasm, Heineman began regularly issuing records for the black clientele, so-called 'race records', and other companies soon followed suit.

Intially the records were made in New York. They featured dance bands, blues singers from the Harlem nightclubs and black evangelical preachers. The Columbia company's most successful race artist was the mighty-voiced Bessie Smith, the 'Empress of the Blues'. New record companies sprang up outside New York in the 1920s. At Grafton, Wisconsin, near Chicago, a former chair factory was converted to a record press, where Paramount records were produced.

The production of race records peaked between 1927 and 1930, when approximately 500 were issued annually. In order to find new artists for their race catalogues, record companies started making field trips outside New York and Chicago, visiting Atlanta, Memphis, New Orleans and other southern cities regularly.

The first blues records had been made by cabaret artists accompanied by small jazz bands, and their style was quite urban. From the mid-twenties, there began to appear in the catalogues of these record companies some guitar-playing singers whose music must have seemed hopelessly outdated to the people in Harlem. These singers had usually been found by a local record dealer, and they were often semi-professional or amateur musicians, barbers, sharecroppers or even beggars, who were earning extra income from music. They would tune their guitars in unorthodox ways and slide a broken bottleneck, stuck on the little finger of the left hand, along the strings; they would break off their verses asymmetrically and pronounce their lyrics in thick southern accents. These records were advertised in the *Chicago Defender* and other newspapers read by blacks, and mail-order companies would send them to southern black sharecroppers and labourers, who would relax with the gramophone on a Saturday evening.

Behind many historic blues records was the figure of Henry Spiers, the owner of a music shop in Jackson, Mississippi. Jackson is where the Mississippi Delta begins, a region with a predominantly black population. The area had large cotton plantations, whose owners would have dozens of black families working for them. Right up until the 1960s, outsiders' movements in the region were kept under surveillance.

Living on the Dockery plantation near Jackson was a guitarist by the name of Charley Patton. He was born in 1880 to a former slave family. On Spiers's initiative, from 1929 onwards, he recorded a number of blues and gospel tunes for the Paramount company. At the time they sold in their hundreds, at best in their thousands. The tunes are mostly traditional folk songs of the region, which many other singers also used, but Patton's interpretations are especially intense.

When the Mississippi blues was 'rediscovered' in the 1960s, Patton became the symbol of the style. In 1986, the University of Liège in Belgium held an international Charley Patton symposium. Among Patton's neighbours were the blues singers Son House and Skip James. Others who came to the fore later, from the Dockery plantation or its vicinity included Tommy Johnson, Roebuck Staples, Robert Johnson, Howlin' Wolf and Muddy Waters. The youngest of them only began their careers after moving to Chicago. These may all be regarded as the heirs of Charley Patton. From the 1960s onwards, many rock bands recorded blues numbers which they learned from their records. Cream recorded Patton's 'Spoonful' and Skip James's 'I'm so glad'. The Rolling Stones reworked Robert Johnson's 'Love in vain'. A famous group took its name from Tommy Johnson's 'Canned heat blues'. Such was the influence of the Dockery plantation.

Sources: Dixon and Godrich (1970, 1982); Titon (1977)

The 'Hot Five'

In the 1920s, jazz had grown in popularity in the United States, and there was a demand for famous bands and soloists. In 1924, Fletcher Henderson had lured Louis Armstrong to move from Chicago to New York to play in his dance band, and Armstrong began to be in demand as a studio musician too, accompanying blues singers. In November 1925, however, he returned to Chicago – probably at the instigation of his wife, Lillian – where he began a four-year busy period of work. Chicago, at that time run by mayor 'Big Bill' Thompson, was an open city, where the prohibition laws were flouted openly in the restaurants and variety theatres. Dozens of restaurants, dance halls and pleasure palaces were offering work for musicians, and the record industry, previously concentrated in New York, was spreading its activities to Chicago. Louis might sometimes play with Carroll Dickerson at the Sunset Café, sometimes in Erskine Tate's band at the Vendome Theatre, and sometimes in both on the same day.

Not surprisingly, the OKeh company took an interest in the rising young musician. In the 1920s this company was the leading producer of blues and jazz records. Its head office was in New York, but its Chicago office was regularly producing recordings, for which a technician was called in from the east coast. The producer and talent scout in Chicago was Richard M. Jones, himself a notable jazz pianist. Between 1925 and 1928 Louis Armstrong recorded about sixty numbers for OKeh, which have become landmarks in the history of jazz and of recording. The first records were made on 12 November 1925, as soon as he arrived in the city.

Armstrong's recording groups, whose names on the labels were the 'Hot Five' or the 'Hot Seven', were simply recording ensembles, who performed only twice in public, at charity concerts given by the local musicians' union. Their composition varied over the years, and the New Orleans players of the early years (including Johnny Dodds, who had played in King Oliver's band) came to be replaced by more modern musicians, notably the brilliant pianist Earl Hines. In 1925, OKeh had just gone over to electric recording. As Armstrong developed artistically and technically between 1925 and 1928, he exchanged his traditional cornet for the crisper-sounding trumpet. It is not possible to date the change on the basis of the records.

Instead of the recording horn there was now a microphone in the studio, but otherwise recording proceeded as before. There was only one microphone, so the relationship between the instruments in the recording could only be adjusted by changing the distance of the instruments from the microphone. The use of multiple microphones, which made it possible to manipulate the relations between the instrumental groupings while recording, came much later. In *Muggles*, Armstrong originally wanted the sound of Zutty Singleton's drum to be more prominent than usual. This was achieved by the producer holding the snare drum in his hand and Zutty playing it right beside the microphone. From the microphone the sound went through an amplifier straight to the disc-cutting machine, which cut a groove into a wax disc. The matrix for pressing was made from the wax plate by the galvanic process. If the recording failed, the whole business had to be repeated. Since sample records would only be available a few days later, the big record companies automatically made two versions of every number being recorded, of which the better one would be issued.

The Hot Five records were made in a very relaxed way. The record company would announce beforehand how many sides it wanted to make at each session, and usually the musicians would agree on the tunes to be recorded at the evening rehearsals – held in Armstrong's living room. Often the compositions would be pieces cobbled together at the last moment by members of the band, and only a few of them (such as Kid Ory's *Muskrat Ramble*) have survived independently as part of the jazz repertoire.

The numbers were rehearsed in the studio for as long as it took to achieve a good recording. The compositions were, after all, only frameworks in which Louis Armstrong could demonstrate his prowess as a soloist, and it could be said that, during these recording sessions, jazz became a soloist's art form. In February 1926 they recorded *Cornet Chop Suey* and *Heebie Jeebies*. The first of these has an astonishing 16-bar solo, in which Armstrong's cornet soars above the rest of the band's 'stop-time' harmonies. *Heebie Jeebies* presented Armstrong, for the first time, as a scat singer; this kind of wordless singing later became his trademark. In the autumn of 1927 they recorded *Hotter Than That*, which Armstrong's biographer James Lincoln Collier regards as the most joyful record in the history of jazz. Among the last recordings by the Hot Five was *West End Blues*, recorded in June 1928, whose introduction, improvised on the trumpet, is one of the great moments in jazz history, just as famous in its own field as the opening bars of Beethoven's fifth symphony.

All the Hot Five recordings originally appeared in the OKeh 8000 'race' series, which was intended only for black customers. The records were advertised conspicuously in the *Chicago Defender* and other black newspapers, and anyone, of any race, could freely buy them in Chicago. But in those parts of the United States where there were no appreciable black populations there was hardly any market for them. By 1928 Armstrong's reputation had grown so much that the Hot Five recordings were moved to the OKeh 41000 series which had a much wider domestic distribution. In 1926 Columbia bought OKeh, and the Hot Five's records soon appeared in Europe too, through Columbia's distribution network. Thanks to these records Louis Armstrong became a model for a whole generation of trumpeters in both the United States and Europe. When Armstrong visited Europe in 1932 he was welcomed by a keen audience which had been following his development on record for several years. Some of the public were disappointed, though, when their idol started 'fooling about' on stage. Although an inseparable part of his act in America, these antics had not come across on the record.

Sources: Priestley (1988); Rust (1978a)

The Singing Brakeman

The man who, in practice, was responsible for issuing Mamie Smith's records was the head of production at OKeh, Ralph Peer. In 1923 he decided to make some recording trips to the southern states of the USA, where suitable artists for his clientele might be found. Among the many hopeful performers who turned up for test sessions, held in Atlanta in June 1923, was a traditional fiddler of the old school, Fiddlin' John Carson, who sang to the accompaniment of his own playing. Peer did not believe that Carson's old-fashioned music would sell, but when the local agent personally undertook to order 500 records, Fiddlin' John was allowed to record 'The Little Old Log Cabin in the Lane'. The success of the record came as a surprise to Peer; it soon ran into many pressings, and the record industry had discovered the Southern White folk tradition. Initially these records were marketed as 'old time tunes' or 'hillbilly', but it was these that eventually grew into the colossal 'country music' industry. Fiddlin' John represents one of the roots of country music: the fiddlers, banjo players and guitarists whose repertoire the record companies eagerly snapped up in the twenties for their rural customers.

Representing another branch of it was Vernon Dalhart, whose real name was Marion Try Slaughter. Dalhart was born on a Texas cattle ranch in 1883, and in 1910 he moved to New York with ideas of an opera-singing career. From 1915 onwards he recorded operetta tunes, comic songs and hit tunes for many different companies with moderate success, until, in 1924, the Victor company, spurred on by Fiddlin' John's success, asked him to record two ballad-like tunes with just guitar and harmonica accompaniment. 'The Prisoner's Song' was a sentimental ballad about a convict's yearnings; 'Wreck of the Old '97' was based on a railway accident that occurred in 1903.

On these recordings Dalhart used the nasal 'country' singing style he had learnt in Texas, which his singing teachers had taken care to eliminate. The record was a success. It was bought by both country and city people. Because of the success of the record, several composers claimed to have written it, and there was a long court case over the copyright. The Victor company was obliged, under oath, to show the court detailed sales figures for it. The documents show that 957,635 copies were sold in 1924–5, and subsequent sales of that order meant that the 'Prisoner's Song' was one of the first records to have proven sales of over a million. The later annals of the Victor company claim that sales exceeded six million, but such figures cannot be relied upon. (There is evidence from the early 1920s that some of the records made for Victor by the Paul Whiteman band also reached the magic million in sales.)

From such ingredients a new musical tradition gradually came into being. Research has shown that among the country records of the twenties there were quite a few English folk ballads, the oldest of them going back to Elizabethan times. But there were just as many contemporary songs by the performers themselves on record, as well as popular tunes from the late nineteenth century which were becoming part of the oral tradition.

The artist who eventually created a new American musical style from these ingredients was also one of Ralph Peer's finds. In August 1927, Peer, who had meanwhile moved over to Victor, was scouting for talent in Bristol, Tennessee. On this visit he came across the Carter Family of singers and performers, who quickly became popular artists, and a guitarist and singer named Jimmie Rodgers. Rodgers was born in Mississippi 30 years earlier. His father was a railwayman, and Jimmie himself was a brakeman on the railways for 14 years and had other temporary jobs until he had to give them up because of his poor health. Eventually he decided to concentrate on music. Rodgers specialized in songs he had penned himself, which had ingredients from many contemporary musical trends. His singing style and his guitar playing were not markedly different from Vernon Dalhart's, but his songs often had a blues structure, borrowed from the black tradition of Mississippi, and between the verses Rodgers often inserted passages of yodelling, an idea he had evidently taken from the Swiss yodellers who used to tour the country's variety theatres. In addition to this, his backing groups occasionally contained, apart from the traditional fiddle and guitar, a Hawaiian guitarist or even a jazz trumpeter. Louis Armstrong was his guest accompanist in the studio in Los Angeles in July 1930.

All this may sound an unlikely combination, but in Rodgers's hands these ingredients were combined into a charismatic, and, above all, a genuinely American whole. He quickly gained a lot of fans, and Jimmie Rodgers may be regarded as the father of modern country music in the sense that he was a singer of his own compositions, rather than a folk musician performing traditional songs.

Jimmie Rodgers's career was short. He had suffered from tuberculosis since 1924, and the disease worsened over the years. Rodgers died in 1933 on a recording trip to New York. He made his last records on the day before he died, thus lending poignancy to the legend of the Singing Brakeman. During Jimmie Rodgers's time, country music established itself alongside black and immigrant music as one of the important branches of the American record industry, with a life of its own concurrent with the main streams of popular and serious music. Most of the country records were made far from New York, and gradually Nashville, Tennessee, became the centre of the country music industry, where all the big record companies had permanent studios and producers.

Ralph Peer became one of the important invisible figures in the background of blues and country music. He was in the habit of buying all the rights to their compositions from his artists for a cash sum and registering them in the name of his own company, Southern Music. The record company would pay a few cents to Southern Music for every record sold. Since many of these compositions have subsequently become favourites of rock musicians, the Southern Music catalogue has become a valuable one.

Even in the 1920s, American dance music was spreading around the world through the medium of records, and it soon became the pattern for modern dance music everywhere. Even records that were issued primarily for the black clientele in the United States were being sold in many European countries shortly after their release. Recordings by immigrant musicians were often also released in their original homelands. On the other hand, country music was so uniquely American that its influence was for a long time restricted to the United States alone. But there is no rule without an exception. Among Australian and New Zealand farmers, country music found a great response as early as the 1930s, and even today Jimmie Rodgers is as well remembered in Australia as in his homeland.

Source: Malone and McCulloh (1975)

The Berlin Schlager Factory

If New York and London were the two leading recording centres in the 1920s, Berlin was certainly the third. We have already noted the role of German record companies in producing classical recordings, but they were equally adept at producing popular music for the world market.

At that time, international record trade had two forms. When Louis Armstrong's records were issued outside the United States, the Columbia company would just send metal stampers to the plants of affiliated companies in Britain, France or Argentina. But many smaller countries had no such factories. The first record factory in Finland, for instance, was opened in 1938, and prior to that, all records sold in Finland, whether by Finnish or international artists, were pressed elsewhere, usually in Germany, which had, by the late 1920s, become the main supplier of recordings for many smaller countries. In 1929, when Germany's domestic sales amounted to 27 million, as many as 14 million records were exported. The biggest importing countries were Sweden, Czechoslovakia and Switzerland, but in that year 887,000 records were shipped to China, 550,000 to Finland, 375,000 to Egypt, and 80,000 to Estonia, to give just a few examples.

A lot of these recordings were made by artists from their respective countries, either during visits to Berlin or by German technicians visiting those countries. Between 1928 and 1943 the Lindström company issued about 600 Finnish records on their Odeon label in a special A228000 series. The A237000 series was reserved for Albania, while A239000 indicated records were marketed in Madagascar. Similar series were produced for most countries in Europe, Asia and Africa. But the sales of such records were inevitably limited, as Albanian records could hardly be sold in Finland. However, German companies were also skilled at producing records which were globally acceptable.

Probably the most productive German recording artist of the twenties was the violinist and bandleader Dajos Bela. Born Leon Holtzmann in Kiev, Ukraine, he became the Lindström company's musical director responsible for the production of popular records in 1920. Over the next decade, his various orchestras recorded several thousand titles which were issued either under his adopted name or under various pseudonyms such as Wiener Boheme Orchester, Sandor Joszi, Orchester Mascotte, and so on. There were medleys from operas and operettas, well-known waltzes and tangos, and current hits. Most of the recordings were instrumental, but Dajos Bela would also provide visiting foreign soloists with suitable accompaniment when required. They were marketed all over the world, and the 1944 Argentinian Odeon catalogue, for instance, still listed over 100 Dajos Bela items.

On the domestic German market, different styles prevailed. Franz Lehár had made a comeback in Berlin in 1927 with the hugely popular operetta *Der Zarewitsch*. This was followed by *Friederike* (1928) and *Das Land des Lächelns* (1929). The star of these operettas was the tenor, Richard Tauber, who was probably the best-selling German recording artist of the decade. Tauber's biggest Schlager was the 'Wolga-Lied' from *Der Zarewitsch*, which sold several hundred thousand copies.

Lehár's operettas reflected a world that had disappeared in the Great War. In Berlin's restaurants, variety shows and dance halls a more modern type of popular song prevailed, combining elements from earlier traditions with new American dance forms, the foxtrot and the tango. The widespread cynicism caused by the hyperinflation of the early 1920s gave rise to numerous comic songs bordering on nonsense:

Wir versaufen unsrer Oma ihr klein Häuschen,
und die erste und die zweite Hypothek!

(We'll drink Grandma's little house,
and the first and second mortgages)

This was followed by song titles such as *Ich hab das Fräul'n Helen baden sehn* (I have seen Miss Helen in the bathing tub), *Tante Paula liegt im Bett und isst Tomaten* (Aunt Paula is lying in bed eating tomatoes) and *Mein Papagei frisst keine harten Eier* (My parakeet doesn't eat hard-boiled eggs). The triumph of recorded music was celebrated in *Ich hab zu Haus ein Grammophon*, where the protagonist shudders at the idea of having to listen to four hours of Richard Strauss at the opera, and prefers the company of his own gramophone.

While crowds foxtrotted in restaurants or flocked to the Metropol to hear Tauber, there was fighting going on in the streets of Berlin, as Nazi brownshirts confronted communist redshirts. Both sides were experts in propaganda, and, for the first time, the gramophone acquired an important role in politics. Hitler's speeches appeared on the Braune Platte ('Brown Disc') label. The German Communist Party also had its own record label, Arbeiter-Kult, which released political songs by groups such as Rote Raketen (Red Rockets) and Das Rote Sprachrohr (Red Megaphone).

From this milieu came one of the greatest theaterical success stories of the decade, *Die Dreigroschenoper* of Bertolt Brecht and Kurt Weill, premiered at the Theater am Schiffbauerdamm in Berlin, in August 1928. Brecht and Weill belonged to the group of radical German artists who believed in the 'liquidation of arts engendered by established society'. They wanted to revolutionize musical theatre, combining elements of classical music with cabaret and popular songs to create a form of contemporary political theatre.

The Threepenny Opera was a runaway success. It was soon presented abroad in many languages, and record companies rushed to issue excerpts from the play. We have a chance to hear on record the original Mackie Messer, Harald Paulsen, and Weill's wife Lotte Lenya as Jenny. Otto Klemperer recorded excerpts from the music with the Berlin Staatsoper orchestra. When the play was revived in New York in September 1955, it became a great hit. It ran for 2706 performances, and the *Moritat* of Mackie Messer (Mack the Knife) was recorded by many performers ranging from Louis Armstrong to Bobby Darin. But the recording which best captures the spirit of Berlin in the twenties is Brecht himself singing the *Moritat* with his street-singer voice, to the accompaniment of the Theo Mackeben orchestra, originally issued on the Orchestrola label in 1929.

Sources: Lammel (1979); Lotz (1991–7); Sperr (1978)

The First Electric Gramophones

The new microphone-recorded discs placed new demands on record players as well. The improved dynamics and the extended range of reproduction went to waste if the records were played on an old acoustic gramophone, which would eventually grind them to dust with its needle, weighing 100g. Yet it was not clear how the problem of improved reproduction should be solved.

Viewed with hindsight, it is now obvious that the natural solution was to make use of the new amplifying techniques which had made microphone recording possible. As early as 1925 the Brunswick company, one of the medium-sized manufacturers of records and players in the United States, had put the first fully-electric record player, the Brunswick Panatrope, on the market. The old soundbox was replaced by a magnetic pick-up, and to amplify the sound, a similar vacuum-tube amplifier and speaker were used as on the best radio receivers of the period. The record was revolved by an electric motor. Also available was a model with an automatic record changer, so that the owner might load a whole symphony recorded on five discs onto his record player and sit back to enjoy the music. Only once, halfway through the performance, would he have to get up and turn the pile of records over.

Victor and the other companies soon followed suit. The largest radio company in the United States, RCA, bought Victor in 1929. It was natural that, instead of the old Victrola cabinet, customers were now offered a radio-gramophone combination. But electrical sound reproduction was still expensive, and not all music lovers in the twenties even possessed electricity. The gramophone fever of the late twenties was undoubtedly due to the microphone and electrical recording, but part of the growth in record sales was accounted for by the spread of cheap portable gramophones at this time.

The basic model of the portable gramophone had already been developed during the First World War by Decca in England, whose simple but durable 'suitcase' model was supplied in the thousands to the British troops at the front. (At this time Decca was only manufacturing gramophones; they went over to records in 1929.) After the Armistice, other manufacturers took their cue from Decca's 'trench model'. Especially light, aluminium-bodied models were manufactured for use in dirigibles. In the technical sense, the portable gramophone was a scaled-down version of the cabinet model, whose ancestor was the Victrola of 1906. The speaker was concealed inside the box, and the record was revolved by a motor equipped with a spring. The device was completely acoustic. It needed neither current nor batteries; the external energy came from the user's muscles.

The acoustic portable gramophones were the cheap popular models. There were also experts, however, who took a dim view of electrical recording. They pointed out that, in principle, the acoustic gramophone is capable of just as faithful sound reproduction as the electric one, while with acoustic reproduction one avoids the hum and other distractions inherent with electricity. The inventors of electric recording, Maxfield and Harrison, had developed a new 'orthophonic' horn for Victor, which was supposed to reproduce microphone-recorded discs as faithfully as possible without electric amplification. Even today there is a small group of collectors who swear by the EMG gramophone, handmade in London by

E.M. Ginn in the twenties and thirties. The unique feature of the EMG was its huge horn, made with scientific precision, with a diameter at the mouth of over a metre. Each soundbox was tuned by hand. The motor that drove the turntable, however, was electric.

The new recording technology of the twenties raises the question of how these records should be heard today. The recording equipment and gramophones of the acoustic period were linear – they realistically reproduced sound as it was (if one discounts the missing high and low frequencies, the unintentional disturbances caused by resonance and other technical shortcomings).

With the advent of electrical recording, the record company engineers began consciously manipulating the recording characteristics of their equipment. Strong bass notes, which could now be captured with the microphone, could easily destroy the groove of the recording. On the other hand the surface noise of a record is strongest in the high frequencies, which the improved amplifiers were now picking up. It was thus necessary to attenuate the low frequencies in recording, and boost the treble. When the record was played, the amplifier performed the same operation in reverse. Thus it was possible to improve the dynamics of the records and reduce background hiss.

This idea was universally accepted by all companies which adopted electrical recording, but they were not able to agree on details. Some companies would set the turnover point (the point at which bass attenuation would begin) at the frequency of 400 Hz. Others would choose 250, 300 or 500 Hz. There were other such discrepancies. It was not until the 1950s that reproduction curves were standardized, and, since then, the RIAA (Recording Industry Association of America) playback curve has been built into every amplifier with a phono input.

At the end of the 1920s most record buyers were content to listen to the new microphone-recorded discs on their acoustic portable gramophones without worrying much about whether the sound was realistic. But a record collector who plugs his gramophone into a modern amplifier built to the RIAA standard will most likely get a false impression of the sound of early electrical recordings. This problem even applies to many LP reissues, which are made according to modern standards but without compensating for the reproduction curve of the original. Serious attention has been paid to this question in recent years, but the comparison of historical reissues produced by different record companies highlights the problem.

Ultimately the choice is a subjective one: are we confronting the historical truth if we listen to music recorded in the twenties as it sounded in the studio at the time, or should we hear it as the record company engineers wanted us to hear it, or as contemporary listeners heard it – played on the typical portable gramophones of the period?

Sources: Chew (1981); Read and Welch (1976)

CHAPTER FOUR

Depression and Resurgence

The Great Crash

For record companies worldwide, 1929 was the best year since the invention of the gramophone. But on Thursday, 24 October, prices crashed on the Wall Street stock exchange in New York, and the crash soon reverberated around the world. The economic life of the United States and other industrialized countries had been too much in the hands of speculators. The house of cards collapsed, and many people lost their savings overnight. The image of a former millionaire jumping from the window of a skyscraper characterized the depth of that collapse. Soup kitchens and queues of unemployed men were everyday scenes in the early 1930s.

All branches of the economy suffered from the slump. The record industry was hit with double force, however. After all, records were a luxury. In the good years, they had been found even in ordinary workmen's homes, but it was easy to give them up when times were hard. Besides, the gramophone record now had two serious competitors. Broadcasting had begun in the United States in 1920. By the end of the decade, radio had become widespread, both in Europe and America. The talking pictures had also secured a place for themselves before the Depression started. With such competition, who would buy records now? It is no coincidence that the first full-length talking pictures were musical ones, such as *The Jazz Singer* (1927).

In 1929, about 150 million records were sold in the United States. RCA Victor, the largest company, had alone sold more than 34 million. By 1933 sales had slumped to 10 million. RCA Victor's share was 3.6 million. All over the world the trend was the same: sales were cut to a fraction of the years of the 'gramophone fever'. One by one, the record companies went bankrupt or merged. The old rivals in England, Gramophone and Columbia, merged on 20 March 1931 under the name Electric & Musical Industries Ltd (EMI), after both companies' turnover had plummeted by 90 per cent. The old enemies, Alfred Clark and Louis Sterling, became chairman of the board and managing director of EMI respectively. They did not get on, and matters were not helped when Sterling was ennobled in 1931. Since both Columbia and the Gramophone had had subsidiaries in many European countries, including the whole Lindström company in Germany, most of the records manufactured in Europe were now EMI products, although outwardly the labels were competitors. In Finland, for instance, the three principal EMI labels all had their own agents and their own roster of exclusive artists.

Throughout the 1930s, EMI had only a few serious competitors in Europe. The most important of these were Decca in England, who had branched into records from making gramophones, and Deutsche Grammophon, which had become independent during the First World War, but at the end of the thirties came into the ownership of the giant electrical goods manufacturer, Siemens (Telefunken). Apart from these there were only a few small local firms in Europe, whose operations were generally restricted to a single country. Sonora, of Sweden, became an important company in its homeland in the thirties. Even Latvia had its own company, Bellaccord. In the Soviet Union, record manufacturing had been resumed after the revolution in the same factories as before, which had begun to become seriously run down, until, in the late 1930s, the country's record industry was finally modernized.

A similar concentration of the record industry took place in the United States, where only the Victor company emerged intact from the Depression. Eldridge Johnson had retired in 1926, a multi-millionaire. Victor had been sold in 1929, before the collapse of the stock market, to the giant Radio Corporation of America. The popularity of radio helped to keep the record side of the business afloat even in hard times, and the radio factory made enough profits to plough into the development of television as well. Victor had to put its flagship into dry dock, however: the famous Red Seal series was abandoned for a few years.

Things were going worse elsewhere. The smaller American record companies simply dropped out of the market. The giant of the film industry, Consolidated Film Laboratories, which owned Republic Films, among others, snapped up the rest like overripe apples. In 1930, Consolidated bought Cameo, the bargain-store label, Plaza, and the American subsidiary of Pathé – which had merged the previous year as the American Record Corporation – for a derisory sum. The following year Brunswick and Vocalion came into its grasp, and in 1934 it snapped up Columbia, which had already changed hands a couple more times. Consolidated was owned by Herbert Yates, proprietor of film laboratories in Hollywood, who had become wealthy by taking over film companies that had got into difficulties and were unable to pay their film development bills.

When Decca, in England, established an American subsidiary in 1934, it had only two serious competitors: RCA Victor and the American Record–Brunswick–Columbia group, owned by Consolidated Films. As a first step, Decca bought all the rights to Gennett's record production for a pittance. No-one bothered about Paramount, the matrices of whose legendary race records were sold for scrap.

The drop in sales was also reflected in the number of new records issued, though fortunately this did not shrink as sharply as did sales. In the early 1930s the record companies even had to cut down on their programme of planned releases, and the less profitable lines were dropped altogether. The emphasis was now to be on certain hits, and classical music, along with all other 'minority' music, was slimmed down. There was a sharp reduction in the amount of jazz, blues and immigrant music being recorded. The recording trips to the South were halted.

Competitors of the Gramophone

In April 1923 the Gramophone Company issued a record on which King George V and Queen Mary greeted the children of the British Empire. On the other side was 'God Save the King'. In its advertisements the record company claimed that there is no other means whereby children in London, Inverness, Calcutta, Ottawa and Fremantle could hear their own King and Queen speaking to them.

This was true at the time. The gramophone record, and before it the wax cylinder, had for a long time been the only means of preserving and disseminating sound. Even the pioneers of the phonograph had tried to capture the voices of the famous people of their day, and Kaiser Wilhelm, Bismarck, Tennyson, Strindberg and others spoke on the phonograph. George V's mother, Queen Victoria, who died in 1901, had, in 1896, sent greetings, by wax cylinder, to Emperor Menelik II of Ethiopia, to promote the diplomatic negotiations then going on between their two countries. This recording, like most of these unique cylinders, has vanished into oblivion, but recently another cylinder alleged to contain her voice has turned up.

With the arrival of the gramophone record, the opportunity to duplicate sound arose, and soon the record companies were boldly offering their customers recordings by the actress Sarah Bernhardt, the Scout leader, Baden-Powell, the suffragette, Christabel Pankhurst, and Queen Elisabeth of Romania – the last of these was better known by her poetic nom de plume, Carmen Sylva. At the turn of the century Leo Tolstoy was an international celebrity thanks to *Anna Karenina* and *War and Peace*, and though he was not, to many people's dismay, the first recipient of the Nobel Prize for literature, the Gramophone Company issued a series of records in 1907 on which the aged count gave voice to his ideas in no less than four languages: Russian, French, German and English.

Soon, however, it became apparent that the public was not particularly interested in these momentary documents. While it is true that nearly all European statesmen have committed themselves to record, these were mainly intended for official purposes. When the Allies conquered Italy at the end of the Second World War, they found piles of unplayed records of Mussolini's speeches. Not even the keenest Fascists could be bothered to listen to Il Duce on record. The spoken word made a comeback with the advent of the LP, when famous comedians started making recordings, but for now, what the public wanted on record was music.

Kings and prime ministers found, in radio, a more effective way of addressing their subjects. But even though King George was able to talk to his subjects in London and Inverness simultaneously on the BBC in the 1930s, on the other side of the Empire, in Fremantle, the clock was half a day ahead of London. The radio companies of the great powers in the thirties were desperately seeking ways to preserve their programmes so that they could be broadcast again later. For this reason German radio used ordinary recording technology and made shellac pressings of its programmes. This process is slow, and unconscionably expensive unless at least 50 to 100 copies are required at the same time. In the thirties, for repeats of its news broadcasts, the BBC used wire recorders, where the job of the tape was done by huge wire spools. By the end of the thirties the modern type of studio tape recorder had finally arrived, but it was only after the Second World War that these became widespread.

The commonest solution to the problem of preserving sound on radio at this time was the direct-to-disc process, developed at the end of the 1920s. The technology was essentially the same as that used by record companies, but while recording studios used wax masters which had to be processed until they could be replayed, the disc recorders used aluminum discs coated with acetate, which could be played back immediately on an ordinary record player. Using disc-recording equipment it was possible to preserve five-minute excerpts from programmes, and using two parallel recorders, a skilled technician could make continuous recordings of long radio programmes. Eventually these recording machines even found their way into the homes of wealthy music lovers. Some models also had a built-in radio, encouraging listeners to record their favourite programmes.

By these methods, the larger radio companies soon acquired considerable material for their archives. Since a fair proportion of all radio stations' programmes have always been made up of music, the archives also came to include a lot of music that was never available on commercial records. Gradually some of this has come into the hands of collectors and been issued on LP, with or without permission. Thus we have the only preserved example of Sibelius himself conducting an orchestra: the *Andante festivo*, broadcast on New Year's Day, 1939. This has now been issued several times. Thanks to radio recordings we have the opportunity to hear entire opera evenings at the New York Metropolitan and the Berlin State Opera in the 1930s and hear the interpretations by such great conductors as Mengelberg, Furtwängler and Toscanini, of works they never recorded.

From the point of view of jazz, the acetate record has been invaluable. Thanks to this method, for example, we have recordings of the famous 'From Spirituals to Swing' concerts organized at Carnegie Hall in 1938 and 1939 by John Hammond, including such musicians as boogie-woogie pianists, Pete Johnson and Albert Ammons, the Count Basie Band, and the King of Swing, Benny Goodman. The legendary blues singer, Robert Johnson, had also been invited to the 1938 concert, but in August of that year, a jealous girlfriend poisoned him. Also recorded from radio onto instantaneous disc was Duke Ellington's first large orchestral composition, *Black, Brown and Beige*.

Though contemporary with the gramophone, movies were silent for a long time, and required live music as accompaniment to theatre showings. The advent of sound in pictures quickly attracted the attention of inventors. The first full-length talking pictures relied on sound recorded on disc, which was synchronized with the movie projector using special equipment.

When viewers flocked to the cinemas in 1927 to hear Al Jolson singing in the movie, *The Jazz Singer*, the sound came from specially-made discs that revolved at 33 r.p.m. However, this 'Vitaphone' process was impractical in many ways. If the film had to be patched up or the needle jumped a groove, sound and picture would get out of synchrony. In 1927 the Fox company bought the rights to the optical sound recording process developed by the Germans, Engl, Massolle and Vogt, in which a sound signal was captured at the edge of the film in the form of different degrees of brightness. Records disappeared from movie theatres, but the speed of 33 r.p.m. is one we shall encounter again in the history of records.

Musical films quickly became popular, and soon they were being mass-produced. A new type of recording artist appeared thanks to the musical picture and the radio, one who was equally at home in all three media. Singers were no longer expected to have a full-throated, operatic style, as it was now possible to commit to record a soft, almost whispering style of delivery, even if a large orchestra was playing in the background. The prototype of the new type of singer was the American, Bing Crosby. Everywhere else where movies were being made, singing movie stars were appearing on record. In the Middle East and India, the arrival of the talking picture gave rise to completely new forms of musical entertainment.

Record companies understood the power of the movies, and rushed to record the most popular songs from the films, both as performed by the original artists and in other versions. Yet film soundtracks came to contain a lot of music that was never released on record. In recent years the soundtracks of some old films have been, with varying degrees of legality, reissued on disc, usually in small pressings for collectors. Thanks to radio and movie soundtracks, a lot of music from the thirties has been preserved which had not been available on record because of the hard times which beset the industry.

Source: DeLong (1980)

Walter Legge and the HMV Society Project

The stock market crash forced the record companies to sharply cut their programmes of releases. Not even the brightest stars in the classical firmament were spared by the Depression. Even Victor and EMI had to drastically prune their programmes of new classical issues, and many distinguished artists' contracts were allowed to lapse. New recordings kept to a 'safe' repertoire.

In 1931 Walter Legge was a 24-year-old copywriter in the advertising department at EMI, keen on classical music and worried about the shrinking recording programme. He came to his superior's notice with an original suggestion. If 500 buyers committed themselves in advance to buying a record album on which Elena Gerhardt performed songs by Hugo Wolf, could one be made? It would not cost much to record a solo singer. Legge was given the green light. One of the first subscribers was John McCormack. In a few months the record salesmen had found 500 members for the Hugo Wolf Society who were prepared to pay 30s. for the Wolf songs – 111 of the subscribers were from Japan. The recordings were made on 5 November and released the following April. Each record was numbered and no further pressings were made. If one of the records broke, the buyer could get a new one only by taking the label of the broken one to a dealer.

The project was such a success that it was decided to continue the activity of the Hugo Wolf Society. Altogether the Wolf series embraced six albums of six records each, including 118 songs in all. The performers included Gerhard Hüsch, Karl Erb, Elisabeth Schumann, Helge Roswaenge, Friedrich Schorr and Alexander Kipnis. Walter Legge was moved from the advertising department to work for Fred Gaisberg. In June 1932 he was Gaisberg's assistant when Yehudi Menuhin was recording Edward Elgar's violin concerto at the new Abbey Road studios under the baton of the composer. The society idea was now applied to other composers. Artur Schnabel was contracted to record Beethoven's piano works. The first record for the Beethoven Sonata Society appeared in 1932, and, oddly enough, it was the composer's last piano sonata, op. 111. Within three years, records had been sold to a value of £80,000. The original idea of limited editions had fortunately been abandoned. The fifteenth and last volume in the series was completed on the eve of the Second World War. At EMI's Abbey Road studios, Schnabel was remembered as a difficult customer, who would slam down his piano lid after unsatisfactory takes and mutter 'Impossible'.

The series for the Haydn Society consisted of the composer's 28 string quartets, played by the Belgian Pro Arte quartet. In 1933 the Society idea spread to France, where Wanda Landowska made recordings on the harpsichord of Bach's *Goldberg Variations* and Scarlatti's sonatas. Before the war brought an end to the Society series, Bach's major works had been recorded. Edwin Fischer played both parts of *Das Wohltemperierte Klavier* on the piano, Casals did the cello series and Albert Schweitzer a number of organ works. Also issued were works by Mahler and Delius. Three Society albums were devoted to the relatively unknown Russian emigrant composer, Nikolai Medtner, for which the composer had to thank the music-loving Maharajah of Mysore, who acted as sponsor.

Also included in the series were Artur Rubinstein's first recordings, of all Chopin's mazurkas, although his piano career had in fact begun in 1900 at a concert conducted by Joseph Joachim. The reason for the late start, according to Rubinstein himself, was that, early in his career, wine and food, beautiful women and good cigars had been more important to him than practising, and he was playing a third of the notes wrong. Only after his quite hostile reception in America and the competition with Rakhmaninov, Hofmann and Horowitz, did he have a late awakening, and began to practise. Thanks to sound films and his large recorded output he soon became as widely known as Stokowski.

The last of Legge's large productions before the war was the Mozart Opera Society, in whose name four of Mozart's operas were recorded. Parts 1 to 3 consisted of *The Marriage of Figaro*, recorded at the Glyndebourne Festival. The orchestra was conducted by Fritz Busch, who had fled from Germany. Parts 4 to 6 were *Cosi fan tutte* and parts 7 to 9 *Don Giovanni*, both of them conducted again by Fritz Busch. Beecham's *The Magic Flute*, recorded in 1937 at the Berlin State Opera, completed the series. The major roles in this recording were played by Tiana Lemnitz, Erna Berger, Gerhard Hüsch and Wilhelm Strienz.

In 1939 Fred Gaisberg retired, and the short-sighted Walter Legge got a posting in the army's entertainment corps. The Society series vanished into the storms of history, but the records remained in the HMV catalogue until 1955, as long as 78 r.p.m. records were being sold, and most of them have successfully made the transition to the CD era.

Sources: Sanders (1984); Schwarzkopf (1982)

The American Supervirtuosi

The most dazzling performing artists of the period ended up in America sooner or later. The Russian Revolution sparked off a wave of musical exiles, and Hitler's rise to power caused a flood of them. American concert fees also attracted those who had no pressing reasons to emigrate. For a few years the Depression had dimmed the attraction of the New World, but after a brief interval, concerts were flourishing again. The large radio companies in the United States, CBS and NBC, offered new opportunities for renowned artists, and in 1934, RCA Victor relaunched the distinguished 'Red Seal' record series, under the management of Charles O'Connell. As long as the other companies were virtually paralysed as a result of the slump, Victor had a virtual monopoly as a manufacturer of classical recordings in the United States.

The trend toward extremes of technical performance and volcanic interpretations reasserted itself in the United States. At the same time as the great swing musicians (such as Benny Goodman, Lionel Hampton, Art Tatum and Roy Eldridge) were, for the first time in the history of jazz, conquering the concert halls right up to Carnegie Hall and developing their own virtuoso styles, the laurels in classical music were being won by Heifetz, Horowitz and Toscanini. The concerts and recordings by Heifetz, Artur Rubinstein and the cellist Gregor Piatigorsky were advertised under the name of the 'Million-dollar trio', and according to *Life* magazine, these famous chamber musicians were, together, earning over a million dollars a year, although this figure was probably exaggerated.

The violin world was ruled by Auer's St Petersburg prodigies: Mischa Elman, with his golden sound and Jascha Heifetz, with his perfect technique. At the age of 14, Elman had recorded a violin arrangement of Chopin's nocturne in E flat major, op. 9, and with its lyrical sweetness, naturalness and freshness this interpretation brings out Elman's best qualities. It is a question of romantic interpretation: the powerful, dynamic gestures are coloured in an archaic way by long *fermati* and the use of *portamento*. In the 1930s Elman recorded an acoustically beautiful reading of Beethoven's romance in F major and a lyrical interpretation of Tchaikovsky's violin concerto.

Heifetz played his way to great public prominence for the first time in 1914 at a concert conducted by Arthur Nikisch in Berlin, when Nikisch pronounced the boy, still only 13, to be the greatest violinist he had heard. Heifetz's playing has often been described with the words 'cold beauty' and 'polished marble' and he has been accused of American superficiality – he even wrote popular songs under the pen-name, Jim Hoyl. This evident misinterpretation of artistic talent is probably due to the fact that Heifetz, like Toscanini and other technical perfectionists, was naturally led, in the thirties, to a remote style that dispensed with sentimentality; one that might even be called Cubist. In his memoirs, Heifetz's record producer Charles O'Connell related how many times Heifetz rejected the recordings he had made, which everyone else thought quite acceptable.

Heifetz's hurried pace in the finale of Tchaikovsky's violin concerto may indeed disturb the romantics, but in works such as Saint-Saëns's *Havanaise* and *Rondo cappricioso*, Wieniawski's *Scherzo tarantella* and *Polonaise brillante*, Sarasate's gypsy songs and Ravel's *Tzigane* he represents violin playing at its best. The German

63

expert on violinists, Joachim Hartnack, names Lalo's *Spanish Symphony* as Heifetz's best recording, with accompaniment from the RCA Orchestra conducted by William Steinberg. But there is just as much artistry and romantic brio to be found in Wieniawski's D minor violin concerto, conducted by Izler Solomon.

Rakhmaninov and Hofmann were the great competing pianists of the twenties and thirties. The relatively few recordings made by Hofmann are not just personal interpretations of the works performed, but in some cases rise decidedly far above the recordings by others. Hofmann's playing of Chopin's B minor scherzo and Liszt's *Tarantella* (abridged), recorded in 1916, were dazzling examples of virtuosity. They even surpass his reading of Moszkowski's *Spanish Caprice*, performed at his fiftieth birthday concert.

The programme for this concert, given at the Metroplitan in 1937, was issued by Columbia, and among the other great interpretations on the record are Chopin's ballade in G minor, the 'Minute Waltz' (a minute and a half) and an unusually rapidly played *Berceuse*. A year later Hofmann gave his Casimir Hall concert, which has become a legend, and was recorded on an acetate disc. This recording, which has technical shortcomings, was subsequently issued by the International Piano Library, which specialized in rarities of piano music. Chopin's B major nocturne, op. 9, was rendered by Hofmann into a mighty piano elegy, and the greatness of his vision is also evident in the ballade no. 4 in F minor.

Sergey Rakhmaninov recorded a few pieces shortly after fleeing Russia in 1919, including Liszt's Hungarian Rhapsody no. 2, with an astonishing lightness of touch. In the meantime he made a few rare Edison records, but his great series for Victor was begun only in 1924, with Chopin's C sharp minor scherzo and A flat major ballade. Rakhmaninov's most remarkable recordings, which have become models of interpretation for many generations of pianists, are Schumann's *Carnaval*, recorded in 1929 and Chopin's B flat minor sonata, recorded in 1930, in which Rakhmaninov, unusually, begins the funeral march pianissimo, ends fortissimo before the trio, and continues after the trio with the same fortissimo, concluding eventually with the pianissimo again. The famous interpretative riddle of the finale he solves by playing it colourfully, as a shimmering carpet of harmonies, where the individual notes can scarcely be made out.

Vladimir Horowitz arrived in America in 1928. His playing was a reflection of the motor-powered 1920s, which had produced such realistic works as Honegger's *Pacific 231* and Mossolov's *Steel Foundry*. At his debut concert in New York, Horowitz played Tchaikovsky's B flat minor piano concerto, and it is said that during the first two movements he grew so annoyed with Beecham's slow tempo (in fact Beecham was cultivating quite a fast tempo) that at the beginning of the finale he rushed ahead like lightning and left the orchestra far behind him – Beecham could not catch up with him throughout the entire movement.

Most of Horowitz's recorded output was produced in the age of the LP, but his production in the twenties and thirties occupies a special place because of its technical perfection. This includes Liszt's Paganini étude in E flat major, from 1930, Liszt's B minor sonata from 1932, and a recording of Rakhmaninov's third piano concerto, recorded in 1930 with the London Symphony Orchestra, conducted by Albert Coates. The technical perfection of the performance is evident, although in the Paganini étude one may notice the pianist exceeding the limit of speed beyond which absolute accuracy cannot exist. In terms of style they represent the kind of machine-gun-like delivery that made Horowitz famous in the twenties.

Later, in the 1930s and early 1940s, Horowitz did studio work with conductors such as Toscanini and Fritz Reiner, who belonged to the same school of interpetation. Reiner accompanied him in Beethoven's fifth piano concerto and again in Rakhmaninov's third concerto, Toscanini in Brahms's B flat major piano concerto and in Tchaikovsky's piano concerto no. 1. A livelier version of the latter work is to be had, however, on a record cut from a 1943 radio broadcast played by the same pair of artists.

Sources: Creighton (1974); Gelatt (1956); Schonberg (1987)

A New Generation of Golden Voices

The appearance on the record market of the instrumental virtuosi had, for a short while, displaced the opera singers who used to dominate it, just as the great swing soloists had left the blues singers in the shade. Still living, from the crop of singing stars of the twenties, was the influential Amelita Galli-Curci, whose heyday had begun ten years before the arrival of the microphone. Galli-Curci's farewell performance took place at the Metropolitan in 1930; after that she began her European tour, which was a failure, and she gave up her career in 1936. Galli-Curci had become famous through her records. There are about 100 of them, several displaying a timeless brilliance. She was self-taught as a singer, and in the later stage of her career she used her own records in teaching. Galli-Curci lived on into the stereo age, dying in 1963.

New singers were now rising to take the place of the older stars. The most famous singer of the period was undoubtedly Beniamino Gigli, the son of an Italian village cobbler, who was more lyrical than Caruso and inclined to a sometimes tearful sentimentality. What had been straightforward for Caruso was achieved by Gigli with deliberation and artifice: Victor and HMV spread this illusion of perfect ease to every corner of the globe.

Gigli's career had got under way when he won the important Parma singing competition in 1914. He made his first records in Milan in 1918 ('Dai campi, dai prati' from Boito's *Mefistofele*, which was one of his favourite operas). The war slowed down his rise, but in 1920 he was contracted to the Metropolitan Opera. In 1921 Caruso died, and the newspapers started writing about 'the new Caruso'. The favourites with journalists were Giovanni Martinelli, Giulio Crimi and the newcomer, Gigli. Gigli rejected these references as blasphemous, but the following autumn the Metropolitan commenced its season with a production of *La Traviata*, with Galli-Curci as Violetta and Gigli in the role of Alfredo. A new star was born.

In ten years Beniamino Gigli became the Metropolitan's leading tenor. At the same time his close recording collaboration with Victor began. He would surely have maintained this position for a long time if the director of the Metropolitan, Gatti-Casazza, had not had to cut the salaries of all the operatic artists by half in 1932, when the Depression was at its deepest. All of them accepted this, except

Gigli and Maria Jeritza. Gigli went to Europe, where he appeared with great success on the operatic stages of several countries and continued recording for His Master's Voice, which had previously been pressing his Victor records in Europe. In 1935 he started on a series of tear-jerking movies in Germany, beginning with *Vergiss mich nicht* and *Ave Maria*, which enjoyed great success. He had not even been particularly highly praised for his acting skills in opera, but his golden voice drew the audiences into the cinemas. His 1938 recording of Schubert's *Ständchen* sung in German with accompaniment from a string orchestra, gives a good idea of this aspect of Gigli's artistry. More significant from an artistic point of view was his contribution to many complete recordings of operas made in the thirties: he played in *Pagliacci*, *La Bohème*, *Tosca*, and *Madama Butterfly*, among others. For many people he remains the greatest lyric tenor of the century; others find him too sentimental.

The female counterpart of Gigli was Maria Jeritza, who hailed from Brno, the queen of the opera singers, a diva among divas and a prima donna in every sense of the world. Jeritza, who began her career in 1912 at the Vienna State Opera, appeared at the Metropolitan at exactly the same time as Galli-Curci and Gigli: in 1931–2. She had a magnificent voice which knew no limits, and dramatic, effulgent interpretation. She sang everything. She had begun her career as Fritzi Massary's successor in Offenbach's operettas, and later she became a great star of the talking pictures. Jeritza's great roles, however, were Richard Strauss's operas *Ariadne auf Naxos* and *Die Frau ohne Schatten*. In Puccini's opinion, Tosca was one of Jeritza's brilliant roles. Recordings have not, however, treated her kindly: her strong personality and exceptional beauty do not come through to us, and her voice sounds ordinary. Her contemporaries also noticed this, and demand for her records was waning by the end of the 1930s.

The departure of Gigli and Jeritza did not in any way undermine the status of the Metropolitan Opera, which continued to attract famous singers. Beginning on Christmas afternoon, 1931, the NBC radio network broadcast, every Saturday afternoon, a matinée performance from the Metropolitan. The broadcasts were sponsored by the American Tobacco Company, Lambert Pharmaceuticals, and RCA, and helped to win opera thousands of new friends. During the worst Depression years, Lucrezia Bori and Geraldine Farrar appealed to listeners to save the Met from financial disaster and raised over $250,000.

Not surprisingly, many of the soloists featured in the broadcasts had recording contracts with RCA Victor. Prominent among them were Rosa Ponselle, Elisabeth Rethberg, Giovanni Martinelli, Ezio Pinza and Lawrence Tibbett. Both Tibbett and Ponselle were American-born, and the three Europeans also spent a sufficiently long time at the Metropolitan to become thoroughly well known to American opera lovers.

Through his records, films and broadcasts, Tibbett undoubtedly became the best-known American singer of the era. The California-born baritone had made his debut at the Metropolitan in 1923, and performed in the premieres of several modern American operas, such as Gruenberg's *The Emperor Jones* ('Standin' in the need of prayer' from this opera was recorded in 1934). His Iago in *Otello* was widely praised both for his singing and acting talents, and with Martinelli he made an abridged version of the opera for Victor. But a look at Victor catalogues reveals strikingly how the status of opera recordings had changed. The 1917 catalogue had listed over 140 Caruso titles. The 1940 Red Seal catalogue, where Tibbett was the most prominently featured singer, listed fewer than 60 titles by him. Caruso, dead for two decades, was still represented by almost as many. The music lover who wants to hear Tibbett in a complete *Otello* must turn to one of the NBC broadcasts which were preserved privately on acetate discs and have subsequently been released for collectors. (There is an *Otello* from 1940 with Martinelli and Tibbett, and another from 1941.)

One great American singer of the thirties who never made it to the Metropolitan until 1955 was the black alto Marian Anderson. Lack of stage experience prevented her from developing dramatic roles, but it is easy to understand her success as a recitalist after hearing her recordings of songs by Sibelius, Schubert and Brahms. Her interpretations of Sibelius's songs such as 'Långsamt som kvälsskyn', recorded in 1936 for RCA Victor with Kosti Vehanen, the Finnish pianist who was her regular accompanist for many years, are still exemplary.

Source: Steane (1974)

The President, the Disc Jockey and the Crooner

It has been said that the microphone brought three voices into the consciousness of every American in the 1930s: Franklin Delano Roosevelt, Martin Block and Bing Crosby. The folksy president developed a whole new type of politician thanks to his use of the microphone in his radio talks. Whereas Hitler and Mussolini would bark at the masses, Roosevelt's 'fireside chats' on the radio created an image of a relaxed 'Father of the Nation', who was a welcome guest in every family's living room.

In the early thirties it was rare to hear records played on the radio. The big radio stations had their own musicians, and famous dance bands would play live every week. Records were regarded as a sign of poverty. Besides, some famous bandleaders, notably Fred Waring, had taken radio stations to court with the aim of a total ban on broadcasting records. In 1939 the Supreme Court of the United States finally settled the matter in the stations' favour. Similar litigation was going on in many European countries, and in most cases the broadcasters won. Only in the United Kingdom, the Court of Appeal decided in 1934 that record makers had the right to authorize the broadcasting of their records, and the BBC was compelled to limit the use of records by 'needle time' quotas.

Martin Block was the first disc jockey in radio history, who played popular records on his programme 'Make-believe Ballroom', creating an image in the minds of his Depression-bound listeners of a dance party to which they were all invited. The programme was first broadcast on station WNEW in New York on 3 February 1935. Block had to buy the records needed for the programme, because the radio station did not own a single record. The first sponsor on the programme (it was a commercial station) were the makers of Retardo slimming pills. Four months later Block had four million listeners, and in five years he became the best-paid –

and most imitated – presenter on radio. The idea was in the air: similar request programmes were soon appearing on many European stations.

The smooth-voiced Bing Crosby rose, in the 1930s, from being an anonymous singer with a band to becoming a great star of movies and radio. He made his first film in 1930 as a member of a singing group called The Rhythm Boys. The following year he made his radio debut on CBS in a programme sponsored by the La Palina cigar company, and established 'Where the blue of the night meets the gold of the day' as his signature tune. Throughout the thirties he regularly made movies and radio programmes, the choicest cuts of which would then appear on record. Bing Crosby may justly be called the father of the modern hit song; he was the first singer who knew how to exploit the microphone, so that the listeners felt that he was singing for them personally, and not for a whole dance hall.

Bing Crosby had made his popular records for Brunswick, and in the Depression he was their best-selling artist. When the head of Decca in England, Edward Lewis, set up an American branch in 1934, he paid Brunswick's record producer Jack Kapp, who had a reputation as an unerring hit-maker after producing Al Jolson's 'Sonny Boy', to run it. Kapp brought Bing Crosby with him to Decca, and he became the new company's leading light. Bing Crosby's big hits included 'Pennies from heaven' (from the movie of the same name), 'Sweet Leilani' (from *Waikiki Wedding*) and 'San Antonio Rose'. Decca guaranteed Crosby a minimum of $40,000 a year for his records, but it is revealing that he earned much more from radio performances and films. The climax of Bing Crosby's career came in 1942 with the film *Holiday Inn*, in which he performed Irving Berlin's 'White Christmas'. It became one of the biggest sales successes in recording history; about 30 million copies of it are estimated to have been sold during four decades.

With the domination by films and radio of its recording programme, the record industry's traditional links with live music were weakened. New York's Broadway was perhaps the most important centre of musical theatre in the world in the 1930s. Jerome Kern, Richard Rodgers, George Gershwin, Cole Porter and Vincent Youmans created their careers by writing music for this street. The most popular of them, Irving Berlin, even had his own theatre on Broadway, the Music Box. At their best, their songs, with their inventive tunes and distinctive harmonies, competed with the works of the great *lieder* composers. Hundreds of recordings have been made of them, but, remarkably, their early recordings have mostly been forgotten.

Ethel Merman was a New York actress whose breakthrough came in 1930 on Broadway in George Gershwin's musical *Girl Crazy*. Her bravura number in that was 'I Got Rhythm'. Merman's voice was untrained and her range was narrow, but she was a powerful personality with a striking stage presence. She became the darling of New York. Irving Berlin was captivated by her style, and Cole Porter wrote a musical for her: *Anything Goes* (1934). In 1946 she was unforgettable in *Annie Get Your Gun*, and later she was still appearing in *Hello, Dolly* on Broadway when it closed its doors after 2718 performances. However, Merman only made a score or so of records in the thirties. 'I Got Rhythm' and 'Anything Goes' became standards, of which countless recordings have been made, but Merman did not record them before the advent of the LP. It is not certain whose version of 'I Got Rhythm' was the first – perhaps Louis Armstrong's in 1931.

Many performers were forgotten due to the fact that few records were being sold in the 1930s. But when Hollywood had lured singers, they attained international popularity. Judy Garland, born Frances Gumm, was the daughter of a show business family, who was pushed by her ambitious mother into the movies at the age of thirteen. Judy Garland's recording of 'Over the Rainbow' (from *The Wizard of Oz*), recorded in 1939 when she was seventeen, is still heard regularly today.

Sales of records started to recover in the mid-thirties. The worst of the slump was over. The increased record sales in the United States were partly due to jukeboxes, which after the end of Prohibition appeared in every little bar and restaurant. According to official estimates, there were 220,000 jukeboxes in the country. Unofficial estimates spoke of half a million. In a noisy bar, the refined love songs of Broadway would not be heard. The first big jukebox hit was the *Beer Barrel Polka*, a Bohemian polka recorded for RCA Victor by the German Will Glahe's orchestra, whose catchy refrains resounded from jukeboxes hundreds of thousands of times.

Soon, other dance tunes began to be heard on jukeboxes. Jazz-influenced dance music – swing – became popular with American youth from the mid-1930s onwards. The big swing bands, with 6 to 10 brass players and a rhythm section, seemed to express the vitality of America as it recovered from the Depression. The roots of the style were in black American music, but this new dance music was played by white bands in dinner suits, of whom anyone could approve.

In 1935, about 25 million records were sold in the United States. In 1938, six swing records sold over a million copies each. They were Harry James's *One O'Clock Jump*, Tommy Dorsey's *Boogie-Woogie*, Ella Fitzgerald's *A-tisket, A-tasket*, and three big hits by Artie Shaw: *Begin the Beguine, Nightmare* and *Black Bay Shuffle*. By 1940, overall record sales in the United States had risen to 100 million, for which the record industry could thank the popularity of swing. The best-known swing bands were invited to Hollywood to make movies and the bandleader, Artie Shaw, married the film star Ava Gardner. Through the media of films and records, swing quickly spread to Europe.

Sources: Pleasants (1974); Rust and Debus (1973)

John Hammond and Jazz on Record

John Hammond was born in 1910 into a wealthy New York family. On his mother's side he was related to the millionaire Vanderbilt family. John attended the finest private schools and took violin lessons. As a teenager he took an interest in the flourishing entertainments in his home city, and discovered Harlem and its jazz musicians just a few blocks away from his family's town house, which had room for sixteen servants and a dining hall for 250 guests. After his violin lessons he would slip away to listen to Bessie Smith at the Alhambra Theater in Harlem.

In 1931 John Hammond gave up his studies at Yale, having decided to devote his life to music. On a trip to London he was taken on by the *Melody Maker* as its United States correspondent. He actually wanted to be a record producer, but in 1931 the record industry did not favour new entrepreneurs. Because of the slump, record sales were virtually nil, and jazz was hardly being recorded at all. The first records he produced, a couple of piano solos by Garland Wilson, had to be paid for out of his own pocket.

In England, jazz was doing a bit better, and the Columbia company there was disappointed at not getting any new jazz recordings from its American subsidiary. Finally the company asked the young Hammond to produce a couple of jazz records for the English market. On 9 December 1932 John Hammond invited the Fletcher Henderson Band, which he admired, to a three-hour recording session, at which, according to Musicians' Union rules, four numbers had to be recorded. As usual, Henderson was two hours late for the recordings, and only three numbers were committed to wax, which eventually appeared in England.

The record producer's career had begun. Thanks to his family's wealth he did not have to earn a living from music, so he was able to concentrate on producing records that interested him. In those days a producer's duties in the studio were fairly simple. The most important job was to contact the artists and agree on the numbers to be recorded. If the band was not a permanent one, he would procure the accompanists and arrangements. A good record producer was, above all, a talent scout. In the studio the music was recorded as 'naturally' as possible, as in a live performance. With the technology available it could not be altered appreciably. There were a few microphones in the studio. The recording was made by etching the performance straight onto a wax disc, and if it did not succeed the first time, the whole thing was done again. (The big record companies generally made two takes of each number recorded as a matter of course. The unissued takes have sometimes been reissued.)

Initially, John Hammond acted as an agent for English record companies, and in this capacity he produced the first records on which the clarinettist, Benny Goodman, led a band. The soloist singing on one of these records was one of Hammond's finds, Billie Holiday. Goodman later married Hammond's sister, and Goodman's and Hammond's collaboration continued up until the 1960s, sometimes clouded by family feuds. In 1933 Hammond also got to fulfil a dream of his youth by producing Bessie Smith's last record. The ageing blues singer died shortly afterwards, in a road accident, on a tour of the South.

By 1935 Benny Goodman had established himself as a bandleader, and John Hammond produced a series of records for Victor which are among Goodman's best. They included 'Sometimes I'm Happy', 'Blue Skies' and 'King Porter Stomp'. His next find was Count Basie's band in Kansas City, and in 1936 Hammond recorded the band's first records for the Columbia subsidiary, Vocalion. Basie was, however, snapped up by a rival record company, Decca, when Columbia hesitated over his contract. Hammond was also responsible for many of Billie Holiday's recordings during this period.

By 1937 record production was on the increase again. The big-sellers now were the swing bands of Benny Goodman, Tommy Dorsey and Artie Shaw. The record companies needed producers who knew jazz, and John Hammond got a permanent contract with the newly resurrected Columbia company, for whom he produced records by Count Basie and Benny Goodman (both of them having meanwhile switched to Columbia). In Oklahoma City he discovered an electric guitarist named Charlie Christian and virtually forced Benny Goodman to sign him on with his band. The electric guitar in those days was still a little-used instrument, and Goodman did not believe in its possibilities, but the dazzling Christian proved to be the most significant new figure in jazz in the late 1930s.

The war temporarily brought the record producer's career to a halt. For a while Hammond was manager of the Keynote company, but in 1960 he returned to Columbia. He never lost his nose for talent. The artists he signed up for Columbia, and whose first records he produced, included Bob Dylan, Leonard Cohen and Bruce Springsteen. John Hammond died on 11 July 1987, at home, listening to an old Billie Holiday record.

Source: Hammond (1977)

Duke Ellington: The Composer in the Studio

The jazz historian could pick out many renowned bands from the 1930s. The decade may truly be called the 'golden age' of the big band. Musicians' wages were relatively low, and even a modest nightclub or dance hall could afford to pay bands of ten to fifteen members. The bandleaders were adored as stars, whereas the solo singers were regarded as mere rank-and-file musicians.

Fletcher Henderson, Jimmie Lunceford, Andy Kirk, Count Basie, Benny Goodman, Tommy Dorsey, Artie Shaw, Glenn Miller – these names are known to anyone with even a slight interest in jazz history. Yet there is one bandleader who rises head and shoulders above the rest: a man who has quite seriously been called the greatest American composer: Edward Kennedy Ellington – 'Duke'.

Duke Ellington was born in 1899 to a well-off Washington family. He had started his career as a pianist in a band he formed with some neighbourhood boys and by 1927 he had risen to become bandleader at the famed Cotton Club in New York. When the Duke Ellington Orchestra was forced to disband in 1973 owing to its leader's serious illness, it could look back on a career spanning virtually the entire history of jazz.

Nearly all the famous bandleaders of the thirties were also composers, and each of them had, with their arrangers, succeeded in creating a distinctive style for their bands. So did Ellington. There is something exceptional about Ellington's music, however. Ellington's role as the first important jazz composer forces a redefinition of the word 'composer'. Ellington's orchestra recorded hundreds of tunes, whose authorship was ascribed to Ellington, and many of them have become jazz standards, played by countless other musicians. But with hindsight it is evident that many of Ellington's best-known themes were the inventions of his band members or other musicians. The famous *Creole Love Call* was apparently the work of King Oliver; *Black and Tan Fantasy* is based on an idea by Bubber Miley – and so on. Towards the end of his career Ellington even had to go to court in copyright cases against various members of his orchestra, and he lost. When the search was on for the scores of Ellington's best-known recordings after his death, only a few scribbled notes were to be found.

Yet among Ellington's hundreds of recordings there are dozens that are part of the core of jazz history. The wild 'jungle rhapsodies' he recorded in 1926/27 capture the atmosphere of the Harlem nightclubs at their best: *East St Louis Toodleoo, Black and Tan Fantasy*. In 1933/34 there were the impressionistic orchestral tone poems such as *Solitude, Daybreak Express* and *Dear Old Southland*. In 1940, when Ellington's orchestra was at its peak in many people's view, it recorded *Ko-Ko, Concerto for Cootie, Conga Brava, Cotton Tail* and half a dozen other masterpieces for Victor. Ellington's best records contain many brilliant solos, but the end result is primarily Ellington's handiwork.

So what did this composer, who was not always a composer in the usual sense of the word, actually do? Ellington's orchestra was one of the longest-lived in jazz. Some of its members were friends from Ellington's youth, who were allowed to stay on, even though, in the critics' view, much better instrumentalists could be found. During Ellington's tour of Finland, drummer Sonny Greer was not even able to come onto the stage, owing to his drinking problem. All of them were personalities, however, whom Ellington had selected himself. Many of the best recordings by the Ellington band are built on the personal playing style of some member or members of the orchestra. For example, Johnny Hodges's alto saxophone was always powerfully charismatic, with an easily recognizable tone. Ellington's *Things ain't what they used to be* is not just a miniature concerto for an alto saxophone, but specifically for Johnny Hodges's alto saxophone. Ellington planned the framework for the performance, often the instrumental groups were left to work out the details of the arrangement, and the finishing touches were the task of the soloists. This close relationship between orchestra and composer can also be seen in Ellington's orchestration. He often changed the sound of the saxophone section by blending in Juan Tizol's trombone. The harmonies had a special Ellington flavour. His way of using all the nuances of the orchestra as his palette, and the small details of the arrangements, make these records immediately recognizable.

Early in his career Ellington frequently recorded the same composition on two or three different labels. Even after the orchestra was contracted to Victor, many of its recordings were made twice. In the different versions of these compositions we can trace how Ellington was actually composing in the studio. He would experiment, change his mind, and adjust the arrangement. In the minds of jazz fans, *Ko-Ko* and *Concerto for Cootie* have crystallized into the forms they took in the Victor studio in March 1940, though we know that on some other occasion they might have sounded quite different. Duke Ellington was a composer, but instead of a written score he used the recording studio as his tool.

Source: Collier (1987)

Jazz Finds a Home in Europe

Having made its first jazz records, the Original Dixieland Jazz Band had hardly become famous in New York when the band was invited to play in London. On 1 April 1919 the ensemble arrived on the liner Adriatic in Liverpool, and continued by train to London, where they had their first engagement at the Hippodrome. By 16 April the Original Dixieland Jazz Band was recording the tune *At the Jazz Band*

Ball for Columbia in London, and the rival Gramophone Company was soon issuing a version of the same tune recorded by the band for Victor in New York. At that time record companies were not taking the trouble to sign recording contracts with jazz bands guaranteeing them exclusive copyright. Although the ODJB's English audience was more astonished than enthusiastic, soon local jazz ensembles began to appear in England, Germany and other European countries, imitating the style of the ODJB.

The spread of jazz to Europe and the rest of the world from the 1920s onwards was the first great trend in musical history to occur mainly through the medium of recordings. Since the time of the Original Dixieland Jazz Band, American jazz recordings have been regularly released in Europe, and thanks to recordings, Louis Armstrong, Duke Ellington and the other great names in jazz became famous there long before their first visits. Indeed, without the records the tours would never have happened.

When they did arrive in Europe in person, they often made records during their visits. And when European musicians in turn began to gain a reputation in the jazz field, they also appeared on record. Being based mainly on improvisation, jazz could not have spread to Europe without the gramophone record. Improvisation cannot be learned from notation, and the American pioneers' tours were short. A record, however, can be played again and again, and one can gradually learn the secrets of jazz playing.

It took some time before it really dawned on either the enthusiasts or their opponents that jazz was neither a new dance step nor a new type of dance band. In the twenties every new dance was 'jazz', especially if there was a saxophone in the band, and the first jazz recordings made in Europe are often pathetic attempts to emulate the outward features of the new music. There is seldom any evidence of improvised solos or other essential features of the jazz idiom.

Knowledge of jazz in Europe grew markedly in the thirties. 'Hot clubs' were set up in the big cities for jazz enthusiasts. In 1932 the Belgian Robert Goffin published his book *Aux frontières du jazz*, and in 1934 the Frenchman Hugues Panassie's *Le jazz hot* appeared, which was translated into English, Danish and Swedish. In the same year the Finnish jazz magazine *Rytmi* started to appear. In 1936 the first jazz discographies appeared – catalogues of jazz recordings aiming at scientific accuracy, which attempted to give the performers, recording dates and other details often missing from the labels of historic jazz recordings; these were Hilton Schleman's *Rhythm on Record* in London and Charles Delaunay's *Hot Discography* in Paris.

Europe was ready to make its contribution to the development of jazz. The first internationally significant European jazz musician was the French guitarist Django Reinhardt. He was born in 1910 in a Gypsy caravan travelling through Belgium, and was so badly injured in a fire as a teenager that only the thumb, index and middle fingers of his left hand, so important for playing the guitar, could be used. Yet he developed a brilliant guitar technique of his own, which he first exploited in small tango groups. Django was a jazz fanatic whose great hero was Louis Armstrong, and in 1934 he set up his own 'Gypsy jazz band' under the aegis of the Hot Club of Paris – the Quintette du Hot Club de France. The group differed from an ordinary jazz band in its instrumentation: a violin, three guitars and a bass, and its repertoire consisted mostly of Django's own compositions. But in solos, Django's guitar soared like an eagle, and in the recordings he made with visiting American musicians of the calibre of Coleman Hawkins, Rex Stewart and Dicky Wells, Django had reason to be proud of his playing.

The QHCF's records appeared mostly on the Swing label, which was the first label in the world exclusively specializing in jazz. Its founders were the young jazz fans Hugues Panassie and Charles Delaunay, who persuaded the French Pathé-Marconi company to give them financial support. The first Swing number was issued in 1937: Coleman Hawkins's and Django Reinhardt's *Crazy Rhythm*. Django's playing had many admirers in the United States too, although his only visit to America ended miserably: he forgot to turn up at a concert where he was supposed to perform as soloist with Duke Ellington's band.

The most interesting contribution from England to the development of jazz in the thirties came from a young bass player and composer named Patrick 'Spike' Hughes. His father was the music critic of the *Daily Telegraph*, and 'Spike' was himself a prolific jazz journalist. Having abandoned his studies at Cambridge, he founded his own dance band and signed a recording contract with Decca under the punning name of Spike Hughes and his Decca-Dents. In 1933 Spike persuaded Decca, which was just setting up operations in the United States, to arrange a recording session for him in New York. In April and May 1933, with John Hammond's help, he put together a studio band, with a number of the best American musicians of the time, including Benny Carter and Coleman Hawkins. The fourteen numbers they recorded were mainly Spike Hughes's own compositions, an original blend of Delius and Ellington. The records were ahead of their time and were not commercial successes, but Coleman Hawkins's solo in *Donegal Cradle Song* is still regarded as one of his best.

In the 1980s the Harlequin label, under the guidance of discographer Rainer Lotz, issued a monumental series of LPs titled 'Jazz and Hot Dance' from various European countries. It traces the diffusion of jazz in Europe between the World Wars, from the first attempts by a Budapest Gypsy orchestra to tackle ragtime in the 1910s to the flowering of highly competent swing bands in Copenhagen, Prague and Moscow by the late 1930s.

Source: Priestley (1988)

Those Were the Days

European record production in the 1930s did not consist only of swing, though developments in the industry did otherwise follow the American pattern. Radio and the microphone brought into being a new type of singer, one whose voice was small but charismatic and with emotional appeal. The movies required a photogenic appearance. Bing Crosby's English counterpart was Al Bowlly, his French one was Tino Rossi and his Finnish one, Tauno Palo. Most of the singers who recorded were chiefly artists who had learned their trade on the stage, in dance halls, in restaurants and even on the streets, like Edith Piaf. The various forms of light musical theatre were still flourishing, and the variety, the cabaret, the vaudeville, the burlesque, the zarzuela, the music hall and other forms of music theatre offered work for countless composers, performers and singers, the best of whom were subsequently picked up by the record producers in the studio.

In those days musical entertainment still had clear national traits, even though most of the records made in Europe were the products of the various subsidiaries of either EMI (HMV–Columbia–Odeon–Pathé) or Siemens (Deutsche Grammophon–Telefunken). It was easy to distinguish the French, German or English styles, even if the popular films were spreading the stars' reputations across Europe, and the most popular songs were translated into other languages. In England, as in America, the dance band leaders were kings: men like Billy Cotton, Ray Noble and Harry Roy. The great names in France were Lucienne Boyer, Mistinguette, Maurice Chevalier and Charles Trenet. With its internal upheavals, Germany came to rely heavily on imported artists. Even in Finland, the stars of the popular UFA films such as the Swede Zarah Leander, the Chilean Rosita Serrano and the Dutch Johannes Heesters had many admirers.

There was even a Russian wave in European light music in the thirties, created by the flood of artists who fled after the revolution. At any European flea market, a pile of old 78s from this era is likely to contain some balalaika orchestras or Russian romances. The most talented of these performers was the singer-songwriter Aleksandr Vertinski. Vertinski had moved to China after the revolution and thence to western Europe, where he earned a living in restaurants patronized by emigrants, singing his own romances with piano accompaniment. The most famous of his recordings, which were mainly made for emigrants, was *Doroga dlinnaya* ('The Long Road'). This was later revived by the Welsh singer Mary Hopkin under the name 'Those Were the Days' and translated into many European languages, but of course Vertinski was not acknowledged as the composer on the labels.

Vertinski never got over his homesickness. He moved back to the Soviet Union in 1943 and died there, a well-loved songwriter, in 1957. Among Vertinski's contemporaries was the Ukrainian Pyotr Leschenko. After the revolution, like many he ended up in Paris, where he studied ballet. Soon, however, he moved to Romania. Leschenko owned a restaurant in Bucharest, from where he ventured forth on tours of Europe. His brisk adaptations of Gypsy songs to a foxtrot style entertained listeners in Russian restaurants in all the big cities of Europe, and many modern performers of Russian or Gypsy songs have sought inspiration from his records. Leschenko died in mysterious circumstances in Romania in the 1950s.

Sources: Leimbach (1991); Rust and Allen (1973)

The First King of the Tango

On 24 June 1935, near the town of Medellín in Colombia, there was an air crash which has passed into the annals of the gramophone. Those who died in the crash were the tango singer, Carlos Gardel, his three accompanists, his lyricist Alfredo le Pera, his masseur, his private secretary, his English teacher, his sound recordist and his manager. It was almost a royal party – and yet the tango singer in question had begun his career in the slums of Montevideo.

In 1935 Carlos Gardel was in the course of a big South American tour aboard his own aircraft. He had just made four films for Paramount and was well on his way to creating a movie career for himself in the United States, even though the English language sometimes seemed to present him with insurmountable obstacles. The son of immigrants born in Toulon, France, had come a long way. Carlos Gardel's official birthday, 11 December, is celebrated in Argentina as 'tango day', although his real birthday is not known. On their arrival in Uruguay as immigrants, at the turn of the century, the boy's mother had given his birth date as 11 December 1890, but the actual year of birth was probably about five years earlier.

Gardel began his career in Montevideo singing duets with an older singer named Juan Razzano, and made his first record in 1917 for Lindström's Nacional label. At that time the tango was dance music performed by small dance bands. Sometimes lyrics were sung on the records, mostly they were not. Carlos developed tango singing into an art form. He often performed on record accompanied by just two or three guitars, and he made his best records at the end of the twenties, when microphone recording brought out every nuance in his voice.

Gardel liked to interpret the tangos written in Buenos Aires slang by Enrique Santos Discepolo, whose mood was balanced on the invisible boundary between romanticism and cynicism. *Esta noche me emborracho* ('Tonight I'll Get Drunk') was a song to the memory of a love lost a decade earlier. *Que vachache?* ('What's to be Done?') is a song with no illusions of a world where money dominates and Jesus is no better than a thief. *Yira...yira* ('Windborne') is also classic Gardel:

You know that everything is a lie, there is no love,
the world doesn't care about anything.

Gardel was also an important tango composer himself; such compositions as *Volver* and *Cuesto abajo* are classics of their genre. Despite his background near the River Plate, Carlos Gardel's popularity knew no borders. He often visited Spain, he made his debut in Paris in 1928 and in the thirties he was on his way to a film career in the United States. In the hope of finding new markets he switched in 1934 to RCA Victor and abandoned Lindström, on whose Odeon label all his records had appeared for over a decade. Inspired by Rudolf Valentino's film career, he studied English eagerly and even made one record in English, which had to be rejected, however, because of his pronunciation. We will never know whether Gardel might have made a career in the Anglo-Saxon world as well. In Argentina and Uruguay he became almost a national saint, whose portrait can be found in homes alongside the Blessed Virgin.

Before the Second World War the tango was South America's most successful musical export. It was, however, only one among many local styles. If one browses through the Latin American record catalogues of those years one encounters brass bands, *zarzuelas* (Spanish operettas) and the local forms of dance music in each country. Rising to a place of honour alongside the tango among the many Latin American regional dance music traditions is the Cuban *son*.

Son is one of the many Afro-Cuban forms which once existed unobserved by the rest of the world. The typical *son* grouping is a sextet or septet containing, in addition to a solo singer, guitar and trumpet, some Cuban rhythm instruments:

claves, maraccas, marimbula, botijeula, bongo drums. With the acoustic method it would not be possible to record such a combination of instruments, but after the advent of electric recording it was possible to strike a balance between the rhythmic and melodic instruments in the studio. The famous Sexteto Habanero made its first record in Havana in November 1925, and Ignazio Pineiro's Sexteto Nacional followed shortly thereafter.

Tourism, recording and the Cuban musicians who had emigrated to the United States aroused interest in Cuban music from the rest of the world in the thirties, although the old *son* compositions generally spread to the United States in the guise of rumba. At the same time Cuban orchestras were also visiting Paris and London, giving Europeans their first contact with the music. Romantic Hollywood movies with a Latin American setting further contributed to the spread of these melodies around the world. By the late thirties, London, Paris and New York all had their resident Cuban orchestras, often, in fact, mixing musicians from many Latin countries.

In recent years the genuine *son* seems to have enjoyed a renaissance both at home and abroad. The old recordings of the Sexteto Nacional from the twenties have been issued on LP and CD for the first time, and new *son* groups have been formed outside Cuba. Yet the recordings of Latin American music from those years are still generally unknown to collectors; the future may still produce some surprises from among them.

Sources: Collier (1986); Diaz Ayala (1994)

The Gramophone in Piraeus

The first Greek records were made at the turn of the century, in Constantinople and Smyrna, cities ruled by the Turkish sultan, whose tea houses and places of entertainment employed hundreds of Turkish, Greek and Armenian musicians. Gramophone, Columbia and Odeon had to compete with Orfeon records, which were pressed locally in Constantinople by the Blumenthal company. Here recordings were made featuring such traditional instruments as *ut* (lute), *kanun* (zither) and *sanduri* (hammered dulcimer), popular among Turks and Greeks alike. Then Turkey collapsed in the World War. Greece went defiantly to war against a weakened Turkey and lost. Hundreds of thousands of Greeks were expelled from Turkey. Piraeus, the port city of Athens, filled up with refugee camps. As Greece struggled with its economic difficulties, those who could afford recorded music had to make do with Greek records made in America.

Gradually, however, in the taverns and cafés of the port, the music brought by refugees from Turkey evolved into a new form. Greeks from the archipelago and the colourful figures of the Piraeus underworld made their own contribution. The lyrics of the songs abandoned the old decorative Byzantine language and instead spoke of everyday life in the port: of the pickpocket from whom the police try to force a confession with a beating, of the hashish dens and wine bars, of the salvation of drunkenness, of the misery of gaol. The accompanying instruments were the stringed bouzouki, and the little baglama, which was even taken into gaol if need be. The new music was called *rebetika*.

In the middle of the Depression, rebetika music was ripe for committing to record, naturally on the various EMI labels, which had their competing representatives even in Greece. The bouzouki player and singer Markos Vamvakaris, from the island of Syros, was one of its first stars. Roza Eskenazi, of Sephardic Jewish extraction, rose to become leading female soloist. Younger musicians, too, gradually came to the fore, such as Vassilis Tsitsanis, who gave up his law studies for the charms of the bouzouki. Tsitsanis's *Sinnefiasmeni kyriaki* ('Cloudy Sunday') is one of the fundamental compositions of rebetika music.

The dictator Metaxas, who seized power in 1936, tried in vain to suppress the proletarian rebetika and put the sophisticated foreign tango in its place (it, too, was just as proletarian in origin). By the end of the fifties, with the natural change of generations, the rebetika began to give way. The slums of Piraeus were pulled down to make way for a modern city, but soon composers of Mikis Theodorakis's generation were starting to make use of rebetika elements in a new way. Today the rebetika is accepted as a part of the national tradition in Greece, but if one wants to seek out the real spirit of the period of its birth, one must look for it on the records of 50 years ago.

Source: Holst (1975)

Calypso: The Singing Newspaper

The rich musical tradition of the Caribbean islands is the result of the blending of many African and European ingredients. France, Spain, England, Holland and even Denmark have all in turn colonized islands there and left their traces in their music. African and European religions, dances, carnivals and even street fights have required their own music. But, apart from Cuba, the islands are so small and poor that they were of little interest to record manufacturers. The Victor company made a couple of recording trips to Trinidad in the early years of the century, but otherwise musical recordings for the region were made only by musicians who emigrated to New York, Paris or London.

Thanks to its oil, Trinidad, with less than a million inhabitants, is one of the richer islands in the Caribbean. The Trinidadian carnival music, the calypso, has been popular all over the English-speaking Caribbean since the 1920s. When the Sa Gomes company in Port of Spain got the franchise for American Decca in 1935, it was natural that the company began regularly recording contemporary calypsos. Decca technicians visited Port of Spain at least once a year, and in the meantime the renowned calypso singers had to travel to New York, where there were Caribbean musicians who were suitable as accompanists. Decca's blue-labelled Trinidad records appeared regularly for a period of about ten years from 1935.

Every year at carnival time the calypso singers competed for the title of 'King of Calypso'. The winners preferred imposing names for themselves such as The Lion, Atilla the Hun, King Radio, or Houdini. The songs were just as likely to deal with local gossip as with great world events. When the black Joe Louis beat the German Max Schmelling in the world heavyweight boxing championship, black Trinidadians identified strongly with the winner, and several calypso records were made about the fight. The abdication of Edward VIII was of course also worth a calypso. But in addition to 'parish pump' news, the subjects were the Spanish Civil War, the Ethiopian war and the gradual spread of the Second World War. In 1940 Atilla even commented on the Finnish Winter War in his calypso called 'Finland', siding with the small nation fighting against dictators.

Many calypsos tell of events that happened in the singer's immediate circle. If a female neighbour left her husband, that would give rise to a song ruminating on the eternal problem of male–female relationships. The hearers of the song might not know the details of the event, but they would enjoy the singer's witty lyrics, which would become catchphrases. In his early novels about Trinidad, V.S. Naipaul gives a lively account of these occasions. But the records would also take a strong line on local politics. The years 1935–40 were a time of political upheaval in Trinidad. In June 1936 the oil workers, led by Uriah Butler, declared a strike and fourteen workers died in the unrest which arose when police tried to break the strike. The Governor had to resign, and this led to a chain of events which eventually brought about Trinidad's independence in 1962. Obviously, the events were immortalized on record, although the British authorities censored the more radical lyrics.

It was particularly galling to the authorities that after the strike Butler managed to go into hiding for three months, despite an intensive police hunt. On his record *Where was Butler?*, Atilla claims to have asked Butler directly where he was hiding:

> He said, '*Atilla, I was right in the city,*
> *Arrest by police is what I really feared*
> *So I just clip me moustache and shave off me beard.*'

The calypso singers were able to mock Hitler with impunity on their records; the war did not actually reach the Caribbean. On the other hand, Trinidad had a large American military base during the war. For a while calypso came into the consciousness of the whole United States, when the popular singing group the Andrews Sisters recorded a song called 'Rum and Coca-Cola', which became one of the hits of 1944. A man named Morey Amsterdam was credited on the label as the composer. Later a court established that the tune was actually from *L'année passée*, by the Trinidadian pianist, Lionel Belasco, and published as long ago as 1906. Some years later the Jamaican-born Harry Belafonte created another calypso wave in the United States, and for a brief period calypsos were played and imitated all over the world.

The Unlikely Rise of Australian Country Music

Australia has never been one of the centres of the musical world, but during the boom years of the 1920s, music-hungry Australians had supported four record-pressing plants. With the Depression, they were closed, one by one, but the

Columbia factory at Homebush, Sydney, managed to continue operations through the lean years. When HMV and Columbia joined their operations in 1931, it became the headquarters of Australian EMI.

During the twenties, Australia had mainly been an importer of British and American recordings. Australians were eager to keep abreast of musical events in London, but they were also prepared to lend an ear to new forms of American popular music. By the 1930s, local artists also emerged. Among the talent recorded were Jim Davidson's Australian Broadcasting Company dance orchestra and Jacko, the 'broadcasting kookaburra'. But in retrospect, the most original Australian recording artist of the 1930s was Tex Morton, the father of Australian country music.

Tex Morton, born Bob Lane in New Zealand in 1916, had acquired a local following as a performer of American hillbilly songs. His first recordings, cut at EMI's Homebush studios in 1936, 'Texas in the Spring' and 'Going Back to Texas', were clearly aimed at audiences which associated country music with cowboy movies and American recordings. But he soon started recording his own compositions such as 'Yodelling Bagman' and 'Murrumbidgee Jack'.

Morton's singing style was based on Jimmie Rodgers and his American followers, but he successfully transferred the idiom to Australian soil. He later became a successful hypnotist and TV actor, but he was followed by a number of singers such as Smokey Dawson, Slim Dusty and Buddy Williams, who continued to write original Australian country songs. The most faithful audience for these records was on isolated farms, where fans would rise at 5 a.m., tune into their favourite country music programmes and hear songs such as Smilin' Billy Blinkhorn's 'Sunny Queensland' before milking the cows:

> Give me my old pony and a saddle
> way out where the sheep and cattle roam,
> Where the waving gum trees sigh,
> the dingo's lonely cries,
> and I know I am in my sunny Queensland home.

The spread of new forms of music from the New World into Europe had been greatly assisted by the gramophone, but it had been spearheaded by visiting artists from the New World who first made Europeans aware of these idioms. European songwriters and performers were usually careful to emulate the dress, language and imagery associated with these styles. Dutch tangos had Spanish titles, and the recordings of Swedish steel guitarists always contained some reference to the South Seas. Australian country music is unique in the way it quickly adopted the imagery of the Australian outback. After the Second World War, many American country singers toured Australia, but the birth of Australian country music is an example of a musical idiom which spread to another continent and acquired a new life there almost exclusively on the strength of recordings.

Source: Hill (1993)

Birth of the Record Library

By the mid-1930s the worst of the Depression was over, and record sales were enjoying a resurgence. Although the sales figures for 1929 were now a distant dream for the manufacturers – in most countries they were only matched again after the Second World War – the resurgence created a new interest in records as cultural artefacts. In the United States, libraries started acquiring records in addition to printed material. The world's first national record archive was established in France. The first discographies – detailed catalogues of records – were appearing.

Andrew Carnegie (1837–1919) was an American steel magnate who left his huge fortune to the trust that bears his name. It was with Carnegie's backing that the famous Carnegie Hall was built in New York. In the twenties the fund donated art collections to several universities to raise the students' cultural standards. In 1925 the foundation decided to start raising the profile of music in universities. Initially, collections of scores and instruments were considered, but in 1929 the standard of mechanical music was deemed to be so high that records could be used in music education. The Carnegie Foundation resolved to donate record archives to selected universities, consisting of records that were available on the market. The first collections were handed over in 1933. They were accompanied by a Capehart record player, which represented the acme of sound reproduction.

The Carnegie series consisted of several hundred records, and was not intended for individual music lovers. Similar ideas were in the air elsewhere, however. In the late twenties the German Parlophone label issued a set of ten records compiled by the musicologist, Curt Sachs, a digest of '200 years of music' before Bach. Columbia, in England, expanded on the idea by issuing an aural history of music on 40 records compiled by Percy Scholes. This still represented a straightforward western concept of the development of music from ancient Greece to modern times, but, at the same time, Erich von Hornbostel assembled a collection of ten discs for the Lindström concern, 'The music of the Orient'. The records covered all of Asia, from the Arab lands to Japan. This was the first time that examples of the vast Lindström output of records for the Oriental market was issued to the European public. In 1933 Curt Sachs, who in the meantime had had to flee to France, began issuing a series of records devoted to ancient music, *L'Anthologie sonore*, which in time ran to several hundreds of records.

Record collectors also became active. In 1932 the International Record Collectors' Club (IRCC) was established to reissue historic vocal recordings, many of them having been unavailable for a quarter of a century. In 1936 Roberto Bauer of Milan published what became a bible for classical record collectors, the *Historical Records* discography, cataloguing operatic records issued before 1909. In the same year Charles Delaunay's *Hot Discography*, a seminal work for jazz record collectors, appeared in France.

The records listed in it were mainly rarities, no longer available, but at the same time books were also starting to appear which assessed records that were on the market. When David Hall's *Record Book* appeared in the United States in 1940, it was a surprising sales success: 60,000 music lovers bought this volume. In the same year, in Berlin, the first doctoral thesis to be presented on the subject of records was published: Dietrich Schulz-Köhn's *Die Schallplatte auf dem Weltmarkt* – still a useful study of the international record trade.

In 1936, Eric Clarke and Philip Miller were given the task of revising the Carnegie record collection, taking into account new discs that had appeared in the meantime. This gave Miller the opportunity of going through the entire catalogue of records then available. In Europe it would have been much more difficult to compile such a collection.

In 1936 it was no longer a problem to acquire the entire core of the concert repertoire on disc, from Bach to Wagner. There were numerous recordings of Beethoven's symphonies available, and for the enlightenment of students there were also three string quartets, the piano concerto no. 4, played by Schnabel, the violin concerto, played by Szigeti, and excerpts from *Fidelio*. Mozart, Brahms, Schubert, Tchaikovsky and Sibelius only caused problems of selection, and many of the recordings selected are still exemplary. It was harder to find more modern music. For example, little of Mahler had been recorded by 1936, and the only piece included in the collection was *Ich bin den Welt abhanden gekommen*. As for Charles Ives, *General Booth Ascends into Heaven* was available. Carillo's microtonal *Preludio de Cristobal Colon* seems just a curiosity from the standpoint of the present day. Older music caused similar problems. In the thirties there was much talk of 'authentic' interpretations of Bach and Haydn, but the recordings available were more representative of arrangements from the Romantic period. The first recordings made on the Baroque organ had just come on the market.

It was mostly American university students who came to benefit from the Carnegie record collection, but many American public libraries began lending records in the 1930s, and the record section of the New York Public Library, under the direction of Philip Miller, soon developed into a pioneering operation in music librarianship. In Europe, France was in the vanguard: in 1938 the Phonotèque Nationale was established there, and a law was passed obliging record companies to submit to the archive one copy of every record it issued. Most other European countries had to wait until the 1960s, or even later, until national sound archives were established.

CHAPTER FIVE

From the Copyright Wars to the World War

Aryan Germany

Since the 1920s, Germany had been the leading musical country in Europe and Berlin had been a musical metropolis ranking with London, Paris and Vienna. Its academy of music had Hindemith and Schoenberg as teachers of composition, Emanuel Feuerman teaching cello and Artur Schnabel piano. Also working in Berlin was the great violin teacher, Carl Flesch. The solo cellist of the Berlin Philharmonic was Gregor Piatigorsky. The State Opera had Erich Kleiber and Leo Blech as its conductors, the Kroll Opera had Otto Klemperer and the Städtische Oper had Bruno Walter.

When Hitler came to power in 1933, not only did such clearly leftist figures as Brecht, Weill and Hanns Eisler have to flee, but also all those mentioned above, as well as dozens of other distinguished artists. Furtwängler put up some opposition, Hitler gave him an hour-long harangue on the Aryan race and placed him under Gestapo surveillance. The ranks of entertainers were thinned out as well. The hugely popular singing group, the Comedian Harmonists, disbanded, since its Jewish members had to leave the country. Most galling of all, though, was that Marlene Dietrich, the daughter of a German officer, proved deaf to the entreaties of the Third Reich and refused to perform ever again in Germany.

The expansion of Greater Germany into Austria resulted in a wave of emigration by operetta composers. Paul Abraham, the composer of *Viktoria and her Hussar*, fled to Cuba, where he had to make a living as a piano teacher. Oscar Straus, the author of the *Waltz Dream*, subsequently had a nervous breakdown in New York. The waltz king, Robert Stolz, fared better, achieving moderate success in the United States as a light music composer. It was no longer permissible to perform the works of exiles, and soon the only living composer good enough for the German operetta stage was Franz Lehár, approaching his seventies but prepared, if the need arose, to mould his works to fit the demands of the new ideology. Even he got into difficulties over his Jewish-born wife, but he was allowed to live in peace, because *The Merry Widow* was Hitler's favourite operetta. Lehár's long-standing librettist, Fritz Löhner (*Schön ist die Welt* and *Giuditta*), was gassed at Auschwitz.

The purge of Jews not only affected artists, but reached record companies too: their international links aroused suspicions of 'international Zionism'. The leading record companies, Electrola (HMV) and Lindström (Odeon and Columbia) were subsidiaries of the English EMI concern until this link was severed on the outbreak of war. The most important German labels were Deutsche Grammophon (Polydor) and Telefunken; both were controlled by the giant Siemens electrical corporation. The music censorship office set up by the Nazis, the Reichsmusik-Prufstelle, made prior examinations of the record companies' publication plans, and the Gestapo went around the record companies' warehouses with their lists, removing the music of Jewish composers. The Aryanized record companies rushed to release Germanic music, and the highlight of these was Telefunken's partial recording, at Bayreuth in 1936, of Wagner's *Lohengrin*, *Siegfried* and *Die Walküre*.

Of those conductors who remained, one who now rose to prominence was Herbert von Karajan, a member of the Nazi party and a favourite of Göring, who was interested in opera. Succeeding Walter as conductor of the Gewandhaus in Leipzig was Hermann Abendroth, who recorded Brahms. The aged composer Richard Strauss, to whom Hitler had given a place of honour as chairman of the Reichsmusikkammer, made recordings for Deutsche Grammophon's Polydor label of his symphonic poems *Don Quixote* and *Ein Heldenleben*. Even such massive works as Bruckner's fourth and fifth symphonies were put on record; the conductor on the Electrola recording was Karl Böhm. The most important of Telefunken's foreign orchestral conductors was Willem Mengelberg who, partly in Berlin and partly in occupied Holland, conducted Beethoven's and Brahms's symphonies, Schubert and Liszt. This conductor, called the Napoleon of the orchestra, because of his virtuosity, had to flee to Switzerland after the war owing to his pro-German sympathies.

The most famous instrumental soloists in the Deutsche Grammophon stable before the war were the Beethoven pianists Wilhelm Kempff and Elly Ney, as well as the only great violinist to remain in Germany, Georg Kulenkampff, whose recording in 1936 of Beethoven's violin concerto ranks in its classicism alongside Kreisler's interpretation made in the same year. Kulenkampff can also be heard on a number of concert recordings from these years, including an outstanding interpretation of Sibelius's violin concerto with Furtwängler. In those days German radio had extremely highly developed recording technology, and since the radio's archives were broken up after the war into both official archives and the collections of music-loving Allied officers, there have been steady streams of reissues of the historical recordings from this period. Many of them have had their origins in recordings taken to the Soviet Union in 1945.

After Artur Schnabel moved to England in 1933, having been ousted from his post at the Berlin Academy of Music, only Kempff and Ney remained to carry on the German tradition of piano playing, focusing on the figures of Beethoven and Schubert. As an interpreter of the latter composer, and ranking with Schnabel, was Eduard Erdmann, who made some recordings for Odeon and DGG.

Of the great singers, those who remained in Germany were Gerhard Hüsch, Tiana Lemnitz, Helge Roswaenge and Heinrich Schlusnus, who was just beginning his career. In the coloratura field there was competition between the celebrated star of the Berlin State Opera, Erna Berger, and Erna Sack of the Dresden State

Opera, whose range extended over four octaves. Of the great vocal works, Beethoven's *Missa solemnis* had been recorded as early as 1928. The complete recording by Bruno Kittel in 1941 for DGG of Bach's *St Matthew Passion* aroused great attention not least because of its cost – 60,000 German marks. The matrices were taken by submarine to Japan, where 17,000 copies of this eighteen-record album were sold before the end of the war. Kittel also recorded Mozart's *Requiem*.

At the same time as the German recording of the *Missa solemnis*, Bach's B minor mass had appeared in England, conducted by Albert Coates, with the solo parts sung by Elisabeth Schumann and Friedrich Schorr. The war put an end to such grand ventures, though in German-occupied France there were still complete recordings of Debussy's opera *Pelléas et Mélisande* and Berlioz's *Damnation of Faust*, the former conducted by Roger Desormière, the latter by Jean Fournet. Fournet also made a 22-sided recording of Berlioz's *Requiem*, with the Paris Radio Orchestra and Choir, later referred to by the American critic David Hall as 'the best recording made in the world during the war years'.

Before the Deluge

The last years before the outbreak of world war witnessed the triumphal progress of Fascism in Europe. Civil war was raging in Spain, ending with the Francoites' victory in 1939. In 1938 Germany annexed Austria. The following year it was Czechoslovakia's turn, and on 3 September 1939 war broke out, following Germany's invasion of Poland. Soon Sweden, Switzerland and Portugal were the only havens of peace in Europe. As the politicians and generals planned their advances, musicians were in retreat. Nevertheless, just before the deluge, in 1937/38, some historic recordings were made in Europe.

In 1937 Fred Gaisberg, who had just turned 64, decided to record Dvořák's cello concerto in the composer's homeland with a Czech orchestra. The natural choice was the Czech Philharmonic Orchestra, whose conductor was George Szell. The recording venue was the Deutsche Haus in Prague, a concert hall famous for its acoustics. Soloists of sufficient calibre were not to be found in Czechoslovakia, however, so Gaisberg's choice fell on Pablo Casals. Casals was, at the time, Minister of Culture in the democratic Catalan government, but he flew from Barcelona to Prague, where he gave first a public concert, and the next day made a recording. After the recording Casals was on the point of collapse, but there is not a trace of his exhaustion on the record; the entry of the cello is like a lion's roar. Soon after the recording George Szell moved to England, and thence on to the United States. Casals returned to Barcelona, but soon had to flee his homeland, to which he never returned.

The following year saw Gaisberg in Vienna, recording Mahler with Bruno Walter. Walter was born in Berlin into a modest middle-class Jewish family. From 1901 to 1913 he worked in Vienna as a conductor in close collaboration with Gustav Mahler. Mahler even gave him permission to make necessary changes in the scores of his works, and after the composer's death he conducted the first performance of his ninth symphony. In the twenties Walter conducted orchestras in various places in Europe and America with great success. After Hitler's rise to power he no longer had a place in Germany, however, and settled in Vienna. On Sunday, 16 January 1938, at the Musikvereinsaal in Vienna, Gaisberg recorded a concert of Mahler's ninth symphony with the Vienna Philharmonic, conducted by Walter. The concert was graced by the presence of Chancellor Schuschnigg, whom the Nazis imprisoned a couple of months later. Recorded at the same time was Mahler's song cycle, *Das Lied von der Erde*, with Kerstin Thorborg and Charles Kullman as soloists. Several of Mahler's symphonies had not been recorded at all, and this was the first recording of the ninth symphony.

After the Anschluss, Walter fled to France, and soon he and Gaisberg met again in the studio, this time with the orchestra of the Paris Conservatoire, recording Berlioz's *Symphonie fantastique*. In 1939 Gaisberg retired. Walter was not able to continue working in France for long, because in 1940 he was obliged to continue his exile in the United States. There he became one of the country's most highly regarded conductors, and over the years he recorded industriously with many American orchestras, including most of Mahler's symphonies. In 1952 Walter encountered the Vienna Philharmonic again, when he recorded the song cycle, *Das Lied von der Erde* for Decca. That, too, has become a famous record, not least because of Kathleen Ferrier, who sang the alto part on this occasion. The 1938 recording, however, is an invaluable historical document of the last days of the old Austria.

Source: Gaisberg (1942)

America: Gathering-place of the Great Musicians

While the Nazis were consolidating their power in Germany and Fascism was advancing in Europe, on the other side of the ocean, people were recovering from the great blow of 1929. As economic life recovered, so too, musical life quickened. In the first part of 1936, RCA Victor was selling between 800,000 and 900,000 records a month. By Christmas it had reached a million. Annual total record sales in the United States were now exceeding twenty million. In Germany in the same year, not even a figure of two million records could be achieved. One result of Hitler's persecution of the Jews was a welcome addition to the ranks of recording artists in the United States. Apart from Furtwängler, all the great conductors were now working in America: Toscanini, Walter, Fritz Busch as well as the Hungarian-born Fritz Reiner and Eugene Ormandy. Of the great living composers, apart from Strauss and Sibelius, a larger proportion were working in the great musical centres of the USA.

Most of the great American orchestras had previously recorded for Victor. When, in 1934, RCA Victor re-established its Red Seal series, Eugene Ormandy's name was new to it. He conducted the Minneapolis Symphony Orchestra, and continued the virtuoso tradition established by Stokowski, recording such works as Kodály's *Háry János* suite and Schoenberg's *Verklärte Nacht*. When the new records were marketed, the public was made familiar with a new term, 'High Fidelity', which promised the buyer a guarantee of the best possible sound. No new invention had actually been made in the industry – it was more a matter of publicity than of technical advancement. The next year Ormandy recorded a live concert performance of Mahler's second symphony, in whose final movement the bells of a nearby church were used. The same year the Boston Symphony Orchestra returned to the Red Seal series playing Strauss's tone poem *Also sprach Zarathustra*, which contained the 'greatest crescendo ever recorded'.

Towering above all the other conductors recording in the thirties, however, was Arturo Toscanini, the former conductor of La Scala, Milan. From 1926 to 1936 he was guest conductor of the New York Philharmonic. Toscanini was one of the greatest conductors of his day; his brisk tempos, his unromantic interpretations, faithful to the score, and his rehearsals which streched the orchestra to its limits, made him a model with whom competitors were inevitably compared. But in a country where modern advertising and public relations had just been invented, he was soon made into a legend. Toscanini's whims and outbursts provided limitless material for the press. He was a political opponent of Mussolini, but otherwise was not politically active. To the public, Toscanini epitomized music, and only works conducted by Toscanini (which included virtually no music of this century) were considered 'great music'.

Toscanini had long been suspicious of gramophone records. He did not understand the technology, and he did not have the patience to familiarize himself with the demands of recording technique, though he had had experience of the studios since 1920. In 1936 he agreed to record again with the New York Philharmonic. Three years earlier, engineers for Victor had secretly made a recording by optical means (the film soundtrack method) of his radio broadcast of Beethoven's fifth and sixth symphonies. The maestro, enraged and also dissatisfied with the result, had demanded that the matrices be destroyed.

The time was now ripe, and Toscanini's great series for Victor began. For the first time, engineers used several wax cutters, so as to avert the need to interrupt works to fit the length of a record side. The recording took three days, and resulted in seven works being issued, which represented the peak of technical achievement of the time. The best of them were the *Siegfried Idyll*, and 'Dawn' and 'Siegfried's Rhine Journey' from Wagner's *Götterdämmerung*; but Toscanini was still not satisfied. However, in New York alone 2500 copies of the Wagner album were sold in the ensuing months, although the sets cost $10 each.

In 1936 Toscanini retired from his post as conductor of the Philharmonic and moved to his villa in Italy, but he soon became bored by the inactivity. In his days at La Scala he had refused to conduct the Fascist hymn, *Giovinezza*, at the end of operatic performances, and as Mussolini consolidated his dictatorship, his position in Italy became dangerous. When, in the following year, David Sarnoff created, for Toscanini's sake, a symphony orchestra for the NBC radio network, which was owned by RCA, the maestro was pleased to return to the platform.

From 1937 to 1939 Toscanini was making records alternately for RCA Victor and HMV. Of these, the English recordings with the BBC Orchestra are generally excellent; the American recordings with the NBC Orchestra are less satisfactory. The superiority of the English records is probably due to the excellent accoustics of the Queen's Hall in London, which was subsequently destroyed in the war. On the other hand, Victor, at Sarnoff's request, had to record in the infamous radio studio 8H at the NBC, where the maestro's Saturday evening concerts were broadcast all over the United States, with numerous reporters covering the events.

The studio was acoustically dry, and lacked reverberation. The orchestra therefore sounded lifeless. The NBC technicians exaggerated the effect of dryness by using microphones placed near the instrumental groups of the orchestra. The LP reissue, made in the sixties, added artificial reverberation, but the newer CD pressings have generally gone back to the sound of the original records. The best records of this period are Weber's *Invitation to the Dance*, the overtures from Rossini's opera, *The Silken Ladder* ('La scala di seta') and Mozart's *The Magic Flute*. Unusually, Toscanini's tempi grew quicker as he got older.

With the outbreak of war, Toscanini remained permanently in America, and in 1940 he recorded Beethoven's violin concerto with Heifetz. With his son-in-law, Horowitz, he recorded Brahms's second piano concerto, in which the orchestra's playing is hardly audible at all, and in the following year Tchaikovsky's piano concerto no. 1, whose sound, the Toscanini expert Robert Charles Marsh claims, is eminently suitable for jukeboxes. Marsh picks out the immolation scene from Wagner's *Götterdämmerung*, sung by Helen Traubel, as the best recording made with the NBC orchestra; it was recorded at Carnegie Hall in 1941. At the end of the war Toscanini recorded as untypical a work as Gershwin's tone poem, *An American in Paris*. It was technically very successful, but otherwise Toscanini's literal adherence to the score in his conducting does not really suit Gershwin's style. Before the ban on recording in 1947, Toscanini also recorded Mozart's divertimento, KV 287, which the critic, Howard Taubman, cites as an example of how Mozart should be played.

The Victor engineers often secretly kept the microphone open during Toscanini's rehearsals, and the documentary recordings subsequently issued bear witness to his Vesuvian outbursts. Circulating among collectors for a long time, too, have been copies of a recording of a rehearsal for *La Traviata* in which Toscanini himself performs all the sung parts, accompanied by the NBC orchestra. Even in the early 1950s, aged over eighty, Toscanini made a large number of recordings, among them many famous overtures, the virtuoso *La Mer* of Debussy, Strauss's *Till Eulenspiegel*, Mussorgsky's *Pictures at an Exhbition*, Schubert's 'Great C major' symphony and his only commercial recording of Sibelius, a simply-styled and direct rendering of *Finlandia*. The recording of Beethoven's ninth symphony, made at Carnegie Hall in 1952, even Toscanini himself regarded as 'almost satisfactory'.

Altogether Toscanini made 262 recordings of 186 different works, as well as 33 so-called 'V-discs', which the US Army distributed to troops during and after the war. Subsequently, numerous radio broadcasts were also released, as well as previously unreleased recordings and other documentary material, the most significant of which are *Falstaff*, *The Magic Flute* and *The Mastersingers*, recorded by Austrian radio at the Salzburg Festival of 1937. Hundreds of hours of his radio broadcasts are still stored away in archives. When Toscanini's phenomenal memory failed him once, in 1954, and he gave up his conducting career for good, twenty million copies of his records had been sold. Charles O'Connell, who produced most of Toscanini's recordings for Victor, later wondered, in an article, whether Toscanini believed he was the greatest conductor in the world, but came to the conclusion that the maestro was convinced he was the only *good* conductor in the world.

Sources: Horowitz (1987); O'Connell (1947)

The Price War of 1940 and the Battle of the Orchestras

In 1938, 33 million records were sold in the United States, in 1941 the figure was 127 million. The slump in the record business was finally over. The man who was responsible for raising artistic standards once again in the record industry was Edward Wallerstein, who took over at the Columbia company in 1938. Wallerstein had started in 1930 as sales manager at Brunswick and, a couple of years later, moved to become head of record production at RCA Victor. There he saw how the old record company rode out the Depression under the wing of the huge radio concern. Wallerstein had rejuvenated record sales after RCA started manufacturing moderately-priced radiograms.

When record sales took a turn for the better in the late thirties, Wallerstein fixed his gaze on Columbia. In the twenties it had been a serious competitor of Victor, but during the Depression it had shrunk to become one of Consolidated Films' many record labels. To give himself a free hand, Wallerstein talked the head of CBS radio, William Paley, into buying Consolidated Films' entire record production for $700,000, including the valuable Columbia label. Wallerstein, of course, became head of Columbia.

Wallerstein had seen that in the classical music field Victor had a virtual monopoly in the United States. All the major classical artists were recording for Victor's Red Seal records. Rival record companies had mainly been relying on importing from Europe. He set about reversing this situation but realized that in order to do so, turnover would have to increase, and the best way to achieve this would be to reduce prices. On 6 August 1940, without warning, Wallerstein started his discount sale. Retail prices were drastically reduced, and retailers were allowed to return their existing stock of older Columbia records if they agreed to buy one new record at the new reduced price, for every three returned. This caused a commotion, during which Wallerstein himself fled to Canada. When he returned ten days later, the battle had been won. RCA was forced to reduce its prices, and since it had bigger stocks, it would have suffered a catastrophe had it not had artists like Toscanini and the NBC Orchestra to fall back on.

The battle for the orchestras was now on. Wallerstein poached the New York Philharmonic from RCA, in addition to which he signed up the Minneapolis Orchestra, conducted by Mitropoulos, the Los Angeles Orchestra, led by Klemperer, Stokowski with the All-American Youth Orchestra, as well as the Cleveland and Chicago Orchestras. Since Columbia also had the big names of swing, Benny Goodman, Duke Ellington and Count Basie, it had virtual control of the orchestral music field.

The orchestras who remained with RCA were by no means bad. Toscanini and the NBC Orchestra, Koussevitzky and the Boston Symphony Orchestra, and the Philadelphia Orchestra with its new conductor, Ormandy, were indeed still the leading names in the country. Furthermore, in 1940 RCA managed to snap Duke Ellington away from Columbia. Nevertheless the head of RCA, David Sarnoff, the Minsk-born radio operator who had created his colossal company out of nothing on arriving in America, started adding to his list of orchestras. It was noted that in many American cities, thanks to the influx of German and Austrian refugees, there were quite excellent orchestras. By winter 1941 there was hardly a single large orchestra in the USA that was not signed either to Columbia or to RCA.

Both Wallerstein's and Sarnoff's operations came to a standstill when two big labour disputes blew up in the music world which forced the competitors to collaborate. ASCAP (the American Society of Composers, Authors and Publishers) and the radio stations of the United States had been negotiating fruitlessly throughout 1940 on the royalties the stations ought to pay composers for playing their works. When the talks broke down without result, ASCAP, representing the big music publishers and famous composers, in early 1941 forbade the stations to play any of the music it represented, in the belief that a public hungry for music would force the stations to yield.

Irving Berlin, Cole Porter and George Gershwin were now out of bounds for the radio. The radio stations had, however, been preparing for the boycott and had founded their own rival copyright agency, BMI (Broadcast Music Inc.). It quickly recruited into its ranks the swing musicians, blues singers and arrangers whom ASCAP had not taken on as members. There were more takers than expected, because ASCAP, which was dominated by music publishers, had never paid much heed to the cause of new, unknown composers. Black composers did not feature; Duke Ellington was only accepted as a member of ASCAP in 1953. The dispute did not affect classical music, because most of it was in the public domain.

The parent companies of both Columbia and RCA were also the largest radio networks in the USA, and the record companies eagerly started recording music represented by BMI, which was then played on the radio. In the first half of 1941 two-thirds of all the hit records sold in the United States were BMI compositions, and there was not a single ASCAP tune in the top twenty. The big hit of the year was the Mexican Alberto Dominguez's 'Frenesi', to which BMI had acquired the rights.

After ten months ASCAP was forced to give up, once the government had intervened. The old popular composers were given a conditional reprieve by the radio stations, but as a result of this battle the United States, unlike other countries, still has two copyright organizations. The success of most of the BMI hits of 1941 was short-lived, but BMI's efforts to support new, unknown composers began to bear fruit in the next decade. With the rise of rock and roll, the BMI catalogue began to accumulate tunes that are today played all over the world.

The squabble between ASCAP and BMI had not directly affected the record industry. The record companies had always had the right to record music from ASCAP, but the industry's close links with radio had disposed it in favour of BMI. Half a dozen recordings of 'Frenesi' promptly appeared, the most popular of them by Artie Shaw. Record companies avoided recording compositions that stood no chance of being played on the radio.

The next dispute affected the record makers directly. Hardly a year had passed since the copyright dispute died down when the president of the American Federation of Musicians, James Caesar Petrillo, announced a recording ban in August 1942. The musicians were trying to get work for 20,000 players who had lost their jobs when talking pictures made their final breakthrough in the movie theatres. The union's demand was that in addition to the hourly wage for recordings, a commission on sales be paid to the musicians, not just the conductors; five cents for every record sold, to aid unemployed musicians. The record industry rejected the demand, and Petrillo declared a strike, which stopped all recording activity for two years.

At first the situation was not at all hard for the record companies, because they had large stocks and a number of unreleased recordings. The situation with shellac was harder. Because of the war, the major raw material for records was being rationed, and during the war years huge numbers of valuable old records were destroyed to recycle the raw material. The buyer of a new record had to bring an old one back to the shop at the same time. Eventually, though, the number of recordings available for issue was becoming depleted. After thirteen months of the strike, the first to give in was the head of American Decca, Jack Kapp. His first recording was an album of songs from the latest hit show, *Oklahoma*, which sold 1,300,000 copies for $5 each. RCA and Columbia held out longer, but when in 1944 Decca managed to break into the hallowed ground of Red Seal records by poaching Jascha Heifetz, who had been recording for Victor since 1918, the depths had been reached, and an agreement was achieved to end the strike. (Another, shorter dispute broke out between the musicians and the record companies in 1947.) When recording activity got started again, RCA Victor's domination of the orchestras was finally at an end. Even during the strike, Wallerstein had been behind the scenes stealing yet another of RCA's leading lights, Eugene Ormandy and the Philadelphia Symphony Orchestra!

Source: Sanjek (1988)

The Recording Industry at War

The effects of the war were evident in the record industry not just in the shortage of materials. In the United States, after Pearl Harbor, a tremendous patriotic surge struck the composers of popular songs. Irving Berlin's 'God Bless America', as performed by the actress Kate Smith, became the unofficial national anthem. The cowboy singer Elton Britt's 'There's a Star-Spangled Banner Waving Somewhere' set off a wave of star-spangled songs in 1942. Kay Kyser's 'Praise the Lord and Pass the Ammunition' was so popular that radio stations had to forbid their announcers from playing it more than once an hour. The cleverest of the wartime records, however, was Spike Jones's 'Der Fuhrer's Face'. Similar patriotic recordings were being produced in all countries. 'There'll Always be an England' and 'Till the Lights of London Shine Again' helped Englishmen to retain their courage.

When it was not possible to make new records in the United States in 1943, owing to the strike, even though the record factories were working at full capacity, pressing out recordings stored away from the previous year, the United States Army started producing its own records for the amusement of the troops, with the keen assistance of the Musicians' Union. The first 100,000 'V-discs' (for Victory) were sent to the front in waterproof packaging in September 1943. Among these records, pressed on unbreakable vinyl, were recordings from radio broadcasts by Kate Smith and Bing Crosby. In 1944, two million 'V-discs' were manufactured, and twice that amount in 1945. The records were also played frequently on American Forces Radio. The operation was run by Captain Robert Vincent, an RCA engineer in civilian life. One of his subordinates was Sergeant Steve Sholes, who later became famous as Elvis Presley's producer. The famous swing bands, the popular singers and of course Spike Jones made hundreds of V-discs. In jazz circles the jam session organized by *Esquire* magazine, held in as unlikely a venue as the Metropolitan Opera on 26 January 1944, has an almost legendary reputation. Playing in the concert were the winners of its readers' poll, including Louis Armstrong, Roy Eldridge, Coleman Hawkins, Art Tatum and Lionel Hampton – a real *Who's Who* of jazz. Excerpts from the concert were issued on ten V-discs, which have since become sought-after collector's items, because such a combination never played on any commercial disc. In principle all the remaining V-discs are the property of the United States Army. The Musicians' Union has not given its approval to the reissue of records that were originally issued free, although illegal 'bootlegs' have been in circulation.

In Germany, the record industry had, since 1933, been forced to adapt to the National Socialist ideology. All music composed or played by Jews, Negroes or politically suspect persons had to be removed from the catalogues. Mendelssohn's music was decadent. The great names of German cabaret, Berthold Brecht, Kurt Weill, Kurt Tucholsky and Friedrich Holländer, were erased from history. After the outbreak of war, the music of the fast-increasing number of enemy countries was also banned. It was not possible to get the opera-going public to give up *Carmen*, but all Bizet's other works were banned. France was, after all, an enemy country, albeit a conquered one. Records of Chopin could no longer be sold – the composer being a member of an inferior race. The only composer good enough for Aryans was Wagner, whose opera, *Siegfried*, had been such an overwhelming musical experience in Hitler's youth. As the bans piled up, issuing records began to be something of a tightrope act. When war broke out, the popular English dance bands went onto the blacklist, but sales of American swing music were allowed for the time being, as long as the performers were neither black nor Jewish. The Jew, Benny Goodman, had been *verboten* since he performed at a benefit event for the Spanish republicans, but Fats Waller's records were for a long time sold quite openly, since no-one at the Reichsmusikkammer had realized that the singing pianist was black.

The bans were not quite free of loopholes. Young German officers liked to listen to swing and did not bother taking the ideological orders from headquarters literally. In occupied France it was possible to play and even record *St Louis Blues*, as long as it went under the name *Tristesse du St Louis*. The only jazz records recorded in Germany itself during the war years were done by a secret group called Charlie and his Orchestra. Playing on the records were well-known Berlin dance musicians, the compositions were authentic 'hot' tunes such as 'Dinah', 'Stormy Weather' and 'You're Driving me Crazy', but new words were put in place of the English refrains, making fun of Churchill, the British Royal Family and the BBC. 'Charlie' himself was the cabaret singer, Karl Schwedler, and some of the song lyrics were written by the famous Lord Haw-Haw (the English Nazi William Joyce), who made German propaganda programmes, and who was hanged in 1946. This is Charlie's version of 'You're Driving me Crazy':

Here is Winston Churchill's latest tear-jerker:

'Yes, the Germans are driving me crazy,
I thought I had brains, but they shattered my planes,
They built up a front against me,
it's quite amazing,
clouding the skies with their planes.
The Jews are the friends who are near me to cheer me,
believe me they do.
But Jews are the kind that now hurt me,
desert me and laugh at me too.
Yes, the Germans are driving me crazy...'

This was followed by Fritz Brocksieper's drum break *à la* Gene Krupa, and the band then played the last verse in their best Goodman style. The discs were usually recorded in the studios of Greater German Radio on Adolf Hitler Platz in Berlin and pressed in batches of 100 at the Deutsche Grammophon works. It was not possible to buy these records in the shops; they were reserved for playing on propaganda broadcasts to England. They were also distributed for amusement in prisoner-of-war camps. In 1945 the SS spread a rumour that any one found in possession of the records would be shot, and many of the records were destroyed. Over the years, though, a few examples of Charlie's songs have been reissued.

Ordinary Germans had to make do with more traditional fare. The Nazi propaganda machine favoured nostalgic and escapist songs such as *Mit Musik geht alles besser* ('With Music Everything will be Better') or *Heimat, deine Sterne* ('The Stars of my Homeland'). As the war advanced, martial music became more and more popular, and the recordings included such numbers as *Die Fahne hoch, Ade Polenland, Wenn wir fahren gegen Engeland, Heil Hitler dir,* and *Von Finnland bis zum Schwarzen Meer*. One cannot but admire the abilities of the German march composers, even if the ideology behind their compositions has fortunately lost its currency. These records, performed by various *Stabmusikkorps* and *SS-Musiksturms* did seem a little forced, with one exception.

A young actress named Lale Andersen, who had performed in the literary cabarets of Munich, recorded Norbert Schultze's atmospheric 'Lili Marleen' before the war, in March 1939. It was not a particular success at the time. It was only when the German military transmitter in Belgrade started playing the tune regularly on its evening programmes in 1940 because of a temporary shortage of suitable material that the miracle happened: the soldiers would wait for 'Lili Marleen' from one evening to the next, and throughout the war they could not get enough of it. Everywhere, from the North Cape to El Alamein, the tune was played where German soldiers were at the front. It was not only the soldiers of the Wehrmacht who were smitten by this unmilitaristic song, it was recorded many times over on both sides of the front – in French, English, Finnish and many other languages. Marlene Dietrich performed it regularly to the American troops on her tours from 1943 onwards, and it is said that it was a favourite of General Eisenhower. In response, Charlie recorded a propaganda version of 'Lili', in which a young British soldier hears the trumpet calling him to desert.

Lili Marleen was one of those who emerged victorious from the war. When the Allied troops occupied Germany in 1945, they wanted to buy 'Lili Marleen' wherever they went. They were in for a disappointment, because the record had sold out long ago. But its singer, Lale Andersen, was asked to perform it for the American troops, and it again went from victory to victory. Subsequently, Lale Andersen made several different recordings of this bravura number of hers, and a couple of million copies of them have been sold over the years.

Amid the madness of war there was one place where the old values were still respected. The Nazis' V-1 rockets razed whole blocks to the ground in London, but at the editorial office of *The Gramophone* they were eagerly studying the latest German record catalogues, sent to them by a reader in neutral Lisbon. In each issue of the journal, they published lists of the latest classical recordings issued in Berlin and Rome, provided with an editorial note that the records were not available at the moment, but the information was published as a matter of general interest.

Sources: Lange (1966a); Sears (1980); Zwerin (1985)

CHAPTER SIX

The Age of the LP

The War is Over

At the end of the war, the European record industry was in a depressed state. In the United States, on the other hand, record manufacturing had survived almost undented, as it had the First World War too. Despite rationing and the two-year musicians' strike, record sales had grown steadily during the war years, and as soon as the war ended the same kind of jump occurred as happened after the previous war. As a result, by the end of the 1940s more than half the records in the world were made and sold in the United States. As the customer base for recorded music grew, the increase in demand was most noticeable in the field of popular music, and nearly 90 per cent of records sold in the United States consisted of popular music, country, and rhythm and blues, as 'race' records were now called.

The ten years after the end of the world war in the history of recording are the history of the American record industry. A record business conscious of its strength was ready for innovations, and in the years 1948–50 two new inventions were indeed adopted which signified a great step forward in both the technical and the artistic senses: tape recording and the LP record.

By the 1940s, the gramophone record had attained a very high technical standard. As a by-product of the war, its reproduction quality was improved still further. During the war the Decca company in England had been given the task of developing listening equipment needed in anti-submarine work, whereby it was possible to distinguish the sounds of the propellors of one's own vessels from the enemy's. At the war's end, Decca's chief engineer, Arthur Haddy, began applying the same technology to record production. The first significant recorded work using the new technique was Stravinsky's electrifying *Firebird* suite, conducted by Ernest Ansermet. On its appearance in 1946 it aroused great admiration among the music critics. As a mark of the extended range of reproduction, the letters 'ffrr' (full frequency range recording) were printed on the label. The records still revolved at 78 r.p.m., and the *Firebird* still had to be divided up into three- to five-minute sections. Making a record was still a slow and difficult process. Recordings had to be cut in the studio directly on a wax disc, and a recording, once made, could not be corrected or edited.

The record industry had learned to live with these limitations, and the customers accepted operas sliced into five-minute portions as a necessary evil. Radio, on the other hand, was feverishly seeking a quicker and handier way of recording programmes. In the thirties, radio broadcasts were mostly live. Acetate records were used where necessary to record short excerpts of programmes. It was clear, though, that if programmes of any length at all could be recorded at moderate expense, quite new opportunities would open up for recording radio programmes. Programmes could be recorded at the most convenient time for the performers and could be repeated at any time, and mistakes could be rectified.

Source: Sanjek (1988)

Table 6.1 *World Record Sales, 1946–60 (Selected Countries)*. (Millions of units sold. For USA, $ value, in millions.)

	USA	UK	Germany (FRG)	Finland
1946	218			0.2
1947	224			0.4
1948	189			0.3
1949	173		4.0	0.2
1950	189		7.6	0.3
1951	199		12.5	0.2
1952	214		17.0	0.5
1953	219		25.0	0.3
1954	213		31.0	0.5
1955	277	59.9	40.0	0.6
1956	377	66.5	56.0	0.9
1957	460	78.4	57.3	0.9
1958	511	71.4	53.4	0.6
1959	603	66.7	..	0.9
1960	600	72.7	..	1.0

Source: Gronow, 1996. Figures from other countries are not available for this period.

The Tape Recorder Arrives

As early as 1898 the Danish engineer, Valdemar Poulsen, had constructed a 'telegraphone', which recorded sound magnetically on a wire. This grandfather of the tape recorder was given an award at the Paris World Exhibition of 1900. At that time, however, amplifiers were not available to exploit the possibilities of the invention. Without a microphone and an amplifier, the 'telegraphone' was useless. With the development of amplifier technology through radio in the thirties, various adaptations of the 'telegraphone' were tried out in practice. The BBC recorded its news bulletins for its colonial service on large wire spools for re-broadcasting.

In 1935 the German company AEG exhibited at the great Berlin radio exhibition a device called a 'Magnetophon', in which the steel wire was replaced by a paper tape coated with a metallic oxide. The speed of the tape was 76 cms/second. The Gestapo was one of the company's best customers. Many radio stations, too, tried out the AEG magnetophone, and even the Finnish Broadcasting Company acquired some for the 1940 Olympic Games, which, for well-known reasons, were not held. The reproduction quality of the first magnetophones was, however, clearly inferior to that of records.

When American troops were examining the radio stations of occupied Germany after the war, to their surprise they found tape recorders that could reproduce sound considerably better than their predecessors. The Germans had discovered that applying a high frequency current to the tape recording head along with the audio signal (high frequency bias) would significantly reduce tape hiss and other forms of distortion.

As a result of the war, AEG's patents had fallen into the hands of the Allied forces. John Mullin, an engineer serving with the US communications corps, brought two tape recorders home from Radio Frankfurt as a memento of war, along with 50 tape spools, and persuaded the Ampex company to manufacture a few copies of the German recorders. Similar machines were shipped to England and other allied countries, where local manufacturers developed their own models.

Mullin's first customer was Bing Crosby, who in autumn 1947 began recording his tremendously popular radio programmes on tape. Crosby enthused over the opportunity presented by tape recording of assembling a programme out of separately recorded parts, cutting the tape and reusing the rejected tape as the occasion demanded. Other radio stations, film companies and recording studios soon adopted the recorder, and although the devices were not yet within the reach of private consumers, early in 1948, American music critics were seriously discussing whether, before long, tapes would replace discs in domestic use. This did not happen, however, because, in June 1948, the LP was born.

The R.P.M. War

In theory there are several alternative solutions to the problem of extending the playing time of gramophone records. The disc may be enlarged, the speed of revolution may be slowed or the grooves may be narrowed. All of these have been tried at some stage. Edison, whose curriculum vitae contained at least as many fiascos as successes, had manufactured the first 'long-playing' records as long ago as 1925. They were the same size as modern LPs, but about a centimetre thick, and even at a speed of 80 r.p.m., twenty minutes of music fitted onto their ultra-fine grooves. They did not work out in practice, however. The stylus would not stay in the grooves, and marketing of the discs had to be curtailed.

The next attempt was made by RCA Victor, who presented their own LP records, revolving at 33 r.p.m., in 1931. The technology was borrowed from a type of disc evolved for talking pictures a few years earlier. Some specially recorded pieces were available on the new discs which would not have fitted onto ordinary records without cutting, such as Beethoven's fifth symphony and some of Duke Ellington's large orchestral compositions. The timing was wrong, however. The Depression had caused record sales to collapse, and these LP discs soon had to be withdrawn from the market. Nevertheless they began making huge 40cm discs by the same method, which were used to distribute background music and popular radio series, the predecessors of television soap operas, to radio stations all over America. These records were extremely fragile, so they were never offered on the domestic market. The idea of the long-playing record was in the air, however.

At the end of the war, when demand for records was increasing quickly, the time was at last ripe for a new type of record. Columbia's dynamic director, Edward Wallerstein, was behind the idea. The head of research at the CBS concern, the Hungarian-born Peter Goldmark, was responsible for its technical development. In 1946 Goldmark was directed to shift from developing television to gramophone records. One beautiful June day in 1948, Wallerstein was ready to present his long-playing record to the press in a suite at the Waldorf Astoria hotel. On one side of him he had a two-metre-high pile of old 78 r.p.m. discs, and on the other a 40cm-high one of the new LP records, both containing the same amount of music.

Those veterans present found a lot that was familiar about the invention. All this had been seen before. The records had Edison's 'microgrooves' and Victor's speed of 33 r.p.m. But Wallerstein had more things to offer. Instead of shellac, the records were pressed on durable vinyl plastic, which did not have the hiss of the old records. Placed on the market at the same time was a new, moderately-priced record-player, on which could be played both 33 and 78 r.p.m. records. They had planned an ambitious series of releases of both light music and the great works of classical music, for which the long-playing time came into its own. The tape recorder, which had just come into use, would ease the recording of such works.

CBS-Columbia put the new invention at the disposal of the entire recording industry. Some small companies expressed their interest and soon their work was issued on LP records, both classical music and jazz. Columbia's most important rival, RCA, was ominously silent, however. The reason was soon clear. Early in 1949 RCA introduced its own novelty to the market, a small 7-inch disc which revolved at 45 r.p.m. RCA announced that it was producing both 'singles', containing two numbers, and EP, or 'extended play', records, containing four, which, like LP records, were packed in individual cardboard sleeves. Another feature was that Columbia LP records could not be played on the new RCA record player.

The public and the record dealers were astonished. There was talk of a 'war of speeds'. In 1948/49 overall record sales in the United States declined. Many customers reacted by refraining from buying either of the new kinds of record. Soon it became evident, though, that the LP was to ensure a place for itself. In their very first year, Columbia sold over three million of their new records. In 1950 RCA relented and issued its first LP record. The directors who had been running the EP operation were sacked. Both speeds, 33 and 45, had come to stay, and, since then, all new record players have been equipped for both. Larger-scale works came to be issued on LP records, while the single established itself as the format for popular hits. Popular music recorded especially for the LP record only became common in the late 1960s.

Elsewhere in the world, it took time for the new speeds to come into use. In the early fifties the European record industry was still suffering from the post-war shortage of materials. Even the demand for shellac records exceeded supply. Sir Louis Sterling of EMI was a record manufacturer of the old school, who had started his career in the age of the wax cylinder. He had seen Edison's and Victor's long-playing records come and go, and he believed the same would happen with Columbia's LP venture. The first to adopt the LP format in Europe were Decca and DGG, in 1950–51. EMI followed them, with its tail between its legs, a couple of years later. In the Soviet Union the 45 r.p.m. format was never adopted, but both singles and LP records revolved at 33. Indeed without the solo venture by RCA the world could have managed with just one speed of revolution until the death of the vinyl disc.

Sources: Beizhuisen (1959); Gelatt (1956); Sanjek (1988)

The Recording Industry Reorganizes

The new speeds were a sign of the power of the big American companies. A quarter of a century earlier they had adopted microphone recording. Now, once again, they were forcing the whole world to dance to their own tune. Paradoxically, this time the new technology did not strengthen their position.

In 1944 record sales in the United States were worth $66 million. In 1946 they amounted to over 200 million. The biggest slices of the cake were claimed by the three giants: Columbia and RCA Victor, who had been in at the beginning, and Decca, established in the Depression years, which in 1945 had fallen into American hands as a pawn in the British war debt. Panting at the heels of the three giants, however, were three robust competitors with ambitious plans. Capitol had been established in 1942 in Hollywood (in 1956 it became an American subsidiary of EMI). MGM was the record department, set up in 1946, of the film company of the same name. Its head office was also in Hollywood. The third new contender was Mercury, in Chicago.

In their operations Capitol, MGM and Mercury imitated the model of the big three. They were trying to produce all kinds of music and sell their products all over the country. Capitol and Mercury were also praised for their issues of classical music. MGM's big star was the country singer Hank Williams. They had their own factories and effective sales organizations. The rock historian, Charlie Gillett, has calculated that of the 163 records whose sales gave them 'gold record' status between 1946 and 1952 in the United States – that is, over a million copies sold – as many as 158 were released by the six biggest companies.

As demand for records grew, many other people realized that producing records was profitable. The country was full of musicians who wanted to appear on record. If a record was made as cheaply as possible, sales of only a couple of thousand would be enough to bring in a small profit. Record salesmen, radio shop owners, managers and other people working on the fringes of the music business started setting up their own record companies. Some came into the record industry by surprising routes. Al Green owned a paint factory and had invented a new varnish-making process. When there was a shortage of shellac, the raw material of gramophone records, during the war, Green set about selling his varnish as a substitute for shellac to the record-pressing plants. He soon bought some pressing plants himself and set up the National company, whose most famous star was the ballad singer Billy Eckstine. National's success lasted a few years, and then Green had to return to the more secure paint industry, but his son Irving later became one of the major shareholders in Mercury.

Within a few years, hundreds of record companies sprang up in the United States, most of them short-lived. They survived by keeping their overheads low and by specializing in one kind of music. In Detroit, record dealer Bernard Besman recorded local blues singers in the back room of his shop. His biggest success was John Lee Hooker's 'Boogie Chillun' (released on the King label) in 1948. The echo effect on the record was achieved by moving Hooker's guitar amplifier to the shop's toilet and recording it over again on another microphone. At Campbellsville, in the coal-mining region of Kentucky, Jim Stanton set up the Rich-R-Tone label in 1945, which specialized in the thriving bluegrass music of that region. In New York, Tetos Demetriades, who had begun his career by recording popular numbers in Greek for Victor, set up the Standard label, whose roster included, apart from the manager himself, other immigrant artists such as the Finnish accordionist, Viola Turpeinen.

Similar things were happening in dozens of other places. Among the little backyard record ventures there gradually came to the fore a dozen or so companies that were stronger than the rest, and which, little by little, extended the distribution of their records all over the United States. The sons of the Turkish Ambassador, Ahmet and Nesuhi Ertegun, borrowed $10,000 from their dentist and set up Atlantic Records in New York, out of which grew, years later, part of the gigantic WEA concern. In Chicago in 1947, Leonard and Phil Chess established the record label named after themselves. In Cincinnati, in 1945, Sydney Nathan's King label was set up. These one-man companies came to have a considerable influence on the future development of the recording industry, and, indeed, of recorded music.

During the war years, Sydney Nathan owned a small record shop in Cincinnati, Ohio. A lot of workers from the South had come to work in the city's industrial plants, and Nathan noticed that they asked for strange records that local people did not care about. Gradually Nathan sold out of his stock of race and hillbilly records, acquired before rationing, and had to face the fact that the big record companies would not put out any more of these. Because of the shortage of materials, they were concentrating on the more popular hit records and the guaranteed market for classical music.

In 1944 Nathan and a few colleagues decided to set up a record company which they called King Records. The old companies were not willing at that time to manufacture records to a competitor's order, and King had to buy old presses that had long been disused. The industry had for many years been so concentrated that it was hard to find a skilled worker to repair the equipment. Nathan had to make a study trip to Louisville, where the United States government manufactured 'talking books' for the blind. He received so much help from this public institution that in 1945 King was making its first records. King 501 was Merle Travis's 'When Mussolini Laid his Pistol Down'. Number 504 was a big hit: Cowboy Copas's 'Filipino Baby'.

King produced both country, and rhythm 'n' blues, as hillbilly and race records were now being called. The leading stars on its country roster were Cowboy Copas, Moon Mullican, Hawkshaw Hawkins and Grandpa Jones, while in rhythm 'n' blues they had Earl Bostic, Wynonie Harris, Ivory Joe Hunter and Hank Ballard. In the early fifties King was making six million records a year, and when the audience for rhythm 'n' blues started to grow in the middle of the decade, records such as Hank Ballard's 'Work with me Annie', Otis Williams's 'Hearts of Stone' and Bill Doggett's 'Honky Tonk' achieved 'gold record' status. In its country series, King's biggest success was Cowboy Copas's 'Tennessee Waltz'. King records were distinguished by a strong influence from the swing era as interpreted by the small bands in nightclubs, bars and dance halls in the forties. King's rhythm 'n' blues artists were mighty-voiced shouters, accompanied by a honking saxophone. Even the country singers had electrified their guitars and preferred the swing rhythms of the previous decade in their accompaniments.

Chess records had quite a different sound. Leonard and Phil Chess were Polish Jews who had encountered the blues world as nightclub owners on the South Side of Chicago and started making records in Leonard's garage. Plenty of immigrants from the south had come to Chicago in the war years, including singers and players who had learned their trade straight from Charley Patton, Robert Johnson and their contemporaries. In the clubs of the South Side the guitars and even the mouth harps were electrified, but it was the blues of the Mississippi delta that emanated from the records of Muddy Waters, Howling Wolf and the other Chess artists, in which the regular rhythms and bar divisions gave way to the tune's own logic when the occasion called for it.

Despite its southern origins, the Chess brothers quickly came to identify with the music they were recording. Leonard would even play the drums, if needed, to accompany his blues singers – he can be heard on Muddy Waters's classic recording, 'Still a Fool' (1951). When a younger generation of musicians playing a lighter and faster-paced blues arose in Chicago in the mid-fifties, the brothers were quick to sign up the more promising talents among them for their label. Chuck Berry and Bo Diddley soon became leading figures in rock, and their Chess records sold in the millions. Like many other family businesses, Chess lasted as long as its founders. Since the brothers' deaths the company has been sold many times over, but reissues of Muddy Waters's and Chuck Berry's historic recordings are constantly appearing on the market.

Sources: Daniels (1986); Gillett (1970); Ruppli (1983); Ruppli and Daniels (1985)

From Rhythm 'n' Blues to Rock 'n' Roll

In the post-war years, in many American states there were still racial segregation laws, as there were in South Africa until recently. In Alabama there were separate seats on buses for blacks, separate schools, hotels, places of amusement and radio stations. It was only in 1964 that racial segregation was forbidden by federal law. Under these conditions, black music lived peacefully in its own ghettoes. Its share of rhythm 'n' blues record sales in the United States in 1953 was about five per cent, which might seem small, but five per cent of overall sales of 300 million records is a larger number than the entire record sales for several European countries at the time. At their height, Muddy Waters and John Lee Hooker were selling hundreds of thousands of copies of their most popular discs. To the chagrin of black leaders, though, nearly all the turnover went into the pockets of the white company owners.

During the immediate post-war years, thousands of rhythm 'n' blues records aimed at the black audience had been turned out, most of them only of local importance. They were put out by Atlantic in New York, King in Cincinnati, Chess in Chicago, Doug Robey's Peacock label in Houston, the Bihari brothers' Modern in Los Angeles and a score of other companies, all of them small family businesses by the standards of the United States. In the mid-fifties, however, there was a breakthrough in music which subsequent historians have interpreted in many ways. In about 1953, certain radio stations in northern cities, whose listeners were mostly young and white, began playing rhythm 'n' blues records regularly. More and more of a white audience began turning up at concerts by black musicians. Records appeared on the market on which white singers sang in a rhythm 'n' blues style or even copied popular rhythm 'n' blues records note for note, often selling more than the original. Pat Boone borrowed Fats Domino's 'Ain't That a Shame', Bill Haley copied Joe Turner's record, 'Shake, Rattle and Roll'. The disc jockey, Alan Freed, invented a term for the phenomenon – 'rock 'n' roll', and thus a musical wave was started whose global influence only began to be felt a few decades later.

The events of these years have been retold many times in histories of rock 'n' roll, and with hindsight it is easy to exaggerate the importance of rock. 'Mambo Italiano', 'The Ballad of Davy Crockett', 'How Much is that Doggie in the Window' and 'Love is a Many-Splendored Thing' were also big hits in the United States in the fifties. Only a part of the record sales of that decade were rock 'n' roll, and there was room in the firmament for such stars of the era as Doris Day, Frank Sinatra, Harry Belafonte and Mantovani. But it was thanks to the influence of rock 'n' roll that big changes took place in the record industry. According to Charlie Gillett's calculations, in the United States Top Ten chart between 1955 and 1959 there were 147 records in all. Of these, only 46 were put out by the old established record companies, 101 came from small independent companies. Chess, Atlantic and other similar labels, which had previously been only small local companies, now took on national significance. Bearing in mind that over the same period the value of record sales in the United States rose from $213 million to $603 million, the effect of rock 'n' roll can be seen in a truer perspective. Classical music, jazz and many other varieties of music were also important for the record industry. Rock was, however, the locomotive which drove the American record industry forward at a furious pace in the fifties. The same trend developed in Europe in the 1960s.

Source: Gillett (1970)

Elvis and Little Richard

Sam Phillips's Sun Records of Memphis, Tennessee, was a typical one-man company. Sun, established in 1952, operated out of a small one-storey building on Union Avenue, Memphis. The owner and managing director also took care of the recording and the bookkeeping; his brother Judd was in charge of sales. Initially Sam Phillips earned extra income by recording weddings and meetings to order, but during the fifties Sun grew into a respectable little business, with artists on its roster such as Carl Perkins, Jerry Lee Lewis and Johnny Cash. Sam Phillips has passed into history, however, as the man who sold Elvis Presley, in 1955, for $35,000.

In 1954 Elvis was a 19-year-old truck driver who was dreaming of a singing career and practising his guitar. He often visited Sam's office in the hope that Phillips would pay him some attention, and even paid a few dollars for the chance to record a couple of songs on an acetate disc. The story often related in the press that Elvis had the record made for his mother is, however, a fable dreamed up later by the PR men – at that time the Presley family did not even own a record player.

Sam Phillips, who was always prepared to try out new talent, invited Elvis to make demonstration recordings on several occasions in Spring 1954. Like other one-man businesses, Phillips did not keep accounts of studio hours, but made one demonstration tape after another on days when he was free. Accompaniment was provided by the company's regular session musicians, who did these extra jobs voluntarily in the hope of getting future work. On 6 June 1954, having tried in vain to record a couple of slow ballads, Elvis did Bill Monroe's bluegrass tune, 'Blue Moon of Kentucky' and Big Boy Crudup's blues number, 'That's All Right Mama'. Elvis played acoustic guitar himself, and his accompanists were Scotty Moore on electric guitar and Bill Black on bass. Depth was added to the singing voice by using tape echo, but on the whole the performances sound spontaneous and lively. Since Elvis's death, all the rehearsal tapes and even the incomplete takes made in the Sun studio have been reissued, and from these we can hear how naturally the records that were released arose as a result of the rehearsals. Sam Phillips was satisfied: he had finally found the 'white boy with a black voice' that he was looking for.

'That's All Right Mama', Sun 209, found favour with the Memphis radio stations, and the record was a local hit. The following winter Elvis recorded a dozen more numbers for Phillips and performed on a concert tour he had arranged – with such success that Atlantic offered him a recording contract. The victory went, however, to the chief producer at RCA's country section, Steve Sholes, who bought Elvis's contract from Phillips in November 1955 for $35,000. At that time Phillips had many rising singers on his books. If he had remained on the Sun label Elvis would probably have had the same kind of short-term popularity as Carl Perkins. RCA had a more effective nationwide sales organization, and after switching labels Elvis's star rose rapidly. Early in 1956 he made his real commercial breakthrough by performing on the popular Ed Sullivan Show on television. The same year he began his movie career and gained his first gold discs when 'Heartbreak Hotel', 'Don't Be Cruel', 'Hound Dog', 'Love Me Tender' and 'I Want You, I Need You, I Love You', all broke the million-selling barrier. Some of these records were recorded in Nashville, some in New York. Some had the same accompanists as before, but the difference between these and the earlier Memphis recordings was enormous. The electric guitar and the drums, used sparingly on the earlier recordings, were now brought into the foreground, the echo was increased greatly, and a male quartet sang in the background to fill in the empty spaces in the arrangement. Compared to Elvis's Sun recordings, the ones he was making for RCA sound almost like a parody of rock 'n' roll, but the public thought differently. In both the United States and Europe, 'Hound Dog' and 'Don't be Cruel' became the symbol of the new music, rock 'n' roll.

In the hands of his clever manager, Colonel Parker, Elvis Presley quickly rose to become one of the most successful singers in recording history. At one stage it was estimated that one fifth of all RCA records sold were sung by Elvis. His repertoire was directed more and more towards his film roles, and a certain kind of turning point came in 1960 with his recording 'It's Now or Never' – an only slightly modernized version of Caruso's old 'O sole mio'. Elvis was unable to handle his own success, however. Over the years he withdrew more and more from the world and died, aged only 42, on 16 August 1977.

Alongside Elvis, Little Richard serves as an example of life at the top of rock 'n' roll. Richard Penniman was a pianist and singer who toured the southern United States in the fifties performing mainly in clubs and dance halls patronized by blacks. He made his first records for RCA in 1952. They were very ordinary rhythm 'n' blues numbers, and did not attract any attention. In 1955, hoping to make a new recording, he sent a demonstration tape to Art Rupe's Specialty label. In the spring, the company's producer Bumps Blackwell invited him to New Orleans to a recording session, to which other hopeful artists were coming. The recording went badly, because the numbers Little Richard was offering were terribly ordinary. During a break, however, Blackwell heard him performing a fast number for his own amusement, in which his voiced jumped suddenly from baritone to falsetto. Blackwell quickly drafted an arrangement for it, and the surrealistic introduction to 'Tutti Frutti' soon became world-famous: 'Awopbopalubopawopbamboom!'

From 1955 to 1957 Little Richard made ten or so hit records which have been taken up by countless subsequent rock singers from Elvis Presley to the Beatles: 'Long Tall Sally', 'Slippin' and Slidin'', 'Good Golly Miss Molly' to name a few. In structure they follow the usual rhythm 'n' blues pattern, their lyrics can be summarized in a couple of lines, but it is their boundless energy that singles them out from other contemporary recordings. The Swedish collector, Johnny Sandberg, has issued an LP of rehearsal tapes, on which Little Richard was preparing the recordings he made with Art Rupe for Specialty. The record has five versions of 'Rip It Up', for example, and we can hear how Little Richard and Art Rupe adjusted the arrangement. Richard had the actual composition and the structure of the arrangement ready when he entered the studio, but in the studio the tempo, the details of the accompaniment and the sung parts were arranged and rearranged time and time again. Although the recordings were made on tape, they were not usually corrected afterwards, but rather the take deemed suitable for a record was lifted from the tape as it was.

In 1957 Little Richard tired of life on the road and entered a seminary, where he did not stay for long. In his memoirs he claims he was inspired to do this by the first Sputnik space flight. Art Rupe had suddenly lost his best-selling artist, to whom, it is true, he had only been paying half of one per cent in royalties on record sales. Rupe was now in a hurry to find new material. Little Richard's last record of the fifties, 'Keep a-knockin'', was cobbled together out of one minute's worth of rehearsal tape. The sharp-eared listener can discern that the record consists of two identical one-minute tapes strung together.

Sources: Jorgensen *et al.* (1986); Shaw (1978)

Congress Investigates

By the end of the fifties, the first wave of rock 'n' roll had burned itself out. Some gold record winners had died of heroin overdoses; many were, like Little Richard, continuing to tour as second-ranking stars. The fifties left only one 'superstar', Elvis Presley. At his death at his palatial residence in Memphis, 'Graceland', in 1977, as a result of overeating and drug abuse, Elvis had 50 gold records on his wall, and the overall sales of his discs were estimated at 170 million. And they have not stopped selling yet.

At the end of the fifties, annual US record sales exceeded $600 million. However, the late fifties is not a very interesting period in the history of American popular music. The wild rockers had been cast aside, and the 'pretty boys' who were elevated into their place, such as Paul Anka and Fabian, mostly sang hits in a more traditional style. The old record companies, with their superior machinery, had won back the large share of the market they had lost to the small fry. Nevertheless, the record business was one of the few areas where the pioneering spirit that was part of the 'American Dream' still prevailed, with all its good and bad aspects. A newcomer to the record industry in the United States could still become a millionaire on a modest investment. This was especially easy, at least in theory, in the fifties, when the LP had not yet displaced the single. All that was needed was a catchy tune, a good, or good-looking, performer and a few hours in the studio, and the record might be one of the 100 or so that each year sold a million copies. This has indeed happened, albeit not often, as the established companies with their organized distribution networks, their advertising departments and their famous artists of course had the advantage over their competitors.

Since about 5000 singles were issued each year and only a few were 'hits', competition was fierce. The producers could not afford to leave things to the whims of the public. Even in the days of barrel organs, American music publishers developed a sales technique they called 'song plugging'. The aim was, by various means, to get a tune to seem so popular that the public would have to become familiar with it. In those days the sheet music was sold, and publishers' agents were in the habit of recommending to famous performers to include their numbers in their repertoire. Sometimes, drinks for the boys in the band would fix it; sometimes cash was called for. It was not possible to make a bad tune popular in this way, but if a melody had 'that certain something', a clever salesman could improve its chances quite a lot.

The key to success in fifties America was radio. With the spread of television, playing records had become the commonest type of programme on radio, and endless stories were told in the business of completely unknown records that became big hits when some radio announcer took a liking to them. In North Carolina, in 1947, a radio announcer named Kurt Webster had found a 15-year-old record by Ted Weems called 'Heartaches'. He liked it. Webster played the record every day on his programme and customers started asking after the record, long since sold out, in the shops. Of course 'Heartaches' was reissued, and for twelve weeks it was the best-selling record in the country.

Everyone in the record business knew these tales, and as competition tightened some record companies started regularly bribing radio announcers to choose their own new issues for their programmes. The record companies would send forged request letters to radio stations, they would buy quantities of their own records to increase the sales figures, and offer their own artists to perform for nothing. Sometimes a well-known radio announcer would be credited as co-composer of a new record, so as to get a royalty for each copy sold. A new word was even coined – 'payola' – which referred to all these forms of bribery whereby the record companies were trying to pump some life into sales of their records.

By the end of the fifties this practice had grown into such a widespread and widely known scandal that Congress appointed a committee to look into the matter. 'Between 1950 and 1954 certain record companies formed a network of radio announcers for the most important markets and paid them a commission on sales of the records they played,' stated the report on Payola and Other Deceptive Practices in the Broadcasting Field, submitted in 1960 to the Committee on Interstate and Foreign Commerce of the House of Representatives. Even in the early stages of the investigation, it was ascertained that manufacturers and wholesalers had made payments to 255 disc jockeys and other radio station employees in at least 56 cities in 26 states. According to the popularity of the disc jockey, payments varied between occasional small sums and weekly or monthly transactions. In Philadelphia, Boston, New York, Cleveland and Chicago the record companies had paid radio announcers sums amounting to thousands of dollars. The famous disc jockey, Alan Freed, was sentenced as a warning to others. After the congressional investigation the situation calmed down for a time, but accusations about payola erupted at regular intervals in the trade press. The opportunity makes the thief: in all those countries where commercial radio, which mainly plays records, is the channel for making new records familiar, the radio announcer is the gatekeeper at the doorway to a record's success.

Sources: Denisoff (1975); US Congress (1960)

The Yardbird Suite

In the early 1940s, a new phase was beginning in the development of jazz. Since the days of Louis Armstrong, the fundamentals of improvisation had remained essentially the same: one takes a tune, either well-known or freshly composed, and new melodies are created on the basis of its harmonic structure. Although this pattern was to survive in use for another couple of decades until the advent of Ornette Coleman, young musicians in the war years had been growing ever more impatient with its limitations. The familiar 32-bar tunes based on functional harmony, which had served the previous generation of jazz musicians excellently, seemed shackling to the musicians of the forties.

As the mid-forties approach one begins gradually to hear on record cautious attempts to extend the familiar patterns: Charlie Parker's one-chorus saxophone solo on Jay McShann's *Hootie Blues* of April 1941, Thelonious Monk accompanying Coleman Hawkins in 1944, Tadd Dameron's harmonic experiments on Harlan Leonard's recordings in 1940. We would certainly have heard more of them if the American Federation of Musicians had not been boycotting recordings throughout 1943. The 'jam sessions' captured on acetates for private jazz enthusiasts from Minton's Bar in Harlem, in which Dizzy Gillespie, Thelonious Monk and Charlie Christian, among others, took part, give us the opportunity to be present at the birth of a new process in music.

By 1945 the new music already had a name – 'bebop' – and its acknowledged leaders were the trumpeter, John 'Dizzy' Gillespie and the alto saxophonist, Charlie 'Yardbird' Parker. The new concept of harmony in bebop, the new technical demands placed on the instruments and the solos progressing at breakneck speed in asymmetrical phrases dismayed the older generation of musicians and critics. In their first reviews in the jazz press, Parker's and Gillespie's music was roundly condemned. But at the same time a circle of fans grew up around Parker and Gillespie, trying to adopt both their heroes' music and their nonconformist way of life. Bebop turned into a cult and an outlook on life. Bebop can be heard bursting into bloom on numerous records from 1945 onwards, most of them issued by small, enthusiastic record companies that were set up after the war.

Ross Russell, who later also wrote a biography of Charlie Parker, had saved up money to set up his own record shop, having spent two years in New Guinea as a naval radio operator. Having heard Parker on the latter's first visit to California in 1946, Russell sold his record shop and established a record company named Dial in order to release the music of his idol. (Dial also issued the first LP by avant-garde composer John Cage.) Even more extreme in his devotion was Dean Benedetti, a former professional musician, who 'dropped everything' on hearing Parker and devoted the ensuing years to capturing his solos on a primitive disc recorder. In Russell's biography, which is not always hictorically accurate, Benedetti has been made into a colourful character who supports his recording activities by selling heroin. If he was not allowed to bring his recorder to the venue of a performance, he would even get into the men's toilet and record it through the walls, wrote Russell.

The Benedetti tapes were long thought to be lost, but dozens of hours of Parker's music have been preserved on recordings made by other enthusiasts. During his lifetime, Parker made only about 100 recordings. By 1976, the number of known Parker recordings had passed 1000, including previously unreleased alternate takes, broadcasts, and on-the-spot live recordings from nightclubs. Most of them are variations of well-known titles, but all bear witness to Parker's boundless inventiveness. In the 1980s, the lost Benedetti tapes (actually discs) were finally discovered in the attic of Dean's brother's house, and they have subsequently been issued on CD. No recordings made through walls were found among them.

Bebop had its strongly nonconformist and antisocial side: it prefigured the Black Panthers and other extreme black tendencies. The bebop musicians were in the avant-garde, and although most of them had no direct links with modern literature or art movements, they perceived themselves in the same way, as being far ahead of public taste. The musicians might turn their backs on the audience while performing, and they regarded meeting contractual obligations to perform and record as petty bourgeois matters. Parker expressed his own pain with the world by taking heroin, which led him to spend long spells in mental hospitals. Many times he was unfit to perform or record, and at best a recording might proceed like this:

> Hipsters and fellow musicians trouped in and out of the studio as if it were a bus depot. Once recording got under way there were breaks to send out for soft drinks, ice, food, liquor, narcotics and girlfriends. Miles Davis took a thirty-minute nap on the floor of the studio. Savoy A&R director Teddy Reig half-dozed through it all like an oriental deity, directing with a minimum of effort. The three-hour union time limit was ignored.

(Ross Russell, *Bird Lives*, London, 1973, p. 195)

Despite everything, this session, when *Parker's Mood*, *Billie's Bounce*, *Ko-ko* and *Now's the Time* were recorded, produced some unforgettable music. The three takes that have been issued of *Parker's Mood* represent a gigantic leap forward in jazz compressed into a few minutes.

By the early fifties Parker had grown from a cult figure into an internationally famous jazz musician. The impresario Norman Granz signed a recording contract with Parker and set about organizing a concert tour for him. A large new jazz club was established in New York, called Birdland. But Parker had already burned himself out. He was banned from Birdland. More and more regularly he was incapable of performing, and in March 1955 he died, at the age of 34, from the combined effects of heroin and alcohol. The doctor who was called to treat him had guessed his age as 60. At least half a dozen famous bop musicians died young from heroin, having followed their role model too literally.

On the basis of the recordings and musical influences he left behind him, Charlie Parker must be regarded as one of the pivotal figures of jazz, and perhaps music in general, in our time. It was largely thanks to him that jazz rose from the dance halls to become a demanding art form, though at the same time it did lose its former popular appeal.

The Jazz Labels

The Hot Club of Berlin, established in 1934, was one of the many jazz enthusiasts' clubs that arose in the big cities of Europe in the thirties. One of the founder members of the club was a young man named Francis Wolff. In Hitler's Germany, however, jazz was not looked upon kindly, and in 1938 the Wolffs, who were Jews, succeeded in escaping to America. Together with a fellow refugee, Alfred Lion, the young Wolff started making a living by setting up a shop in New York called Blue Note, which specialized in jazz records. The partners in the business also released the occasional record themselves, and among the first contracts they signed was one with the Sidney Bechet Quartet in 1940.

During the war years Blue Note was inactive, but when record sales picked up again after the end of the war, Blue Note started issuing discs with increasing regularity. Their producer was Ike Quebec, himself a notable tenor saxophonist, whose finds included the pianist, Thelonious Monk. During the twenties, many jazz records had been issued solely for the black population in the United States, in the record companies' race series. Like immigrant music, they were music that was produced for one minority group. During the thirties, jazz had become part of the popular music of the era. Over a million copies were sold of the more popular swing records, and Columbia, Decca and RCA Victor competed for recording contracts with the well-known bands.

Bebop made jazz into a minority music again, although its enthusiasts did not constitute any clearly definable social group. The old established companies, which had previously tried to offer something for everyone, were no longer as interested in jazz as they had been. Production of jazz records moved into the hands of small labels like Blue Note. The founders of these companies were generally keen jazz enthusiasts themselves, for whom record production was a mixture of business and pleasure. The small companies could survive by selling a few thousand copies of their records. Ten thousand copies was considered a success by them, whereas the big companies would not have covered their costs with such an amount.

The real rise of Blue Note began with the arrival of the LP, when the company began regularly recording such luminaries of the bebop era as Monk and Bud Powell. In the late fifties, Blue Note came up with a new generation of bebop artists such as Horace Silver and Art Blakey, and it has been said that the company played a crucial role in the rise of the style known as 'hard bop' which they represented. Among the new Blue Note artists of the sixties were Wayne Shorter and Herbie Hancock.

Alongside Blue Note there were other important jazz labels in the early years of the LP: Prestige, Riverside and Verve. They were all 'one-man shows' which had come into being out of their owners' love of music. Bill Grauer and Orrie Keepnews were collectors who edited the magazine, *Record Changer*. In 1953 they set up the Riverside label to bring out reissues of forgotten jazz and blues records of the twenties, which had been unavailable for a quarter of a century. Riverside's 25-cent LP discs saved the historic Paramount and Gennett recordings for a new generation. Soon the company started issuing modern jazz too, and among its more important artists were Bill Evans, Cannonball Adderley and Wes Montgomery.

Bob Weinstock's Prestige label started in 1949. The company's first record, recorded on 11 January, was Lennie Tristano's *Tautology*. Among its artists during the fifties were Miles Davis, Sonny Rollins, Stan Getz, John Coltrane and Gene Ammons – musicians who at that time were all playing straightforward modern jazz.

Norman Granz had originally worked in the Los Angeles film industry, and was keen on jazz. In 1944 he arranged a concert in aid of Mexican immigrants, *chicanos*, and Illinois Jacquet's saxophone solo recorded at that concert became a surprise hit on the West Coast. Encouraged by its popularity, Granz began arranging concert tours known as 'Jazz at the Philharmonic' (JATP). The concerts aimed for a jam session atmosphere, with musicians playing familiar numbers for their own enjoyment. At their best the JATP concerts did indeed warm up to a frenetic pace, when soloists of the calibre of Lester Young and Illinois Jacquet would try to outblow each other for dozens of verses at a stretch. This was also a way of cutting arrangement and rehearsal costs. The JATP concert tours soon became worldwide, with concerts as far afield as Finland and Japan.

Granz recorded the best of his concerts, and, initially, he sold the tapes to other record companies. His first partner in this was Moses Asch. However, by 1951 he thought it would be best to set up his own record company, whose products appeared on the Clef and Verve labels. Verve was the label that issued Charlie Parker's last records. But with Prestige and Riverside concentrating on modern trends, Verve soon became known as a 'middle-of-the-road' jazz label. The company's major drawcards were the singer, Ella Fitzgerald and the pianist, Oscar Peterson, but Granz also faithfully recorded Billie Holiday, who was struggling with a heroin problem, and offered recording opportunities to fading soloists of the swing era such as Art Tatum.

Smaller specialist jazz labels came and went, but jazz was also being issued regularly by companies that concentrated on black music such as Savoy and Atlantic. The Ertegun brothers, the founders of Atlantic, were long-standing jazz fans, and although their label concentrated on rhythm 'n' blues, the recordings by the Modern Jazz Quartet seemed to naturally fit their profile. Savoy came from a different background. The owner of the company, Herman Lubinsky, was a middle-aged Jewish businessman who had started off with a radio shop in New Jersey, on the other side of the Hudson from New York. Lubinsky did understand black music, however, and after the war he became a leading producer of Gospel music for black audiences. The jazz records were the responsibility of his other producers, such as the keen bebop fan, Ozzie Cadena. Savoy has a place in history mainly because of the recordings made by Charlie Parker in September 1948. At that time small companies like Savoy had not yet made the jump into the LP age, and these performances originally appeared on 78 r.p.m. discs, but since Parker's death, every inch of tape of his Savoy recordings has been issued on LP, even the incomplete takes.

But not all jazz musicians are Parkers. Sales of jazz records have always been uncertain, and often only a few thousand copies of a record would be sold. A record produced according to the Musicians' Union's minimum fees might just cover its production costs with sales like that, but often, even this was not achieved. These jazz specialist companies were small, often run on a tight budget. Weinstock, Granz and Wolff knew jazz well, and the musicians who played it. Their styles were never completely undifferentiated, but, at their worst, they sound somewhat similar.

For economic reasons, large bands could not be considered, nor were there many of them in the fifties. Playing on most of the jazz records of this era are small groups of four to six, specially assembled for the recordings. Sometimes the bandleader might recruit participants over morning coffee in Manhattan just before going into the studio. Many of these discs were even recorded in same place – Rudy van Gelder's popular studio in Hackensack, New Jersey, just a half hour's drive from Manhattan. For budgetary reasons, rehearsals, too, had to be kept to a minimum. Usually, though, this merely enhanced the spontaneous character of the improvised music. The task of the producer and the recording engineer was simply to capture the music on tape as authentically as possible. By the 1980s these recordings made by Rudy van Gelder in the fifties were being held up as examples of natural sound reproduction at its best – from a forgotten golden age of recording.

Sources: Cuscuna and Ruppli (1988); Priestley (1988); Ruppli (1980)

West Coast Jazz: The Gramophone Creates a Style

The companies operating out of New York were able to take advantage of the city's vibrant jazz culture. Since the 1920s New York had been a centre of jazz; the city to which the best musicians made their way, and where the new trends started. The west coast of the United States had never been known for jazz, but in the mid-fifties 'West Coast jazz' was making jazz enthusiasts, even in Europe, prick up their ears. Behind this new current were the new jazz labels centred mainly around Los Angeles: Contemporary, Fantasy and Pacific Jazz.

California is the centre of the United States film industry, and as such it employs plenty of studio musicians, with diverse professional skills. Many of these musicians like to play jazz in their spare time; often a refined, sometimes cerebral, music, onto which might be grafted ideas from modern concert music (the same kind of ideas as are sometimes heard on film soundtracks). The results of such pursuits were sometimes heard in local nightclubs and jazz clubs, where musicians would gather to relax in their spare time. Capitol, whose head office was in Hollywood, released the first records by Shorty Rogers and Gerry Mulligan in the early fifties. On these one can hear the first examples of the new jazz being played on the West Coast.

Most of the harvest was reaped, however, by the small local companies in California. The oldest of these was Fantasy, which had been set up in Berkeley in 1949 by the brothers, Max and Sol Weiss. Lester Koenig established Contemporary in Los Angeles in 1951, and Richard Bock began issuing records on the Pacific Jazz label the following year. But whereas the New York companies were documenting the music that was flourishing around them, West Coast jazz was largely born in the studio. All three, to a large extent, made use of the same circle of musicians: Rogers, Mulligan, Chet Baker, Art Pepper, Jim Hall, Bud Shank and others. West Coast jazz was a collective name for the products of these companies. Heard in retrospect they are often somewhat tame, but they found support as far afield as Europe at a time when the first bebop revival generation had burned itself out and radical innovators were no longer on the horizon.

From the big companies' viewpoint this music was not interesting, though for a few years it caused quite a storm in jazz circles. In the fifties they were content now and then to pick up some of the more prominent names from the small companies' rosters for themselves. The biggest commercial success from their ranks was Dave Brubeck, who was signed to Columbia in 1953 after becoming a popular jazz musician on the college circuit. Brubeck's springboard to fame had been Fantasy, which had released his first disc – initially straight from tapes recorded by Brubeck himself from performances.

As the West Coast jazz wave flattened out, the companies extended their operations to other areas. Pacific released Ravi Shankar's first American recordings; Fantasy was, for a long time, the comedian Lenny Bruce's label. After the owners died or retired, these one-man companies were, one by one, sold off, and the records they released have become, except for the better-known ones, rare collectors' items. Fantasy enjoyed a revival as a rock label. Alfred Lion retired in 1967, and Francis Wolff died in 1971. Blue Note was sold first to Liberty and then to EMI. Bill Grauer died in 1963, and the following year Riverside went bankrupt. In 1960 Norman Granz sold Verve to MGM and moved to Switzerland to live. Thanks to the CD, however, these records have been reissued more and more often, and since much more music fits on a CD than on an old LP, in many cases we have had the bonus of previously unissued recordings.

Source: Gordon (1986)

Classical Music Moves into the LP Age

The increase in record sales in the 1940s also made possible the production of recordings of the more obscure classical repertoire. Even during the Depression, true devotees had scraped together the money to buy Kreisler's latest recording, but now there were buyers even for Dufay or 17th-century Spanish lute music. The biggest specialist classical shop in New York, the Gramophone Shop, was pressing such discs as the Anthologie Sonore series, a range of records specially devoted to ancient music, compiled by the refugee German musicologist, Curt Sachs, for the American market. At the other extreme, the *New Music Quarterly* was issuing ultra-modern experimental music for its subscribers. The *Encyclopaedia of Recorded Music*, published by the Gramophone Shop, and the *Record Book*, compiled by David Hall (1940), attempted to catalogue every available record and present it to classical music fans. Over 60,000 copies were sold of the first edition of the *Record Book*.

The new edition of the *Record Book*, which appeared in 1948, just before the advent of the LP, contained 1200 pages. In his introduction, David Hall stated that American classical music devotees had about 25,000 records to choose from, ranging from Gregorian chant to modern music. Some of these were records imported from Europe, which were only available from specialists like the Gramophone Shop, but there were also gems put out by small American labels. The Artist label, operating from the West Coast, released excerpts from Berg's *Wozzeck*, while Continental offered Béla Bartók interpreting his own piano works. The Disc label issued John Cage's first recordings. Among the more esoteric enterprises was Paraclete, of East Haven, Connecticut, which, in 1947, released

50 records solely of Scriabin's piano music. In the late forties an unbelievably wide range of 78 r.p.m. records was available, though only in the United States. Seen from this standpoint, the arrival of the LP, despite all its new advantages, was initially a step backwards.

The development of the repertoire can be traced by glancing through the Schwann LP catalogue, which William Schwann began publishing in 1949. Since then it has been cataloguing all the LP records available on the United States market each month. The first catalogue was a thin booklet, which included eleven companies: Allegro, Artist, Capitol, Cetra Soria, Columbia, Concert Hall, Decca, London, Mercury, Polydor and Vox.

The first LP recordings to be made were reissues of the basic classical music repertoire as interpreted by renowned artists. The lesser-known repertoire had to wait its turn. Unfortunately, every conductor thought the same way. By 1954, according to the Schwann catalogue, 21 different versions of Beethoven's *Eroica* had appeared on the LP market, both new recordings and pressings transferred from old 78 r.p.m. discs. Tchaikovsky's *Romeo and Juliet* was available in just as many versions. There were ten recordings of Mozart's D minor piano concerto, and five interpretations of the *St Matthew Passion*.

At its best the new technology did indeed inspire the conductors to performances of superb quality. Toscanini, in particular, appreciated the possibilities offered by the tape recorder of recording large orchestral works in longer sections. His 1952 recording of Beethoven's ninth was both an artistic and a commercial success: in two years it sold nearly 150,000 copies. Ten years earlier such a work would have had to be issued in an album containing eight 78 r.p.m. discs, and it would have sold a few thousand copies.

Toscanini already had a contract with RCA. With the new technology, the company extended its roster of artists. One of its notable new signings was the Chicago Symphony Orchestra, conducted by Fritz Reiner, whose RCA records are regarded as among the best orchestral recordings, both technically and artistically. The original pressings of them have become collectors' items, which are snapped up just like original pressings of Caruso; the less purist collectors can hear Reiner's renderings transferred onto CD. Among the new signings for CBS were Bruno Walter and George Szell. Mercury, which had grown rich on polkas and rhythm 'n' blues, made the grand gesture of a contract with Antal Dorati and the Minneapolis Symphony Orchestra for 100 LPs. With the London Symphony Orchestra the industrious Dorati recorded another 50 LPs for Mercury.

Thanks to the new technology, the sound reproduction of records had improved considerably. This was most evident on the recordings of classical music. On an LP record it was possible at the optimum to capture a frequency of as much as 18,000 Hz and dynamics of over 50 decibels. This meant that the highest harmonics on the violin and most of the variations in volume in the orchestra, from pianissimo to fortissimo, could, in principle, be captured on record. Correspondingly, the quality of domestic sound reproduction equipment improved. Appearing on the market alongside the mass-produced radiograms were amplifiers and speakers of high quality which were able to faithfully reproduce what was etched onto disc. Wealthy music lovers were prepared to invest more and more in high-quality sound reproduction – high fidelity.

Mercury records became known among classical music enthusiasts for their excellent sound reproduction. The recordings were of top quality, all sections of the orchestra could be heard in the right perspective and in the finest detail. The discs themselves were of fine quality, made with care from first-class materials and without superfluous frills. Mercury did not hide its technical light under a bushel either; on the record sleeves, in addition to the usual information about the musicians performing, there were details of the microphones used and other technical matters. In this way the company was consciously feeding the hi-fi enthusiast, and advocating high-quality sound equipment.

The advent of the LP also provided opportunities for new entrepreneurs specializing in classical music. One of these was James Grayson, an English businessman who had come to the United States during the war to take charge of food consignments to hungry Britain and stayed there. Grayson realized that there was room for others in the growing classical music market. In 1949, with Michael Naida and Henry Gage, he established the Westminster company. Grayson's business idea was to make recordings cheaply in impoverished Europe at the mimimal musicians' union rates and sell the records to rich Americans. Naturally, the venue chosen for the company's European headquarters was Vienna, where for many years Grayson had his own box at the Konzerthaus.

Over a period of fifteen years Westminster issued more than a thousand LP records. These included an exemplary series of works conducted by Hermann Scherchen. In addition to the basic classical repertoire, Westminster was instrumental in making Baroque music known on record. In the 1960s, the rising standard of living in Europe and competition between record companies raised conductors' and soloists' fees, and Westminster was no longer able to adjust to the stereo age. The advent of the compact disc, however, has given a new lease of life to the company's best recordings, reissued in a new form.

Source: Gelatt (1956)

Dario Soria and the Resurgence of the Opera Record

Although many of the brightest stars in the early years of recording were Italians, the Italian record industry had been almost entirely in foreign hands. Even the famous Fonotipia label, for which so many legendary singers had recorded, was English-owned. In the nationalist-minded 1930s, to promote domestic production, the Italian radio company RAI established its own record label, named Cetra. Its purpose was to exploit the resources of the radio's music department and offer conductors such as Victor de Sabata and Bernardino Molinari an opportunity to perform on record.

The war curtailed Cetra's operations, however, and set in motion a new phase in its development. Dario Soria (1912–80) was a Jewish-Italian businessman who had fled to America as Hitler was consolidating his collaboration with Mussolini. Soria worked in advertising in New York, but his great love was opera. When peace was re-established he managed to join an American trade delegation that was visiting Rome to negotiate the reconstruction of trading links. The result of the trip was Cetra-Soria, a company that undertook to record Cetra's discs in the United States. If we recall that at that time more than half the records produced in the world were sold in the United States, we can understand that this was also of some significance to the development of the Italian recording industry.

Classical music had just begun to appear on LP records in the United States, and in 1949 Soria started pressing LP records directly from the tapes he had brought back from Italy (where records were still being pressed in 78 r.p.m. format). 1951 was Giuseppe Verdi's anniversary year. Cetra and Soria celebrated the occasion by issuing, over the next seven years, a total of sixteen complete Verdi operas, including such rarities as *La Battaglia di Legnano* and *Un Giorno di Regno*. The most prominent of Cetra's singers at that time was a tenor named Ferruccio Tagliavini, whose sales in America were promoted by his appearance at the Metropolitan Opera. Subsequent generations remember Cetra better for Maria Callas's debut record.

By the 1950s, other record companies had started producing operatic records. Soria shrewdly sold his business to Capitol and moved himself onto the EMI payroll. Cetra itself merged in 1957 with another Italian record label, Fonit, which had achieved success with dance music. Times had changed: the first international hit for the new Cetra-Fonit company was Domenico Modugno's 'Nel blu dipinto di blu', the winning tune at the San Remo Song Festival of 1958.

Source: Hall (1980)

Sinatra's Empire

The American hit tunes of the forties and fifties, of which many have lived on in translation in a multitude of languages, may be roughly divided into two main groups. On the one hand were records whose appeal lay in a simple catchy melody. Bing Crosby, Nat King Cole, Doris Day, Perry Como, Frankie Laine, Rosemary Clooney and Patti Page were selling millions of this type of record each year. The same records were familiar all over Europe. On the top-selling list for 1952, even in Finland, were Nat King Cole's 'Too Young' and Doris Day's 'Domino'.

A second significant group consisted of the tunes from Broadway shows, which were often considerably subtler on record. Often the most important compositions from the musicals were issued on 'original cast' records, performed by the Broadway artists. *Oklahoma, An American in Paris, High Society, My Fair Lady, West Side Story, South Pacific* and *The Sound of Music* were hits on record as well as on stage. When musicals enjoyed a long first run in the Broadway theatres of New York, then transferred to other theatres, and often subsequently to the screen, record sales got a colossal boost. When the songs were further re-recorded as 'soundtrack' versions, the tunes were marketed twice over, to the great satisfaction of composer and publisher alike.

Among the popular singers of post-war America there is one, however, who is difficult to place in any pigeon-hole. Francis Sinatra was born in the Hoboken, New Jersey, to an Italian immigrant family in 1915. In 1939 he signed a contract

115

as a solo singer with Harry James's band, moving to Tommy Dorsey's outfit the following year.

Solo singers with popular swing bands of that era were something of a necessary evil, being required to perform the refrains. The real stars were the bandleaders and instrumental soloists. There was something about the slim, boyish Sinatra, however, that was especially attractive to female audiences. In 1943 Columbia signed a personal recording contract with him, and Sinatra left the band for a solo career, which was soon boosted by a film contract (his first speaking role was in 1944; before that he sang in three films). In the forties Sinatra became an especially popular interpreter of love songs, and almost hysterical audience reactions were witnessed at his concerts on a scale not to be repeated until the age of rock 'n' roll. When Sinatra arrived in California for the first time in 1943, one of his women fans bit the arm of a journalist who was obstructing her view of her idol.

Sinatra's career seemed to be ending with the forties. He already had a fairly long singing career behind him. His records were no longer selling at their former rate, and the tempestuous Sinatra had irritated all the influential figures in his record company. In 1952 Columbia suspended his contract, and it was only with great difficulty that his manager got him a new one with Capitol. Only his failing marriage, to Ava Gardner, and his successful role in the film *From Here to Eternity* seemed to be keeping Sinatra in the limelight.

In his Capitol period, however, Sinatra began a successful new recording career supported by his permanent arranger, Nelson Riddle. Sinatra was one of the first singers of the LP era who made albums that were complete thematic entities. In 1954 his *Songs for Young Lovers* came out; in 1955, *In the Wee Small Hours*; in 1956, *Songs for Swinging Lovers*; in 1957, *A Swinging Affair*; in 1958, *Come Fly with Me*; in 1959, *Come Dance with Me*; in 1960, *Nice and Easy* – records that sound completely fresh even in the CD age. In the same period he had time to make more than ten movies, from musicals to serious speaking roles.

Sinatra's recordings and film performances began to do so well that in 1960 he established his own record company, Reprise. Previously it had only been budding artists who could not get a recording contract that put out their own records. Dizzy Gillespie's and Charles Mingus's effort to set up their own record business had been stillborn. Reprise, however, was, from the beginning, a company to be taken seriously. The first album released on the label featured tenor saxophonist, Ben Webster, and other Reprise artists included Duke Ellington, Rosemary Clooney and Sammy Davis Jr. In fact, Sinatra was intially prevented from recording for his own company by his old contract, and had to finish four 'contractual obligation' albums for Capitol.

On the new label Sinatra began the third successful phase of his singing career. The new Sinatra was perhaps not as artistically ambitious as the Sinatra of the Capitol era. His albums ranged from show tunes to a soft rock suite (*Watertown*, 1969) and included jazz with Count Basie and bossa nova with Antonio Carlos Jobim. But commercially the new phase was a great success: 'Strangers in the Night' was a number one hit in 1966, and 'Somethin' Stupid', made with his daughter Nancy, was an even bigger success the following year.

By this time, though, Reprise was no longer Sinatra's own label. He sold Reprise to Warner's in 1963, the reason being not unprofitability but rather the film roles offered in addition by this film company which had expanded into the record business. (Sinatra also got a share of Warner's overall record output, which over the years proved to be an incredible investment.) Since Sinatra many other famous entertainers have started putting out records on their own labels though usually they have left distribution to the bigger companies. Harry Belafonte established his own production company in 1961; distribution of the records was done by RCA. Paul Anka even bought the rights to all his records from his first label, ABC-Paramount, so as to be able to decide on any future reissues.

Frank Sinatra died on 14 May 1998. He was the friend of politicians, film stars and sometimes shady businessmen, a man whose whims and outbursts were reported in detail in the American press. He was not merely a singer, but an interpreter of songs, in whose hands the nuances of a tune and lyrics came to life. He might be called the Fischer-Dieskau of American popular song.

Sources: Friedwald (1995); Shaw (1968)

Moses Asch and Folkways

Moses Asch was born in Warsaw in 1905, the son of the well-known Jewish writer, Sholem Asch. He was educated in France, Germany and the United States and then settled in New York as an electrical engineer. In the late thirties, when the record business was expanding, 'Mo' Asch set up his own record company, Asch Records. The company's first release was a collection of modernized Jewish folk songs performed by the Bagelman Sisters. In the war years Moses Asch came into close contact with the left-wing folk music movement in New York, and among Asch's record releases were songs by Woody Guthrie, Pete Seeger, Burl Ives and Leadbelly, and jazz recordings by Coleman Hawkins and James P. Johnson. In 1947 Asch tried to expand his operations by signing a contract with the poular singer, Nat King Cole, but this was too much for the company. Asch Records went bankrupt, but the same year Moses Asch set up a new company, named Folkways.

Folkways was to become the world's leading specialist folk music label. Asch continued to document the American folk movement and released a six-LP set, _Anthology of American Folk Music_, a selection compiled by Harry Smith of commercial labels' folk music releases from the 1920s, which was to become a model for many folk musicians of the sixties. At the same time Asch formed close relations with representatives of a new branch of science that was burgeoning at the time – ethnomusicology.

Ethnomusicologists were making field recordings as part of their research into the traditional music of many parts of the globe, and Asch released the most interesting pieces on record. Over the years Folkways put out more than 2000 LPs, on which practically every country in the world is represented. Although new companies have sprung up since the 1960s in Europe, such as Bärenreiter in Germany and Ocora in France, which have released newer and technically superior recordings from the same areas, in many cases the old Folkways records are, even today, the only available samples of some particular tribe's or nation's music. In addition to folk music, Folkways also released other documentary records, such as the tape recording of Bertolt Brecht's statement before the Congressional Committee on UnAmerican Activities.

Although Moses Asch had close links with the American folk scene, Folkways did not benefit much from the commercial popularity of folk in the 1960s. Old and new stars of the genre, such as Pete Seeger, Bob Dylan and Joan Baez, were drawn toward the bigger labels, which had more effective distribution and marketing organizations. Moses Asch had once burnt his fingers with Nat King Cole, and Folkways remained to the end a small, one-man operation. In *Sing Out* magazine, the mouthpiece of the folk music movement, Asch warned readers of a 'personality cult in folk music'.

If one had to choose a typical record from the extensive Folkways catalogue, it might be the collection of music of the aboriginal Ona population of Tierra del Fuego, released in 1972. At the turn of the century, Argentine and Chilean cattle breeders mercilessly exterminated these aborigines of the southern tip of South America and paid a bounty for the Indians, as Bruce Chatwin relates in his book, *In Patagonia*. In the sixties there was only one surviving representative of the aboriginal population of Tierra del Fuego, whose sung repertoire was recorded on tape by the ethnomusicologist, Annie Chapman. This shamanic music, based on two or three main tones, is hardly what anyone would listen to for enjoyment, but it is part of humanity's common culture. Thanks to Moses Asch, it has been preserved.

Moses Asch was a colourful personality, of whom many tales have been told. Though he selflessly released many records that were guaranteed not to sell, he was on the other hand an extremely stingy businessman, who was prone to endless delays in paying royalties to artists. Mo was active in the record industry almost until the age of 80. One of Folkways' last releases was also a homage to his father: a collection of old recordings of Jewish *klezmer* music from the turn of the century. Moses Asch died on 19 October 1986. He bequeathed his record company to his adopted homeland. In 1987 the Folkways archives passed to the Smithsonian Institution, the national museum of the United States.

Europe Rises to its Feet

In the United States the record industry had got through the war almost unscathed. In Europe, when the war ended, it had to be rebuilt almost from scratch. Both Columbia's headquarters in London and the Deutsche Grammophon office in Berlin had been destroyed by bombing. Record production in the war years had had to be reduced for the sake of the armaments industry. After the war rationing continued for a long time, and many Europeans were too poor to think of buying records. In 1950, representatives of EMI calculated that overall record sales in the world were worth £66 million. As much as £37 million of this was in the United States record market. Sales in England were worth only two-and-a-half million, and about the same in West Germany and France. By 1955 overall sales in the industry had risen to £96 million, but the proportions for each country remained much the same.

Berliner's workshop

William
Owen

Shalyapin at
Hayes with the
Gaisberg
Brothers

The Voice of the Victor

The Lindström factory in the 1920s

Louis Armstrong

Paramount advertisement for 'race records'

John Hammond

Duke Ellington
Orchestra

Bruno Walter

David Sarnoff

Peter Goldmark with a pile of LP records; beside him the equivalent
amount of music on 78 r.p.m. discs.
Courtesy of Columbia Records.

Walter Legge and Herbert von Karajan

Clive Davis

The Fugs: Reprise Records advertisement

Fritz Reiner
recording

Wanda
Landowska

After the war the record industry in the United States had immediately exploded into rapid growth, as a result of which hundreds of new record companies sprang up across the country. Such a development only took place in the sixties in Europe; the old companies maintained their dominance for a long time. Those in the best position at the end of the war were EMI and Decca. Their manufacturing plants had not suffered badly, and even EMI's irreplaceable archives at Hayes had survived intact. As representatives of the victorious allies, it was easy for the companies to re-establish business links with their agents elsewhere in Europe. Relations with America were already basically sound. On the strength of its historical ties, EMI represented the record production of both RCA and CBS in Europe. Record manufacturing had continued to decline throughout the war, and it was easy to expand it as soon as rationing allowed. The biggest problem for EMI, in fact, was that both Sir Louis Sterling and Sir Alfred Clark were elderly gentlemen who did not approve of any innovations. Sir Alfred retired in September 1946, but Sir Louis stayed on as managing director, delaying the switch to LPs for many years to come. Thus EMI lost some of its competitive lead: the first LPs in Europe were released by Decca.

Soon EMI was losing ground in another sphere. In 1951 the omnipotent president of RCA, General Sarnoff (the rank had been granted for his wartime services) had visited the EMI headquarters at Hayes, near London. His hosts had kept the General waiting for over an hour, and he had plenty of time to study the holes in the linoleum on the floors. Word spread rapidly in America. In 1952 CBS terminated its agreement with EMI, the following year RCA did the same. CBS moved its representation to Philips, and RCA to Decca.

American connections were vital for the European record companies in those years, because a large proportion of the records sold in Europe were of American origin. To post-war Europe, America was a dream of freedom and wealth. The bandleader, Glenn Miller, called up to serve in the United States Army, had disappeared with his aircraft somewhere over the English Channel. In the war years American swing music had been played in Nazi-occupied countries, and when the war ended, records by long-since disbanded swing bands were bought up feverishly. In England EMI had sold as many as 460,000 copies of Major Miller's *Moonlight Serenade* (originally issued by RCA). After the war the new American singing stars automatically became famous in Europe too, thanks at least partly to the American forces radio stations operating in Germany. Now EMI had to be content with its own wares or to buy recordings from the smaller American companies (which proved to be a sound move, due to the burgeoning number of small companies in the US at the time). It was only by 1955 that EMI had recovered enough to buy American Capitol in recompense.

Connections with America were important because European popular music was suffering a serious identity crisis in the wake of the war. The two best-selling records for EMI up to 1955 were 'O mein Papa', by the honey-voiced trumpeter, Eddie Calvert (1,120,000 copies) and Richard Addinsell's super-romantic *Warsaw Concerto*, performed by the London Symphony Orchestra (1,025,000 copies). The runners-up were the British dance bands of Victor Silvester and Joe Loss.

Traditional national popular music was of course still being produced in all European countries. Neapolitan songs and Scottish bagpipers were available on

119

record, but the younger generation (which has always bought the largest numbers of records) had turned its back on this kind of music. When, in 1955, the English paper, *Record Mirror*, began collating lists of the top ten best-selling records, they were dominated by American singers: Johnnie Ray, Rosemary Clooney, Tony Bennett, Frankie Laine and Doris Day. Number three in January 1955 was a harbinger of what was to come: Bill Haley's 'Rock Around the Clock'.

Soon the European record companies had to start producing domestic rock stars just to be able to stay in the competition. Before long every western European country had its own miniature Elvis competing for a share of the market, but the lion's share still went to the Americans. Since the discs were, after all, being pressed in Europe from American matrices, even Elvis and Bill Haley were helping, in their own way, to resurrect the record industry in the Old World. Between 1955 and 1960 European record sales doubled once again.

Sources: Batten (1956); Gelatt (1956); Pandit (1996)

Walter Legge Returns to Civilian Life

In the sphere of classical music, which offered export opportunities to the United States, the European record industry recovered more quickly. At the end of the war the most influential producer of classical music records in Europe was undoubtedly Walter Legge of EMI. Legge, who had poor eyesight, was drafted into ENSA, the British Army's entertainment unit, during the war years, where his responsibility was to arrange classical concerts for the troops. At Legge's initiative the BBC Symphony Orchestra played a concert in Portsmouth, conducted by Sir Adrian Boult, for 20,000 seamen, and the pianist Solomon toured North Africa, playing the piano in soldiers' quarters and bars. No-one took offence at the fact that the usual repertoire consisted of works by Beethoven, Brahms, Wagner, Richard Strauss and other 'enemy' composers. Occasionally a little Elgar was included in the programme.

Production of classical records was in abeyance during the war but ENSA offered Legge the opportunity to continue his work as a talent scout. As soon as the Allies had conquered Paris, Legge was ordered to travel there. His old friend, Jacques Thibaud, introduced him to a promising young violinist named Ginette Neveu. As a result of this meeting Neveu got both an invitation to perform in soldiers' quarters and a contract with EMI. As early as November 1945 Ginette Neveu went to London to make a recording of Sibelius's violin concerto, which is still regarded as one of the best. The young Belgian, Arthur Grumiaux, was discovered for EMI in the same way.

With the war over, it was time to set up a new recording programme. In January 1946 Walter Legge travelled to occupied Vienna, where he arranged recording contracts for Irmgard Seefried, Ljuba Welitsch, Maria Cebotari, Elisabeth Schwarzkopf, Hans Hotter and the Vienna Philharmonic, among others. He managed to procure the services of the conductors Wilhelm Furtwängler and Herbert von Karajan. Some years later, Legge married the singer, Elisabeth Schwarzkopf.

In 1946 Legge had been able to pick up the best artists in Europe almost without competition, since they badly needed the opportunities to record and the extra income which records offered. When other companies joined in the game, the competition for artists intensified. Nevertheless, even in the fifties, Legge succeeded in contracting both Maria Callas and David Oistrakh for EMI, and raised the relatively unknown conductor Otto Klemperer to world fame.

Among Legge's other accomplishments was the recording of the Philharmonia Orchestra, even though he did not need to arrange a special contract for it. The Philharmonia was Legge's 'own' orchestra. It grew out of the assemblage he had put together in the forties, in which he had expressly intended to gather the country's best musicians. In order to keep the orchestra together he arranged concert tours and film music recordings for the Philharmonia, and, of course, as many recording sessions as possible. Its permanent conductor was, originally, Karajan, and later, Klemperer, and Toscanini agreed to be its guest conductor. Legge's aim was to maintain a symphony orchestra on a purely commercial basis with his slogan 'Democracy has nothing to do with art'. As the 'owner' of the orchestra he had the right to expel musicians at any time, if their playing left anything to be desired, and hire better ones. When Walter Legge retired from EMI in 1964, he coldly disbanded the Philharmonia Orchestra and sacked all its members. His dumbfounded players set up their own co-operative, the New Philharmonia Orchestra; Legge forbade the use of the old name.

The role of the classical music producer is more like that of an impresario than the task of a pop music producer. The producer signs up the artists, agrees on their repertoire with them and arranges the recordings to fit the artists' hectic timetables (which in the case of opera recordings can be an extremely difficult task). He also has to be a diplomat. One of Walter Legge's greatest accomplishments was to keep Karajan and Furtwängler on the EMI roster at the same time, although the maestri did not get on. (Furtwängler never referred to his younger rival by any other name than 'Herr K'.)

The classical music producer is not expected to make improvements to compositions by adding new parts or finding new 'sounds' in the symphony orchestra. The arrival of the tape recorder in the studio did not necessarily signify a revolution in classical music production. However, correcting performances in the studio was not unknown in the production of classical records. One of the most famous instances was Furtwängler's recording of *Tristan and Isolde* for EMI, on which Elisabeth Schwarzkopf had to fill in all the high Cs in the second act which the ageing Kirsten Flagstad could not attain. Large-scale classical works are hardly ever recorded in their entirety unless they are concert recordings. Mistakes occur in nearly every performance. Most often they are so slight that they do not disturb anyone in the concert hall, but when heard over and over again on record they can be annoying. In order that the illusion of a perfect performance could be captured, the large orchestral works, for example, were cut up into 3- to 5-minute sections in recording, rehearsed separately and recorded several times. The length of the sections was originally dictated by the playing time of a 78 r.p.m. record.

Thanks to the tape recorder and the LP, the tasks of the producer increased. Some producers started cutting the pieces to be recorded into small parts, some only a few bars long. If mistakes occurred, the part to be re-recorded was never long. Studio musicians who were used to recording practices learned to preserve tempi and sound so well in their playing that the cuts were undetectable. Other producers thought they could achieve better results by recording entire sections of works. The mistakes were patched up either by re-recording only the faulty part later, or by cutting a piece of matching length from another take to replace an unsuccessful one.

The working practices of different producers and conductors tended to differ sharply. In any case the musicians' and singers' studio performances were only the raw material from which the producer assembled the final interpretation. Co-operation between producer, recording engineer and conductor must proceed so well that the parts form a seamless whole, which has the best features of both an impassioned concert and a faultless studio performance. Finally, the producer is also responsible for the transfer of the completed tape to disc. Even at this stage it might prove necessary to alter a soloist's tone by electronic means.

Many artists have related what an important part Legge played in the shaping of the final interpretation of a work in the studio. He was able to involve himself in the smallest details of an interpretation and to discipline a temperamental Italian tenor. Legge had never studied music formally, but on the strength of the records he produced he must be counted among the great musicians of the century. Nevertheless, he benefited from an exceptional historic opportunity. At the beginning of the century, Fred Gaisberg had been the first to yoke the world's most famous musicians into the service of the gramophone. In the same way, during the Depression and the war years, Legge was virtually without competition as a producer for the greatest record company in Europe.

Source: Schwarzkopf (1982)

Decca and DGG

It was not long before EMI had competitors in making classical records. Its most serious rivals were Decca and DGG (Deutsche Grammophon Gesellschaft). Soon Philips in the Netherlands also became a significant player in the classical music field, and in time, several small enterprises exclusively devoted to classical music were appearing in the western European market. Apart from Walter Legge, the most prominent classical record producer of the post-war years was John Culshaw, of Decca.

When John Culshaw began working in the publicity department of Decca on 11 November 1946, he was a former fighter pilot who was interested in music, with a few published articles in the music press to his credit. His job was to write biographies of Decca artists for the press to use – the same job, incidentally, with which Legge had started his career. The head of Decca, and its chief shareholder, was Sir Edward Lewis, a former stockbroker who had bought the company when gramophone fever was at its height in 1929, and believed in its possibilities, even in the Depression years, so much that he had set up a subsidiary in the United States. The company's chief engineer was Arthur Haddy, who had developed the 'ffrr' recording technology. The producer of its classical repertoire was Victor Olof.

He had just completed a recording of Stravinsky's *The Firebird* and *Petrushka*, using the new technique, with Ernest Ansermet conducting, and Decca had received much praise from the critics. Production was increasing, and the young producer sometimes had to help out with recording. In 1949 Decca started making LP records, at first for the American market and soon for Europe as well. One producer could not do everything, and eventually Culshaw had to leave the publicity department.

Like many other British companies, Decca had had to dispose of its American subsidiary during the war. In 1949 Sir Edward resumed operations in the United States, this time with the London label, and at the same time he came to an agreement with Capitol in America. Decca had its own agents in various European countries, the most active of whom was the Swiss Maurice Rosengarten. Rosengarten had a finger in many pies, but he had good connections in central European musical life. It was through him that such artists as Tebaldi, Knappertsbusch and del Monaco were signed to Decca. Soon Decca ranked alongside EMI and DGG as one of the most important producers of classical music in Europe, and Culshaw and Olof were fully occupied in recording in all the great musical centres of the continent. In ten years Decca grew into a serious competitor to EMI, and in 1959 the company crowned its achievements by poaching Herbert von Karajan from EMI.

Things were not going so well in Germany. The Deutsche Grammophon factory in Hanover was only able to function when the Allies had found in a gravel pit 1000 record matrices of speeches by Nazi leaders and the war crimes investigators wanted test pressings made from them. By autumn 1946 records were being made for the civilian market as well, and by 1948 production had reached two million records. At the great German radio exhibition of 1951, DGG proudly presented its first LPs, including Felix Mendelssohn's *A Midsummer Night's Dream*, banned during the Nazi era.

The most popular DGG artist during the fifties was Freddy Quinn, whose saccharine, langorous ballads, such as *Heimatlos* ('Homeless'), *Heimweh* ('Homesickness') and *Unter fremden Sternen* ('Under alien stars'), earned the company no less than seven gold records, illustrating the uncertainty of the Germans in the period of reconstruction. Production of popular music elsewhere in post-war Europe was just as conservative, which might perhaps explain the rapid breakthrough of rock 'n' roll in the Old World a few years later. But in the field of classical music, DGG was soon to demonstrate its superiority.

In 1949 DGG had secured Dr Fred Hamel, a well-known musicologist and critic, as its chief classical music producer. Hamel was particularly interested in early music, and under his guidance, DGG established its early music series, with its own trademark, Archiv Produktion. Early music was, it is true, not entirely unknown on record – the French Anthologie Sonore, managed by Curt Sachs, had produced many distinguished records in the thirties. Under Hamel's direction, however, DGG set about its task with typical German thoroughness. The covers of the Archiv records had a clinical asceticism about them; illustrations were not used at all; instead there were exhaustive background notes about the record. What appeared on the records were both previously unknown Baroque music and older music from the Middle Ages onwards.

One of its ambitious aims was to put onto record the entire colossal output of Johann Sebastian Bach, starting with the organ compositions, which Helmut Walcha recorded for Archiv in their entirety. Hamel was so devoted to ancient music that in 1952 he devolved his production jobs to others, and dedicated himself to the Archiv series until his death in 1957. His successor as producer of the Archiv programme was the musicologist, Hans Hickmann, among whose notable signings were the Bach specialists Karl Richter and Nikolaus Harnoncourt.

In 1967 Archiv celebrated the bicentenary of Telemann's death with a large-scale recording project. By this time early music was no longer the exclusive province of DGG; every self-respecting large record company had started to produce it. The chief producer for the mainstream classical programme at DGG was, from 1952, Elsa Schiller, a Hungarian-born professor of the piano, and one of the few women in the business. Under her direction DGG undertook an ambitious recording programme, involving artists such as Dietrich Fischer-Dieskau, Annelies Kupper, Enrico Mainardi, Wolfgang Windgassen and Wilhelm Kempff. The Finnish bass, Kim Borg, recorded for DGG from 1952.

The large classical productions were mainly conducted by Ferenc Fricsay in the early stages. After the war Fricsay had been invited from Hungary to set up the Berlin RIAS Radio Symphony Orchestra, which was to represent the future for a Germany rising from the ashes. He was conducting at the Berlin State Opera as soon as it resumed operations, and in 1949 he also became artistic director of the Munich Opera. In the fifties he was a central figure in many musical ventures, but had to withdraw from most of them owing to differences of opinion. He died in 1963.

Fricsay's career with DGG lasted longer than with most other companies, since Elsa Schiller acted as a 'stabilizer' of her countryman's fiery temperament. A gigantic programme was committed to record, mostly Romantic music, which was Fricsay's main strength. Records were made at such places as the Dahlem Church in Berlin and the Residenz Herkules in Munich; wherever Fricsay performed. Not all the recordings have stood the test of time, but his incomparable rendering of Tchaikovsky's sixth symphony is still exemplary. Fricsay also played a central role in the creation of a new operatic programme for DGG. The first opera to appear on one of the company's LPs was Lortzing's *Zar und Zimmermann*, in 1952, and subsequently Fricsay conducted recordings of *Don Giovanni*, *Fidelio* and *The Flying Dutchman*, among others. Over the years the entire central repertoire of Italian and German opera appeared on record. By this time, of course, there were other conductors as well, since DGG had managed to lure back artists who had signed up with the British labels after the war. In 1960 DGG signed a contract with La Scala, Milan for opera recordings, and DGG also released complete German-language versions of *Tosca*, *Madama Butterfly* and *La Bohème* for the domestic market.

Sources: Culshaw (1981); Riess (1966); Rutz (1963)

Callas

The great stars of the early years of the century had been singers. Caruso was a household name, Tetrazzini had popular songs composed for her and Melba had a dessert named after her. With the improvements in recording technology and the advent of the LP, instrumentalists and conductors had risen to prominence in the making of classical records; the great name of the thirties was Toscanini. In the fifties the world once again saw a singer in whom artistic perfection and a high public profile were united. She was the Greek soprano, Maria Anna Kalogeropoulou, or Maria Callas (1923–77).

After studying singing in Athens she made her debut in Italy, and in the fifties she created a magnificent international career for herself in London, Chicago, New York and Milan. Maria Callas was one of those rare talents in whom brilliant vocal resources and an exceptional singing technique were united with an unusual gift for acting. After Lilli Lehmann she was the first singer to appear with equal success in the central roles of both Wagnerian and Italian opera. Just as legendary as Callas's interpretations were her quarrels with opera directors, her poodles, her divorce and her great love affair with the multimillionaire shipowner, Aristoteles Onassis. In Maria Callas the world's press found a star who provided just as much material for the gossip columns as Elizabeth Taylor at her best.

Callas had started her recording career in the late forties, on the Italian Cetra label. In the summer of 1951 Walter Legge heard her singing in Bellini's *Norma* at the Rome Opera and rushed to the diva's dressing room after the performance to offer her a recording contract. The contractual negotiations between Legge and Maria's husband at the time, Giovanni Meneghini, were among the most colourful in the history of recording. Meneghini was aware of his wife's abilities and held out for the highest price, causing Legge to bring flowers for Callas for weeks on end. It was a year before a contract was signed.

Legge was engaged in a large operatic recording project in conjunction with La Scala, and in the fifties Callas was involved in the recording of many significant operas, with conductors such as de Sabata, Karajan and Serafin – *I Puritani, Cavalleria Rusticana, Tosca, Norma, La Forza del Destino, Il Turco in Italia, Madama Butterfly, Rigoletto, Il Trovatore, La Bohème, Un Ballo in Maschera, La Sonnambula, Manon Lescaut* – as well as a few operas recorded without the help of La Scala. These recordings, later to become legendary, were appearing with such regularity in the fifties that in 1958 the unappreciative critic of *The Gramophone* complained that EMI and La Scala were producing Callas records as if on a conveyor belt, and that he would like to hear some other soprano for a change.

Perhaps the most famous of the recordings is the *Tosca* made in 1953, on which the conductor was Victor de Sabata, with Tito Gobbi and Giuseppe di Stefano in the male roles. The *Tosca* recording in Milan took eleven feverish days, during which Gobbi's part in the first act was recorded no less than 30 times. After hearing this realization of Puccini's score, 'all other performances, whether in the opera house or on record, seem frustratingly inadequate or even irrelevant,' wrote the opera critic David Lowe.

Callas's *La Traviata*, on the other hand, is the most famous non-existent record in history, just as historic in its way as Jean de Reszke's vanished Fonotipia records.

EMI had long been planning for Callas to record this Verdi opera, after Callas had appeared in Luchino Visconti's and Carlo Maria Giulini's sensational production at La Scala. By 1968 the time should have been ripe. Peter Andry, Legge's successor, had done a colossal amount of preparatory work. The conductor was to be Giulini, and Luciano Pavarotti had been secured for the role of Alfredo after Callas had rejected Placido Domingo. The studio was booked for three weeks and the musicians and choir had been paid. A day before recording was due to start, Callas cancelled the engagement, because she thought Rome was too cold in September.

Since 1964 Callas had not appeared on stage. In the same year Walter Legge had left EMI. Now her recording career came to an end as well, though she did record a few operatic arias subsequently. The reason for Callas's final silence is known. In 1968 Aristoteles Onassis fell for Jacqueline Kennedy, and they were married on 20 October 1968. Maria Callas was only heard a few times in public after that. In 1973/74 she arranged a sort of farewell tour, which took her as far as Japan, but her voice was no longer as it had been; according to David Lowe, 'she was guilty of the kind of wailing that can give opera a bad name'. Callas died in Paris in 1977; the ultimate reason for her death remains unclear. Her ashes lay in a French bank vault for two years, until, in 1979, the Greek government had them scattered over the Aegean.

With a little bit of effort we can hear Callas, on record, in *La Traviata*, as Violetta. In 1953, contractually obliged by her old company Cetra, she had recorded this opera in Turin under Santini, and the record is still available. Since Callas's death her legend has grown to such proportions that all her recordings are valuable. Record releases, lawful and unlawful, include dozens of her radio broadcasts, tape recordings of opera performances, and even the lectures she gave to a master-class at the Juilliard School of Music in New York in 1971/72. We can hear Callas as Violetta in Buenos Aires in 1951, Mexico City in 1952, at La Scala in 1955, 1956 and 1958, and at Covent Garden in 1958. Even EMI, the company she let down, finally succeeded, a few years ago, in releasing a *Traviata* sung by Callas, when the company got hold of a performance recorded in Lisbon in 1958, which is more than satisfactory. Alfredo was played by Alfredo Kraus. But thanks to Jacqueline Kennedy we will never hear the most celebrated Violetta of the century singing with Pavarotti on what was supposed to be the most magnificent opera record of all time.

Sources: Ardoin (1982); Lowe (1987)

Pianists from Behind the Iron Curtain

For a long time the Soviet Union and its record industry were an unknown quantity to Western music lovers. After the Second World War it took nearly ten years before Soviet musicians began performing in the west in any great number; some never had this opportunity. The Soviet Union was indeed producing huge numbers of records, but for a long period their technical quality was inferior to western standards, and obviously the Soviets could not market them abroad. A nation that was used to importing and exporting goods by the trainload could not understand the fluctuations in demand in the western record market.

In fact there were old traditions of record manufacturing in the Soviet Union. The ten or so record companies operating in the country had been nationalized after the revolution, and the first products of the socialist record industry were, of course, speeches by Lenin. Once this shortcoming had been rectified, the country had more pressing matters to attend to than making records. The nationalized record industry had, for a long time, to make do mainly with pressing reissues of old recordings by Shalyapin and his ilk, and new records rarely appeared. In 1926, total production was only 900,000 copies. Things went so badly that in September 1933, the Soviet government (Council of People's Commissars) issued a statement that 'the state of the gramophone and the gramophone record industry is absolutely unsatisfactory'. When John Hammond visited Moscow in 1935, they were only conducting their first experiments in microphone recording.

As the Soviet Union was becoming wealthier in the late thirties, a new impetus was given to record manufacturing. In 1936, a group of engineers was sent to RCA Victor in New York to study advanced recording technology, and the Aprelevka record factory near Moscow was modernized. Within a few years the entire gamut of music was appearing on record, from the soloists of the Bolshoi to the latest accomplishments in Soviet jazz, and for the first time since the revolution an effort was made to systematically record the music of the country's minority Asiatic nationalities. Recording expeditions were sent to Kiev, Tashkent, Alma-Ata, Simferopol and Pyatigorsk. But then came the war, which overturned any grander plans.

In the 1950s the gramophone record was seen in the Soviet Union as a by-product of radio. Record manufacturing was the responsibility of the State Radio Committee. Records pressed in factories in Moscow, Leningrad, Riga and Tashkent all appeared on the SSSR label. In the other communist bloc countries the record industry was also concentrated in the hands of one state-owned company. Polskie Nagranie in Poland, Supraphon in Czechoslovakia, Hungaroton in Hungary, Electrecord in Romania and Balkanton in Bulgaria all followed similar policies.

LPs gradually came into use in the Soviet Union in the mid-fifties, but the last 78 r.p.m. records were made as late as 1969, the same year that India abandoned the old speed. The records hissed, they were issued in anonymous wrappers, but they often contained fascinating music. Light music was dominated by heavy-voiced Russian females like Ludmila Zykina, accompanied by accordion and balalaika ensembles. Jazz was suspect, and modern light music was represented by hits such as Solovyev-Sedov's *Moscow Nights*. In fact as many as eight million copies of *Moscow Nights* were sold over the years, and the tune became so popular that its opening bars were eventually adopted as the signature tune for Radio Moscow.

Nevertheless record production was dominated by educational and cultural-political goals, rather like those prevailing in the musical programmes of western European state broadcasters. The Composers' Union had a big say in planning the recording programme, and indeed the music of composers wedded to socialist realism is prominently represented on record. Time has been kinder to the performing arts of the fifties in the Soviet Union. It was possible to buy ridiculously cheap records by Gilels, Oistrakh (father and son), Lemeshev and Dolukhanova. And when chinks began to gradually appear in the iron curtain that was put up between east and west after the second world war, many of them could be heard on western stages as well.

The pianist, Sviatoslav Richter, was one of those Soviet musicians around whom an almost legendary aura grew up in the fifties in the west. The master pianist, Emil Gilels, was well known thanks to his very extensive tours. Richter was known to be a world-class pianist of at least the same stature, but in the west he could only be heard from his recordings, which were hard to procure. Between 1952 and 1959 he made 23 LP records for the domestic market, mostly of Russian composers' music. Since the mountain would not come to Mohammed, in 1959 Deutsche Grammophon sent its technicians to Warsaw expressly to record a concert by Richter. Richter's first performance in the west was given in Helsinki in 1960; people came from further afield to hear him. After that Richter was allowed to travel more widely. The master, not used to the ways of the west, signed contracts with all the producers who were interested, and in three years, 32 Richter albums appeared on nearly as many labels. Only in 1964, when the Soviet recording industry was reorganized and the Melodiya company was established, could the marketing of Soviet artists' recordings be organized abroad on a large scale.

Sources: Solomatin (1989); Volkov-Lannit (1963)

The Finnish Tango King

When the war was over in 1945, there were only two small record companies in Finland, Rytmi and Sointu. During the conflict, international companies had severed their ties with the country. Raw materials were difficult to obtain, yet more than 50 new records were released. The biggest hit of the year was *Hiljaa soivat balalaikat* ('Balalaikas are Playing Softly'), a tango written by the young jazz pianist Toivo Kärki. In 1939 Kärki had won a songwriting contest organized by the British *Melody Maker* magazine and dreamed of an international career, but instead he had had to spend five years in the artillery. The Slavonic mood of the song perfectly caught the spirit of the times, and the record eventually sold 11,800 copies to war-weary Finns.

By 1951, annual record sales had reached a quarter of a million copies, and nearly 200 new domestic releases appeared. There were now five Finnish record companies competing for this small market. Several of them also acted as representatives for the major international companies. The best-selling foreign record of that year was *Tennessee Waltz*, played by Les Paul and Mary Ford, but domestic records outsold imports considerably.

The most popular Finnish records of the early fifties have a strikingly traditional sound. Many of them were written by Toivo Kärki, using a variety of pseudonyms. They are sentimental waltzes and tangos or humorous *schottisches* featuring accordions, violins and clarinets prominently in the accompaniment. In 1950, only one third of the country's population was urban. The lyrics of the songs tell us of the beauty of the northern woods and roving woodcutters, sailors, and farmhands who meet beautiful maids. The best-selling record of the decade was *Muistatko Monrepos'n*, a dreamy waltz celebrating a famous park in Viborg, a city that Finland had lost to the Soviet Union in 1944. It sold 34,620 copies in the original 78 r.p.m. form and a few thousand copies at 45 r.p.m. The LP version only sold a few hundred copies, proving that the LP era had not yet really come to Finland.

In 1951, the Finnish music papers had begun publishing Top Ten charts of popular records. After 1953, the artist most frequently appearing in the charts was Olavi Virta (1915–72), a baritone with a powerful voice and striking good looks. Trained as an electrician in his youth, he soon found jobs as a dance band vocalist and made his first records in 1938. After the war he became a highly successful entertainer, especially after he made his first film in 1950. In spring 1954, the three best-selling records in Finland were all performed by Virta.

Number one was a Finnish cover version of *Istambul*, a novelty tune originally popularized by the Four Lads, but numbers two and three, *Täysikuu* ('The Full Moon') and *Sokeripala* ('A Lump of Sugar') were tangos written by Toivo Kärki. The tango had come to Finland in the 1920s, and at first it had only been moderately popular, but during the war several Finnish composers had started writing tangos that differed markedly from their Latin American and continental models. Slower in tempo and frequently in a minor key, their nostalgic lyrics dealt with the Northern landscape and lost or unattainable love. The form reached its full maturity in the mid-fifties when Toivo Kärki added his sophisticated sense of harmony to the Finnish tango.

Olavi Virta remained popular throughout the fifties. Towards the end of the decade he started recording more frequently cover versions of foreign hits such as *Mambo Italiano*, *Banana Boat Song* and even the *Rock and Roll Waltz*. By 1960, Finland's annual record sales had grown to a million copies, and imported recordings were beginning to outsell domestic ones. Virta started drinking heavily, spent some time in jail for drunken driving, but continued to perform almost to the end of his life, a tragic figure half paralysed and blinded by alcoholism and diabetes. The subsequent generations have crowned him posthumously as the Finnish tango king. Although only a relatively small proportion of his recordings were tangos, it is the tangos which continue to be reissued and played on request programmes on the radio.

Similar developments were taking place in all European countries. When the damage caused by the war had been repaired, people began to spend a greater part of their income on leisure. A significant part of the record market consisted of American imports (pressed locally under licence arrangements to save foreign currency), but all European countries steadfastly continued producing popular music in national idioms. Although most of the output never crossed national borders, some of it became quite successful on a European scale. In the Finnish top ten charts of the decade we can find the German comedienne, Evelyn Kuenneke, the British trumpeter, Eddie Calvert, and the French chanteuse, Edith Piaf. In the late 1950s, the Italian *canzone* enjoyed a period of considerable popularity all over central and northern Europe.

Even the onslaught of rock 'n' roll could not force these nationalistic trends into the background. In 1964, the best-selling record in Finland was *All My Loving*, by the Beatles, but number two was the tango *Tähdet meren yllä* ('The Stars Above the Sea'), by Reijo Taipale. Since the 1980s, Finland's commercial television channel has annually sponsored a tango festival in the town of Seinäjoki. It has grown into the country's biggest musical event, and every summer thousands of tango fans cheer as a new tango king is crowned. But many Finns still consider Virta the world's greatest tango singer, and his collected recordings have been reissued on 30 CDs.

Sources: Koski *et al.* (1977); Kukkonen (1996)

India: The Last Refuge of the Shellac Disc

During the 1920s, there had been several competing record companies in India. But as the Depression began to affect record sales, and films became the most popular form of musical entertainment, the Gramophone Company of India gained a practically monopolistic position in the country. With a factory in Dum Dum, near Calcutta, and production units in Calcutta and Bombay, the company continued to record the country's prominent classical artists and popular film stars. After the creation of EMI, the records appeared on the Columbia and His Master's Voice labels. Sales figures are not generally available, but the 1957 yearbook of the International Federation of the Phonographic Industry estimated India's annual record production as 3–4 million copies – about one-tenth of Germany's total sales in the same year.

India has an indigenous classical music tradition which is very much alive. Until the 1960s, it was little known in the west. In its 2000-year history, Indian classical music has turned many times in different directions to European art music. Whereas the west gradually moved from medieval monophony towards polyphony, and ever more precise notation, India abandoned harmony and chose an increasingly refined development of melody and rhythm. In both cultures, over the centuries, more sophisticated performing techniques were demanded of professional musicians, but in India a combination of virtuosity and improvisational skill was required. The Indian musician was expected to soar to dizzy heights of imagination in performances lasting half an hour, an hour or even several hours, with only the *raga* and the *tala*, the mode and the rhythmic cycle prescribed beforehand. In the sixties many jazz and rock musicians discovered, to their surprise, that the Indians had long ago found something that they were seeking. It had taken a long time for the west to discover the east.

In theory, Indian music had been available on record ever since Fred Gaisberg recorded Indian music in Calcutta in December 1902. Yet for over half a century the only market for these records had been India. It must be admitted that it would have been been hard for a European listener to get a true picture of Indian music from these early discs. It was not easy to capture the essence of Indian classical music in three minutes, any more than for a European symphony. These records were addressed to the Indian listener, who already knew the artists appearing on the disc and wanted to recapture the atmosphere of a concert already heard. To an outsider they gave only a hazy image of the music.

Nevertheless we can be thankful that many of the now dead legendary Indian artists of the twenties and thirties were captured on record. On large 30cm discs, with a playing time of five minutes a side, we may hear, for example, Ravi Shankar's father-in-law and teacher Allauddin Khan, who was said to be the most important Indian musician of his generation and a significant innovator of the improvisational style. The famous singers, Abdul Karim Khan and Roshan Ara Begum, are likewise preserved on disc. In addition to the 'great tradition' of classical music we can hear the folk music of the many peoples of India and music from its neighbours, Nepal, Burma and Tibet, dating back to the beginning of the century. In the early fifties an important series of recordings was made in Lhasa, to where the recording equipment was transported by caravan.

G. N. Joshi joined the Bombay branch of the company as a producer in 1938, and stayed until the 1970s. Originally trained both as a lawyer and a singer in the classical Indian tradition, he was the perfect man for the job, and throughout the years he produced innumerable recordings ranging from classical Indian music to educational songs advocating prohibition. Reading his memoirs, one is struck by the similarities between the Indian and Western musical cultures, rather than differences. The big money was in film music, and getting a popular actress to sign a contract could be decisive for a record producer's career. But negotiating with classical artists could be even more difficult. Under British rule, Indian states had been ruled by princes, and artists were used to royal patronage. The potential royalties from record sales were usually modest, and artists had to be cajoled into the recording studio by various means. Joshi had to record the famous singer, Bade Gulam Ali Khan, secretly on the pretext of inviting him into the studio for dinner and asking him to demonstrate certain aspects of his style. After a good dinner, topped by Scotch, the recordings were played back and the singer graciously permitted their release. Another famous singer, Surashri Kesarbai Kerkar, broke her contract with the company and never recorded again after one of her recordings had been released without her approval.

The introduction of tape made it possible to edit improvised performances. Until 1959, all records produced in India were 78 r.p.m. In that year, the Indian *sarod* virtuoso, Ali Akbar Khan, had made an LP in England, introduced by Yehudi Menuhin, who had recently become interested in Indian music. The first shipment of 300 copies soon sold out, and Joshi decided that the time had come to introduce the new format in India. The golden age of recording classical Indian music now began, and artists such as Nazakat Ali, Salamat Ali, Bhimsen Joshi, Ustad Amir Khan and Bismillah Khan were able to make recordings which were of almost the same length as their concert performances. As Indian music was now becoming better known abroad, many of these recordings were also distributed worldwide.

Sources: Danielou (1952); Joshi (1984)

Africa

Africa's share of world trade is only a few per cent. It is no wonder, then, that the interest of record companies in sub-Saharan Africa was, for a long time, slight compared with the lively record industry on other continents. Nevertheless, the gramophone record came to Africa before the First World War. As early as 1912 the first African records were made by the Gramophone Company in Johannesburg, including a Swazi version of 'What a Friend We Have in Jesus'. In Nigeria, in 1914, recordings were made of Yoruba spiritual songs performed by the Reverend J.J. Ransome-Kuti, grandfather of the future 'Afro-pop' star, Fela Anikulapo-Kuti.

In the boom years of gramophone fever in the twenties, European companies tried to enter the small record markets of such exotic places as Madagascar and the Gold Coast. In 1926, 42,714 records were sold in Kenya, and the Gramophone Company's local agent, P.B.Vatcha reported to head office that although the natives' songs have no tunes, they are all mad about music. In particular, a dance called the *gomo* would be worth recording. Not only the British, but the French and Germans as well were trying to enter the market, and records were made in several African countries.

During the Depression, the record companies' interest in Africa waned. Even in the thirties, production continued only in South Africa. The Boer population, which had long lived in isolation, wanted to hear its own Afrikaans-language songs on record, and the growing urban black population was becoming wealthy enough to create a demand for records. The Johannesburg businessman, Eric Gallo, sent both black and white artists on the long sea voyage to the studios of London, and thus the birthpangs of black South African popular music began.

After the Second World War the urban population of Africa grew, and with recording technology becoming simpler at the same time, soon both branches of international companies and home-grown local record companies were springing up. In the Belgian Congo (later Zaire) a Greek businessman named Geronomidis established the first local record company. New entrepreneurs soon joined the fray, and in the fifties there were annual sales of about 800,000 records in the Belgian Congo. In 1955 the guitarist and bandleader, Franco Luambo Makiadi, began a long string of recordings for the Loningisa company, run by another Greek, Antonopoulos. Franco's guitar-based 'jazz' was for a long time the dominant trend in Central and East African popular music. The company's plans to market the style in Europe came to grief when it was revealed that Franco had contracts with four other companies as well.

In West Africa, more specifically Nigeria, Sierra Leone and Ghana, a musical style known as 'highlife' had developed in the thirties, spearheaded by E.T. Mensah and his band in Accra. Highlife music brought in saxophones and trumpets borrowed from swing music, and married them to African drums. Decca and EMI were for a long time the leading companies in the region, but in the sixties Philips became a serious competitor. The threat was removed, however, when, during the civil war in 1966, the government troops found out that the Philips factory at Onitsha had been pressing records praising the Biafran leader, General Ojukwu, and the pressing plant was burned to the ground.

During the sixties Nigeria became one of the most interesting musical countries in Africa. Under the influence of American soul music, new trends grew up alongside highlife, such as 'Afro-pop', whose most celebrated exponent is Fela Anikulapo-Kuti, and *juju* music, combining traditional drums and modern electric guitars, of whom Sunny Adé became the best-known performer internationally.

The fastest growth after the war was to be seen, however, in South Africa, where both Eric Gallo's Gallotone company and EMI had set up studios and pressing plants. By local standards, Gallotone grew into a significant enterprise in the forties. Gallo commissioned the black theatre director, Griffith Motsieloa, to take charge of producing local music for the rapidly expanding population of the black slums of Johannesburg and Cape Town. Motsieloa's first find was a Zulu group called The Manhattan Brothers, who performed swing numbers of the Mills Brothers kind in Zulu and Sotho to the accompaniment of outstanding jazz musicians.

In the late fifties a new, more popularly-based kind of music sprang up alongside Zulu jazz – *kwela*. Kwela was a youth music movement born on the streets. Its main instrument was the penny whistle, a tin whistle which could be picked up for a few pence, and its main performers were teenage musicians, who blew at the instrument like the best jazz soloists despite its technical limitations. The best-known kwela star on record was Spokes Mashiyane, who began his career as a small boy. Although his records were selling more than fifty thousand copies at their height, the artist himself only got a flat payment of £20 a time. In the sixties, kwela gave way to *mbaqanga*, an electrically amplified form of popular music, and new styles are continually being created.

African music was released on 78 r.p.m. records well into the sixties. Outside Africa these records were sold only in Paris, London and other capitals of former colonial powers, where there are considerable African communities. During the 1980s, however, African music entered the public consciousness in new ways, while there was an acknowledgement of the influence that African music has indirectly exercised on the music of this century. Stern's African record shop in London, which started in the fifties, selling records for the city's small African community, alongside its electric lamps and toasters, has become almost a place of pilgrimage, where one might encounter famous rock musicians poaching new ideas. Numerous books have been published in the past few years about African music, which was totally unknown outside the continent just a few years ago. The first compilations of historic African recordings are already on the market, and we can expect, with the help of reissues, to make a broader acquaintance with the history of African recording.

Sources: Anderson (1981); Collins (1985); Coplan (1985)

Electronic Music

The advent of the tape recorder and the LP also made possible the creation of a whole new kind of music – electronic music. While the modernists of the turn of the century, such as Schoenberg, Ives and Stravinsky, were writing music for the traditional instruments of the orchestra, which sounded strange and unmusical to the ears of their contemporaries, another, smaller group of composers was attempting to develop entirely new kinds of instruments which could be adapted for performing the music of the age of technology. As early as 1906 an American, Thaddeus Cahill, had constructed an electric instrument called the telharmonium, which was meant to transmit music along telephone lines to New Yorkers. Cahill's electric organ really worked, but it required an entire warehouseful of space. These were the times before radio, amplifiers and speakers. Cahill was many decades ahead of his time. His 'cable music' company went bankrupt, and the telharmonium was sold for scrap. Much later, its principles were adapted to the Hammond organ.

The idea of electric instruments was not dead, however. The Russian scientist, Leon Theremin, in 1920 constructed a one-stringed electric instrument to which he gave his own name. Theremin brought his instrument with him to the west, and in the United States it found a few adherents (the theremin can be heard on the Beach Boys' record, 'Good Vibrations', for instance). In 1928, in France, Maurice Martenot constructed a more sophisticated instrument along the same lines, which was called the ondes martenot. Olivier Messiaen used it in his 1946 composition, the *Turangalîla-Symphonie*. Other musical inventors constructed similar devices, but they were all monophonic, limited in range and difficult to handle.

The general spread of the tape recorder after 1948 opened quite new possibilities for electronic music. Electrically produced sound could now be stored, cut, shaped and mixed with other sounds. Several experimental music studios were created under the auspices of the larger European national radio companies, in which young composers were given the opportunity to play with instruments constructed by engineers. For example, tape recorders with variable speeds were available. The most important experimental music centres in the fifties were at the French Radio in Paris and Westdeutsche Rundfunk in Cologne. The Cologne studio used as its sound source the sine-wave oscillator, from whose whine an almost limitless range of new sounds could be shaped.

The Parisians called their works 'concrete music': its source was natural sound captured on tape and subjected to the same kind of treatment. The main brains behind 'musique concrète' were Pierre Schaeffer and Pierre Henry; among their important guest users were Pierre Boulez and Edgar Varèse. Schaeffer's early works included an étude for locomotives and another for saucepans. The most significant product of the Cologne school was Karlheinz Stockhausen, whose *Gesang der Jünglinge* (1956) was undoubtedly the most significant German electronic work of the decade. It was also released directly onto record, even though it exceeded the limitations of recording technology at the time: the work is intended for performance in a space where sound emanates from five channels, surrounding the audience on all sides.

The methods developed in Paris and Cologne – which were fairly simple adaptations of the electronic technology available – spread quickly to other parts of the world once composers interested in new worlds of sound started employing them. In the United States, the old radical, John Cage, was among the first of them. The acme of experimentation in the fifties, however, must surely be Edgar Varèse's *Poème électronique* (1957–8), whose sponsor was the electronics giant, Philips. Varèse composed his electronic poem for the Philips stand at the 1958 Brussels World Exhibition. The world-famous architect, Le Corbusier, designed the Philips pavilion especially 'around' Varèse's music. The *Poème* was also released directly on record.

Source: Holmes (1985)

CHAPTER SEVEN

The Age of Growth

By the early 1960s the record industry was able to look confidently to the future. The last of the 78s had been consigned to the second-hand stores. Sound reproduction on LP records had been improved by moving to stereophony, but this time the improvement had been made so cleverly that it was possible to play the new stereophonic records even on old record players and *vice versa*.

Barriers to international trade were falling. The big names in both classical and popular music could expect to have worldwide success with their records. Growth was the main theme in the record industry of the sixties. A business that was doing well in all the big industrial countries in 1960 was, by 1970, overweight.

Record sales in the United States in 1960 were worth $600 million; the figure in 1970 was $1660 million. Even accounting for inflation, that amounts to a considerable growth, and the growth continued through the seventies. The peak was reached in 1978, when 762 million records and cassettes were sold in that country, worth over $4000 million. It was only then that a slight downturn was experienced.

In England, 72 million copies of records were sold in 1960; the figure was 114 million in 1970. In the peak years of the seventies, sales exceeded 200 million records and cassettes. In France the sales figures were 28 million in 1960, 62 million in 1970 and 157 million in 1978. In the German Federal Republic, Japan, Sweden and many other countries, sales doubled in ten years. In the Soviet Union, too, record production grew over the decade by more than 50 per cent, and by 1970 the Soviet Union, having produced 173 million records, was, in fact, the world's second biggest record manufacturer. In relative terms the biggest growth, however, was seen in the developing countries, where large sections of the population were now able to buy recordings. In the world as a whole, ten times more records were sold in 1970 than in 1950; in a speech in 1971 the new head of record production at EMI, Len Wood, described the growth as 'astonishing'. Right up to the end of the seventies the growth continued all over the world.

The main reason for the growth was, of course, the general increase in the standard of living, which encouraged a demand for other consumer goods as well. Another important factor was the arrival of cheap cassette recorders, which expanded the customer base of recorded music. Production of recordings was also inflated by the maturation of the baby-boom generation and the contemporary internationalization of youth music. The rise of rock 'n' roll in the fifties had taken the big record companies very much by surprise; by the sixties they had the situation under control. The British government took note, in the sixties, that EMI had played a significant role in improving the country's balance of payments, and the company's main stars, the long-haired Beatles, were awarded OBE medals. But Herbert von Karajan's Swiss bank account was also expanding nicely, and Decca, Philips-PolyGram, CBS and RCA were in good shape. A rising tide carried with it both the optimistic dinghy and the great ocean liner: alongside the big names, many a little record company grew into a middle-sized one in the boom period – or headed for bankruptcy.

At the same time, records were making new inroads. Playing records had, by the fifties, become the most important form of radio programme in the United States, as television forced radio to change its programme content. In Europe, however, public radio stations had a reserved attitude to playing records. Nevertheless, the American pattern now began to spread into Europe. It was first adopted by the commercial radio stations such as Radio Luxembourg and Radio Monte Carlo, which took as their model the American Forces radio stations operating in Europe. In the sixties they were followed by numerous illegal 'pirate' stations. Although most of these stations were soon suppressed by the state, the 'official' stations had to increase the record content of their programming considerably, both in Britain and on the continent. The old monopolies ended officially when most European countries legalized commercial broadcasting in the 1970s. At the same time recorded music was coming into restaurants, dance halls and department stores as background music. The discotheque was an invention of the sixties. The number of jukeboxes increased. In the 1960s the gramophone record became the most important means of disseminating music.

No great revolutions were occurring in the structure of the record industry, but the business was experiencing change. To put it briefly, the big were becoming bigger still and the number of small operators continued to grow. In the United States, Victor and CBS were still the market leaders, while in Europe they were EMI and Decca. After the war they had initially been working in harmony, each on their own continent, and representing each other in their own regions. In 1955 EMI had bought Capitol, a significant American record company. In the sixties RCA and CBS responded by establishing their own subsidiaries in England and other important European countries. Thus all four giants extended their operations systematically into all continents.

By the 1970s Decca's star was starting to wane, and it gradually descended into the middle ranks. In the meantime, however, two new multinational giants entered the firmament, each with even bigger electronics and entertainment concerns behind them. In 1962, Deutsche Grammophon of Germany and Philips in the Netherlands began a collaboration which led to the establishment of the PolyGram company in the seventies. In the United States, the Warner movie company rose to the stature of RCA and CBS in the sixties by buying up a cluster of successful medium-sized firms. By the 1970s the five big international concerns in the record business were CBS, EMI, PolyGram, Warner and RCA – more or less in that order. While the smaller companies created in the fifties were gradually dying out or merging with larger companies, hopeful new entrepreneurs were continually arriving on the scene.

Source: Sanjek (1988)

Table 7.1 *World Record Sales, 1961–80 (Selected Countries).* (Million of Units Sold. For USA, both units and $ value, in millions.)

	USA $	units	UK	Germany	France	Japan
1961	640		76.4	..	34.1	..
1962	687		77.5	47.4	40.1	
1963	698		85.5	42.3	43.2	45.9
1964	758		101.2	43.0	47.6	..
1965	862		93.8	49.2	47.5	72.7
1966	959		84.9	47.5	43.3	75.6
1967	1173		90.2	57.5	48.7	80.7
1968	1358		98.9	68.9	52.6	96.3
1969	1586		106.4	76.6	60.1	105.4
1970	1660		114.0	87.0	62.3	153.9
1971	1744		126.0	86.9	76.5	171.3
1972	1924		148.3	107.1	89.4	..
1973	2016	616.0	177.9	109.1	90.9	159.0
1974	2200	539.9	198.4	120.9	102.9	164.6
1975	2391	533.3	202.1	127.0	120.8	162.9
1976	2737	591.6	223.7	139.3	121.0	184.8
1977	3500	698.2	231.6	161.1	148.1	218.7
1978	4131	762.2	195.9	206.1	157.0	203.4
1979	3676	683.0	187.0	202.4	144.4	208.0
1980	3682	649.0	170.4	199.1	143.9	219.8

Table 7.1 (continued) (Millions of units sold)

	Italy	Sweden	Nether-lands	USSR	Czecho-slovakia	Poland
1961	..	..		..	..	..
1962	..	..		..	..	..
1963	25.0	..			..	..
1964	..	..		132.7	7.6	6.3
1965	28.5	4.0		140.7	8.3	7.5
1966	32.0	6.2		163.7	7.1	6.1
1967	37.4	8.2		189.2	7.1	4.9
1968	39.8	8.8	..	196.9	7.8	4.9
1969	..	9.7	..	193.8	9.0	5.4
1970	31.0	10.2	15.3	172.6	9.6	6.1
1971	33.2	10.8	24.3	175.3	10.0	5.1
1972	28.2	11.5	25.2	183.6	10.1	5.4
1973	27.6	12.3	26.8	187.0	10.3	5.8
1974	28.0	13.9	24.2	192.2	10.1	7.3
1975	31.5	16.3	27.7	196.7	10.2	7.0
1976	39.4	17.4	33.4	198.3	10.4	7.7
1977	41.8	17.7	48.3	202.3	10.6	..
1978	43.7	15.6	55.8	204.0	10.4	6.3
1979	50.1	15.0	53.0	..	..	..
1980	44.2	15.1	45.5	..	..	..

Table 7.1 (continued) (Millions of units sold)

	Canada	Mexico	Brazil	Australia	South Africa
1961	..	..	..	5.7	..
1962				..	
1963	..	..	..	6.4	..
1964	28.9	..	..		
1965	36.4	..	6.9	..	5.5
1966	43.8	..	..	..	5.8
1967	47.2	14.8	..	..	5.9
1968	39.1	17.2	13.6	..	6.7
1969	<u>41.3</u>	21.9	16.1	18.2	7.8
1970	43.5	21.9	16.6	..	7.5
1971	45.3	..	20.3	..	..
1972	53.1	..	..		
1973	..	32.5	..	..	10.2
1974	74.9	33.4	..	..	11.4
1975	74.4	..	..	..	..
1976	82.4	..	..	43.1	..
1977	85.3	67.4	..	46.5	13.1
1978	94.0	..	58.0	38.3	11.2
1979	94.5	79.1	46.7	..	..
1980	84.5	82.6	56.0	..	..

Source: Gronow, 1996

Note: For most countries, the figures refer to sales by IFPI member companies only. Underlining indicates a change in the definition of the figures quoted. For at least part of this period, sales data are available from several other countries as well.

The Rome Convention

The 1960s also brought about a change in the legal status of the gramophone record which was not immediately evident to music lovers, but was to have far-reaching consequences on the development of the industry. Since the time of Queen Anne, copyright has protected the rights of authors and book publishers against the unauthorized reproduction of their works. Such laws also protected publishers of sheet music, and during the nineteenth century, copyright was gradually extended to cover the public performance of music, giving composers the right to compensation when their works were performed in concert halls or restaurants.

A record is not a reproduction of sheet music, and record companies at first were reluctant to pay royalties to composers and publishers for the music captured mechanically in the grooves of a recording. The first conflicts actually arose between piano roll manufacturers and music publishers. In the United States, the copyright law was revised in 1909 to cover also the recording of musical works, and, sooner or later, record companies in other countries were also obliged to pay composers for the use of their works. But what rights did the record companies themselves have, and the artists whose singing and playing could be heard on the recording? Piracy, or unauthorized copying of gramophone records, appeared quite early in history, despite the technically inferior quality of the copies. In 1908, at an international copyright conference, the British government proposed international protection for gramophone records, but the conference decided that 'the subject was on the borderline between industrial property and copyright and might conceivably be held to belong more properly to the former category'.

During the 78 r.p.m. era, records made from the original stampers were clearly superior to copies, as an illegal copy or 'dubbing' would inevitably contain a higher degree of surface noise. This tended to limit the extent of illegal copying. In the 1930s the record industry initiated a campaign to control the broadcasting of records, but outside the United Kingdom it had little success. After the war, and with the subsequent growth of the recording industry, the leading record-producing countries joined forces in 1961 to draft an International Convention for the Protection of Performers, Producers of Phonograms and Broadcasting Organizations, the so-called Rome Convention.

The Rome Convention grants performing artists and record companies certain rights. Countries that have signed the convention are obliged to grant these rights to their own citizens and the nationals of other signatory countries. These rights are known as 'neighbouring rights', as they differ in some respects from the rights of authors and publishers. It is illegal to record an artist's performance without his or her permission, or to reproduce published recordings. Record companies and performers also received the right to be compensated for the broadcasting and public performance of their products, but cannot prohibit such use; this state of affairs is known as 'compulsory licensing'.

The Rome convention also protects broadcasters against unauthorized re-transmission and copying, but this right became important only after the development of cable TV. Originally, broadcasters felt that they had lost rather than gained in the bargain.

The first signatories of the convention were the United Kingdom, Germany, Denmark, Sweden, Czechoslovakia, Brazil, and Ecuador, and, somewhat suprisingly, Niger and Congo. Since the latter two are hardly among the leading record producers, there was some suspicion that their participation was the result of diplomatic manoeuvres rather than a need to protect artists. The United States also participated in preparations, but still has not signed the convention, no doubt due to the powerful influence of the country's broadcasters. The US Copyright Act was revised in 1972 to curb piracy, but it still does not require broadcasters to compensate record companies, as European laws do.

With the passing of time, most European countries joined the convention, and in 1995 the EC made it mandatory for member states. The convention has helped to keep record piracy under control, and guaranteed producers and artists a source of secondary income in the form of fees paid by radio stations, discotheques, and jukebox operators. The way in which this income is distributed varies from country to country. In some countries the collecting societies established for this purpose gather detailed information on airplay, while in Germany, for instance, it is distributed on the basis of sales figures, with the assumption that best-selling records will be broadcast most frequently.

Although such secondary income forms a relatively small percentage of the industry's total turnover, its significance has grown over the years. According to IFPI, the industry's international trade organization, in 1992 performance royalties amounted to $200 million, which is only about one per cent of world record sales. But the percentage is considerably higher if we exclude countries (such as the US) where this right does exist. Unlike income from sales, performance royalties are almost pure income without costs.

Sources: Frith (1993); Stewart (1983)

The Case of Clive Davis

In the 1960s the United States was still the undisputed leader of the recording industry. The colourful career of Clive Davis is a signal illustration of the development of the record business during this decade. Davis came to work for CBS in 1960 as a lawyer, and in 1965 he became the company's head of record production. CBS-Columbia was at that time one of the four big record companies in the United States, and one of the biggest record companies in the world.

Record sales in the United States in 1965 were valued at $862 million, of which CBS's share was 11 per cent. When Davis was sacked in 1973, overall record sales in the United States amounted to more than $2000 million, with CBS taking nearly one-fifth. It had become the biggest record company in the United States and the world.

While Davis was employed by CBS, the record industry was going through a big structural change. In the early sixties CBS's big stars included Andy Williams and Johnny Cash, who both had their own regular TV series. The company's biggest sellers were the Broadway musical recordings and Mitch Miller's 'Sing Along' albums, which repeatedly achieved gold record status. The record companies believed that rock 'n' roll was a passing fashion. The portion of singles in overall sales was considerable, and many of the LPs on the market were merely compilations, consisting of old singles.

When sales of Mitch Miller and the popular Broadway albums fell below 100,000 in the mid-sixties, alarm bells began to ring. For a small company, sales of 10,000 were a lot, even in the United States. However, in a company the size of CBS, the administrative and marketing costs alone, quite apart from the shareholders' expectations, are so great that the company needs annual sales of over 100,000 for quite a number of records, as well as several that achieve gold record status. In the United States a gold record means wholesale LP record income of a million dollars, or about a quarter of a million discs. It was obvious that both CBS and the other big companies would have to radically modernize their repertoires.

Rock 'n' roll had not been a passing whim after all. By the beginning of the seventies, over half the record sales in the United States consisted of rock music. RCA had had Elvis all along, and Capitol had the Beatles, but the first actual signing for CBS was Paul Revere and the Raiders, contracted in 1963, who have not exactly carved a niche for themselves in the annals of music. From the mid-sixties onwards, the CBS catalogue began to fill up with the likes of Dylan,

Donovan, Janis Joplin, Simon and Garfunkel, Blood Sweat and Tears, Chicago, Santana, Johnny Winter, John McLaughlin, The Grateful Dead, Sly Stone and Bruce Springsteen. Rock replaced the Broadway tunes. The structural change not only meant a new roster of artists, but a transformation of the whole economy of record production. As record sales increased, the artists learned to be aware of their own value, and artists' fees increased as well. The most expensive signing during Davis's period was Neil Diamond, whom CBS contracted for a fee of four million dollars. It was a huge amount of money, even if the contract was for ten LP records, and, as is American practice, the agreed sum was also to cover production costs for the records. To get a return on its investment the company had to be able to sell at least a quarter of a million copies of each of these ten LPs.

Rock does not, of course, account for all record sales, not even in the United States. One of the biggest sellers for CBS, even in the seventies, was Barbra Streisand, whose individual interpretations of show tunes and other MOR (middle-of-the-road) numbers have always found listeners. CBS has also been well represented in Nashville, the centre of country music. Despite the changes that have occurred in other fields of music, country music has remained a genre that respects tradition, which has its own loyal audience, and even its own radio stations, in the United States. New trends in black music, on the other hand, largely passed CBS by. In the jazz field, the company's big name was, for a long time, Miles Davis, in addition to which the company has, at regular intervals, repackaged compilations of the historic jazz recordings it owns, from Louis Armstrong's Hot Five onwards.

Classical music was a problem for the big companies for a long time, despite the increase in overall sales. Among the competition, RCA Victor clung tightly to its honourable traditions in this sphere, whereas Warner never even seriously attempted to develop its classical music production. In the sixties, CBS had contracts with the Philadelphia Orchestra, conducted by Ormandy, and the New York Philharmonic, conducted by Bernstein. When the Philadelphia contract came up for renegotiation in 1967, CBS studied its accounts and concluded that it could not afford the two million dollars the orchestra was claiming for a long-term contract. CBS's classical drawcard had for many years been its Christmas albums, on which well-known orchestras played familiar Christmas tunes. There were not enough Christmas songs to go on recording indefinitely, however. Classical 'hits' like Ravel's *Bolero* might sell 50,000–100,000 copies. The basic classical catalogue, such as the familiar symphonies, might, on the other hand, sell only a few tens of thousands at best, even though the sales area encompassed the whole world and the selling period was much longer than for rock music.

CBS thus jettisoned Ormandy and the Philadelphia Orchestra, which signed a contract with RCA in 1968, but it kept Bernstein and the New York Philharmonic. The company also dared to issue works by Ives, Cage, Riley, Stockhausen, Xenakis and other modern composers, although their sales were modest. On the other hand, their production costs were not high either, and they raised the company's profile in the critics' eyes.

CBS also had the legendary Vladimir Horowitz, who had left RCA in 1961, having recorded for them since the 1920s. Horowitz had given up his concert career in 1953 after a nervous breakdown, and his admirers were able to hear his astounding piano performances only on rarely-issued discs. Despite this – or perhaps because of it – by the 1960s he had become the best-known pianist in the United States, a legend on the scale of his father-in-law, Toscanini. When Horowitz returned to the limelight in 1965, the queue for tickets at Carnegie Hall began to form a full day before they went on sale. Over 50,000 copies of the recording of the concert were sold. Nevertheless, taken as a whole Horowitz's records brought losses to the company, because the pianist was wont to spend months on recording one work and then change his mind as to the interpretation even at the stage when the factory had begun pressing the records. CBS held firmly onto its contract with Horowitz; he was 'the Greta Garbo of classical music', as Davis put it.

Clive Davis was dismissed from the job of head of CBS record production in 1975. The reason given was misuse of expenses, but what lay behind it were deeper differences of opinion on company policy. Since then he has been a prominent figure in other companies.

Source: Davis and Willwerth (1975)

Clive Davis's Competitors

CBS was a typical example of the state of the record industry in the 1960s. Five American and European companies were making half of the records sold in the world. They were all parts of large conglomerates for whom records only constituted one sector of their operations. Alongside CBS the most established leaders were RCA in America and EMI in England, whom we have encountered many times already in the history of recording. Television had superseded radio as the main area of activity for RCA and CBS. In addition to all its other holdings, RCA owned a carpet factory and a car hire business; CBS manufactured guitars and published books. They are large, bureaucratic organizations, which have to sell huge numbers of records just to cover their administrative expenses. These companies have on their books the biggest names in both classical and popular music, because as multinational organizations they are able to sell their records throughout the world and guarantee princely sums to successful artists. In the less popular areas of music, such as jazz, they pick out a few internationally-known names.

Alongside CBS, RCA and EMI in the sixties there arose two new giants: PolyGram in Europe and Warner in America. Of these two, PolyGram had old roots in the recording industry. It was owned by two giant electrical concerns, Philips of the Netherlands and Siemens of Germany. Philips had started releasing records in 1950 and, thereafter, bought up several smaller record companies; in 1961 it bought Mercury in the United States. Siemens's empire included the legendary DGG – Deutsche Grammophon. Philips began collaborating with DGG in 1962, when each gained a 50 per cent share in the other company. By this stage the company was starting to become a serious competitor for the other three on a worldwide scale. The final merger occurred in 1972.

These four companies were able to look back on a history that began in the early years of recording. Compared with them Warner was a young company, which lacked a classical range almost entirely, but perhaps for this very reason it was able to exploit the new musical trends of the sixties and seventies to its own advantage in an unprejudiced way. While the other giants conducted their operations from New York, the Warner head office was in Burbank, California, near the homes of many of the leading rock groups of the sixties.

Warner was originally a film company. It was one of the pioneers of sound film. In 1958, inspired by the example of its rival, MGM, Warner established its own record division, whose initial success was modest. However, Warner continued its determined assault on the record market by buying the Reprise label from Frank Sinatra in 1963, and Atlantic from the Ertegun brothers in 1967. That same year the entire company, with its film and record divisions, was sold to another, bigger concern, the Kinney Corporation, which had earned its wealth through funeral parlours, laundries and car parks.

Warner waxed fat and successful in the record business, cushioned by its new capital. The company bought out the Elektra and Asylum record labels. Artists sharing the roster with Frank Sinatra included the hippie group, The Grateful Dead, Black Sabbath, Deep Purple, Jethro Tull, Joni Mitchell, Frank Zappa and, for a short time, Bob Dylan. The company became famous for its appeal to the 'counter-culture' by taking out advertisements in the underground papers. In one of them, a long-haired hippie declared, 'the man can't bust our music'; another one stated that 'Joni Mitchell is 90% virgin'. One of Warner's most expensive failures was neatly turned into a propaganda campaign when Van Dyke Parks's revolutionary record, Song Cycle, proved too 'difficult' and wound up gathering dust in the warehouses. Warner distributed thousands of copies of the record at a dollar apiece, declaring in newspaper advertisements that art was more important than business. The funeral parlours and car parks were forgotten, the Warner concern became known as a progressive and youthful company, and by the end of the sixties it had grown into one of the world's five big record manufacturers.

Thus the five giants, with their various branches in other countries, made half of the records sold in the world. The other half – leaving to one side the socialist countries – was divided between a few dozen middle-sized, and thousands of small companies. Even in the 1940s, founding record companies had become something of a hobby for many entrepeneurs in the United States. By the 1960s Europe, too, had begun to sprout hundreds of little record companies based on the most diverse ideas: to produce the music of the ethnic separatists in Brittany or the Basque country, to reissue historic opera records, to spread the Word of God in its countless variations, or simply to make as much money as possible. In many cases they are the work of one person dedicated to a particular cause. Thanks to their smaller administrative costs and their more flexible organization, they are able, when occasion demands, to produce records for a far smaller audience than the big companies, and in this way they are able to quickly latch onto new trends in music, to nurture local traditions and to produce music for minorities.

There is a continuous interaction between the large and the small companies. Even though competition for the market is often bloody, the large and the small live in a sort of symbiosis, with each needing the other. Walter Yetnikoff, Clive Davis's successor at CBS, once declared, 'If an artist can only sell 100,000 records, then this company is not interested in pursuing that artist.' Yet there was also a lot of business in selling records in quantities of fewer than 100,000 copies. A small company can contract with a bigger one for the international distribution of its records. If a small company does well, one of the big ones can buy it or poach the company's best artists with a better contract. The boundary between a large and a small company is not a firm one, of course. In smaller countries, the local subsidiaries of the multinational concerns often behave like the small local companies and produce records for the local market while also taking care of the distribution of the parent company's products.

Sources: Clurman (1992); Wallis and Malm (1984)

Stereo and Multi-track Recording: Realism and Romanticism

In the 1960s and 1970s, strong economic growth was the prevailing trend in the business. At the same time, important technical developments were taking place in the record industry which came to have an ever greater influence, over the years, on the music we hear on record. Stereo, two-channel sound, was soon to be heard in every music lover's living room. Consequently, two speakers now had to be bought instead of one. The arrival of stereophony, and the other developments in sound reproduction at the same time, offered the opportunity, at least in principle, for a more realistic and natural sound production.

With two ears a human being both hears sound and identifies its source. Thanks to them we can hear in the concert hall, even with our eyes closed, how the instruments of the orchestra are arranged, and it is this that is the basis of that sense of depth which is characteristic of live music at its best. For over half a century, though, record buyers had had to adapt to the fact that recorded music reproduced sound only in a 'one-eared' (monaural) way, without the sense of its source. In a similar way, black-and-white movies were accepted as long as colour was not technically or economically feasible.

The principle of 'binaural', or stereophonic, sound recording had, in fact, been known for a long time. As early as 1931 the British engineer Alan Blumlein had patented two alternative stereo systems, whereby aural signals were captured on record simultaneously, from two different angles – the left ear and the right ear. The other of Blumlein's inventions was based on the simultaneous use of Edison's vertical cut and Berliner's horizontal version. In the case of the second alternative, on which present-day stereophony is based, the signals were stored one on each side of the groove of the disc, at an angle of 45 degrees. Recently found in the EMI archives were two test recordings made by Blumlein on 19 January 1934, on which Sir Thomas Beecham rehearses Mozart's 'Jupiter' symphony with the Royal Philharmonic Orchestra. The magnificent sound of the record testifies that a technically quite satisfactory stereo process was available more than 50 years ago. The discs revolved, of course, at 78 r.p.m.

The record industry of the Depression years was not, however, interested in Blumlein's invention, believing that a public which was still generally using acoustic gramophones would not be ready to go over to sound reproduction that required a new kind of pick-up and amplifier. Blumlein was transferred to making improvements in television and radar, which were more relevant fields of development for EMI at the time. He died in an air crash on 7 June 1942, in a bomber which was testing the radar he had been developing. By that time the world had had its first taste of stereo sound – in the movies. Walt Disney's animated musical, *Fantasia*, had a soundtrack conducted by Leopold Stokowski in real stereo. Only a few cinemas, however, were able to show the film in this form.

The arrival of tape recording made stereo relevant once more. Recording sound in stereo on tape was simple. All that was needed were two recording heads to store the left and right channels, in parallel, on tape. The big record companies even started systematically making their important recordings using both the old method and the stereophonic one simultaneously. For some time in the fifties it was even supposed that production of recordings would go over completely from discs to stereo tapes. Reel-to-reel tapes did not win the favour of the broad public, however. It was more complicated to make a stereo record, as both a new cutting process and new sound equipment that could be marketed to the consumer had to be devised for it. In the mid-fifties there were several competing stereo processes available. One system, which even came onto the market, required a record player equipped with two arms for stereo listening. A record industry made wiser by the r.p.m. war now sat down at the negotiating table for once. In 1958 an international agreement was achieved on a uniform stereo process, and the first stereo records appeared on the market in the summer of that year. In autumn 1958 the record industry press was full of articles about stereo. 'All one hears in the American record world these days is stereo and its ramifications,' wrote the correspondent for *The Gramophone*. In September 1958 the American record market was 'in turmoil'; by October it was 'in a positive uproar'.

To play the new stereo records, the consumer was, of course, obliged to acquire new equipment. A new record player and a two-channel amplifier were needed to play them, but at least the new system had features in common with the old one. The old mono records could be played as before on the new player, and it was also possible to play the new stereo records on an old record player, though of course only monaural sound would be heard. The big record companies already had stereo recordings going back several years in their warehouses, so the transfer to the new technology was an effortless process for them. The biggest difficulties were created for the record dealers, who were obliged to keep double stocks of the same records, in both mono and stereo versions. Stereo records were more expensive, until, in 1966, the head of CBS, Clive Davis, raised the prices of mono records to the level of stereophonic ones. The other companies had to follow suit, and within a few years the mono versions disappeared altogether from the market. Only a few resisted the change, notably the producer Phil Spector, who for a long time refused to make stereo records, and, to make his point, wore a badge saying 'BACK TO MONO'.

It was also hard for the ageing Walter Legge to get used to the new thinking, and he preferred to leave stereo record production in younger hands. Legge's recording of *Der Rosenkavalier*, made at Kingsway Hall, London, in December 1956 for EMI, is a typical record of the transition period. The conductor was Herbert von Karajan, and the orchestra was the Philharmonia. In 1956 all records were still being released in mono, and Legge, together with his recording engineer, Douglas Larter, made sure that the singers and the orchestra were committed to tape specifically for monaural listening. It was so expensive to record the opera that the idea of dozens of highly-paid artists standing idle for a day because of a technical fault in the tape recorder could not be countenanced. For this reason a second recording desk and tape recorder, operated by assistant engineer, Christopher Parker, was placed in an adjoining room. For experimental purposes Parker was using a two-channel stereo recorder. When stereophonic records became common a couple of years later, the stereo version of *Der Rosenkavalier* was compiled from his tapes.

The placement of microphones and the entire recording session were planned with monaural reproduction in mind. There is a scene in the first act of *Der Rosenkavalier* where the Marschallin and Octavian (Elisabeth Schwarzkopf and Christa Ludwig) sing a duet in bed. In stereo the scene sounded as if the singers were in opposite corners of a large room. By adjusting the relationship between the channels, however, it was subsequently possible to bring the couple closer together. The result can be heard in a recent CD pressing of the opera in all its stereophonic glory. A purist might, nevertheless, wonder whether Legge's original monaural version was not more authentic after all.

The older generation of record men did have their grounds for being suspicious of stereophony. Some of the first stereophonic records were just made for effect, with the instruments jumping like ping-pong balls from one speaker to the other. 'Simulated stereo' records also appeared on the market, on which old mono recordings were 'enhanced' to create an artificial stereophonic sound using echo and other electrically-produced effects.

Simultaneous with the arrival of stereophony, in the recording studios, and out of the sight of the average music lover, far more thoroughgoing developments were occurring with equipment. Recording was making use of the new multi-track technique, which offered the opportunity to record music in a completely new way: layer on layer. The rapidly developing electronics industry was bringing ever newer devices into use for musicians and recording engineers, whereby sound could be shaped and diffused. Alongside the realism in record production there was soon flourishing a quite new kind of romanticism, one which constructed imaginary and artificial sound worlds. If the classics recorded for RCA by Fritz Reiner represent a still unparalleled realism in record production, the Beatles's *Sergeant Pepper* was the acme of the new romanticism.

Fritz Reiner and RCA's Stereo Symphonies

The Hungarian-born conductor, Fritz Reiner (1888–1963), had emigrated to the United States in the 1920s, when he was offered the post of conductor of the Cincinnati Symphony Orchestra. He conducted with many of the leading orchestras in the United States, and from 1949 to 1953 he conducted at the Metropolitan Opera. His career culminated in his term as conductor of the Chicago Symphony Orchestra (1953–62). During Reiner's period with it, the orchestra was regarded as one of the world's best; he was praised for his exceptionally exact, lustrous interpretations. Reiner had been making records since the thirties. In 1950 he signed a contract with RCA, but he was not satisfied with the results he achieved with the studio orchestra (the NBC Symphony Orchestra), because there was never enough time for rehearsal. In 1953, when Reiner was contracted in Chicago, RCA signed a new contract, which bound the orchestra and its conductor together. Now Reiner had an opportunity to plan recordings in tandem with his concert repertoire. Virtually all the works he recorded were performed publicly in concert at least twice beforehand so that the orchestra would get a proper feeling for them.

RCA was not just a record company; it was, and is, also one of the world's biggest electronics companies. In the fifties the company developed many high-quality microphones, tape recorders and speakers intended for professional use. In 1953 RCA began experimenting with stereo recording, and from 1955 onwards the company regularly recorded orchestral music in stereo. Although records continued for many years to appear in mono versions, some of the recordings were issued in stereo on reel-to-reel tapes. One of the RCA stereo studios was at Orchestra Hall in Chicago, the home of Reiner's orchestra.

The chief technician for RCA's classical music recordings was Lewis Layton. Microphones were used extremely sparingly, mostly the legendary Neumann U47 model. The placement of microphones in the hall was the result of lengthy experimentation, and musicians were expressly forbidden to move the microphones located in front of the groups of instruments. In this way Layton wished to ensure that the acoustic properties of the hall were captured correctly on tape. RCA used three-track studio tape machines in recording. The idea was to record in monaural sound on one channel, with the left and right stereo channels on the other two, but the system also allowed a few possibilities for reprocessing the sound afterwards, before the records were manufactured.

Reiner's contract with RCA was worded so that the less time he spent on recording, the greater was his conductor's fee. This suited Reiner wonderfully; his aim was to conduct on record the same way as in concert. As far as possible the music was recorded in one sequence, without pauses. Faulty passages were patched up afterwards only in dire emergencies. For Heifetz's sake Reiner was prepared to make an exception to the rule, but his collaboration with Rubinstein came to grief because of the pianist's inability, or unwillingness, to record the movements of a concerto in their entirety.

With the Chicago Symphony, Reiner concentrated on recording the basic 19th-century repertoire: most of Beethoven's symphonies, Tchaikovsky, Dvořák, Brahms's violin concerto (with Heifetz) and operatic overtures. The music of our own century was represented by Mahler, Rakhmaninov and Richard Strauss.

Reiner's records were characterized by a brilliant orchestra, an excellent concert hall and the best and most realistic recording technology available at the time. Subsequent processing – the cutting and copying of tapes, which inevitably increases the amount of interference in a recording – was kept to a minimum. In addition, RCA had at its disposal superlative record manufacturing technology for its time. The cutting of the discs, subsequent to taping, did not suffer losses in the dynamic fluctuations, as so often happens, nor was there any intrusive snap and crackle in the records made at RCA's four pressing plants.

In the opinion of many experts Reiner's RCA records are among the best orchestral discs ever recorded. The development of recording technology since the sixties has not necessarily brought any greater realism, and at the same time the phases subsequent to recording – tape editing, mastering, pressing – have often deteriorated considerably in quality. After the great oil crisis the quality of the vinyl used in record manufacturing declined.

The original pressings of Reiner's records are now among the LPs most sought-after by classical music collectors. Those most in demand are the works in which the nuances of the orchestra come to the fore: Respighi's *Pines of Rome*, Rimsky-Korsakov's *Sheherazade*, Strauss's waltzes. Later pressings will not suffice, and there are minute differences even among RCA's own products. One may see collectors looking for the factory's markings stamped into the vinyl beside the label, to see whether the pressing is one from the first, virginal matrix, or a later one, whose sound quality leaves something to be desired. The differences in quality are real, though subtle. Truly high-quality sound equipment is needed to hear the difference between two pressings of Reiner's *Sheherazade*.

Source: Gray (1987)

The Opera Stage Through the Speakers

Many classical records are produced in the United States, but the recording of opera has, for a long time, been virtually a European monopoly. In this field the first great masterpiece of stereo technology was the series of twenty LPs made for Decca between 1958 and 1965 by John Culshaw, on which Georg Solti conducted Richard Wagner's *Ring of the Nibelung* cycle.

The *Ring of the Nibelung* encompasses the four central Wagner operas: *The Rhinegold*, *The Valkyrie*, *Siegfried* and *The Twilight of the Gods*. These works, inspired by ancient Germanic mythology, are gigantic in many senses. Their length, the size of the ensembles, and the ideas they embrace are greater than those of most other operas. Excerpts from them and individual arias have been recorded many times, from the very earliest days of recording. To record the entire cycle on 78 r.p.m. discs, however, would have required an album of 120 records. The advent of the LP opened up new opportunities for recording Wagner, but even so, *The Twilight of the Gods* alone takes up six LP discs. Classical music accounted for about 10 per cent of overall record sales, depending on the country concerned. In the mid-fifties, no-one would have dared to put an operatic package of six LP records on the market. With the growth in the market, by the end of the decade the idea no longer seemed impossible.

There were many problems associated with the recording of the *Ring of the Nibelung*, some of them being common in the production of opera records, some peculiar to Wagner's operas. The scores had to be checked through for accuracy. It is common to find printing errors in the parts used by the orchestral players. In public concerts they pass unnoticed, but when immortalized on record they remain to trouble the sharp-eared critic. Among the problems peculiar to the recording of Wagner were the many unusual instrumental combinations and effects. Not even in a musical city like Vienna is it easy to find six harpists available for a recording at the same time. Also needed for the recordings were eighteen anvils and their players, peals of thunder and other effects. The alphorns scored in the *Twilight of the Gods* are usually replaced in performances of the opera by bassoons, but Culshaw ordered reproductions of the horns once used by Wagner at Bayreuth from a German instrument maker.

Recording an opera requires plenty of studio time. Contracts have to be drawn up with the orchestra, the conductor and the singers, and a timetable has to be worked out which everyone can observe. The entire *Ring* was conducted by Georg Solti, with the Vienna Philharmonic, which also had its normal concert season in progress. Changes had to be made in the roster of singers as the *Ring* progressed from one section to another. Nevertheless the records contain a selection of singers who could never have been heard together on the opera stage. The important role of Fricka in the first opera to be recorded, *The Rhinegold*, was sung by one of the greatest Wagnerian singers of our time, Kirsten Flagstad, whom Culshaw managed to coax into the studio after she had already announced her complete retirement from performing following the revelation that Elisabeth Schwarzkopf had covered her role in the celebrated Furtwängler recording of *Tristan and Isolde*. In the other three operas, Brünnhilde was played by Birgit Nilsson. Among Culshaw's other choices were Dietrich Fischer-Dieskau, a well-known lied singer whose voice was perfectly suited to this role, as Gunther. Although operas are recorded in short sections and the overture might even be saved until last, the planning of studio work so that each singer is in place at the right time can be a logistical nightmare.

In recording the *Ring*, John Culshaw wanted longer sections of 15 to 20 minutes' duration, as opposed to the normal three to five minutes which had been the custom, because in his view the internal tensions in the music came better to the fore in this way. Even more important, however, was that he was the first to use stereophony as an artistic element on record. Opera is, after all, a form of theatre. On the stage the singers take up their own different places. Movement is often an integral part of the performance. Yet for over half a century it had been taken for granted that the stage cannot be transferred onto disc in an operatic recording. The singers came forward, each in turn, to perform their role into the same microphone. Using stereo, Culshaw brought the 'sonic stage' onto record.

Many in the record industry regarded Culshaw's and Decca's *Ring* as a foolhardy effort. The buying public reacted positively to the recordings, however, and the critics praised the final result. The operas were initially sold as separate albums, and finally as a gigantic set of 16 LPs. Early in 1967, *The Valkyrie* was the best-selling classical record in the United States. Nowadays the cycle is available in several recordings. There are special studio recordings, as well as those taped from stage performances, such as Furtwängler's monumental series at La Scala from 1950, which has been preserved thanks to Italian radio. Culshaw's *Ring* has become available again on a set of 15 CDs. It remains one of the great landmarks in recording history.

Source: Culshaw (1967)

Les Paul and the Multi-track Recorder

Classical music recording has long exploited the possibilities offered by recording tape and stereophony to enhance a performance. The interpretation heard on record may be stuck together from tens or hundreds of small pieces, to create the illusion of a perfect interpretation. Ultimately, though, the aim is to get the musicians to play as naturally as possible. On the other hand, tape presented opportunities to create music that had never been, and could never be, performed live. Such experiments were being made with records even before recording tape was adopted. In February 1941 the soprano saxophonist, Sidney Bechet, and RCA Victor technicians had the idea of making a novelty record on which Bechet would stand in for an entire band on his own. Apart from his main instrument, Bechet also played the tenor saxophone, clarinet, piano and bass tolerably well. He played all these as a one-man band on the record, *Blues of Bechet*. The recording was made on an acetate disc, one instrument at a time, like a many-layered sandwich. When the first instrument's part was recorded, Bechet listened to it through headphones and played the next part along with it. Thanks to the excellent recording equipment at RCA Victor, one can hardly hear on the record the inevitable hiss which accumulated as the number of recorded layers increased.

There were other similar many-layered recordings. Another famous example is Bach's double violin concerto, in which Heifetz played both violin parts. The process of recording direct onto disc was laborious, however, and the number of layers that could be recorded was limited. Only with the advent of recording tape was it possible to make full use of such recording techniques in the studio. The man who established this method in studio practice was Les Paul, real name Lester Polfus (b. 1916).

Les Paul began his career at the age of 17, playing country music on Midwestern radio stations, at a time when most music on the radio was still broadcast live. He was a self-taught electronics enthusiast, and built his first guitar amplifier himself. The electric guitar was still at the experimental stage, and Les Paul began to think about the design of a guitar specifically intended for electric amplification. In 1941 he built his first solid-bodied guitar, which had no resonating chamber at all; rather the sound was conveyed straight from the strings to the amplifier by a magnetic pick-up. The 'Les Paul' guitar became the prototype of the electric guitar, and it is still listed in the catalogue of the Gibson guitar factory.

In 1948 Les Paul married the singer, Mary Ford (real name Colleen Summers), and at the same time began recording for Capitol. The records were made in Paul's own home studio, and they were based on Sidney Bechet's old idea. Les Paul was a one-man band with a guitar; Mary Ford sang duets with herself, occasionally becoming a full-blown women's choir. The couple's first record, 'Brazil', was fairly successful, and 1951 was a vintage year for Les Paul and Mary Ford, when 'Mockin' Bird Hill', 'How High the Moon' and 'The World is Waiting for the Sunrise' achieved gold record status. The secret behind these records was the studio tape recorder adopted in 1948, to which Les Paul had made small adjustments, such as adding a fourth tape head in such a way that, when recording, the machine did not erase the previous recording, but the performer could listen to it through headphones and record a new part over it. Even this method had its limitations, and in 1954 the Ampex company built, to Les Paul's special order, the first eight-track tape recorder, which could record eight bands of sound side-by-side, on wider tape than normal.

At first Paul's new recording methods were regarded as curiosities, mainly suited to making novelty records. In 1955 a Dane, Carl Weissman, put together a record in the studio on which dogs barked to the tune of 'Jingle Bells'. The trick was done by recording the dogs' barking, raising or lowering the pitch of the barks by altering the speed of the tape, and finally copying the song thus created against an orchestral background. With modern digital technology all this would be an hour's work, but in the fifties it took several days. The effort paid off: the 'Singing Dogs' got a gold record in the United States. In 1958 it was the chipmunks' turn, with David Seville's 'Chipmunk Song'. This record also made use of multi-track recording and alterations in the tape speed.

Despite these experiments, throughout the fifties the studios' philosophy remained the same as in the days of the shellac disc. The tape recorder was welcomed into the studio, because faulty recordings could be erased and the tape used again, and it was easy to record large works in small sections. The aim and the ideal, however, was to record music as naturally as possible, just as it was performed. In the early sixties, multi-track technology and layered recordings began to become more common. In the mid-fifties RCA had experimented with three-track tape recorders, which recorded music on one band in mono and the other two in stereo. Capitol had a three-track recorder in use at its Hollywood studio in 1958, the Atlantic studio in New York adopted one in 1960. At the famous EMI Abbey Road studios, where the Beatles' records were made, the first four-track machines were acquired in the mid-sixties; eight tracks came into use in 1967.

In the early stages two tracks sufficed; after all, popular music was to be released in mono for a long time to come. The accompanying band was recorded first on one track, so that the expensive studio musicians could be released from their duties. Thereafter the solo singer would be able to sing the vocal part as many times as was necessary to achieve an entire faultless performance. On a four-track machine it was even possible to record the rhythm section on one track, a solo guitarist on another, a solo vocalist on a third and the background vocalists on a fourth, and, if necessary, to adjust the interplay between them afterwards or re-record one individual part. In the sixties it was still the custom to release singles in mono, but as popular music became more generally available in stereo from the mid-decade onwards, the number of channels needed was doubled. From four-track recorders there was soon a trend towards 8-, 24- and even 32-track systems, and at the same time the attitude in studio work shifted to the new 'layered' thinking. It is usual to record just the rhythm section first, with several channels being given over just to recording the drums. In the second phase, the other instruments are added, such as wind instruments or violins. Third comes the solo vocalist, and fourthly the background vocalists, if any. In the fifth phase on, say, a 24-track machine, the recording is mixed onto two tracks as the stereo recording that the record buyer ultimately hears. The possibilities of recording technology were further expanded by many electronic devices that became available at this time.

The Dolby noise reduction system, invented by Raymond M. Dolby in 1966, removed the problem of the extraneous hiss which had until then troubled multi-track studios. Using equalizers it was possible to change the sound quality of vocalists or intrumentalists, and compressors and limiters controlled the volume during signal peaks. Rock could now be recorded at full volume without the peaks causing problems in the cutting of a disc. As new instruments based on synthesized sound were also coming into use at the time, from improved electric organs to drum machines that could keep the beat without faltering, the result was a new sonic ideal. Records no longer strove to imitate live music, but rather new worlds of sound were created in the studio, which musicians would then try to recreate on stage. Les Paul had been the initiator of these developments. Its first flowering dates from the second half of the sixties, firstly on the records produced by Phil Spector in the United States, and thereafter on George Martin's Beatles records.

Source: Cunningham (1996)

Phil Spector and the Wall of Sound

Harvey Phillip Spector (b. 1940) had a marvellous initial contact with the record industry when, as an 18-year-old, he established a singing group named The Teddy Bears with his school friend, Annette Kleinbard. The Teddy Bears were a trio who only had two singers at first, as the future master studio technician sang both male parts. The group's first record, Phil's composition, 'To Know Him is to Love Him', sold over a million singles. When requests to perform started coming in on the strength of its success, a third singer had to be brought in so that the group could perform in concert the arrangements it had sung on record.

The Teddy Bears were a one-hit wonder: their subsequent records did not make the charts. Flushed with success, Phil Spector moved to New York, the centre of the record industry, where his gold record was a passport to getting temporary jobs as a studio musician, producer and composer with various record companies. His best-known composition from these years is 'Spanish Harlem', recorded by a singing group called The Drifters. After a couple of years' apprenticeship he was ready to fly solo. Together with Lester Sills he set up a record company which they called Philles Records. Girl groups were in vogue in the early sixties, and Philles's first signing was an unknown singing group called The Crystals. On 16 November 1961 the group's first record, 'There's No Other One', entered the charts in the leading record industry publication, *Billboard*. Between 1961 and 1966 Philles, which had meanwhile shifted its headquarters from New York to Hollywood, released 37 singles, of which 29 made the charts. It was an incredible achievement in a business where the chances of a hit were one in fifty at best. The label's most popular records were 'He's A Rebel' (The Crystals), 'Da Doo Ron Ron' (The Crystals), 'Then He Kissed Me' (The Crystals), 'Be My Baby' (The Ronettes), and 'You've Lost that Lovin' Feelin'' (The Righteous Brothers), which reached number one in the United States.

All these records were, first and foremost, Spector's work. Not one of the singers achieved much of a reputation before or after Spector. The compositions, many of them by Spector himself, were ordinary teenage pop songs. What made these records historic was their sound, and the way Spector created this sound in the studio. People began to talk of a special 'Phil Spector sound'.

At that time, multi-track technology in the studio was becoming common. Spector had a permanent arranger, Jack Nitzsche, and a permanent recording engineer, Larry Levine, of the Gold Star studio in Hollywood. Spector's aim was to construct a many-layered 'wall of sound' in the studio. The basis of the Spector sound was provided by percussion and guitars, over which was spread a carpet of strings. Wind instruments were needed to provide extra colour. The singers were really only the icing on the cake. Once the label had established its position, Spector might spend days on end in the studio looking for the right placement of a microphone to get just the right sound from the drums or the guitar. Sometimes the desired effect was found by pure chance, as for example with the strange-sounding guitar break on 'Zip-a-dee-doo-dah' (Bob B. Soxx and the Blue Jeans). It was captured on tape when the recording engineer accidentally turned on the wrong microphone channel and recorded the guitar on a microphone at the opposite end of the studio. It was no longer the producer's philosophy to capture music as 'naturally' as possible, but to create new, artificial worlds of sound.

Spector's last effort for Philles was Tina Turner's 'River Deep Mountain High' in 1966. Like other Philles singers, Tina was then a more or less unknown rhythm 'n' blues singer in her husband Ike's band. Spector heard hidden possibilities in her voice, however, and spent a month in the studio perfecting the record to the last detail. The final result (released as 'by Ike and Tina Turner', although Spector did not allow Ike in the studio) has elicited paeans of praise from one critic after another. If there had sometimes been a sickly sweet flavour to Spector's earlier records, this time he found a perfect balance between Tina Turner's 'volcanic' voice and the accompaniment, which was crafted to the finest tolerances.

'River Deep Mountain High' was not, however, the success that Spector had hoped for. It reached number 88 in the *Billboard* chart, only to drop out again. Spector was not consoled by the fact that the record was a hit in England. At the age of 27 the disappointed former teenage millionaire decided to retire, and disappeared entirely from the scene for a few years. But he was not able to leave the business for good. In 1970 the Beatles, who were breaking up, called him in to rescue their half-completed album, *Let it Be*, and Spector put the finishing touches to the tapes the Beatles had recorded in the studio, adding the controversial string background to 'The Long and Winding Road', for instance. After the group disbanded, he became John Lennon's and George Harrison's 'court producer'; since then he has occasionally left his mark on some provocative records: for Leonard Cohen in 1977 ('Death of a Ladies' Man'), the Ramones in 1980 ('End of the Century') and Yoko Ono in 1981 ('Seasons of Glass'). In 1969 he appeared in a minor role in the film *Midnight Cowboy*.

Phil Spector's ideas have been repeated on record to the point of exhaustion over the past twenty years. Abba and many of the other commercially successful groups of the seventies would not have existed without Spector. That is why some of Spector's Philles records sound dated today. The best of them, such as 'You've Lost that Lovin' Feelin'' and 'River Deep Mountain High', always seem just as fresh. But Phil Spector's name will go down in recording history for at least two more general reasons. Phil Spector was the first to bring young people into a responsible position in the record industry. Before Spector, young people's music had been produced by middle-aged, cigar-chomping producers who rarely showed a lively interest in the music they produced. Nowadays every record company sees the vital importance of having young producers to keep in touch with contemporary music. Although the directors of the large record companies are often still middle-aged, there are many people under twenty who set up record companies, and this becomes apparent in the music they produce.

Phil Spector was to recording what David Wark Griffith was to the cinema. Griffith was the first film director to realize that film is quite different from theatre. With Spector, the producer became the 'author' of the record, who moulded the ingredients of the record into an ultimate whole in the studio. Among Spector's admirers were such seminal groups of the sixties as the Beatles and the Beach Boys, and without his influence there would scarcely have been such classics as 'Good Vibrations' or *Sergeant Pepper*.

Sources: Spector (1991); Williams (1974)

George Martin and the Beatles

The great turning points in music are usually connected with social and philosophical movements. Rock 'n' roll had reached Europe in the mid-fifties, and every country in Europe nurtured its own little Elvis. The influence of rock was still limited, however. The record industry regarded rock as it did any other form of popular music. Routine studio musicians were hired to accompany and sometimes even play it.

For a short time in the early sixties, instrumental groups were in vogue, consisting of electric guitar, bass and drums. The trend was set by the Ventures in America and the Shadows in England. When a solo singer was added to this combination, the basic pattern was set for the popular musical groups of the sixties. Hundreds of these groups sprang up within a few years, particularly in England. In a short time the best of them had entered the studios and the charts: the Hollies, the Honeycombs, the Kinks, the Yardbirds, the Swinging Blue Jeans, the Rolling Stones, the Animals, the Beatles and a host of others. The music of these bands was initially quite ordinary American rock 'n' roll. The best of them aimed at composing their own material. What was really new about these groups, however, was that all the members had equal status. There were no soloists or accompanists.

The Beatles rose above all other groups around 1963, creating a phenomenon of mass hysteria among their fans. Although the Beatles' early records reveal both original melodies and good lyrics, usually the work of John Lennon and Paul McCartney, no-one has really compared them with other groups of the same period to examine whether the Beatles' output really was superior. The reason for their success cannot have been merely musical. Even in Finland the fan magazine, *Suosikki*, raised its circulation in one year from 20,000 to over a 100,000 simply by publishing bedsheet-sized pictures of the Beatles. There are always arbitrary, inexplicable factors which account for success in popular music. No-one could really explain in full why the Beatles became so popular in the mid-sixties. What is exceptional about the Beatles, though, is what they did with their popularity. It is largely due to them that the sixties were such a watershed in popular music. The group's members did not just think of music as a pleasant way to make money, but they considered themselves to be artists.

The immense popularity of the Beatles offered them unique opportunities. Studio technology progressed rapidly in the sixties. Record sales were enjoying strong growth, and the Beatles played their own part in this. In 1966 John Lennon half-seriously told an interviewer, 'We're more popular than Jesus'. By that time the group had earned eleven gold LPs and a score of gold singles. The group was of vital importance both to their own company, EMI, and to Britain's exports. No-one at EMI really understood the reasons for the group's success. So when the band wanted to make records of a kind that had not been made before, nobody opposed them.

The Beatles' artistic ambition blossomed gradually between 1964 and 1967. It was not limited to music; in 1964 John Lennon had published his well-received volume, *In His Own Write*. In 1966 the group gave up live performance altogether and concentracted on recording. The change can be heard on the albums *Help!*, *Rubber Soul*, *Revolver* and *Sergeant Pepper's Lonely Hearts Club Band*, which also demonstrated the influence on rock of the new recording technology and production methods.

The Beatles' records had, from the beginning, been produced by George Martin, who had been with EMI since 1950. In the early stages his task was mainly to choose the numbers and see that the recordings went smoothly. By the time of the albums *Help!* and *Rubber Soul*, there were conscious attempts made by him at innovation. On 'Yesterday', the electric guitars were replaced by a string quartet. On 'Norwegian Wood', instead of an electric guitar George Harrison played an Indian sitar.

Revolver continued to use new musical influences. The melodies improved, and the song lyrics strayed still further away from the 'She loves you, yeah, yeah, yeah' of the early years. The members of the group – mainly Lennon and McCartney – wrote the songs and planned the records. The other members played and sang their own parts. George Martin, who had both a thorough musical training and long studio experience, was responsible for the practical aspects. Where necessary he wrote orchestral arrangements or found the right sound in the studio. From the point of view of what was to come, the most interesting number on the album is the last one, 'Tomorrow Never Knows'. John Lennon had got the idea for it from the *Tibetan Book of the Dead*, and wanted his voice to sound 'like the Dalai Lama singing on the mountain-tops'. George Martin achieved this with echo effects. The impression, reminiscent of electronic music, was achieved by having all the members of the group record various effects and passages of music on their home tape recorders, from which Martin then made the final 'mix'. Some of the recordings were played backwards or at the wrong speed.

A great turning point in the history of rock came with *Sergeant Pepper's Lonely Hearts Club Band* in 1967. It was the group's first LP on which the songs formed a consistent whole; they can be seen as parts of a song cycle. Secondly, it exploited all the technical possibilities of the studio then available – though by today's standards they are rather modest. The recordings were made using two four-track machines, and copies from one recorder were made onto another where occasion demanded, so that the result presaged the impression one gains nowadays from 24- and 32-track systems. There was also the use of a 42-strong symphony orchestra on the final track, 'A Day in the Life'. The conductor was dressed in a gorilla costume for this track – a fact which, when later passed to the press, attracted further publicity.

Sergeant Pepper even took dogs into consideration; on the end-groove of the record there is a brief 20,000-Hz signal – too high for the human ear. The cover picture, designed by Peter Blake, was a collage gathering together all the influential celebrities of the past century, from Karl Marx to Shirley Temple, and including Bob Dylan, Oscar Wilde, Albert Einstein, Marlene Dietrich, Lenny Bruce and Jean Cocteau. Indeed the release of the record nearly foundered over its cover, when EMI lawyers, fearing lawsuits, insisted on written permission from everyone included on it. Leonard Bernstein telegraphed to say he was charmed by the tribute; ultimately the company, tired of hunting signatures, went ahead anyway.

After *Sergeant Pepper* the Beatles released three more LPs. They contain many fine moments, but also convey a picture of the group's gradual fragmentation. All the members of the group continued with solo careers after the group's demise.

From 1964 onwards the Beatles had complete artistic independence and were given a free hand to develop themselves in the EMI studios. When the group's manager and friend, Brian Epstein, died in 1967, they decided to free themselves financially as well. The Beatles set up the Apple Corps, to produce records and much else. Apple succeeded in releasing a few good records. Mary Hopkin's 'Those Were the Days' was an international hit, and after the Beatles broke up, Apple also produced John Lennon's records. Soon, however, it became clear that the business could not be conducted with the same degree of creative freedom as the music had been. The Beatles had insisted that the company's accounting department be situated in another building, because figures were so boring. The company's PR man spent his time floating rubber ducks in his bathtub, the electronics division never completed anything, and the Apple fashion boutique soon had to close. The author of the history of the company later described it as 'the longest cocktail party'. Gradually, all the former Beatles moved onto the rosters of 'old' record companies.

Sources: Lewisohn (1988); Martin (1979)

Electronic Music Comes into the Dance Hall

Rubber Soul, Revolver and *Sergeant Pepper* revolutionized young people's thinking about music all over the world. In the United States the Beach Boys had been one of the most popular teenage pop groups of the decade, whose harmless lyrics dealt with surfing, fast cars and pretty girls. In 1965 the artistic soul of the group, Brian Wilson, inspired by *Rubber Soul*, decided to do something just as daring. The result was 'Pet Sounds', a unique record on which teenage romance was replaced by psychodrama, and electric guitars were supplemented by new electronic sounds.

It cost $70,000 to produce 'Pet Sounds' – at that time an unprecedented sum for a rock record. The record sold moderately well, though nowhere near as well as the Beach Boys' previous records, and the critics praised it. The management of the record company was dubious and refused to invest money in promoting the record. The Beatles were fascinated by the album, and on the strength of their recommendation the record sold better in England than in America. What followed was a new Beach Boys single, 'Good Vibrations'. Brian Wilson worked on refining this soundscape, 3 minutes 35 seconds long, for six months. According to those who were present, twenty recording sessions and 90 hours of tape were needed for the record. The strange-sounding instrument on the record was a theremin, borrowed from the effects department of a film company. In December 1966, *Good Vibrations* was the best-selling record in the United States.

From here things went downhill for the Beach Boys. The next album, whose working title was *Smile*, was hailed as the most magnificent record of all time. Throughout 1966 Brian Wilson and his new co-writer, Van Dyke Parks, were writing songs and recording them in the studio. Brian speeded up the process by buying $2,000 worth of hash. Encouraged by the success of the single, 'Good Vibrations', the Capitol company printed 468,000 copies of the record cover in advance with the Christmas market in mind. In May 1967 Capitol had to officially announce that the project had been abandoned. In the meantime *Sergeant Pepper* had been completed. A couple of attractive glimpses from the abandoned album, 'Heroes and Villains' and 'Surf's Up', later appeared in other compilations.

The 1960s also saw a breakthrough in the use of new instruments and studio technology. The Hammond electric organ had been developed out of Thaddeus Cahill's teleharmonium, but so far its use had been limited to background music in cocktail bars. Ambitious attempts to make electronic music were restricted to the experimental studios of universities and radio stations. In 1966 a New York engineer, Robert Moog, constructed an electric instrument using the latest electronics, to which he gave his name. The new instrument attracted the composer, Walter Carlos, who had been working for several years in the electronic music studio at Princeton University. He became interested in trying out the Moog's infinite tonal possibilities with the music of a classical composer who had traditionally been performed on a variety of instruments – Johann Sebastian Bach. Walter Carlos's *Switched-on Bach*, on the CBS label, was one of the successes of the late sixties (a gold record in 1968). Nowadays, Walter Carlos, having had a sex-change operation, is the successful female composer Wendy Carlos.

The Moog and other electric instruments which came on the market at the same time were greeted with joy by rock musicians. Some of the devices were so heavy and complex that they were more suited to studio work. Keith Emerson, of the group Emerson, Lake and Palmer, dragged one of the early models of Moog around with him on tour. The Moody Blues created their own unique sound using a Mellotron, one of the competing inventions. In addition to keyboard instruments based on completely synthetic, artificial sound production, the new technology was also used to alter and shape the sound of ordinary instruments. The electric guitar was a suitable subject for experimentation by musicians interested in electronics; its sound could be altered with a 'sound breaker', an echo device, a phasing device or a pitch changer. An even stranger invention was the Vocorder, a device which can render a singer's voice completely unrecognizable. The first group known to have used it was one called United States of America.

A good example of the possibilities offered by the new technology on the stage and in the studio is provided by the recordings, made between 1967 and 1970, of Jimi Hendrix, who died young. Hendrix was a guitar virtuoso in the traditional sense, but in his hands, using the new electronic devices, the guitar became a new instrument. In the studio he picked up from where he left off on stage. The famous *Are You Experienced* begins with a passage on which tapes played backwards alternate with snatches recorded in the normal way, without the effect seeming for a moment artificial. 'Third Stone from the Sun' makes clever use of tape speed fluctuations to alter the sound. On the album *Axis: Bold as Love* he makes constant use of 'phasing', on which the same note recorded on two channels is mixed with small but fluctuating delays.

Another way of exploiting the new technology was exemplified by the composer and guitarist Frank Zappa. The first album by Zappa's group, The Mothers of Invention, *Freak Out!*, was the first double LP in the history of rock to be planned as a continuous whole. It soon became a cult record, and the Mothers of Invention began putting out a couple of records a year. Zappa made records that were a mixture of concrete music, modern concert music and rock and pop parodies, in a collage-like style, the whole stamped with his unique brand of humour.

In the late sixties these methods were new and untested; their use on the concert stage demanded boldness, skill and imagination. The results were often arbitrary, in the spirit of John Cage. Over the ensuing decade electronic instruments became standardized and mass-produced. Electronic keyboards were followed by drum machines with pre-programmed disco rhythms. What had been considered avant-garde in the sixties became an ingredient in the dance and popular music of the eighties.

Sources: Cunningham (1996); Gaines (1988)

The Motown Sound

The radical youth culture of the sixties created a broad 'underground' publishing network in the United States and other countries. The underground papers supplemented the news disseminated by the mainstream press, broke taboos and created new forms of graphic expression. Underground comics created a whole new art form. Against this background it is rather surprising that, with a few rare exceptions, there were no 'underground records'. The most radical records of the decade mostly appeared from under the wings of the big established record companies. They had learned their lesson from the upheavals of the fifties and wanted to assure their position by producing music for the baby boomers.

Likewise the most successful new companies established in the sixties and seventies came about in very traditional ways. ABC, MCA and United Artists were created as the record divisions of American film and television companies. Arista was set up by Clive Davis after he was sacked from CBS. A&M started up in trumpeter Herb Alpert's garage, and thanks to its records of light popular music

(Tijuana Brass, Sergio Mendes, The Carpenters) it achieved an annual turnover of $70 million. Only Motown was created clearly to satisfy the cultural needs of a particular sector of the population.

Detroit – Motortown – is the centre of the American car industry. Berry Gordy was a moderately successful black businessman who had moved to the city from the South in 1922, like thousands of other blacks. He also wanted his son to be a businessman, but Berry Junior could not seem to find the right business. The son's record shop went bust, his career as a boxer only brought him bruises, and temporary work in a car factory seemed like a dead end. In the mid-fifties Berry Gordy Jr started to make a name for himself as a composer. Among his biggest hits were 'Money' and 'Reet Petite', which have become rhythm 'n' blues standards. From composing it was a short path to producing records, and from producing, a short step to his own record company. In 1959 Gordy junior set up Motown Records with his friend the singer, Smokey Robinson, modelled on Gordy senior's building firm. In 1961 Motown scored its first hit, when Smokey Robinson and the Miracles' 'Shop Around' was for a time the second-best-selling record in the United States, and number one in the rhythm 'n' blues charts.

When one considers what an important part black music has played in the United States record industry, it is hardly surprising that black companies have entered the record business. As early as 1921, W.C. Handy, the composer of *St Louis Blues*, and Harry Pace, who had got rich in the insurance business, set up the Black Swan company, which rode the crest of the blues wave for a few years. Since the Second World War there have been many black-owned companies, but most of them have been short-lived. Among the more successful were Vee-Jay in Chicago, which collapsed in the sixties. Motown was an exception. In the sixties the company had one hit after another, and by the start of the seventies Motown was the largest black-owned company in the United States.

In many ways Motown was a family business. Many of the company's 399 employees, and even its artists, were relatives, acquaintances or members of the Gordy family. The label's most important artists were from Detroit or its vicinity, and in the early years the Motown Records office was a place constantly teeming with the company's artists, aspiring singers or just interested neighbours. Berry Gordy's secretary, Martha Reeves, became one of the company's most popular artists. A blind 11-year-old musical prodigy, Steveland Morris, for whom Gordy invented the stage name, Little Stevie Wonder, used to come and play in the company's office after school, and the label's studio musicians taught him in their spare time.

Other famous Motown artists included the Four Tops, Marvin Gaye, Gladys Knight, the Marvelettes, the Supremes, the Temptations and the child group, the Jackson Five, whose solo singer was the young Michael Jackson. Their influence on the music of the sixties and even the following decade was so strong that people started talking of a special 'Motown sound'. The style was not completely original; its models were the many popular black singing groups of the previous decade, and also Phil Spector's records, but the Motown sound is both easy to recognize and hard to imitate. Its secret lay in its artists, who originated from the city and often appeared together, the same permanent background musicians, and a team of composer-producers – above all the famous trio of Holland–Dozier–Holland, who were responsible for the production of their own songs on record. The composers' participation in the production process was natural at Motown, because often the compositions were only given their final form in the studio. Although the Motown style did not favour improvised solos or jazz elements, but preferred to be a smoothed-down 'wall of sound' after the fashion of Phil Spector, the accompaniment on record was at least as important as the solo singer. The drummer, Uriel Jones, described producer Norman Whitfield's working method as follows:

> *Cloud Nine* began as a beat on the cymbal. Norman would come and tell you this is what he wanted on the cymbal. He'd have you sit and play that two or three minutes by itself, and he'd tell you to add a certain beat on the foot. Actually, what he's doing is just listening to see what he wants to add to it. Then he turns the whole band down on this tune. He may hear a little something else that he wants and then tell you to change this to this. Norman had in mind what he wanted, but the tune really materialized once we started playing it.

Many ideas were born in the Motown studio that later came into general use in the record industry. The company's regular bassist was James Jamerson, whose bass lines can be heard on many hit records. The secret of the Motown bass sound was that the label's studio was the first to record the electric bass directly from the pick-up of the instrument without a separate microphone. But the secret of the success of the cosy 'family firm' also lay in the fact that musicians often played for considerably lower rates than union contracts would have allowed. Artists had contracts with both the record company and the Gordy family's concert agency and music publishing business, and artists' fees were often lower than normal.

In 1972 Motown moved to Los Angeles. With the decline in the car industry, Detroit had developed some bad slums, and Philadelphia was growing into the creative centre of black music. In the 1970s many of the major Motown artists moved to other record companies, some accompanied by bitter lawsuits. Instead of records, Berry Gordy became interested in racehorses and movies – he produced, for instance, the film biography of Billie Holiday with Diana Ross, former singer in the Supremes, in the leading role. In 1986 Motown was sold to MCA.

Source: George (1986; quote pp. 170–1)

Messages From Satan

In 1982 a bill was drafted in the United States Congress for a law providing that record covers have a prominent warning affixed to them if the record contained 'secret Satanic messages'. The bill never led to any action, nor was it intended to. It was more or less comparable to the hundreds of private members' bills proposed each year in the world's various parliaments for propagandist purposes, but it was the visible culmination of a campaign kept up over decades by certain fundamentalist preachers who claimed that rock records contain secret Satanic messages which are audible when the record is played backwards. These messages were claimed to have a subconscious effect on the listener, even when played in the normal way. The most frequently mentioned example of such a message is in the song 'Stairway to Heaven' by the heavy-rock band, Led Zeppelin, on which the line 'There's still time to change' sounds to some people's ears like 'Here's to my sweet Satan' when played backwards.

Much had changed in the record industry since the days when the biggest-selling international records were *Moonlight Serenade* and *Kiss of Fire*. Even in the early fifties the most popular hit records were still innocent love stories in which a boy and a girl either loved or left each other. Musically these records adhered to the familiar patterns established by the popular and folk music of the last century. By the end of the fifties the breakthrough of rock 'n' roll had separated youth music from other popular music and introduced influences from black music, which to some older listeners seemed threatening and aggressive. Even Elvis Presley's swinging hips attracted wide condemnation.

In the ten years following the middle of the sixties, rock 'n' roll had been transformed, and the rapidly growing record industry had spread its message everywhere. The late sixties were, in both the United States and Europe, a time of great intellectual ferment. It was evident in films, comic strips and politics; it had to come out in music too. After the Beatles and Dylan, successful rock musicians began to think of themselves as artists, who had important things to say. Music that had once been so clear and simple underwent a change: it took on board influences from electronic music, eastern music, blues and jazz. Song lyrics no longer told of love, but took a stand on the Vietnam War, politics, feminism, ecology, religion, drugs and everything that was being publicly debated.

In Europe the change was primarily a musical one. Studio technology encouraged musicians to try out new effects; the lyrics of the songs were often ambiguous or disappeared behind a barrage of electric noise. The new songs were sung in English; their lyrics were incomprehensible except to a small circle. Some years were to pass before the new rock was to be sung in German, Finnish or Icelandic. But in the United States, rock singers were striking at the most tender spots in society. Country Joe McDonald's 'Fixin' to Die' and Barry McGuire's 'Eve of Destruction' were unequivocal protest songs against the Vietnam War, and the listener was forced to take a stand for or against them. Singers with differing opinions composed responses, records were burned in public and radio stations were threatened with the loss of their licences.

Led Zeppelin was one of the British groups who rose to world fame as a result of the breakthrough of the late sixties. The founder of the group, Jimmy Page, had become known in a group called the Yardbirds, whose original idea was to offer real blues to British audiences. Led Zeppelin, founded in 1968, had a different aim, however. The development of amplifier technology in the sixties made it possible for groups using electric instruments to play at ear-splitting volume even in large venues, and this opportunity was exploited by Led Zeppelin to the full. The total power of the group's amplifying equipment amounted to 70,000 watts. Led Zeppelin became the kings of stadium rock. Of course it was not possible to capture pure volume on record, but the new studio technology, with its compressors and limiters, made the illusion of colossal power possible on disc as well. Heavy rock was born. Led Zeppelin became the most popular rock group of the early seventies, possibly even more popular in the United States than in Europe. Led

Zeppelin's popularity was no mere passing fad either. Despite their preference for overblown manifestations of power, its members were also skilled musicians, and the group demonstrated its mastery of softer tones on record as well as louder ones. In the music of Led Zeppelin, the lyrics took second place. It is difficult to say whether the discussion of 'messages from the Devil', which went as far as the United States Congress, was just a fuss dreamed up by some fundamentalist preachers. Jimmy Page was personally genuinely interested in occultism. He collected literature relating to 'secret knowledge' and even bought a small house in Scotland that had once belonged to a group of English 'Satan worshippers', led by Aleister Crowley, at the turn of the century. It was in this house that Led Zeppelin's drummer, John Bonham, died in 1980, not from Satanic influence, but from drinking 40 shots of vodka at a stretch. Perhaps it is possible to find messages hidden in the records of Led Zeppelin and a few other groups, either seriously or as a joke, but these messages scarcely have any more significance than Paul McCartney's message to dogs at the end of *Sergeant Pepper*.

The campaign against Satan worship had an excellent effect on the sales of Led Zeppelin's records. Over eighteen million copies of the group's records were sold in all. The album *Led Zeppelin IV* alone, which contains the controversial 'Stairway to Heaven', sold three million copies. No wonder many heavy rock groups starting out on their careers still believe in the power of Satanic subjects.

Source: Denisoff (1975; 1986)

One-chord Wonders

In 1976 Led Zeppelin were the main stars in a big-budget film called *The Song Remains the Same*. Three-and-a-half million hopeful fans tried to book advance tickets for the Swedish pop group Abba's world concert tour. With a great advertising fanfare, EMI reissued all 22 of the old Beatles singles. Princess Margaret graced a Rolling Stones concert in London with her presence. Rock 'n' roll had become middle-aged.

Led Zeppelin's records appeared on Warner's Atlantic label. Two-thirds of the records sold in Great Britain were issued by six multinational conglomerates, led by EMI, CBS and PolyGram with about 15 per cent, followed by Warner, RCA and Decca with about five per cent each. Record sales were going badly, however, in the companies' view. Overall sales were declining. Opinions differed in the business as to whether the main cause was the prevailing slump in England with the resultant youth unemployment, or a lack of new superstars.

In February an unknown new rock group named the Sex Pistols was thrown out of the Marquee Club in London after a fight broke out during the group's performance. In October EMI, which was desperately looking for new talent, signed a recording contract with the Pistols. In November the group's first record, 'Anarchy in the UK', was released. In December the group caused a scandal by uttering well-known four-letter words on a live TV broadcast. EMI, protective of its public image, cancelled the band's contract, but the record sold 50,000 copies. The Sex Pistols were the visible tip of a rising generation in rock. The Pistols' music was punk – simple, loud, aggressive, consciously irritating. It was associated with its own style of dress, which made punks the darlings of press photographers. The punk style aimed at a surrealistically ragged look, with ripped garments, safety pins and carefully planned clashes of style, aiming to give the impression of clothing found in a rubbish bin.

At the same time other new trends were on the rise, ones which did not attract the same kind of attention in the national press. British pub rock was a return to simple, basic rock – loud, rhythmic music without brilliant amplifying systems or 32-track recording studios. What these trends had in common was a suspicion of the big record companies and their partiality for superstars. (The suspicion was mutual, as the number of new signings for the depressed companies was waning.)

Similar trends were developing elsewhere in the world. The outcome was that in the late seventies a huge number of self-financed rock records were vying for public attention, mostly singles. Whereas the rock stars of the late sixties had refined their discs in the studio for months on end and, if necessary, paid entire symphony orchestras for the sake of a few effects, the self-financed records of the punk labels were made for a few hundred pounds. A punk group called Scritti Politti printed an account on the sleeve of its first single of how much it had cost to produce the record. Fourteen hours of studio time and 2500 singles cost £542. The aim was to encourage other bands to do the same.

A punk discography issued in 1982 (International Discography of the New Wave) catalogued 16,000 records, issued by no less than 3000 different labels. For each label this works out at about five records, many of the 'companies' issuing only one record (put out by the founders of the label). Most of the record companies were in Great Britain and the United States, but there were issues from Iceland, New Zealand, Finland and other exotic places. Some of these self-financed records turned out to be surprising hits. 'Spiral Scratch', a record by the Buzzcocks (on the New Hormones label), sold 15,000 copies, at which stage the 'real' record shops grew interested. Most of them were distributed by hand or by mail order. Distribution of the records was helped by new magazines run by fans, 'fanzines', which achieved respectable circulations when the wave was at its peak.

In the late 1970s rock was dominated by smooth disco dance music. The former manager of The Who, Robert Stigwood, a young business genius, conceived the idea of a film whose subject was fanatical disco dancers. The movie was produced by Paramount, the record of songs from the show was released by PolyGram. The film, *Saturday Night Fever*, became an international phenomenon, once again testifying to the combined power of the record and film industries. The star of the film, John Travolta, decorated the colour pages of the world's weekly magazines. At the same time there evolved in the rock world an international distribution system which was an alternative to the old record companies. Of course this did not prevent the most successful groups from recording for the multinational conglomerates. Encouraged by their success, the Buzzcocks signed a contract with United Artists. The Clash and the Vibrators recorded for CBS. EMI could boast 4-Skins, X-Ray Specs, the Human League and the Angelic Upstarts (the names of the groups were an important part of their image). Gradually, though, between the giants of the business and the one-record, backstreet amateurs there arose companies to be taken seriously in the sphere of the new music just like those in the United States in the fifties.

Stiff Records was set up in 1976 by two young men who had grown up on the fringes of the rock business: Dave Robinson and Jake Jakeman. The founders borrowed £45 from a well-known group (Dr Feelgood) and released Nick Lowe's single, 'So It Goes', which did not attract very much attention. Their first records were mainly sold by post. The publicity being given to punk rock was just then on the increase, and the label's sixth single, featuring the punk group, The Damned, was already a modest hit. Encouraged by this, Stiff signed a distribution agreement with the Island label, which had growth wealthy from reggae music. Later, EMI, and subsequently CBS, took over the wholesale side of Stiff Records in England. In five years Stiff grew into a business to be taken seriously. Among its finds were Elvis Costello, Madness and Ian Dury. All three established conspicuous international careers, although Elvis Costello soon changed labels.

By the 1980s, the concept of independent labels had become so deeply entrenched that 'indie' (or 'alternative' in the US) rock had almost become a musical genre. In the United Kingdom, a long succession of four-man guitar groups made recordings for small aspiring labels, whose products were delivered to record shops by independent distributors, and often praised by specialist magazines. But the winners of the game were usually the multinationals, who learned to buy out any new label that had nurtured a successful group.

Sources: DeFoe (1982); Laing (1985); Muirhead (1983)

Volksmusik with the Virgin Mary

Anglo-American pop music had, by the 1960s, become the prevailing style in the international record industry. When the Beatles were at the height of their career, the release of a new record by the group was hailed as a great news event on most of the world's radio stations. Local representatives of EMI would, of course, rub their hands with glee, but the four other multinational giants were also well represented in all those countries where imports were freely available at all. By the end of the sixties, in many European countries, two-thirds of the most popular records were of English or American origin. Thanks to rock music, English was well on the way to becoming a real international language.

This trend should not be exaggerated, however. Whereas in the Netherlands 80 per cent, and in West Germany 60 per cent of the most popular records were in English, in France the proportions were reversed and the *chanson* dominated the record market. Italian record buyers were almost equally patriotic. In Finland and Sweden, half of the records sold continued to be of domestic music.

The boundary between domestic and foreign is, of course, blurred: in every country Anglo-American hits were eagerly translated into the vernacular, and the rhythms of rock had an effect even on purely indigenous music. In France *la nouvelle chanson* adopted the electric guitar and the leather jacket, and Jean-Philippe Smet sold millions of records (in French) under the name Johnny Hallyday.

In various parts of Europe there are still many indigenous musical traditions that have their own faithful followers. In the 1970s many of them took on new influences and new blood from rock. This occurred in many small cultural regions. Ideas of nationality and kinship were attractive to the young, but their grandparents' music seemed hopelessly old-fashioned. And so was born the folk rock of the Basques, the Faeroese, the Lapps, the Welsh, the Luxemburgers and the Gaels; old melodies with new, partisan lyrics; electric guitars and bagpipes in the same package. These records were released by small labels in Thorshavn, Bayonne, Aberystwyth and other regional centres. The pressings were mostly small batches, but the records had an enthusiastic following. In Wales the Welsh language protest singer, Dafydd Iwan, achieved surprising success with his record 'Carlo', ridiculing Charles, Prince of Wales, though of course it was banned by the local BBC station. There were hundreds of such records appearing in Europe in the 1970s.

Alongside the radical separatist movements in Europe there is also a genuine, hard-wearing rural conservatism, which will have no truck with frivolous foreign music. German-speaking Switzerland, Christian-Social Bavaria and the western mountain regions of Austria constitute a single cultural region where people are not ashamed to wear folk costume even on working days. Speaking in dialect is a matter of honour here, the roadsides are festooned with Catholic saints' images, and the suspicion of the North still survives as a relic of the Thirty Years' War.

Obviously this region has also clung to its own music. Yodellers, brass bands and accordion groups are still the popular favourites. New songs and ditties are written in the local dialects. Even though the electric bass and saxophone are approved of in arrangements, the style is pure oompah, and the lyrics are often straight out of Catholic mythology. Saints perform miracles, the Virgin Mary grows roses in the snow, heavenly love is better than the earthly variety. After the war the big German labels were producing hundreds of these *Volksmusik* records, as they were called on the local market, in the same spirit as Americans make country music. The oompah records of the Austrian Slovene Slavko Avsenik sold in their hundreds of thousands in Germany.

In the seventies numerous small local enterprises entered the field. In Austria alone, twelve record companies specializing in indigenous music sprang up, located in places like Wörgl, Elbigenalp, Kufstein, Otztal, and such like. The German, Austrian and Swiss television networks picked up the trend by introducing an annual Grand Prix der Volksmusik contest. The winner of the 1988 contest, 'Patrona Bavariae' by the Original Naabtal Duo, became so popular that it was considered the 'coming out' of thousands of Volksmusik fans in the rest of Germany who were now ready to reveal their preference for traditional music.

Sources: Bardong *et al.* (1992); Staubmann (1984); Wallis and Malm (1984)

The Liberation of Jazz

The revolutionary jazz records by Charlie Parker and Dizzy Gillespie of the late 1940s were originally issued on 78 r.p.m. discs. In terms of harmony and rhythm they caused an upheaval in jazz, but in terms of formal structure they were bound by the three-minute playing time of the discs. When jazz began to appear on LP in the fifties, it was mainly soloists who benefited, having more room to improvise. The formal structures at the basis of the music derived from the age of the 78 r.p.m. record.

In the sixties, however, a new generation in jazz was spawned, one whose concepts of form and time were shaped by the LP age. Some of these musicians were prepared to introduce large-scale compositions to jazz along the lines of western art music. Some others wanted to free themselves completely from the fetters of composed forms and move to free improvisation, along the lines of stream-of-consciousness poetry or action painting. Among the important names spearheading the new trend were John Coltrane, Charles Mingus and Ornette Coleman. What they had in common was that they received their most important support from record labels specializing in jazz and kindred forms. A vital part in popularizing the new trend was played by the old familiar labels, Atlantic and Blue Note, along with the new jazz specialists Candid and Impulse. Contemporary, owned by Lester Koenig, released the record *Something Else*, by the alto saxophonist Ornette Coleman, which heralded a change. Coleman made his subsequent records for Atlantic and Blue Note.

Ornette Coleman was a natural child of the new jazz. He had little theoretical training in music, but he had an exceptional creative talent, guided by an inner voice. Coleman's aggressive saxophone sound and the configurations of notes he uses testify to his having listened carefully to Parker. Yet his music is completely different. The traditional 12- or 32-beat formal structures of jazz have been done away with. It is as if a poet had decided to move from rhymed to free verse while yet preserving the traditional imagery. In Ornette Coleman's solos the melody is allowed to grow freely, following its own inner logic.

Ornette Coleman's records got a mixed reception. Coleman usually played with a quartet or a trio, and the music did not demand long studio sessions, so the records were cheap to make. Nevertheless he had to take long breaks from recording. It took over a decade before his ideas gained wider currency. Yet Coleman was not the only one to examine the possibilities of expanding the freedom of the soloist. Among the slightly older musicians, Miles Davis, Charles Mingus and John Coltrane had been seeking a solution to the problem of the 'liberation of jazz' at the same time. As the LP became the established medium for the dissemination of jazz, there were opportunities to use more ambitious structures than before. Miles Davis, the only one of this group of musicians to record for the big CBS label, made use of Gil Evans's skilful orchestration as a framework for his solos and brought a sort of concerto form to jazz, in which the soloist's part was improvised, often on the basis of modal scales. In the sixties he returned to small groups, and at the end of the decade developed an original fusion of jazz and rock, including the electronic distortion of the trumpet sound.

Charles Mingus was a bassist and composer who had a long musical career behind him, stretching back to the forties. He had written bold arrangements for Lionel Hampton's band and had played with Charlie Parker. At one stage in the early fifties he owned the Debut record company together with drummer Max Roach, but this was short-lived. When one looks at Mingus's discography one finds that from the early fifties onwards he was making a couple of LP records a year. His collaboration with the record companies, however, never lasted beyond a second record. In 1964/65 he again had to resort to starting up his own label to get his music released. This time its name was Charles Mingus Records.

Mingus was a man torn by inner conflicts, one whose ambition outstripped his ability to fulfil it in practice. The records often seem half-finished, the arrangements were rehearsed in the studio only when recording was due to start, the lists of musicians vary from one record to the next. All the same, records like *Tijuana Moods* (1957, RCA), *Mingus Dynasty* (1959, CBS), *Charles Mingus Presents Charles Mingus* (on the short-lived Candid label, 1960) and *Mingus, Mingus, Mingus, Mingus, Mingus* (1963, Impulse) still sound fresh and bold. As a bassist Mingus was one of the greatest of his time. As a composer and bandleader he painted with a broad brush. In the mid-fifties he gave up musical notation, at which he was very skilled, and began teaching his compositions orally to his musicians. He would build his compositions on previously planned solo passages, collective improvisations and written parts which often quoted from different eras of jazz. His method was reminiscent of Duke Ellington's way of working, even though Mingus never had a regular orchestra at his disposal as Ellington did. He was also among the first to link jazz to the political debate of his time, with compositions bearing names like *Faubus Fables* (after a well-known racist politician), *Oh Lord, don't let them drop that atomic bomb on me* and *All the things you could be by now if Sigmund Freud's wife was your mother*. Mingus was not fully able to realize all his ideas, and some of them are buried on records that have been rarities for a long time, but he may be regarded as the first composer to develop large forms drawn purely from the traditions of jazz.

If Ornette Coleman was a pioneer, John Coltrane was, until his death in 1967, the most brilliant soloist of the new jazz. Coltrane, a tenor saxophonist, had been a practising musician since 1945, and in the late fifties had played in Miles Davis's respected band. Under his own name he was, at the same time, making a series of fairly ordinary records, first for Prestige and then for Atlantic. In 1960 Coltrane established his own quartet, including the pianist, McCoy Tyner, and drummer, Elvin Jones. The quartet marked a rebirth for Coltrane. Out of the former sideman a soloist had grown, rising above all the rest. Unlike Ornette Coleman, Coltrane did not entirely abandon the traditional harmonic and formal structures of jazz, but he favoured simple folk tunes or themes akin to them (*Greensleeves, My Favorite Things*), from which he concentrated the basic scales as the framework for his solos. And Coltrane's solos grew; in his final phase one number took up both sides of an LP.

The first records by Coltrane's new quartet appeared on the Atlantic label in 1960, but the following year he moved to ABC Paramount's brand new jazz specialist label, Impulse, which released all the rest of his work. The chief producer at Impulse was Bob Thiele, under whose direction it became the most important jazz label of the sixties. In five years Impulse put out over 100 LP discs. The records had stylish folding covers and they cost a dollar more than ordinary records. Impulse and Coltrane grew side by side. Coltrane became the most influential new jazz musician of the sixties, a model for young jazz musicians all over the world. On Coltrane's recommendation, Thiele also released records by many then still unknown soloists, and in this way Archie Shepp, among others, came to public notice. But not even Impulse was able to release everything. Bob Thiele has recalled that Coltrane brought him a list of 400 promising musicians.

Sales figures for the new jazz records were generally modest. Coltrane's influence, however, was so broad that his most famous record, *A Love Supreme*, has sold a million copies over twenty years. When Coltrane died in 1967, Impulse could not find another soloist of such brilliance, and Thiele had to negotiate with the saxophonist's widow over the release of the tapes he left behind. In recompense, Impulse had to release a number of records by Mrs Alice Coltrane which might not otherwise have seen the light of day. Impulse gave up its activities in the seventies, having lived for a long time off Coltrane's heritage.

The new jazz was difficult. For the jazz-loving public it was hard to get to grips with a music which lacked so many of the familiar elements. Although, at its best, it radiated an almost hypnotic power, not all soloists had Coltrane's charisma. For lesser-known musicians it was difficult to get work, and audiences walking out of jazz concerts began to become a familiar sight. In this situation some of the musicians had to resort to self-financed records, which they then sold at their concerts or by post. In Chicago, the bandleader-composer, Sun Ra (Herman Blount), had to put out his entire production of music tinged with space mysticism at his own expense (as far as is known over 50 records of his own music have appeared on Sun Ra's Saturn label). Young musicians often had to make their first records themselves. Under these circumstances there was an opportunity waiting for ESP-Disc, founded in 1963 by the New York lawyer, Bernard Grossman. Grossman, who was, incidentally, Dizzy Gillespie's lawyer, was interested in many esoteric cultural manifestations. The label's first release was a collection of songs sung in Esperanto, the aim of which was to promote the spread of this international language. Soon ESP-Disc was specializing in the work of radical young New York jazz musicians, who had taken many steps forward from the reforms of Ornette Coleman and John Coltrane.

The most important ESP-Disc artist was the tenor saxophonist, Albert Ayler. Ayler, born in 1936 in Cleveland, had played in local jazz and rhythm 'n' blues bands as a young man. In 1962 he wandered around Europe. On his first ESP disc, released in 1964, he had already broken his ties with tradition. Ayler believed he had got his music from higher powers, magnificent angels whose brightness exceeded even that of the sun. His themes, which were often quotations, were simple, almost childish. The solos sounded as if in his hands the saxophone had changed into a new, unknown instrument. It emitted notes that rarely even had an identifiable pitch, but were rather a mass of sound rushing forward, howling, screeching, whining or whispering, driven onward by the drums and bass. In November 1970 Ayler disappeared, and three weeks later his body was found in the East River in New York.

ESP-Disc eventually gave up its activities, but before it closed its catalogue was graced by the radical New York groups, the Fugs and Pearls Before Swine. Tuli Kupferberg, the leader of the Fugs, had previously published literary magazines, and the group constituted a bridge between rock and modern poetry. Thanks to the pioneers of the sixties, the barriers between the various modes of music began to lose their significance in the seventies. Jazz and rock musicians began to play more often together, and the differences between their musics became ever harder to distinguish. Miles Davis experienced a revival with rock musicians. When CBS released a record in 1977, produced by Phil Spector, on which the poets Leonard Cohen, Allen Ginsberg and Bob Dylan sang together, hardly anyone raised an eyebrow. But just like poets who have to publish their own debut volumes, more and more musicians nowadays have to release their own records for their music to reach the public.

Source: Priestley (1988)

Chris Strachwitz and the Blues Renaissance

Chris Strachwitz's family was among the millions of Germans from eastern Europe who had to move westwards out of the path of the Red Army as a consequence of the Second World War. The Strachwitz's journey was longer than most: the family moved to the United States, and young Chris went to school in California, where the tall, thin German boy was taunted with the nickname 'Pencil'. In his spare time he listened to the exotic sounds of small radio stations: rhythm 'n' blues on the black stations; Mexican accordionists on the Hispanic stations. Throughout the fifties he also assembled a considerable collection of old blues records, which could be bought cheaply at flea markets.

In the early sixties, traditional blues was not being released on record at all. The black public was listening to the Motown sound; jazz lovers would only accept jazz-related singers such as Bessie Smith and Jimmy Witherspoon. Chris Strachwitz decided to set up his own record label, and chose its name, Arhoolie, from on old work song. He made his first recording on a tape recorder in Clarksdale and Dallas in 1960. The performers were lesser-known old singers who had only made a few records in their time, such as Mance Lipscomb, Mercy Dee Walton and Alex Moore. Arhoolie LP 1001, Mance Lipscomb's *Texas Songster*, was released in November 1960. The first pressing of the record was 250 copies. Chris Strachwitz had sold part of his record collection to finance the release of his first records. Arhoolie operated on a shoestring for a long time; records were sold to collectors by post and through small specialist shops.

Soon, however, Strachwitz noticed that things were turning in his favour. Many other young music enthusiasts and musicians began to take an interest in blues. In 1963 the journal *Blues Unlimited* began to appear in England. A couple of years later, new groups such as the Butterfield Blues Band, Canned Heat and the Blues Project in the United States, and Fleetwood Mac, John Mayall and Alexis Korner in England, were starting to play blues to ever greater audiences. Old blues legends from the twenties, thought to be long dead, were discovered to be alive and fit to play. The new blues bands gravitated towards the big record labels as their popularity grew. Vanguard snapped up renowned blues singers of the older generation such as Son House and Mississippi John Hurt. It fell to Arhoolie to present the lesser-known singers and to reissue historic blues records in its specially created Blues Classics series. The company's sales went on growing steadily as groups that had risen to the top of the rock world recorded tunes borrowed from old blues records.

In the 1970s Chris Strachwitz's interest turned more and more towards the music of other minorities in the United States. Ever since Napoleonic times there had been a French population, *cajuns*, living in Louisiana, whose music had, over the years, blended with the blues. Arhoolie's most significant find in Louisiana was Clifton Chenier, whose rock sung in French dialect to accordion accompaniment is worth hearing. California and Texas, on the other hand, had once belonged to Mexico, and in the boom years after the war new immigrants came pouring over the southern boundary into these states in an unbroken stream – some of them legal immigrants, some secretly swimming across the river – 'wetbacks'. Ever since the thirties the Mexicans of Texas had been developing their own musical tradition, which Strachwitz began to capture in his extensive 'Tex-Mex' series.

In the 1980s Arhoolie, like many other small labels, got into financial difficulties, and the range of its issues had to be restricted. Nevertheless it continues on a smaller scale. Arhoolie is an example of how one man's efforts in the right place at the right time can move mountains. The Arhoolie tradition is carried on by the Austrian blues fanatic, Johnny Partch, who has started to release – at his own expense – a series of records whose eventual aim is to reissue every single blues record released before the Second World War (about 30,000 recordings).

The Pirates

In the early 1970s *Newsweek* magazine estimated that in the United States over 200 million dollars' worth of illegally manufactured records and cassettes are sold annually. The figure meant that over ten per cent of the country's record sales were of 'bootleg' products, copied without the permission of the record company or the artist, for which no royalties had been paid to the performer or the composer, or to the taxman either.

Ever since musical performances have been recorded on tape, the manufacturing of records has been a relatively simple and cheap business. To this of course must be added the printing of the covers by a printer, but what one pays for on a record is not the vinyl on which it is pressed but the music captured in its grooves. This was understood in the sixties, as the record market grew, by scores of shady dealers who started releasing unlicensed copies of hit records. The records were made 'on the side' after working hours at some well-known record-pressing plant and usually sold through ordinary record stores. Particularly in the United States, Italy and many Third World countries, pirate production has at times reached industrial proportions.

Most of the pirates released records which were forgeries – copies made as faithfully as possible of records available on the market. Of course it was easiest to sell records that were already 'in the charts'. Usually organized crime was behind the forgeries, record manufacturing being an easy way to make money. There were also operators in a 'grey area' of the industry, however, who were involved more from a love of the music than for financial gain. They began releasing records made from tapes of concerts, radio broadcasts or other performances by famous artists which were not available at all on record. Those most frequently 'bootlegged' artist of the sixties was Bob Dylan, a singer who had become a cult figure.

The late sixties were a revolutionary period in American culture. The Vietnam War was being bitterly opposed by students, and student organizations were radicalized. The hippie movement spawned its own counter-culture with its underground magazines. Dylan himself was a withdrawn, mysterious figure who, in his ambiguous statements, refused to offer easy solutions. 'Don't follow leaders, watch the parkin' meters,' he sang in his 'Subterranean Homesick Blues'. But the alternative movements needed a prophet. Dylan's songs became the hallmarks of the radicalized youth of the decade. The extreme left-wing Weathermen group, which blew up draft offices and army premises during the Vietnam War, even took its name from one of Dylan's songs.

In 1965 Dylan had released his album, *Highway 61 Revisited*, on which he had radically changed his style. Electric guitars and drums appeared behind the harmonica-playing folk singer. The new style was continued on *Blonde on Blonde*, which appeared the following year. His disciples were perplexed; it was as if the Pope had got married. Articles appeared in the underground press whose authors claimed to know what Dylan *really* meant. A.J.Weberman, who ran a Dylan column in the *East Village Other* paper, gathered material for his column by regularly rummaging through the garbage bins in Dylan's back yard.

In the midst of all the fuss, on 29 June 1966 Dylan had a motorcycle accident. There were conflicting reports about Dylan's injuries, but the singer cancelled all his concerts and withdrew from the public eye completely for a year and a half. His fans were desperate. In summer 1967 Dylan was present at some rehearsals with The Band in the cellar of a house in Woodstock, New York, and there he recorded a number of new songs. They included 'I Shall Be Released', 'Tears of Rage' and 'This Wheel's on Fire'. He sent copies of the tape to Manfred Mann, The Byrds and other artists who had previously recorded his songs, but it was not his intention to issue the tapes otherwise. (Manfred Mann's version of the song 'Mighty Quinn' sold two million copies.)

These second-hand interpretations were not enough for the fans, however. It was as if a prophet had kept his latest revelation from his disciples. Copies of the copies of the tape were made, and hidden messages were sought in them. In summer 1969 a record, packaged in a white sleeve, without a label, appeared in a few Los Angeles record shops; it rapidly became known as the 'Great White Wonder'. On the record were Dylan's 'Basement Tapes'.

According to *Rolling Stone* magazine, the record had been put out by 'Patrick' and 'Merlin', two young men who were evading the draft and Vietnam, and who subsequently fled to Canada on the proceeds of the record. They had 'seen it as their duty to put Dylan's songs into the hands of the people'. It was a painful job to distribute the 8000 copies they pressed, because the 'businessmen' did not even have a car, and deliveries to the shops had to be made in borrowed vehicles. The original pressing soon sold out, and once the entrepreneurs had left the country new pressings appeared on the market, which Dylan's record company, CBS, did its best to stop. It is claimed that over 40,000 copies of the various pressings of the record were sold (other sources claim 300,000). As usual, Dylan kept silent, and his many fans accepted the new record as the word of a god.

The success of the 'Great White Wonder' set a whole underground record industry in motion. Recordings made without permission were called 'bootlegs' –

'bootlegger' originally referred to an illicit distiller during the Prohibition era. More tapes of Dylan appeared on the market, as did concert recordings of the Beatles, the Rolling Stones and other rock artists. A long-haired entrepreneur known as 'Bud' even set up a record company named Rubber Dubber, which specialized in almost publicly releasing illegal concert recordings. The company was alleged to have 50 employees. The nature of the business is indicated somewhat by the fact that one of its salesmen was shot on a visit to a customer. Dylan's biographer, Robert Shelton, calculates that, altogether, 160 bootleg albums of Dylan appeared on the market. The fun ended in 1971, when United States copyright law was revised and heavy penalties were imposed for unlicensed publications. In 1975 Dylan's Basement Tapes were finally given official release (though slightly altered); they can be bought in a record shop, but the sweet taste of forbidden fruit is gone.

The activity of the pirates was by no means restricted to rock. Keen collectors of opera records will know of Edward J. Smith (1913–84), an opera fanatic who, from 1956 to 1983, issued nearly 800 LPs of radio broadcasts by famous singers, reissues of long deleted historic records and even first recordings of such rarities as Sibelius's opera, *The Maid in the Tower*.

Eddie Smith's mother had been a concert pianist and a pupil of Josef Hoffman, and in the 1920s the family spent each summer touring the musical centres of Europe listening to Gigli, Godowsky, Shalyapin and the other celebrities of the decade. Giovanni Martinelli was a close friend of the family. Having tried his hand at journalism, in 1951 Eddie Smith became a record producer, and was commissioned by American companies to record operas in Rome. From 1954 to 1958 he worked for the Allegro label in New York, which released cheap records for cut-price stores. Allegro is notorious among collectors for its many recordings of famous artists under assumed names. At the same time he set up as a producer himself. The records appeared on the E.J.S., A.N.N.A. and Unique Opera Recordings labels. The pressings were small and the covers as austere as possible. The first E.J.S. records were reissues of historic operatic records, which were distributed among collectors, but soon Eddie Smith started also releasing unique recordings: radio broadcasts from the Metropolitan and La Scala from the thirties onward, home recordings and other rarities. Often he was allowed by grateful customers to use their own tapes. Entire recordings of operas released by E.J.S. included Korngold's *Die tote Stadt* and *Violanta*, Gomes's *Il Guarany* and Massenet's *Hériodade*, all of them works that were rarely seen in commercial record catalogues at the time. Among the curiosities there is also Frank Sinatra singing *Don Giovanni* – that too taken from a radio broadcast. Evidently Smith was often able to borrow tapes directly from the staff of American radio stations; in this way, for example, the Finnish Broadcasting Company's tape of Sibelius's rarely-heard opera, *The Maid in the Tower*, ended up on record, having been sent from Finland to the United States as part of a programme exchange.

Smith's activities were known throughout the business, but he was regarded as doing cultural work of little economic significance, so that his efforts were not seriously hampered even after the change in the law in 1971. Today it is impossible to write the history of opera singing without reference to the records he released. In 1971 Eddie Smith contracted cancer and gave up his activities for a time. A friend of his once asked him which operatic aria he would like to hear if he could hear only one before his death. The answer was easy: 'Che gelida manina', Rodolfo's famous aria from *La Bohème*. But performed by whom? Ever since Caruso all the important tenors have recorded it – there are nearly 500 versions. It was impossible to choose the best one. Instead Eddie Smith responded by compiling as his testament a series of six LPs on which are what he considered the 100 best interpretations of this aria, including several which have never been released elsewhere.

Sources: Davis (1981); Heylin (1994); Shaman (1994)

Ten Million Lieder

As late as 1971 the head of EMI Records, Len Wood, calculated that of the company's sales throughout the world, about eleven per cent was of concert or classical music. In England the share of serious music was then as much as fourteen per cent; it was about the same in Japan and West Germany. Relatively speaking, EMI produced more classical music than most other record companies. Furthermore, we can assume that by far the greatest share in the growth of the record business since 1971 has applied to music other than classical. Overall, the proportion of classical music in record sales worldwide is between five and ten per cent. This may seem slight, but if 2500 million recordings are sold in the world each year, then even five per cent of that figure is quite substantial.

In some respects the world of concert music can be compared to professional sport. It too has its world champions, its national stars and its provincial series, and the competition is at least as fierce. It is expensive to record orchestral music and opera: a large infrastructure is needed for the performers, and plenty of studio time, and internationally renowned conductors and soloists do not come cheap. On the other hand concert music forms only a relatively small sector of the record market. To cover the production costs of records, they have to be sold worldwide. This is best achieved by the large multinational companies which have also signed contracts with the most famous artists in the industry.

It may be instructive to look more closely at the careers of three internationally known artists of the record industry. All three are in their own fields among the most brilliant talents of their generation, but their relations with recording differ markedly from one another. These are the German singer, Dietrich Fischer-Dieskau (b. 1925), the Austrian conductor, Herbert von Karajan (1908–89) and the Canadian pianist, Glenn Gould (1932–82).

Dietrich Fischer-Dieskau's youth was passed in the war – he was a prisoner of war in Italy – but in 1949 he was ready to start his singing career. He got his first engagement with the Vienna State Opera in 1949, and since then he has regularly appeared on the leading operatic stages of Europe in the major baritone roles. Besides his operatic career, however, he has continuously appeared with great success as a solo singer in concerts. The lieder of Schubert, Brahms and Schumann enjoy popular favour in the German-speaking area, and in the 1950s, Fischer-Dieskau became known as their greatest interpreter. The great singers of the previous generation had created a style which emphasized the beautiful, smooth execution of these songs. Fischer-Dieskau brought to the concert platform a new, psychological mode of interpretation, which emphasizes the content of the text without consigning the music to second place. It depends on the listener's mood and temperament to which aspect he gives priority, but Fischer-Dieskau's interpretations have indisputably been just as significant a transformation in lied singing as was the arrival of the new generation of singers for Italian opera after the turn of the century.

Fischer-Dieskau made his first record for Deutsche Grammophon in the late 1940s. He was involved in the recording of the first Bach recordings for the Archiv series and he also recorded lieder for DGG, but that company, which was gradually recovering from the war, could not offer the rising young star such favourable terms as its competitors. In 1951 he visited London at the invitation of Sir Thomas Beecham to sing in a performance of Delius's *A Mass of Life*, and gave his own Schubert concert at the same time. Walter Legge of EMI engaged him to record Schubert's song cycle, *Die schöne Müllerin* for His Master's Voice. At the same time he also recorded songs by Beethoven and Schumann. The accompanist was Gerald Moore.

Thus began ten years of fruitful collaboration between EMI and Fischer-Dieskau, the artistic culmination of which may be seen as the recording of Schubert's *Winterreise* cycle in 1955, again accompanied by Gerald Moore. Fischer-Dieskau took part in many of EMI's large opera productions, and continued his solo recordings alongside these. Thus he was involved in Furtwängler's recording of *Tristan and Isolde* in London in June 1952 – one which has since acquired a legendary reputation – and stayed on for another day in the studio to record Schumann's *Liederkreis*. Fischer-Dieskau's lied records were a great success, and he went on to record some of the central sung repertoire, again for EMI, after the arrival of stereo. In the 1960s he went back to Deutsche Grammophon, recording again the same repertoire. Fischer-Dieskau has recorded, from beginning to end, the entire vocal output of Schubert, Schumann and Wolf, as well as a large number of songs by Brahms, Beethoven, Loewe, Liszt and Mendelssohn. Of the *Winterreise* we have a choice of four readings by Fischer-Dieskau with different pianists, of the *Schwanengesang* three. Naturally he has also recorded a large body of more exotic vocal works, for example by Hans Werner Henze and Charles Ives. In the 1970s he became keen on orchestral conducting, and in 1973 he recorded for the first time as a conductor, for EMI again (Schubert's fifth symphony). According to the latest figures, more than ten million of Dietrich Fischer-Dieskau's records have been sold. The huge number can be seen in perspective when we recall that his career spans forty years, during which he has made hundreds of records. Many of these are of the best-known classical vocal repertoire, and many critics have regarded Fischer-Dieskau's interpretations as the best recordings of these songs. Elvis Presley's 'It's Now or Never' alone has sold more than twice as many copies as Fischer-Dieskau's entire output. All the same, ten million records is about the same as Finland's annual record sales.

Source: Sanders (1984)

The Karajan Phenomenon

Herbert von Karajan (1908–89) was an Austrian conductor who, perhaps more clearly than anyone else, became an idol of the musical world on the scale of Toscanini after the war. The young musician had decided to become a conductor after hearing Toscanini conducting in Vienna, and even in the 1930s he had embarked on a promising career in the musical centres of Greater Germany. In 1935 he was appointed leader of the Aachen city orchestra and in 1938 conductor of the Berlin State Opera, and he made his first records for Polydor the same year.

Between 1939 and 1943 Karajan recorded a considerable body of work, including Tchaikovsky's *Pathétique* symphony, Beethoven's seventh and Brahms's first symphonies, all of course on 78 r.p.m. discs. From 1933 Karajan had been a member of the Nazi Party, and after the defeat of Germany the occupying American forces banned him from performing until 1947. In 1946 Walter Legge travelled to Vienna to sign up new artists for EMI. He had heard Karajan in Aachen before the war and definitely wanted him as an artist for his label. As interpreted by the British occupation officials, the ban on Karajan only applied to public performances and not to recording for a British record company, and so on 3 September 1946 he conducted the Vienna Philharmonic at the Musikvereinsaal, when they recorded Beethoven's eighth symphony. The petrol to run the motor of the recording equipment was bought on the black market. Culture – and business – rapidly wiped away the memory of hostilities during the war, but Karajan was never welcomed in Israel.

Overcoming this obstacle, Karajan quickly rose to become one of the leading conductors in Europe. In the early fifties Wilhelm Furtwängler was conductor of both the Berlin and the Vienna Philharmonic, so Karajan, being his junior, had to content himself with the guest role with both orchestras. On the other hand he did conduct the rival Vienna Symphony, visited Bayreuth and La Scala and recorded regularly in London with Walter Legge's Philharmonia Orchestra. When Furtwängler died in 1954, Karajan ascended rapidly to his throne and extended his empire still further: in 1955 he was appointed conductor of the Berlin Philharmonic for life, in 1957 artistic director of the Vienna State Opera, and in the same year to the same post with the Salzburg Festival. He now had in his hands the core of Central European musical life. Not even Toscanini before him had held such power in his grasp.

In 1959 Karajan left EMI, made a series of recordings for Decca with the Vienna Philharmonic and the same year embarked on an extensive series of recordings with the Berlin Philharmonic for Deutsche Grammophon. He now recorded a vast series of operas and a large proportion of the classical orchestral repertoire, some of it several times. During his career he recorded all Beethoven's symphonies at least four times, in mono, in stereo, with the Vienna Philharmonic, the Berlin Philharmonic and the Philharmonia Orchestra. (He made as many as six recordings of the seventh symphony.) In the sixties Karajan's reputation had reached almost supernatural proportions. His sports cars, jet planes and yachts were a regular subject for magazine articles.

Karajan said on various occasions that he regarded records as a better means of disseminating music than the traditional concert. He was always interested in technology and participated in the processing of recordings himself. (After Karajan's death, when the original tapes of his recordings were examined with a view to reissues, it was noted that sometimes he had drastically altered the dynamics of the orchestra on the tape afterwards.) In the classical record industry he took on a status that could perhaps best be compared to that of the Beatles in the rock business.

At one stage, one-third of the DGG records sold in England were Karajan's recordings. It was time to aim for greater financial independence. In 1965 Karajan established a company called Cosmotel to produce operatic films for European television companies. *La Bohème* was directed by Franco Zeffirelli, *Otello* by Karajan himself. Production costs for the film, however, exceeded all prior estimates, and plans for further productions were thus dropped. In 1968 his contract binding him exclusively to record for DGG ran out. Karajan no longer agreed to sign similar contracts. Instead he began producing his own records, and for their release he contracted with no less than three big labels: EMI, DGG and Decca. He was himself responsible for the choice of repertoire and soloists, the production schedule and even for the design of the record covers (which often included paintings by Mrs Eliette von Karajan).

In 1983 Karajan returned to films, this time with immortality in mind. He set up the Telemondial company, whose aim was to film the maestro's entire repertoire. According to a press release from the company, the performances will be issued on videodisc once this new medium has reached the required level of perfection. When Karajan died in 1989 he left behind him on record the entire central repertoire of symphonies and operas, a considerable proportion of it recorded twice or three times. The catalogue of well-known orchestral works which Karajan has not recorded is indeed small. Karajan's readings of Mozart have been called superficial. He recorded painfully little of the music of our own century, but the blame evidently lies more with the record companies than with the conductor. Some of the famous 'Karajan sound' is definitely just as much due to the brilliant orchestras, as to their Kapellmeister. But Karajan will live long: he had already prepared for the eventual advent of the videodisc.

Sources: Hunt (1987); Sanders (1984)

Glenn Gould and the Idea of North

Even in the era of the gramophone record there are influential artists who are reluctant to perform on disc or do not do it at all. The conductor Sergiu Celibidache is one example of these men of strong principle. Apart from in his misspent youth (with the Berlin Philharmonic, 1945–50), he has stubbornly refused to record, because listening to records is 'like going to bed with a picture of Brigitte Bardot'. If one wants to hear Celibidache conducting and cannot hear him live or on the radio, the only possibility is to get hold of one of the pirate recordings of his radio broadcasts made for collectors. A completely opposite view is represented by the Canadian pianist, Glenn Gould. Having toured the concert platforms of the world between 1955 and 1964 he came to the conclusion that public performance before an audience was degrading.

Glenn Gould's retirement from the concert platform was by no means due to a lack of success on it. He had been one of the superstars of the piano, an eccentric of the order of Pachmann, who might fiddle with endless adjustments to the height of his stool or play in a cold concert hall with gloves cut off at the fingers. The tempos he chose were often extremely slow or extremely fast. The public accepted unquestioningly his extraordinary choices of repertoire. For Gould, there had been nothing in the history of music between Bach and Wagner. Beethoven was a composer 'whose reputation was based entirely on rumour'. Once when he deigned to play Beethoven's fourth piano concerto in New York, he had with him a glass of water from which he took refreshment during the orchestral passages. The public loved him, and his engagement calendar was full. But he gave his last concert in Chicago on 28 March 1964.

The microphone was his best friend, and Gould also enjoyed writing (often under the pen-name Dr Herbert von Hockmeister). He continued his career in the studio and the newspaper columns, as a producer of records and radio programmes and as a music journalist. Even his first records in 1955 had aroused great interest. Since Wanda Landowska the harpsichord had been thought the only proper means of interpreting Bach, but Gould was unashamed to play Bach on a modern piano. His *Goldberg Variations* are perhaps not 'authentic' but they are masterful and original. After 1964 Gould's recorded output continued with renewed vigour. His entire recorded production was released through CBS; yet in the memoirs of the company's director, Clive Davis, he rates no more than a passing mention.

Glenn Gould had always been interested in recording technology. Only in a studio, he thought, could a musician give of his best. He once wrote of the famous Culshaw/Solti *Ring* cycle that it 'attains a more effective unity between intensity of action and displacement of sound than could be afforded by the best of all seasons at Bayreuth'. Gould claimed that during his concerts he frequently felt the need to interrupt his performance and repeat a particular section of a work again, because the first take didn't work. When he got involved in record production, he found to his delight that he could do just that.

Gould's most famous record in this respect is his interpretation of the fugue in A minor in Bach's *Das wohltemperierte Klavier*. When Gould recorded it in the studio in 1965, he played it eight times. Two of them, takes 6 and 8, were technically faultless, but different in tone. Take 6 was played in a solemn legato, take 8 in a playful staccato. Each of them, however, was monotonous in Gould's opinion. But why not join them together?

Once this decision had been made, it was a simple matter to expedite it. It was obvious that the somewhat overbearing posture of take 6 was entirely suitable for the opening exposition as well as for the concluding statements of the fugue, while the more effervescent character of take 8 was a welcome relief in the episodic modulations with which the center portion of the fugue is concerned. And so two rudimentary splices were made, one which jumps from take 6 to take 8 in bar 14 and another which at the return to A minor (I forget in which measure, but you are invited to look for it) returns as well to take 6. What had been achieved was a performance of this particular fugue far superior to anything that we could at the time have done in the studio.

(*High Fidelity* magazine in 1966)

Later he planned even more far-reaching experiments. Why not, for example, record piano works using a different microphone and different acoustics for each part: one with the close microphone favoured by Gould himself, another from slightly further away (the 'DGG sound', as he put it) and, the third at the end of the hall? This would give the impression of the pianist moving as the performance progressed. The idea was carried out for the first time in France on one of his television programmes. On record it can be heard at least in his recording of Sibelius's sonatinas. In programmes made for Canadian radio he continued his exploitation of recording technology. One famous programme was called *The Idea of North*. It has nothing to do with music, but is a documentary about the people of the polar regions. Yet it was made in a musical way: Gould cut and copied people's narratives on top of one another so that they composed a sort of fugue.

Having given up public performance Gould made recordings for twenty years. His recordings of Schoenberg's piano works, particularly, are regarded as a breakthrough. He recorded plenty of Bach, English virginal music, most of Beethoven's piano sonatas (despite his disdain for the composer), Liszt's piano arrangement of Beethoven's fifth symphony, which is regarded as a curiosity, as well as an interesting interpretation of Sibelius's *Kyllikki*. Gould had promised to give up completely at the age of 50. He died of a heart attack on 4 October 1982, just after his fiftieth birthday.

As an interpreter of classical music Gould has proved an exception. Scarcely anyone else has, to such a great extent, been able to build a career on recording (even Gould had a short but brilliant concert career as a basis for his record sales). Yet perhaps a time will come when someone will take Gould's ideas to their logical conclusion.

Source: Page (1984, quote pp. 338–9)

Putting Ragas on the World Map

The Monterey Pop Festival of 16–18 June 1967 in California has passed into history for many reasons. The roster of performers was impressive, although many of the artists on it only became more widely known after the festival. It included Jimi Hendrix, Otis Redding, Janis Joplin, The Doors, The Who, Jefferson Airplane, The Butterfield Blues Band and Ravi Shankar.

Ten years earlier an Indian sitar player at a rock festival would have seemed just as serious a breach of style as an electric guitar at a symphony concert. In the sixties, however, Indian music had become known in the west primarily thanks to the records and tours by the virtuoso player, Ravi Shankar. George Harrison had studied under Shankar and, inspired by him, had played sitar on the Beatles' records. The previous year, the Butterfield Blues Band had recorded an album called *East/West*, on the title track of which the guitarists Mike Bloomfield and Elvin Bishop had done their best to create the atmosphere of Indian music. As early as 1961 John Coltrane had recorded a number called *India*, and in the sixties many jazz and rock musicians discovered, to their surprise, that the Indians had long ago found something they they were still seeking.

It was no wonder that Ravi Shankar became the best-known representative of ˙Indian music throughout the world. His father-in-law and teacher was Allauddin Khan, who was said to be the most important Indian musician of his generation and a significant innovator of the improvisational style. His brother, Uday Shankar, was one of the first to popularize Indian music, travelling the world with his dance ensemble in the forties. Brother Ravi was part of the group, thus getting an opportunity to get acquainted with western musical taste. Ravi Shankar made his first record in the 78 r.p.m. era, and in 1955 he performed for the first time for a European record company in a recorded anthology of Indian music compiled by Alain Danielou, which was the first of its kind.

Ravi Shankar's discography (compiled by the Australian, Michael Kinnear) encompasses several dozen records. They include film music, duets with Yehudi Menuhin, teaching records and concert recordings from Monterey and Woodstock. The best of them, however, are interpretations of classical ragas, in which the sitar is accompanied only by the ever-present *tambura*, which plays a continuous ostinato, and the *tabla* drummer. Through Ravi Shankar, Indian music found its way into European record shops in the seventies.

In other ways, too, that decade was the golden age for recordings of Oriental music. Indigenous classical music was now being released fairly extensively on LP records in the Arab countries, Iran, India, Korea, Japan and other urbanized eastern countries. These records were not made for western audiences, but for the concert-going public in their own countries, who knew their own artists and demanded the best from them. The prime element of turnover for the record companies was popular music – in Asian countries it was film music – but there were enough customers for art music as well. In the eighties the cassette displaced the gramophone record in all Asian countries except Japan. At the same time the old record companies lost their position, and the market has been flooded with cassettes produced by small backstreet operators. It may be that future music historians will see the LP era as the last great flourishing of the traditional music of Asia.

Source: Kinnear (1985)

Melodiya

In 1964 a reorganization of the Soviet record industry was undertaken. The Ministry of Culture concentrated all record production in one enterprise, the All-Union Gramophone Record Enterprise Melodiya (Vsesoyuznaya Firma Grammofonnykh Plastinok Melodiya). Thereby Melodiya became one of the six biggest record companies in the world, though its operations encompassed only one country. During the 1960s Soviet record production grew from 100 to 200 million copies, and records were sold in more than 30,000 retail outlets. Every one of these records was made by Melodiya.

In the fifties Soviet record production had lagged far behind the western record industry in technical quality. After the reorganization, and the establishment of Melodiya, record production was modernized and diversified. Modern studio equipment was purchased from the West. Now the record industry was fully able to exploit the high standard of the performing arts in the country. Internationally-known pianists, violinists and conductors made one record after another. Melodiya even had its own orchestra, the USSR Ministry of Culture Symphony Orchestra, conducted by Svetlanov and Rozhdestvensky, which was formally part of the company. Melodiya was soon able to create a flourishing export business, usually in the form of licensing arrangements, and the company's excellent classical recordings became well known in the west. Several of the company's recordings of the compositions of Glinka, Prokofiev and Shostakovich won the Charles Cros award in France. David Oistrakh's recording of Sibelius's violin concerto, for Melodiya, ranks among the finest performances of this work.

Although all Soviet record shops were well stocked with classical music, the largest part of Melodiya's sales came from popular music. The changes that took place in Soviet popular music in the seventies are well represented by the names of Alla Pugachova and Zanna Bichevskaya. Pugachova was probably the company's best-selling artist in the seventies and eighties. Every one of her records sold millions, and would evidently have sold even more if Melodiya had been able to press them. Her biggest hit was *Million roz* ('A Million Roses'), written by the Latvian pianist, Raimonds Pauls. Pugachova combined sentimental minor-keyed Slavonic melodies with soft-rock accompaniment and a modern studio sound. It was modern entertainment for people whose musical tastes were not particularly modern. Evidently, the secret of Alla Pugachova's colossal success also lay partly in the fact that she was the first purely Russian popular singer in a field long dominated by Georgians, Jews and Moldavians.

Compared to Pugachova, Bichevskaya's sales were quite modest. Her speciality was Russian folk songs, but the difference between her and the favourite of the previous generation, Ludmila Zykina, is marked. Gone are the accordions, balalaikas and the throaty Russian voices, now the songs are performed in a bright, clear voice with the sole accompaniment of a single guitar. Ludmila Zykina's interpretations attracted the older generation who grew up on the *kolkhoz*. Bichevskaya was the Joan Baez of the Soviet Union, representing the folk song as viewed by the new urban intelligentsia.

After a cautious start, modern jazz was given the official blessing in the 1970s, and since it no longer had the taste of 'forbidden fruit' about it, the demand for jazz records gradually settled down to a small number of cognoscenti. In a land of 200 million people, even these were sufficient in number to assure continued production. After jazz, Soviet rock also eventually joined the ranks of the officially approved arts (preferably folk rock performed in Russian by groups such as Pesnyary), and thereafter the only ones excluded from studios were heavy rock groups, songwriters who were openly critical of the social order and those artists who had emigrated. (Emigration automatically meant the removal of an artist's records from the market.)

The more exotic side of Melodiya's products is represented by the artists from the Asian Soviet republics and the national minorities. Almost half the population of the Soviet Union were not Russian, and one of Melodiya's best-selling artists was the Azerbaijanian singer, Zainab Khanlarova. Ten million Uzbeks bought so many records that the Tashkent branch of Melodiya had its hands full bringing out everything from traditional folk music to Uzbek disco. One of the more unique Melodiya records of this era is an anthology of solo throat singing from the Tuva Autonomous Republic. Tuva is an area bordering on Mongolia where the ancient Mongolian singing style, in which the singer creates simultaneously a low throat sound and a second flute-like sound originating in the nasal cavity, is practised. On first hearing, the effect is striking. There was also a considerable production of the music of the Chechens and the other small nations of the Caucasus mountains, but these were hard to find even then, since they were usually released in small pressings of less than 1000 copies and soon disappeared from the market. Not many copies are likely to survive today.

Until the mid-eighties, the centralized production system of the Soviet Union worked relatively well in the record industry. The Melodiya monopoly made production economic, and records were considerably cheaper than in the west. Nearly every pop record that got onto the Melodiya release schedule sold hundreds of thousands of copies. The income from that went to support a broad, if somewhat conservative, classical music schedule, and at times has also supported the needs of the ethnic minorities. And since there were no competitors on the market peddling a dozen different interpretations of the major symphonies and concertos, even the basic classical repertoire sold in respectable amounts.

At Melodiya, the vinyl era lasted right until the end of Soviet regime. Throughout the seventies, annual sales had been close to 200 million records. In the early eighties, there appeared both signs of change and breakdown. Sales were declining, not because of lack of demand but because of production problems. In the Gorbachev era new winds began to blow. The most obvious sign of reform was the return of Vladimir Vysotsky to the record catalogues. The actor had been the Bob Dylan of the Soviet Union, a cult figure whose grave is still visited daily by fans. During his life he made a few records for Melodiya, but most of his tapes lay gathering dust on the shelves. His songs, critical and often descriptive of the underworld, and his brusque manner of performing did not suit the label's line. Vysotsky's songs, on the other hand, were disseminated throughout the country in versions by amateurs and on home-made tape recordings. With the advent of *perestroika*, however, extensive series of Vysotsky's rare tape recordings appeared in the record shops. And as banned books by Solzhenitsyn, Pasternak and others began to come into the bookshops, songs by former political prisoners and ever wilder avant-garde creations were brought out on disc. One Melodiya record that perfectly illustrated the mood of 1989 was a mix of Stalin's speeches with drum solos over the top of them.

Sources: Bennett (1981); Solomatin (1989)

The Cassette – Too Good an Invention?

Recording tape had, by the 1960s, established itself as an indispensable adjunct in record production. Tape recorders were also being sold to some extent to private music lovers, but even though prices were moderate, recording tape had not attained the significance as a means of disseminating music that had been predicted for it in the late forties. Efforts to release music recorded on reel-to-reel tape had failed many times. Evidently, the easily tangled tape was an annoyance to the average citizen.

The Dutch company, Philips, however, decided to market a new, 'idiot-proof' tape recorder, which combined the easy handling of a disc with the possibility offered by tape of making recordings oneself. Legend has it that the head of the company's domestic appliance division, Coen Solleveldt, only approved the prototype of the new recorder for production after smashing it on the floor and finding that it still worked. In the Philips recorder the tape was concealed in a plastic cassette, allowing it to withstand rough handling. The cassette recorder came onto the market in 1963. Slightly different 'cartridge' models were manufactured in the United States especially for motorists, but it was not possible to record on them. Both Philips and the American inventors offered their idea to other manufacturers, and encouraged record companies to release their recordings on cassette as well as LP disc.

The first cassette players were virtually toys. Because of the slow speed of revolution the standard of sound reproduction was modest, and serious music lovers turned their noses up at the cassette player. But cassette players were cheap and easy to use, and they happened to appear at a time when European broadcasters were starting to increase the proportion of light music in their programming. After the introduction of the Dolby noise reduction system in 1966, the sound quality of cassettes dramatically improved.

Record companies soon adopted the practice of releasing new popular recordings simultaneously in LP and cassette formats. In many cases the cassettes were purchased by people who previously had not even owned a record player. In the United States, many cassettes were sold to rural country music fans. But for the international recording market the arrival of the cassette had much more dramatic consequences. Record manufacturing is a complex job, demanding professional skills. The copying of cassettes, on the other hand, is relatively simple, and can even be done in small, backyard premises. It was easy for a dishonest businessman to buy a new hit record and start making cassette copies of it at his own expense, without permission and, of course, without paying any royalties to the composer, the artist or the record company. Soon the 'piracy' of cassettes reached such proportions in many countries that the old record companies were in crisis. This trend took different forms in different countries. In the law-abiding northern European countries illegal cassette production was swiftly brought under control when the copyright laws were tightened. On the other hand, in countries where copyright was not strictly enforced, piracy in recordings reached huge proportions. In the seventies, many developing countries still had not joined the international copyright convention, and duplicating foreign recordings was not technically illegal. As a consequence, cassette players almost entirely ousted record players in the

Arab countries, in Asia, Africa and parts of South America. Cassette players were so cheap that even in the poorest developing countries a domestic cassette industry was spawned. In Ghana, where the local representatives of multinational companies had successfully sold recordings of highlife music, record production was, by the early 1990s, taken over by 2700 'dubbing shops' which turned out an estimated two million cassettes a year. Within a few years the international record companies lost the markets in the developing countries they had so patiently been hewing out ever since the days of Fred Gaisberg.

Cassette recorders were introduced to India by migrant workers returning from the affluent Gulf states. In the 1980s, the domestic consumer electronics industry started producing cassette recorders, and by 1991 the country was the world's second largest manufacturer of blank cassettes, with an annual output of 217 million cassettes (including exports). When betel-nut vendors appeared to be taking over the distribution of recorded music, record shops turned to cassettes. After 1982, vinyl records practically disappeared from the market. The Gramophone Company of India, which once had a practical monopoly in the country, now had over 200 competitors. The company sank deep into debt, until it released, in 1989, the soundtrack of the film *Mainne Pyar Kiyta*, which sold over five million cassette copies.

Film music still dominates the Indian cassette market, but a large share of it has now been taken over by devotional and regional music. At best the cassettes became the natural heir to the oral folk tradition. Regional Indian folk singers might be able to make a profit by selling just 100 copies of a self-produced cassette. In the villages on Bali, the gamelan orchestras studied multi-track recording so as to produce their own cassettes, which were then sold at the market among the vegetables and chickens. But the same vendor might also be offering home-made copies of international hits, made using the same technology.

In any event, the cassette has established itself as a cheap and versatile form of preserving sound. Portable Walkman cassette players have enabled people to take recorded music with them anywhere. Before the introduction of the compact disc, more than half of all legitimate sound recordings sold in the world were cassettes. It is an irony that, in the 1980s, Coen Solleveldt was elected chairman of the International Federation of the Phonographic Industry. In this capacity he had to make countless dire warnings of the destructive effects of the cassette piracy. The cassette turned out to be too good an invention. By the nineties, one developing country after another had yielded to pressure from the big powers to tighten their legislation, but the multinational companies still have not regained the foothold they had in the Third World before the advent of the cassette.

Sources: Manuel (1993); Wallis and Malm (1984)

From the Equator to the North Pole

With the spread of cheap cassette players in the seventies and eighties, there was hardly a corner of the world without some sort of local recording industry. One significant trend of this period was that recordings now became important even in the smallest and most distant Third World countries.

New Guinea is situated on the Equator, to the north of Australia. In the distant valleys of the island, cut off by mountains and rain forests, there are still peoples whose contacts with the outside world are intermittent. The western part of New Guinea, Irian Jaya, is occupied by Indonesia, but the eastern part became independent under the name Papua New Guinea in 1975. The country's official language is English, but the natives, who speak dozens of local languages, get on best in Pidgin, or Tok Pisin, which is a mixture of English and local languages.

The native music of New Guinea has been released in Europe and America on documentary musicological records. In the 1970s, New Guineans started buying radio sets and Hong Kong-made cassette players, and eventually an indigenous recording industry was born, whose leading figure is a Port Moresby-based Chinese businessman, Chin H. Meen, and his sons.

Cassette production in New Guinea – they do not make records – consists mostly of Christian devotional music and local rock. Most of what is put out on cassette are indigenous compositions in Tok Pisin. The bands have colourful names, such as Blue Banana Band, Ayurox, Bluff Inn Soles and Ula Ula Band. With effort, even an outsider can grasp the names of their compositions: 'Braun ais blong Ifira' is of course 'Ifira's Brown Eyes'.

The most popular group in New Guinea in the eighties was the Black Brothers, a rock group consisting of five musicians who fled from Irian Jaya, whose cassettes are a mixture of romance and Black Power politics sung in Tok Pisin. The Black Brothers are also popular in nearby Vanuatu and French New Caledonia, where the local Kanak independence movement identifies with the Brothers' ideas. But away from the Equator hardly anyone is familiar with the band.

The first Greenlandic LP, on the other hand, appeared in 1973. It was made in Denmark by a group of Eskimos studying there. They had formed a group called Sume, which performed new Greenlandic rock in the Eskimo, or Inuit, language. On the cover of the first Sume record is an ancient woodcut of a wickedly smiling Eskimo hunter who, with a knife, is cutting off the hand of a European trader he has just killed. The title track of the record, *Pivfit nutat*, gives an idea of the song lyrics:

Iternialerpunga sinissimangaarama
Ulloq ataaseq tassa ukiut untritillit

(I am waking, I have slept a long time,
The new times have begun, we have left the old behind)

(Malik Høegh)

In 1979 Greenland was given autonomous status. Inuit became the country's official language. Sume was succeeded by numerous young musicians who sang Inuit songs accompanied by electric guitars. The Greenland record industry was born. Greenland has 40,000 inhabitants. Yet in the 1980s dozens of Greenlandic records were released, with music ranging from religious songs to political rock. The Greenlanders themselves believe that records have been of great significance in creating a new Greenlandic culture, and when, in 1981, the country's government convened an 'Inuit Circumpolar Conference' in the capital, Nuuk, the event was commemorated with the release of recordings of Inuit music from Greenland, Alaska and Canada.

Sources: Lynge (1981); Niles (1984); Webb (1993)

Two or Four Channels?

Ever since the invention of sound recording the industry has always brought onto the market, every second decade or so, some technical innovation with the announcement that it signifies the perfection of sound reproduction. Electrical recording was followed by the LP disc in 1948; in 1958 was the turn of stereo. Manufacturers of both equipment and recordings have gained quite a fillip to their sales from the new technology. Their basic repertoire has had to be recorded anew three times.

The cassette had broadened the market for recordings, but had not created the need for a new repertoire. Early in the seventies, however, a new invention appeared on the market which was going to change everything again. In place of stereophony, the idea was now to introduce quadrophony – four channels instead of two. The first quadrophonic records and sound equipment were presented in New York and London in 1971, and marketing of the records began the following year.

In principle, four-channel sound reproduction was a logical continuation from the two channels of stereophony. Where two channels had created an impression of direction, four channels would also bring a sense of depth into the listener's living room. The music lover might imagine his living room transformed into a concert hall, when four speakers brought to the room an authentic impression of the listening experience, with all its reverberations. The principle had already been tried out in the cinema with good results, and the new multi-track technology in the studio offered good opportunities to produce multi-channel recordings.

And yet, relatively few music lovers had the opportunity to reserve an entire room just for listening to records, with a speaker cabinet placed permanently in every corner. The critics pointed out, mockingly, that most rooms have a door in one corner, and the hi-fi magazines were full of stories of critics' wives who had had to duck under a speaker with the coffee tray. To cap it all, a new conflict was breaking out in the industry. CBS and EMI were releasing records using their own SQ system, whereas a number of other record companies aligned themselves with the Japanese equipment manufacturer, Sansui, and produced four-channel records under the QS insignia. Of course the systems were not compatible, so that SQ equipment could not play QS records. The result was that quadrophonic sound lasted only a couple of years and was given a quiet burial. We will probably never again get the chance to hear Jascha Horenstein conducting Mahler's third symphony for Unicorn in four channels.

Thus the record makers had to await the arrival of the compact disc. The equipment manufacturers, on the other hand, had their hands full. The radiogram of the fifties had disappeared from the market once television displaced radio as the most important medium of home entertainment, and the substantial mahogany receiver in the living room was replaced by the little transistor radio in the kitchen, which might include a cassette player as well. The advent of transistors and printed circuits made the manufacture of sound recording equipment cheaper and easier, so that every person even remotely interested in music had a chance to acquire a 'stereo'.

Listening to records requires a record player, an amplifier and speakers. The same unit may also include a tape recorder – reel-to-reel or cassette – and a radio receiver. Ready-made stereo systems became the sound reproduction equivalent of the Skoda, fulfilling the basic requirements at a moderate price. For the more discriminating and wealthy listener, 'high end' equipment came onto the market, equipment of high quality made in small numbers, the Volvo, Mercedes or Rolls-Royce of sound reproduction. Although most people do buy their sound systems as a single unit, the equipment actually consists of several independent elements. The better the sound reproduction required, the greater the demands placed on each link in the chain. One of the more recent discoveries by hi-fi enthusiasts has been that when top-quality equipment is used, the quality of the cables between its elements is also significant in producing the result. Consequently, gilded plugs and cables made of silver or deoxidized copper are made to allow the electrons free movement without the resistance of normal cords. A real enthusiast can spend the same amount merely on cables that a layman pays for a radio-cassette player from a cut-price store.

Like many enthusiasms, high-end sound reproduction has its lunatic fringe, music lovers who place on their equipment greater demands than the professional sound engineer. But there is a definite need for specialized manufacturers of quality sound equipment. By the end of the 1990s, it is becoming clear that we must safeguard the continous availablity of good-quality analog record players, to ensure that we will be able to enjoy in the future also those hundreds of thousands of vinyl records which will most likely never be transferred to a digital format.

CHAPTER EIGHT

The Digital Era

The 1980s: Another Period of Transition

In 1977 the record industry celebrated the centenary of Edison's phonograph (in France, of course, they celebrated Charles Cros's invention). It was easy to believe in progress: the phonograph cylinders of the last century and the early gramophone records aroused feelings of pity and amusement in the hi-fi enthusiast of the 1970s. In fact, the record player of 1977 was based on exactly the same technology as the phonograph of 1877. The quality had improved, but the basic principle of mechanical recording was the same. In the history of inventions the gramophone record had long since passed maturity. Far-sighted observers were already anticipating change.

An era came to an end in the history of the gramophone record when John Lennon was shot in New York in December 1980. As the new decade began it was clear that the record business had entered a new phase. After the rapid increase in record sales of the sixties and seventies, the growth had turned to decline. Record industry organizations blamed this on the spread of cheap cassette recorders and the opportunities they offered to record music directly from the radio, although as likely an explanation would be normal fluctuations in the economy. In 1982 the United States economy was at its weakest point since the Depression of the 1930s. Over ten per cent of Americans were unemployed. Things were on a downward turn elsewhere in the world too. It was a wonder that records were, in fact, selling so well.

Record production was still dominated by the 'Saturday Night Fever' of the late seventies. The big international names in the business were Olivia Newton-John, Lionel Richie, Madonna and Prince – all of them singers of fast-paced dance music who looked good in colour photographs but did not create anything revolutionary in the music business. The greatest star of the decade was big-eyed Michael Jackson, who had gained his first gold record as long ago as 1971, as a 12-year-old child star. Jackson's album, *Thriller*, made for Warner, sold ten million copies in the United States and even more elsewhere in the world. The secret of its success lay largely in Jackson's attractive music videos, eagerly shown by the new music TV channels.

The record business was on a huge financial merry-go-round, with one company after another changing hands. Old Sir Edward Lewis, who had bought Decca in 1929, died in 1980. A few days before his death he witnessed the transfer of Decca into PolyGram's ownership. An honourable history was not enough; Decca had not run fast enough in the record-selling race. In the seventies Decca had not produced enough hits, and the shareholders drew the inevitable conclusions. An even greater fuss attended the transfer of EMI into the ownership of the English television concern, Thorn, the same year.

The company which had seemed inviolable in the Beatles' heyday in the 1960s had fallen on hard times. A concern whose parent companies had founded the record industry in England in 1898, discovered Caruso and signed up nearly all the renowned artists in European classical music, had become a subsidiary of a television manufacturer. The depths of humiliation were reached when EMI, in its straitened circumstances, had to sell off its collection of historic gramophones at auction.

Nevertheless EMI's record output even in the seventies was moderately successful, and only the previous year EMI had bought the record division of United Artists. But, as with the other big record companies, records were only a part of EMI's operations. It was the risks the company took in the field of hospital electronics that proved EMI's undoing: the company had lost a fortune in marketing the computerized axial tomography (CAT) scanner it had developed. As a result of the deals, there were, in the early 1980s, five companies that together produced over half of the records sold in the world. Apart from Thorn-EMI, these were CBS, PolyGram, Warner and RCA. What they had in common was that they were giant concerns in the electronics and communications industries, in whose operations records only figured as one among many products.

These five names were still leading the industry's development at the end of the decade, but during the ten years their ownership had changed significantly. The first to change hands was RCA Records. The Radio Corporation of America was still one of the biggest electronics companies in the United States, including one of the country's national television networks. RCA had entered the record business as early as 1928 by buying the Victor company. RCA's main areas of business were electronics and television, and records were of no more significance to it than the Hertz car rental company or the Coronet carpet factory, which it also owned. As long as the company's founder, General David Sarnoff, was at the helm, he could feel a certain sentimental affection for his old record division, which had, at the General's command, rushed the records of his favourite conductor, Toscanini, onto the market in record time, but with Sarnoff's retirement in 1969 the situation changed. In 1986 RCA sold its record division of 80 years' standing to the West German Bertelsmann publishing company. Bertelsmann AG, established in 1835, had grown from a small firm publishing hymn-books into the world's biggest publisher, which, in 1988, had 42,000 employees in 25 countries. Previously the company had released records in Germany on the Ariola label. In the United States it already owned the Arista label.

CBS, the Columbia Broadcasting System, whose vicissitudes have already been covered at length, owned, in addition to its record division, another of the three national television networks in the United States. In the early 1980s CBS also owned instrument factories (including Gibson guitars), toy factories, publishing businesses and much else. In 1987 CBS sold its record division for two billion dollars to the Japanese company, Sony. Thus both of the old American record businesses, whose histories reached back to the last century, passed into foreign hands.

The fourth of the recording giants was the Warner concern, or WEA. Warner's roots were in the movie company of the same name, which had set up its own record division in 1958. Over the years Warner had also taken over the Reprise (1964), Atlantic (1967), Elektra (1970) and Asylum (1972) record labels. In 1989 Warner merged with the Time corporation, one of the biggest publishers in the United States. Both have considerable interests in television.

Thus by the end of the decade only one of the big five was in the same hands. PolyGram's 'parents' were the Dutch Philips and German Siemens companies, both giant electronics concerns. The companies began collaborating in the record business in 1962 and started using the present name, PolyGram, in 1972. As Siemens's part of the dowry, PolyGram got Deutsche Grammophon; Philips' share was the company's own record output. Over the years the family has been joined by such labels as Mercury (1962), MGM (1972), and Decca (1980). In 1989 PolyGram also bought the English label, Island; in the seventies it had waxed fat on the records of Bob Marley, Jethro Tull and Emerson, Lake and Palmer.

In addition to these five giants there are a score or so of other sizeable record companies with significant international operations. In a class of its own is Melodiya, whose monopoly position once guaranteed it a respectable turnover, but even it could not compete with the big five. Of the thousands of record companies that have sprung up since the Second World War only a few have grown big enough to be called middle-sized in international terms. Most of the successful companies have transferred into the hands of a bigger company once they reached maturity. A good example of this is the Motown company, which we examined earlier, and which may serve as a model of a good business idea successfully exploited. In 1993 it passed into the hands of PolyGram.

A smaller merry-go-round (at least as far as the record business was concerned) began with the fall of the Berlin Wall in November 1989. In all the Eastern European countries, the state-owned record companies which once had monopoly status lost their position. The former East German VEB Deutsche Schallplatten company was sold to a successful motor trade retailer in Hamburg. Hungaroton was broken into parts and privatized. Romanian Electrecord was still pressing vinyl discs in 1996. The fate of Melodiya, like so many other Russian enterprises, is not quite clear, but at least parts of the catalogue have been sold to foreign investors.

Mergers of record companies with other giants in the entertainment and electronics industries are sure to continue. The significance of national borders continues to wane as the giants of the Japanese electronics industry continue to wax. During the 1980s Japan became the world's leading manufacturer of leisure electronics. Japan also has the second largest record market in the world. Yet Japan has no opportunities to supply music for the international market: Japan's own domestic record production is too much geared to national tastes. The solution is to buy companies. Since Sony bought CBS, the Fujisankei company bought a share in Virgin Records in England (Virgin subsequently sold out to EMI), Matsushita acquired MCA Records and later sold it to the Canadian company Seagram, and Denon entered into close collaboration with the Czech Supraphon label. The buying up of companies will certainly continue.

The big five, together with a handful of middle-sized companies, produce almost two-thirds of the records sold in the world. The remainder of record sales are shared between several thousand smaller companies. Some of these will become middle-sized over the years and will probably be bought out by some bigger company. Some will stick stubbornly to their own territory, turning out records for some clearly restricted market. Most of them will die sooner or later. The history of the gramophone record has taught us something, however, about the roles of larger and smaller companies. New technology usually comes on the initiative of the large ones; new music, on the other hand, from the small ones. The development of the whole industry depends on their interaction. This basic law of the record industry was demonstrated once again in the 1980s, when the transfer to digital technology came.

Sources: Pandit (1996); Poyser (1996)

Digital Technology and the Laser Disc

As a background to the business merry-go-round of the 1980s, a profound technical transition was going on. The gramophone record, pressed on vinyl, and the cassette, using magnetic recording tape, represented two different methods of preserving sound. At the deeper level of principle, however, they were of the same generation. On a gramophone record the sound is captured mechanically, while on a tape it is done magnetically, but both the modulations in the grooves of a record and the variations in the magnetic field on a tape are analogous, corresponding to the original sound. Both record and tape are examples of analogue technology.

In the late seventies several new inventions had come onto the market which aimed at further improving the sound reproduction of analogue recordings. Direct-cut discs were recorded straight onto the lacquer disc used in the manufacture of matrices, bypassing the taping stage. The quality of sound reproduction improved when the tape hiss vanished completely, but the price of records rose considerably. For some time the manufacture of records using the *dbx* noise reduction process was also tried out. The dynamics increased, but the purchaser had to buy additional special equipment. The efforts to improve the quality of analog records proved fruitless, however. Even the most brilliant inventions were useless when, at the same time, the quality of work at pressing plants in many countries (especially the United States) was declining. It was time for the analog record to go, and make room for the digital compact disc.

The compact disc was a result of the digital technology which advanced with the development of computers. Computers process all the data fed into them as binary digits, in series composed of alternations of noughts and ones. When these digits are changed into electrical form, the computer is able to process and store vast amounts of them. Even a cheap personal computer is able to store a book many hundreds of pages thick on a small magnetic disc.

Everything that can be measured can also be stored on a computer in digital, or numeric, form: figures, letters, images, the sound waves that make up music. Music, with its countless nuances, is of course very much more complex than, say, a written text. Present-day digital sound recording processes typically take 44,100 or 48,000 samples of music – or any other sound – a second, each one of which is transformed into digital form. This makes possible a reproducible range from zero to more than 20,000 Hz, and a dynamic range of 90 decibels. Digital technology was first adapted for sound recording in Japan in 1967.

Sound converted into digital form can be further stored. In principle there are several different methods of doing this. Computer technology generally uses various forms of magnetic recording; the small diskettes used with personal computers have the same type of magnetic coating as audio tape cassettes. Originally, digital recording adopted the U-matic video recorder developed for television (the number of samples, 44,100, actually derives from some peculiarities of videotape recording).

There are also several types of tape recorders which are specifically designed for digital sound recording. In 1988 some Japanese equipment manufacturers began offering DAT (digital audio tape) recorders for domestic use. The high price of the equipment and the resistance of the record industry means, however, that, so far, digital audio tape has been restricted to professional use. Another problem has been the durability of recordings.

The record industry's response to the challenge of digital technology was the compact disc (CD), on which an audio signal, converted into binary digits, is stored using a laser beam and engraved in microscopically small pits in the disc's surface. The speed varies from 500 to 200 r.p.m., slowing down steadily from the beginning to the end; the recorded part of the disc, which is visible to the naked eye, starts in the middle and ends on the outer edge. The CD player does not have a stylus; the information stored on the disc (which, expressed in computer language, amounts to 15,000 million bits) is read by a laser beam, which does not wear out the disc, but, in practice, it is at least as vulnerable to fingerprints, scratches, dirt and chips as the traditional LP.

In 1979 Philips presented the prototype of the CD it had developed with Sony of Japan. This was followed by a few years' intensive campaigning, during which Philips and Sony tried to convince the record industry that their disc held the key to the future. At a press conference in Salzburg in August 1980, the new discs were introduced to the press by Herbert von Karajan with the famous words, 'All else is gaslight'.

The campaign was successful. Other competing methods were also being developed, but the business did not want to get involved in another 'war of the speeds'. The first CDs were put on the market in Tokyo in October 1982. In Europe the new disc was introduced in March 1983 and in the United States in August of the same year. Philips already had PolyGram to take charge of recording and marketing the discs. When Sony opened the first CD factory in Europe in 1985, it was strategically placed in Herbert von Karajan's Austrian home village, Anif. It was natural that the company also wanted to get involved in the creative side of the record business; the solution was to buy CBS.

By 1986 the breakthrough of the CD was being regarded in the United States as an unshakeable fact. About 130 million compact discs were being made each year worldwide. This was not much compared to the annual overall world production of recordings, at 2500 million, but in that year 53 million compact discs were sold in the United States, one tenth of the country's record sales, and it was obvious that the most active record buyers had chosen the CD. In 1988 more compact discs were sold in the United States than LPs, and since the CD cost considerably more than the LP, the income from them was correspondingly bigger. The following year many record companies started phasing out LP record production. (At this time more cassettes were still being sold than both types of disc together.)

In Japan the CD had overtaken the LP as early as 1986. In the other centres of the record industry, West Germany and England, sales of laser discs were also fast gaining ground. By autumn 1989, LPs were on special offer in the big record stores in London and New York. Although the technology was still unknown in developing countries, the trend was clear. The death throes of vinyl had begun. It had taken ten years for the LP to displace the 78 r.p.m. record, and it took the same amount of time for the CD to replace the LP.

Analogue technology is not likely to vanish for some time. Cheap cassette players are so common and versatile that many recordings will be released both on compact disc and cassette. Developing countries, where hundreds of millions of cassettes are sold each year, will have to wait a long time for the new technology to arrive. On the other hand the compact disc is not the only adaptation of digital technology, nor does it by any means represent the apogee of recording technology. Among professionals in the sound industry there is a significant group which believes that the CD was marketed too early, leaving it with certain technical shortcomings.

Since DAT recorders failed on the home market, several new competitors of the CD have already appeared. The Minidisc (MD) is a smaller digital disc format; certain types of MD players can also make recordings. The Digital Compact Cassette (DCC) is a compromise between DAT and the compact cassette, as DCC players can also reproduce analogue cassettes. So far they have not had any real impact on the consumer market, although the MD has certain professional applications on radio stations.

Meanwhile, the compact disc has also acquired new applications. Recordable compact discs (CD-R) have been available for some years, but because of their cost, they are still beyond the reach of the ordinary consumer. The CD-ROM, which can store texts and images in addition to sounds, has wide applications in the computer world. The coexistence of the audio CD and the CD-ROM guarantees that the format will be around for a few decades, although their lifetime will hardly exceed that of the LP. However, digital audio has come to stay. Digital technology has already become dominant in the telephone industry, and digital radio (DAB) is currently being introduced in several countries. In principle, a recording in digital form can be transferred to any equipment possessing a computer memory. Before long, digital technology will be applied to all sound reproduction and storage, and it is quite likely that in the long run it will give birth both to new ways of marketing music and to new forms of music.

In any case the arrival of digital technology meant a wonderful boost for the record industry. The manufacture of a CD originally cost slightly more than that of an LP record. For volume production, however, the difference is negligible. In 1995, only one per cent of world record sales consisted of LPs, yet in the record shops compact discs originally cost nearly twice as much as LP discs. The new technology offered the industry a marvellous opportunity to raise prices, which had fallen below the limit of profitability. Thanks to the new technology a huge number of old, deleted recordings were brought back onto the market.

Table 8.1 *World Record Sales, 1981–95 (Selected countries).* (Millions of units)

	1981	1986	1991	1995
USA	593	618.3	794.9	1100.5
UK	170.2	197.7	198.8	266.9
Germany (FRG)	202.0	176.1	226.1 /	252.8
France	149.3	111.0	137.2	149.5
Japan	202.5	177.6	281.5	416.6
Italy	58.0	41.9	51.7	44.4
Spain	39.6	37.4	54.1	52.7
Sweden	14.3	20.1	25.8	26.5
Netherlands	40.0	33.5	45.8	44.3
Russia/USSR	199.0	136.0	92.2 /	83.2
Czechoslovakia	12.7	14.0	10.0 /	8.1
Poland	10.0	11.6	4.8	22.4
Canada	85.8	78.9	62.6	77.0
Mexico	..	20.5	67.9	60.9
Brazil	42.8	71.0	44.9	75.0
Colombia	..	15.0	7.9	20.9
Australia	46.0	30.9	45.4	49.4
New Zealand	8.7	6.2	7.1	8.9
South Africa	13.3	..	12.7	18.2
Nigeria	4.5	5.5	8.5	12.0
India	..	8.0 /	154.0	303.0
China	..	110.0	..	123.3
Indonesia	..	34.1	39.4	83.0
South Korea	..	19.5	90.5	57.8
Turkey	2.2	.. /	51.5	37.7
Egypt	..	10.0	..	18.1
Saudi Arabia	..	..	10.4	23.4
WORLD TOTAL (number of countries	2044.5	2290	2804	3349
included in total)	(35)	(50)	(60)	(68)

Source: IFPI; Poyser, 1996

Note: Figures usually refer to sales by IFPI members or legitimate products only. The countries omitted from the world total, from which no figures are available, are mainly African and Arab countries, and a large number of very small countries. A slash indicates a change in the definition of data.

By the end of the eighties the record industry had ceased bemoaning its difficulties: it had become extremely profitable again. In the nineties, the upward trend continued. A statistical compendium of world record sales published by IFPI, the International Federation of the Phonographic Industry, recently noted that 'in 1995 annual sales of pre-recorded music reached an all time high, with sales of some 3.8 billion units worldwide, valued at almost US $40 billion. Unit sales are currently 80 per cent higher than a decade ago and the real value of the world music market has more than doubled in the same period.'

Sources: Pohlman (1989); Poyser (1996); Rumsey (1990)

Classical Music Moves onto Compact Disc

Buyers of classical records are generally quality-conscious music lovers who are prepared to invest large sums in audio equipment. The buyer who will pay twenty pounds or more for a complete recording of an opera will also demand good recordings. The first record companies to give up LP records altogether in favour of the CD were those who specialize in classical music. Again, the spread of CD players brought into the market place a whole new generation of customers who were basically interested in acquiring the entire basic classical repertoire. Classical music does not age. If the recordings are of sufficient technical quality, they can be sold over and over again to new generations of customers. The big record companies suddenly noticed that they had in their archives thousands of deleted recordings which could now be sold in a new form at a higher price than before.

The proportion of classical music in the world's record market is less than ten per cent. Industry sources estimate it as 11% in Hungary and the Netherlands, 10% in Germany and Switzerland, 8% in France and 7% in the United Kingdom. In the United States it is only about 3%. But since at least 1000 million records are sold in that country annually, even three per cent is a substantial amount.

Previously many large record companies had regarded their classical music producers as slightly eccentric types who made records for their minority customers. The record put a pleasant gloss on the companies' image as long as they did not make a loss. But in the latter half of the 1980s, they began to see classical music in a new way; as a profitable investment for the record business and one which would shore up company finances in the future when sales of rock records were unpredictable. In autumn 1989 the American *Opera News* remarked that compact discs have a 'profit margin that would even make an arms dealer envious'. The big company deals of the decade were accompanied by a producers' merry-go-round, with companies that had changed hands trying to ensure the continuity of their classical catalogues. As soon as it had bought CBS, Sony hired, as head of its classical department, Gunther Breest, who had been responsible for the Deutsche Grammophon–PolyGram catalogue for eighteen years. Breest had produced records by Karajan, Giulini and Abbado, and Sony believed that his experience and connections would help the company sign up new artists. As his first task Breest signed a contract with the Berlin Philharmonic for new recordings, and there were even rumours of Karajan defecting to CBS, but the conductor's death brought the venture to an end.

PolyGram lost another key figure when Bertelsmann hired Gunter Hensler, who had been responsible for PolyGram's American operations, to head the renowned 'Red Seal' department of RCA. Peter Andry, the long-serving head of the classical department at EMI, moved to Warners to start up the company's classical music production. Of the giants of the record industry Warners had been the only one up until the 1980s not to have a classical catalogue worth mentioning, so Andry's first task was to negotiate the purchase of the French specialist classical music label, Erato. This was followed by the acquisition of Nonesuch and Finlandia.

When the compact disc was being developed, the researchers had to decide how much music should fit onto a disc; this would have an effect on the size of the disc. An ordinary LP generally has about 20 to 25 minutes of music on each side, about 40 to 50 minutes altogether (records of more than 70 minutes' length have been made, but they are extremely vulnerable to manufacturing faults). Often the length of a record is considerably less. But with compact discs it was possible to fit Beethoven's long ninth symphony, the 'Choral', onto one disc. The interpretations by most conductors of this work last about 70 to 75 minutes, although Weingartner, for example, in the 1930s tossed it off in 62 minutes.

By 1988 Beethoven's ninth symphony had appeared in 70 different readings on CD (many of them have already been deleted). Altogether, according to J.F. Weber's discography, this work had been recorded nearly 150 times since Bruno Seidler-Winkler first committed it to acoustic disc in Berlin in 1923. The record buyer can choose from among the world's best conductors. Those on offer include Toscanini, Mengelberg, Karajan, Stokowski, Beecham, Solti, Bernstein and Haitink. As many as nine different interpretations by Furtwängler of this work are available, though all of them are from radio broadcasts. And if one is after real luxury, one could buy the majestically sweeping performance by Karl Böhm and the Vienna Philharmonic, drawn out to 76 minutes, and thus needing two compact discs! (As manufacturing technology has developed it has been issued on only one as well.)

These figures serve to indicate the superabundance that greets the music lover in the record market nowadays. In the United States, England, Germany and Japan tens of thousands of compact discs are available, and 1000 new ones come out each month. As well as the new recordings, old ones are continually appearing in a new guise. Although not as many recordings have been made of every significant classical work as there have of Beethoven's ninth, 150 recordings of one work is by no means unusual. No doubt in the future, every new international conductor will want to immortalize his own reading of Beethoven's symphonies on disc. There is not room for all of them, however; by the mid-1990s there were clear signs that the five largest companies were cutting down classical releases.

One solution is to make recordings that are sure to differ from their predecessors. Competition between record companies has given a wonderful stimulus to the widespread efforts in the 1980s to play 19th-century music on original instruments. In the discography for Beethoven's ninth one finds, among others, Roger Norrington's recording, which, with its instruments dating back to the early nineteenth century, differs markedly from many of the other recordings.

The compact disc has also brought a large number of historical recordings back onto the market, in some cases dating back 100 years. Although it was possible in the LP era to hear samples of Sarasate and Caruso without owning the rare originals, today we are pampered with the complete recordings of many significant early artists and other reissues which would have been unthinkable a quarter of a century ago. The flood of reissues of older material on CD is only partly explained by the growing demand for new releases. To some extent it is due to the development of new digital sound restoration systems such as Cedar and NoNoise which significantly improve the sound of old recordings by removing scratch and hiss.

Sources: Lebrecht (1996); Umbach (1990)

The Complete Sibelius, Mozart, Bach...

Certain works recur at regular intervals in the repertoires of most symphony orchestras, and recordings of the same work have been made over and over again in the history of the gramophone record. All of Beethoven's symphonies have been recorded at least 100 times. In the catalogue of Beethoven's works, however, there are 135 compositions, and, in addition, he wrote numerous smaller works to which he did not assign opus numbers. Naturally not all of them are masterpieces, and a considerable number of them remained unrecorded for a long time. As record production increased in the 1960s, however, record companies began recording ever more obscure works, and gradually the list of omissions decreased. The bicentenary of Beethoven's birth in 1970 spurred the companies on to new efforts. When the sesquicentenary of the composer's death was commemorated in 1977, Beethoven's collected works were already available as a 111-LP set.

The extra playing time offered by the CD and the continuous growth in the record market have given incentive to the recording of 'complete works'. By 1991 (the bicentenary of Mozart's death) PolyGram had released the composer's entire output on 180 compact discs. Most of these have appeared on other records previously, but for the complete recordings, a number of small pieces which have never been heard on record before were included. In 1981 the pianist Leslie Howard began recording Liszt's entire piano works for the Hyperion label. With foresight he included, from the outset, a mixture of favourites and rarities. If the favourites had been recorded first, it would have been hard to find buyers for the later records. All of Domenico Scarlatti's 555 keyboard sonatas have already been recorded for the Erato label; the man behind this laborious job was Scott Ross.

Johann Sebastian Bach lived at a time when a composer was expected to produce new works weekly. Schmieder's *Bach-Werke-Verzeichnis*, the catalogue of the composer's works, runs to over 1000 numbers. Though there is no shortage of recordings of the Brandenburg concertos or the Toccata and fugue in D minor, among Bach's 200 cantatas there are many that have gone unrecorded. This shortcoming is being remedied, for example by the conductors Nikolaus Harnoncourt and Gustav Leonhardt, who have for a long time now been busily recording all of Bach's cantatas for Telefunken. We will probably never hear Bach's works as a complete collection; some have probably vanished forever, some have not been identified with certainty, and some are extant in several versions whose authenticity will be disputed by musicologists indefinitely.

The problems of recording Bach's collected works can be seen in perspective if we examine the catalogue of the works of Jean Sibelius. Sibelius's complete works are currently being recorded by Robert von Bahr's Swedish label, BIS. BIS has wisely divided Sibelius's oeuvre into easily handled portions. The piano works are being recorded by Erik T. Tawaststjerna and the orchestral works by Neeme Järvi with the Gothenburg Symphony Orchestra. However, there is plenty of other music, provisional works and commissioned ones, including works which remained unpublished in the composer's lifetime. 'When I say complete, I mean complete,' says von Bahr. But 70 years have not yet passed since Sibelius's death, so his works are still protected by copyright, and unpublished works may not be recorded without the permission of his estate. In 1991 the estate finally allowed the Lahti Symphony Orchestra to record the first, unpublished version of the violin concerto, but there are still unrecorded works in archives.

Nevertheless the striving for completeness is one sign of the maturity that the record industry has reached. In literature it is common for a collected edition of significant authors' works to be published. With especially important authors there is a critical edition, which is supplemented with notes and alternate versions (for example, when the author changed his work on the appearance of a new edition). Likewise, the output of important composers is being recorded in complete form.

Provincial Orchestras and Provincial Labels

Ever since Fred Gaisberg signed up Caruso to the Gramophone Company, it has been the custom for the best-known singers and orchestras to be under contract to the big international record companies. The Berlin, Vienna and New York Philharmonic are all signed to one of the big international record companies. They are not necessarily the world's best orchestras, but they are of top quality, and their members have long experience of studio work, which guarantees that they are able to put out a considerable number of recordings each year. In return, the worldwide distribution network of the big record companies guarantees the orchestras handsome extra earnings. There has been no place for small record companies and unknown orchestras in recording the central orchestral repertoire.

In recent years, however, this circle has opened out. A phenomenon has occurred which may be described as the advance of the provincial orchestra. Numerous new orchestras have entered the record catalogues, having made fresh and successful recordings of the old standard orchestral works. These orchestras have more to gain; they often spend more time and energy on recording. Many of them have been taken up by new, smaller record labels. Neeme Järvi and BIS have made the Gothenburg Symphony Orchestra well known. Likewise, Mariss Jansons and the Oslo Symphony Orchestra have recorded Tchaikovsky's symphonies for Chandos.

A good example of how such an enterprise can come about is the rather unlikely collaboration between the Naxos label in Hong Kong and the Slovak Philharmonic Orchestra. The man behind the Marco Polo, Hong Kong and Naxos labels is Klaus Heymann, a German journalist who was sent as a correspondent to Hong Kong in 1967. Over the years he began importing first tape recorders and then records to Hong Kong. In 1974 he married the Japanese violinist Takako Nishizaki and started producing his wife's records, on which she performed light music for Hong Kong tastes. At that time the Hong Kong Philharmonic Orchestra was also anxious for an opportunity to record. The orchestra is a normal, western-style symphony orchestra, though obviously without the same kind of traditions as, say, the Vienna Philharmonic. The members of the orchestra were competent musicans, but the string section's playing left something to be desired – as with many European orchestras. Heymann reasoned that it would not be worthwhile for an unknown orchestra to record Beethoven's symphonies or the other old 'warhorses', but the orchestra's style was better adapted to interpreting the lesser-known Romantic works. (The Russian Romantics had had to work with less than perfect orchestras.) And so the Hong Kong Philharmonic recorded Glazunov and Cui, lesser-known works by Richard Strauss and marches by Wagner. In charge of recording was a Japanese, Hiroshi Isaka, who had his own small record company, and the compact discs were also made in Japan. Distribution outside Hong Kong was handled by an American and a French distributor.

The records sold satisfactorily, and Naxos expanded its operations. Heymann's next partners were the Slovak Philharmonic Orchestra in Bratislava and the Bratislava Radio Symphony Orchestra, which were eager to acquire western currency. The recordings were made at a local concert hall using a Dutch recording engineer. The result was more Russian Romantic music, some Dvořák and symphonies by the early 20th-century Austrian composer, Franz Schmidt. Naxos came onto the market at a time when the owners of CD players were starting to look for newer, more obscure works. The records were of a high technical quality, and many of them sold well for classical records.

In 1992, Naxos was already the best-selling classical label in the world after the big five, and by 1996 it had reached the first place in the UK. Heymann has extended his co-operation to other European symphony orchestras and soloists. As well as rarities, the repertoire will also include familiar symphonies. The conductors and soloists are rising international talents of the younger generation. Heymann is in charge of marketing the records and the recordings are made by freelance producers.

Naxos is a good example of how even a small record label can operate on a worldwide scale. Capital is needed to produce the records, but no more than is needed to set up a plumbing business. What is important is the intellectual capital. Records are lightweight freight; the original tapes are even lighter. Theoretically, it would also be possible to transmit a digital recording by telephone line from the studio to the pressing plant without impairing the quality. In an age of air travel it is not necessary for the artists, the record company and the customers to be on the same continent, but the company's thinking must be internationally oriented from the start.

Source: Lebrecht (1996)

The Revival of Early Music

In 1928 Leopold Stokowski recorded his own arrangement of Bach's Toccata and fugue with the Philadelphia Orchestra. The record is a mighty, Romantic orchestral work, still worth hearing, but having little to do with the spirit of Bach. Rather, it relates to the 19th-century practice of 'modernizing' Bach's music.

By 1928 Wanda Landowska had already made her first recordings with the aim of performing the music of Bach's period according to the manner of its time.

Landowska played the harpsichord, the favourite instrument of the eighteenth century, which fell out of fashion with the arrival of the modern pianoforte. Landowska was part of a gathering musical-historical movement, which aimed to purge the Baroque music that was still in the repertoire of the 'modernization' inflicted on it in the Romantic period, and to revive older music that had passed into oblivion.

Regarded as the founder of this movement was the instrument maker, Arnold Dolmetsch, who started making reproductions of historic instruments in London in the 1880s.

By the 1950s the movement had grown so much that there were plenty of musicians in Europe playing the pommer, the shawm, the crumhorn, the viola da gamba, and other almost forgotten instruments, professionally and in a more or less authentic way. The harpsichord replaced the piano in rendering Baroque music. The result was a large number of meritorious recordings which revived our acquaintanceship with the forgotten music of the Baroque, Renaissance and medieval periods. The DGG Archiv and Telefunken's Das Alte Werk series played a central part in this.

Meanwhile, the revivers of ancient music direct their attention to our own time. The modern symphony orchestra developed in the eighteenth and nineteenth centuries. By Beethoven's time the symphony orchestra consisted of much the same instruments as it does today. The harpsichord was replaced by the pianoforte. As new instruments established themselves composers ceased writing music for instruments that were no longer part of an ordinary musician's training.

Familiar instruments and the manner of playing them have, however, changed quite a lot in a century and a half. Beethoven's piano sounded quite different to a modern one, let alone his orchestra. Instead of metal, violins had strings made of gut, which gave a softer sound. Woodwinds used a different system of fingering. Brass instruments were only equipped with valves from the 1820s onwards. Practically all modern instruments have undergone changes since Beethoven's death, even if their outward appearance has remained much the same.

In 1957 the pianist, Paul Badura-Skoda, wrote in his book on interpreting Mozart's works that they should not really be played on a modern piano, but the rarity of historic instruments prevents the aim of authenticity being achieved in practice. Since then the situation has changed radically. Old pianos have been restored; new ones have been built based on old models. The term 'fortepiano' has come into use to refer to pianos of the kind used in the late eighteenth and early nineteenth centuries. Their acoustics are more resonant than those of the modern piano, more 'tinkling' according to some. Badura-Skoda himself has changed his attitude, and he has indeed recorded piano concertos by Beethoven and Mozart on the fortepiano. For Beethoven he used an instrument built in 1820 by Conrad Graf of Vienna (the same kind that Beethoven played). The only instrumental suitable for the Mozart works was an instrument built in the previous century by Johann Schantz.

After Wanda Landowska the record companies thought twice before recording Bach on a modern piano. The same attitude is beginning to be seen in regard to other composers. EMI, which half a century ago had issued all of Beethoven's piano sonatas as rendered by Schnabel, began recording the same works in 1988 with Melvyn Tan playing a fortepiano.

The same is true of orchestral music. In the 1980s several recordings were made of Beethoven's symphonies using historic instruments with the aim of attaining the sound and performing style of Beethoven's era. They are by Roger Norrington's London Classical Players, Roy Goodman's Hanover Band and Christopher Hogwood's Academy of Ancient Music. Symphony orchestras that use modern instruments have remained outside this competition, and the financing of the projects has come from various sponsors, primarily record companies, for whom the movement has presented opportunities to re-release the basic repertoire in a different interpretative framework.

After Beethoven, Mozart and Haydn, the music of Mendelssohn (1809–47) and Berlioz (1803–69) was recorded on historic instruments. Particular praise has been heaped on the recording by the London Classical Players of Berlioz's *Symphonie fantastique*, composed in 1830. This is not ancient music at all, but Romanticism at its most florid. But with a 'corrected' ensemble the relationship between the sections of players changes from what we are used to in modern orchestras' interpretations, and completely new tones are revealed, intended by the composer but hitherto unheard by the listener.

Styles of performance are changing all the time. We already have recordings by Sibelius's contemporary, Kajanus. Perhaps there is no point in trying to establish an orchestra that plays Sibelius's music in the authentic 1920s style, but it is interesting to note that, recently, new recordings of Stokowski's arrangements of Bach have appeared – not as documents of Bach's era but of how Stokowski's generation viewed Bach's music.

Sound and Vision

In the 1930s, when record players were still rare in Europe, new tunes were better disseminated through movies than through records. Swing fans would go night after night to see movies in which Glenn Miller and Benny Goodman were performing. Bing Crosby and Elvis Presley were also successful film artists, so were Beniamino Gigli and Richard Tauber.

In 1949 the NBC network in the USA inaugurated its Television Opera Theatre, starting with Kurt Weill's *Down in the Valley*. Within fifteen years, the series presented both traditional opera and new works. Menotti's *Amahl and the Night Visitors* was specially commissioned by NBC. In Europe, especially in Italy and Germany, national broadcasting companies have a long tradition of presenting opera on television. From direct broadcasts of stage performances, television opera gradually grew into an independent expressive form, and some of the most impressive television operas have never been performed on stage.

Television also brought new dimensions to popular music. In the United States Dick Clark's *American Bandstand* created stars overnight. In England the television series *Top of the Pops* and *Ready, Steady, Go* helped to launch the new pop music of the sixties. As this type of programme became common, record companies started making short film clips or 'promos' of their popular artists, which were offered free, or almost, to the television stations. In 1966 the clever American producer, Don Kirshner, created a new pop group out of nothing by letting four nice-looking boys act as musicians in the series *The Monkees*. Monkees records sold by the million. But one could not buy a copy of a film or television show.

Plans to develop a videodisc, however, were now afoot. RCA, known for its records, was also in the sixties one of the biggest manufacturers of television receivers in the United States. Americans were happy to trade in their old black-and-white receivers for colour, and RCA's shares grew. The company was aware, however, that the growth would not go on forever. In 1964 its president, David Sarnoff, told an annual stockholders' meeting that, at most, there were ten good years ahead; after that the market would be saturated. A new product would have to be developed; one that would sell as well as colour television. The product would be the videodisc player.

It was already technically possible to record television images. In 1956 Ampex had prepared a videotape recorder for professional use, which the world's television companies quickly adopted. RCA did not, however, believe in the domestic possibilities of the video recorder; rather, the company's research division was ordered to develop the videodisc. Over the next fifteen years, feverish work was done in the RCA laboratories to develop the recording of moving images. In 1981 the long-awaited infant was born: accompanied by a massive advertising campaign, RCA's Selectavision VideoDisc was released onto the United States market.

RCA's videodisc was a technical triumph. The moderately-priced player, which played discs the size of an LP, offered the viewer a better picture than a normal television broadcast. Available on videodisc were feature films, music programmes and educational programmes, including Dr Benjamin Spock advising on child care. But the videodisc was a commercial failure. In three years RCA only managed to sell 550,000 videodisc players, and in April 1984 production was stopped. It never went on sale in Europe, and, one day, the RCA VideoDisc will be a collector's item, like the first LPs marketed by Edison in 1927.

The videodisc was, of course, defeated by the videotape recorder, developed by the Japanese and put on the market in the early eighties. By 1985 20 million video recorders had been sold in the United States, and, gradually, video recorders have become as indispensable a domestic appliance as the cassette recorder in all developed countries. Videotape won over the videodisc because it had one overwhelming advantage: it can record television programmes, which the videodisc could not do.

On 1 August 1981 the first music television channel in the United States was launched: MTV, which broadcasts rock music around the clock. The broadcasts are beamed, by satellite, to the cable networks, and in 1986 it was available in 28 million homes. In the United States, MTV already has several rivals, such as the Nashville channel, specializing in country music, and in Europe the same kind of broadcasts by satellite through the cable network have been available on several commercial satellite channels. MTV's programmes consist mainly of music videotapes put out by record companies, visual versions of the records, aimed at enhancing sales. A score or so of video clips are repeated around the clock, accompanied by presenters and supplemented with advertisements.

Most music videos succeed in promoting record sales. The colossal success of Michael Jackson's *Thriller* was evidently due in large measure to the videotape accompanying the record, which the television channels plugged heavily. The best music videos, however, can be regarded as a new art form, and they are sold and hired like other video programmes. At the same time other music videotapes have come onto the market: concert recordings, operas, old musical films. Gradually a market for visualized music is taking shape on the fringes of the record business.

By the end of the 1980s in the United States video sales had become a more lucrative market than video hiring. Videos cost about as much as compact discs, and many have sold hundreds of thousands of copies. The most popular videotapes up to now have been concerned with physical fitness: Jane Fonda's aerobic video is one of the most successful. Films made for normal cinema distribution have also done well, although they usually appear on video long after their first screenings. Music videos form a third big group. In February 1997 the two best-selling videos in the United States were *Independence Day* and *The Nutty Professor*. In third place was the musical *Riverdance*, and among the 40 best-selling videos there were also Bruce Springsteen, The Rolling Stones, *Les Miserables* and *Grease*.

Although video has become an important element, it does not seem likely that visual music will ever replace plain sound recordings.

Sources: Graham (1986); Kaplan (1987)

From the Disco Back to Nature

In the early fifties the real breakthrough for the LP occurred in the classical music market, whereas light music was keen to adopt the cheap single format. Likewise the CD was, in its early stages, regarded as a medium for classical music. For rock musicians, records still had an A and a B side. It was only in the late 1980s that musicians like Brian Eno began to seriously consider the aesthetics of the compact disc. The new medium for rock was the 12-inch maxi-single. The first maxi-singles appeared in the United States in the mid-seventies. Technically there was nothing new about them: they were LP-sized discs that revolved at 45 r.p.m. Yet they did open up certain new opportunities for record producers. It had become the custom to put three to five minutes of music on each side of a single. Greater lengths were possible: in the sixties an LP might even contain 70 minutes of music, but at the cost of some dynamic quality. The maxi-single could accommodate, at great volume, over ten minutes of dance music, and its arrival was closely linked to the rise of disco music in popularity.

By this time the recording studios of the United States and Europe were equipped with at least a 24-track analogue tape deck as standard equipment. Electric instruments had been making use of the new digital methods of creating sound for some time. In 1982, the MIDI (Musical Instruments Digital Interface) standard was introduced in order to facilitate the linking of computers and electronic instruments. Much of the popular music of the eighties arose from the exploitation of these possibilities. Layer on layer, backing tracks were mixed out of sounds produced on electronic instruments; a hypnotic, rhythmic accompaniment in which the artificial effects of the extreme bass sound and the higher notes enhance their power. On top of everything else a sensual voice was added. The same recipe, with slight adjustments, applies to thousands of the records of the eighties: high technology yoked to emotions expressed with abandon.

A notorious example of this trend was the album *Girl You Know It's True* by the group Milli Vanilli. It was a worldwide hit and one of the ten best-selling records in the USA in 1989. Created by German record producer, Frank Farian, who had earlier been responsible for the hugely successful recordings of Boney M, it was a synthetic studio product, a mix of electronic instruments and anonymous voices. But for the video made to promote the record, the producers hired two good-looking young dancers named Rob Pilatus and Fab Morvan.

Milli Vanilli became so popular that they received the prestigious Grammy award in the USA for 'Best New Artist of the Year', but then word got out that the recipients had actually not participated in the recording. Rob and Fab had to return their trophies, and an American court ruled that the record company had been guilty of deceptive packaging and ordered it to pay all Milli Vanilli fans back their money. Remarkably few made use of this opportunity. They were satisfied with the imaginary Milli Vanilli.

But at the same time a new simplicity was raising its head in the record industry. In 1986 the Cooking Vinyl label brought out a record called *The Texas Campfire Tapes*, on which a singer named Michelle Shocked played her own songs to guitar accompaniment. It represented an aesthetic diametrically opposed to disco music. The recording was made outdoors, according to the record company, on a cheap Walkman cassette recorder. Only the natural sounds of the night can be heard behind the tender female voice. The sound quality of The Texas Campfire Tapes may leave something to be desired, though this hardly troubled the hundreds of thousands who bought the record. In fact the 'naturalness' of the recording was one of the record's best selling points.

Since then we have been able to see and hear how recordings of better quality can be made, in the age of digital technology, simply and at modest cost. The album, *The Trinity Session*, by the Canadian group, The Cowboy Junkies, which appeared in 1988, was recorded on a portable DAT recorder using one stereo microphone. The recordings were made at the Church of the Holy Trinity in Toronto, which has excellent acoustics. The recording equipment cost a few hundred dollars to procure. The interesting thing is that the record sold well in CD form. Recordings like this presage a return to the ideals of the twenties. The music is all recorded at once from one point, with the musicians alone responsible for the sound balance between the instruments. Recordings are not edited, the best takes are released as they are. The new simplicity of the Cowboy Junkies' folk rock was aimed precisely at the right gap in the market: by 1989 it had earned a gold disc.

Such recordings are likely to become more common. From synthetic, multi-track music we are returning to the ideals of simple technology and live music. We should not anticipate a return to the old days, however. In these days of multiple values, no single philosophy can hold sway, even in recording technology.

Digital technology makes possible a realistic recording of good quality at lower cost than before, but it can just as well lead to more imaginative studio productions, alongside which, analogue, multi-track taping is child's play. It can even erase the borders between live and recorded music.

Source: Hughes (1992)

Karaoke, Dub and Rap

There are hundreds of little bars in Tokyo that are known by the name 'karaoke' – literally 'orchestra without words'. Regular customers have their own whisky bottle waiting for them behind the bar, from which they pour drinks for themselves and their friends. Most of the customers are well known to each other. The most important equipment in the bars is a cassette player of hi-fi quality and a collection of cassettes of the backing tracks of popular Japanese hits, without the vocals. As the evening progresses, the microphone passes from hand to hand and each customer at the bar takes turns to be a star, getting applause from his listeners. In the 1980s, karaoke spread to Europe, and the cassettes were frequently replaced with videodiscs which contain the lyrics of the songs, to assist the performers.

Karaoke is a good example of how the spread of mechanized music does not necessarily mean the death of live music. In Jamaica, the home of reggae, live music has not been heard at dances since the sixties; the dance music is provided by a mobile discotheque, a 'sound system'. The disc jockey is not content to merely play records and introduce them, instead, as the music plays, he comments on them in verse. In Jamaica it was customary for the B side of a single to have the same performance without the vocals, a so-called 'dub' version, for use by the sound systems. This way the singer does not get in the way of the disc jockey's art. The more popular disc jockeys, such as Prince Buster, Big Youth and U-Roy became recording stars in their own right, as they put their dubs on record. The original instrumental background was electronically processed, the bass and drums brought forward and effects added before the disc jockey recorded his own part. At their best these 'talkover' records sound like Dadaist poetry. U-Roy's performances have been likened to the sound of a hundred angry parrots squawking.

Performing these rhymes or 'toasting' is an old Afro-American tradition which still lives on in various forms in the United States. In the early 1990s it burst forth in the South Bronx of New York, where local disc jockeys developed it into an art. Many of the area's inhabitants are Caribbean immigrants. The South Bronx is one of New York's worst slums, and events there are not generally reported elsewhere in New York. It was here, at the turn of the eighties, that hip-hop music and break-dancing grew up, as well as 'rap', a new way of turning record playing into an art form.

During the seventies the playing of records at dance halls and clubs had become a worldwide phenomenon. At a typical discotheque there were two record players wired to the same amplifier and a disc jockey to choose and introduce the records.

The Bronx disc jockeys were in the habit of talking over the records, in the Jamaican way. Instead of reggae music they used local disco hits, and the whole style was called rap. Gradually the more verbally-agile disc jockeys started making records of their own. The first big rap hit was 'Rapper's Delight' by the Sugarhill Gang, in 1979.

At the same time the Bronx disc jockeys, in hot competition with each other, were developing new ideas for playing records. Grandmaster Flash, a Barbados-born disc jockey, had just completed an electrical engineering course at a technical college. He started making adjustments to his disco equipment so that it was easy while playing one record to mix in parts of another. He started playing short breaks from each of two records in turn, moved the turntable back and forward by hand if necessary, scratched the needle rhythmically, altered the revolution speed of the records to change the pitch, and altogether started making collages – new entities – out of the discs. The technique was given the name 'scratching'. On top of all this he added his own rhymed commentary.

The new style started being exploited commercially. Rap and scratch were brought together in the studio. In the early eighties Grandmaster Flash, Afrika Bambaataa and other popular disc jockeys made numerous hit records which aimed at recreating the disco atmosphere. Rap became a movement. What was spontaneous and magical at a disco often palled when created with studio technology, but rap became one of the most controversial trends of American popular music in the eighties, as rappers turned to violence.

The idea itself – of making a collage of records – has come to stay. The new digital keyboard instruments that came into use in the eighties, the 'samplers', were virtually created for this purpose. These instruments were originally invented as replacements for the old-fashioned electric organ and piano. Digital technology made it possible to store in the instruments' 'memory' the sounds of real instruments, so that by changing a memory disc the same keyboard can conjure up a Steinway grand, a harpsichord, a baroque organ or an accordion. But by the same technique an instrument's memory can be programmed with percussion, natural sounds, singing, excerpts from old records, anything at all. In concerts and recordings it is now easy to use any sounds as raw material, even snatches of other records.

If necessary a disc jockey can create his own record out of these materials – or the record company does it for him. One of the most outrageous advocates of this trend was the British group, The JAM's (The Justified Ancients of Mu Mu), founded by Bill Drummond and Jimmy Cauty. In 1987 they produced their first single, 'All You Need is Love', on the KLF label (distributed by Warner). It was a collage consisting of the well-known Beatles song; 'Touch Me', by the sex goddess, Samantha Fox; a lullaby about an HIV-infected mother and her dying child; and a number of other records.

KLF stood for 'Kopyright Liberation Front', and their next production was 'The Queen and I', a combination of Abba's 'Dancing Queen', the Sex Pistols' 'God Save the Queen' and the British national anthem. It had to be withdrawn after protests from the Swedish group, but the practice has become widespread. The legal status of sampling is not yet completely clear. Ideally, the party wishing to use a sample should obtain the permission of the rights owner and pay a royalty.

This is not always done, and in many cases the culprits have settled the matter afterwards, out of court. But there is also at least one court case (from the United States) where the judge found that quoting with a satirical intent was acceptable.

Sources: Beadle (1993); Frith (1993); Toop (1984)

Techno: The Music of the Future?

The study of sales charts published in trade papers shows that there exists a virtually universal style of rock-based popular music in the English language which is widely accepted all over the world. During any chosen week, we may find the same records among the ten best-sellers in Canada, Argentina, Poland, Norway, South Africa and New Zealand. These recordings do not necessarily represent a unified style; they may just as well be 'unplugged' ballads as strongly amplified heavy metal sounds, but they would all be unthinkable without the rock 'n' roll revolution of the fifties. Most of these recordings originate from the United States or the United Kingdom, but Sweden, Germany and other European countries seem increasingly capable of producing recordings with a 'Mid-Atlantic' sound.

The United States is still the biggest record market in the world, but in 1995, North America only accounted for 33% of world record sales, while Europe was responsible for 34%. When we include Japan's 19% share, this only leaves the rest of the world 14%. But, within this sector, Brazil had grown into the seventh largest record market in the world, surpassing Italy, Spain and the Netherlands in total sales. South Korea, Taiwan, Mexico, India, Indonesia and China had also developed into significant record-producing countries. But in some Asian and African countries, the proportion of pirated records exceeds 50% of the market. These records do not appear in official industry statistics, but they do emphasize the role of recorded music in everyday life.

A significant part of the record market consists of music in local and regional idioms which are hardly known across borders, but can be immensely popular in their native countries. The six biggest hits in Germany in 1990 included _Pump ab das Bier_ by Werner Wichtig and _Verdammt, ich lieb' dich_ by Matthias Reim, along with Suzanne Vega and Sinead O'Connor. In most European countries, the market share of domestic popular music exceeds 30%. In France it was 47% in 1995, and in Greece, 56%. Granted, these figures may include English-language recordings by local artists and such new developments as French- and German-language rap (_Alpenrap_ was a big hit in Austria in the late 1980s); nevertheless, national traditions are still important in the record business.

It would be impossible to discuss all the trends that have appeared in popular music since the introduction of the compact disc. However, there is one phenomenon which epitomizes many of the developments in recording technology since the Second World War, and also raises questions about the future of recorded music: 'techno'.

Techno, or 'house', as it is often called in the United States, has its roots in the same technological and social trends which gave rise to disco and rap in the 1970s and 1980s. One driving force was the widespread adoption of recorded, rather than live, music as the preferred accompaniment for dancing. Another was the rapid development of electronic instruments and the increasing ease of using them. But there were also numerous other factors, ranging from the popularity of new drugs to 'gay liberation', which introduced gay clubs as new venues for dance music.

In the early 1980s, dancers could choose between the highly-polished sounds of disco records, the 'industrial' sounds of electronic rock groups, and the angry scratching of rappers. By the mid-eighties, several young musicians and disc jockeys found that they could produce similar sounds on the programmable electronic instruments which had recently appeared on the market. The Roland 808 drum machine, its companion TB-303 Bass Line, and computer-based sequencers, synthesizers and samplers could be used by anyone with modest means, a little musical training and an interest in computers to produce credible dance music which was unique to a particular club. Soon these products were also put out on records in limited edition, 'white label' pressings, and in some cases sold tens of thousands of copies. By the late eighties, techno had spread all over the world and made a successful transition to CD.

As falling prices have put sophisticated electronic instruments into anybody's hands, techno has developed into a kind of vernacular electronic music. It is probably the first type of popular music which consciously attempts to de-emphasize the personality of the performer. There are hardly ever realistic human figures on the sleeves of techno records. Some are published in plain white covers. Promotional videos feature animation of computer graphics. The creators of the recordings are typically identified by street names such as Sleazy D or DJ Force, or science fiction names like Nebulla 2 or Chemical Vacation.

Techno has quickly branched into a large number of quickly evolving local variants. There is Chicago house, acidhouse, hiphouse, garagehouse, newbeat, hardcore, Germanbeat and Goa trance, to name just a few. Instead of turning electronic music into a branch of computer science, the creators of techno are concerned with such matters as the uniquely individual characteristics of the Alesis Midiverb reverberation unit, as compared to AMS or Lexicon. For those interested in ancient music, the sound of a genuine fifties Hammond organ is an unattainable ideal.

It seems unlikely that techno will ever achieve a dominant position in popular music. Its clannishness keeps sales moderate, and it remains the music of various dance-loving subcultures. But it is unique as the first example of popular music which is completely a product of electronic instruments and recording technology, and its inventions will continue to influence other areas of popular music.

Source: Kempster (1996)

World Music Arrives

One of the most surprising sales successes of the 1980s in the United States was a record known by the French name, *Le mystère des voix bulgares* ('The Mystery of Bulgarian Voices'). This record of Bulgarian folk choirs had nothing to do with

France other than the fact that it had come to the world through the mediation of a Frenchman. In an American record shop the original Bulgarian name in Cyrillic letters would have been too much of a mystery, but the Slavonic women's choir on the record (the Folk Choir of Bulgarian Radio) with its strange dissonances attracted tens of thousands of buyers.

Moving in a different direction, the Navaho flute player, R. Carlos Nakai, has had an astonishing success as a composer of 'new age' music. His record company, Canyon Records of Arizona, which, since the 1960s, has marketed its products almost exclusively for native Americans, suddenly found itself producing music for mass audiences. Nakai's success has also led to a revival of traditional flute music, an almost vanished tradition, among Plains Indians.

In recent years there has appeared in many large record shops a special section labelled 'World Music'. Naturally it contains only a microscopic fraction of the tens of thousands of records that are released in the world each year, and it is probably useless to look there for cassettes from New Guinea, for instance. Nevertheless the birth of the concept of World Music signifies a change that has occurred in the relations between the musics of the world, mostly due to the influence of records.

During the past couple of decades, international contacts have expanded rapidly. Thousands of immigrants from independent former colonies have flocked to the big cities of the former colonial powers, England and France. Large numbers of students from Asian and African countries also live there. The same relationship exists between the United States and the countries of Latin America and the Pacific, although it has not been a colonial power in the formal sense. These immigrants are not from remote villages; they were urban dwellers in their home countries too, and their music has long been absorbing western influences. Early this century the United States was called the melting-pot of nations; at present that appellation applies better to London or Paris. The musical needs of the new immigrants are served by musicians who have come from their former home cities. Some came with the immigrants, some only come to visit London or Paris, to play concerts and to record. Records are also imported for the immigrants, and soon the immigrants themselves start making music. In the suburbs of London there are discotheques specializing in Pakistani *bhangra* music. Amsterdam has Surinamese record shops; Paris has record companies that produce music specifically for Francophone African immigrants.

At the same time as the east (and the south) has come to the west, so western music-teaching has reached a turning point. At a time when the United Nations organization has more than 150 members, it is no longer possible to teach the history of music as simply a development from Gregorian chant to the Second Viennese School. As early as the 1950s there was instruction in Javanese gamelan music at the University of California in Los Angeles, and the LP by the University's gamelan orchestra, *The Venerable Dark Cloud*, was one of the first recordings of 'new' world music. In the sixties the American singer and musicologist, Jon Higgins, studied South Indian music for a long period in Madras, and achieved such proficiency that EMI of India asked him to record songs by the 18th-century South Indian classical composer, Thyagaraja (which should not really be any more surprising than the Indian conductor, Zubin

Mehta, recording Beethoven). Yehudi Menuhin started studying Indian music and recorded with Ravi Shankar.

Over the past 25 years, more and more music academies have started teaching non-European musical cultures. As a result of these contacts a new kind of 'world music' has arisen, the interpretation by western musicians of the musical traditions of Asia and Africa. The records that have been made have been more accessible to European ears than records made for the local market by indigenous musicians in their own countries.

World music is thus the result of a current process of merging: music arising from the interaction of Third World musicians and western music. But at the same time, our musical image of the world has expanded, new channels have opened up in the record market and even records such as the one by the Bulgarian folk choir have opportunities to reach listeners outside their own countries. Purity of tradition and scientific accuracy very often have to be sacrificed in this process, but perhaps the next wave will make room for them as well.

Japan: The Second Largest Market

Japan, with a population of over 120 million, is the second most powerful industrial country in the world. It is not suprising that, since the 1980s, it is also the world's second largest record market. In 1995, 416 million records were sold in Japan, almost as many as in Germany and the United Kingdom together. (The third largest market is actually India, with over 300 million cassettes sold annually, but in terms of value it cannot compete with most European countries.) 72 per cent of Japanese sales consist of domestic product, yet hardly any of it is known outside the borders of the country. Japanese music is not 'world music'.

Actually, the Japanese were early converts to recorded music. The first record factories were built before the First World War, and by the 1930s, there were six significant record companies, which had licensing arrangements with major US and German firms. In 1936, total annual production was 30 million. The best-selling records were Japanese popular songs, but large numbers of European and American classical and popular records were also issued on the Japanese market until rising nationalism led to isolationism, censorship and eventually war.

In the Second World War, the record industry was totally devastated, but by 1951 the economy had recovered, and the LP was introduced to the Japanese market. The number of record companies increased. The most significant companies were joint ventures set up by major Japanese electronics companies and the largest multinationals (Sony-CBS, Matsushita-PolyGram, Toshiba-EMI, JVC-RCA), but like elsewhere in the world, there was also an increasing number of smaller local companies.

The majors were helped by the fact that, during the fifties and sixties, there was a great demand for foreign music. Hidemaro Konoye had already recorded Mahler's symphony no. 4 for Japanese Parlophone in 1930, and Japan has long had a highly knowledgeable audience for classical music. But the biggest demand was for western popular music. Rock 'n' roll has been quite popular in Japan since the sixties, and Japan has also smaller, extremely devoted audiences for other genres, ranging from jazz to Hawaiian music, and many reissue albums compiled for the Japanese market witness to a high degree of expertise among both Japanese record company executives and their customers. It is only because of the high prices of Japanese records and the unfavourable exchange rates for the yen that these records – which often contain material which is not currently available in any other country – are not more widely distributed in the West.

Since the 1970s the proportion between Japanese (*ho-gaku*) and western (*yo-gaku*) music has gradually changed, and, today, domestic products considerably outsell imports. *Enka*, traditional popular music, is losing ground to *kayokyoku*, modern Japanese, which, today, is moving towards rock.

Japan is the world leader in electronics, and a large proportion of the world's CD and video cassette players, radios and televisions are produced by Japanese firms or their subsidiaries in other countries. CBS, one of the world's largest record companies, is owned by the Japanese. Yet Japanese recordings are practically unknown abroad. Unlike some highly rhythmic varieties of world music which appeal to record buyers of the rock generation, traditional Japanese music is often subtle and meditative and emphasizes the importance of the lyrics. It was quite exceptional that the well-known *kayokyoku* song, *Ue o muite aruko*, became an international novelty hit under the name *Sukiyaki*, in 1963. More recently, modern Japanese composers such as Ryuichi Sakamoto have gained some degree of success with their neutral brand of electronic sounds.

Now there is some indication that Japanese music may after all be finding international response on a more limited scale. Following the lead of Japan, other East Asian countries such as South Korea, China, Taiwan, Singapore, Indonesia and the Philippines have also seen a considerable increase in record sales since the 1980s. The traditional musics of this area have a lot in common. Memories of wartime Japanese occupation have, until recently, hindered the acceptance of Japanese culture, but today we can already find pop singers in China and Taiwan recording cover versions of Japanese hits, and as China becames more closely integrated into world trade, we can well see the ancient cultural connections between these countries renewed in the record trade.

Source: Kawabata (1991)

Death of the Gramophone Record?

The life-span of the shellac 78 r.p.m. disc was 60 years. The vinyl disc was born in 1948, and the manufacturing of vinyl records has, for all practical purposes, ceased. The CD may well have an even shorter life.

A hint as to the future can be acquired from the recording studios, which, thanks to digital recording, are moving to quite new methods of processing sound. Digital recording does not need to be stored on tape in the traditional way. It consists of numbers which can be stored in a computer's memory. In broadcasting studios, tape recorders are already becoming obsolete, and many recording studios have also gone over to 'tapeless recording'. For the present, it is true, even a computer needs a magnetic tape or disc to assist its memory.

The editing of a recording in digital form opens up quite new possibilities for processing it. The recordings in the memory of the computer, which correspond to the tracks of a multi-track tape recorder, can be made visible in a graphic form on the screen of a terminal. In subsequent processing they can be mixed together at whim; passages of the recording can be shifted with extreme precision from one place to another, material can be constructed from different versions and then deconstructed. Most of these operations can of course also be done with analogue technology, but digital technology obviates the need for endless moving back and forwards of tape spools, there is greater precision and the danger of extraneous disturbance is removed.

The final result can be encoded onto a compact disc and marketed in that form, but there are other possibilities too. As the new millennium approaches there are at least four exciting avenues for development in recorded sound. First, it is certain that new types of sound carriers will become available. They may not differ that much from the CD, but it is possible to extend the length of a sound recording considerably from what it is now. Instead of an hour, it should, in theory, be possible to store on one disc the entire output of, say, Maria Callas or Elvis Presley. But it would also cost considerably more than a one-hour disc.

Secondly, it is likely that the videodisc (or at least video tape) will to some extent replace the gramophone record. This trend is already well advanced, and it is only a question of the extent to which it will happen. The inclusion of images increases production costs, and it is not necessarily an essential addition from the customer's point of view. Ultimately, the breakthrough of the videodisc is only likely to occur when the quality of sound and vision in television receivers improves from the present level.

Thirdly, we may achieve some kind of interactive disc, one on which the listener can have an influence. It could be compared to a multi-track recording where the listener performs the final mixing. The disc jockey, playing with two record players and a drum machine, is already exploiting this technique in a primitive form. In the 1980s the practice become common of releasing disco music in various versions simultaneously, from which the consumer could choose: the basic rhythm track (in the Jamaican style), a long (dance floor) and a short (radio) vocal version, as well as an edited version supplemented with extra effects. Why not let the consumer do this? Such a technique would be most popular with rock or experimental music listeners; it hardly fits the ideology of classical music to be able to change the interpretation of a Beethoven symphony from Toscanini-esque to Furtwängler-esque in the middle of a performance!

Fourthly, it is feasible that at some point in the future, recordings, as such, will no longer be produced at all, but that music will be supplied to the listener on request. After all, this is the principle on which radio works, but its shortcoming is that the listener cannot choose the programme himself. In theory it should be possible to develop a sort of gigantic jukebox from which the listener could choose the music he wants at the time he wants it, working either by telephone lines, by cable or on the air waves. Payment would be levied subsequently, as with a telephone bill, or when ordering, by credit card.

This fourth alternative deserves closer scrutiny. The global jukebox would enable record companies to sell music direct to consumers. It would reduce distribution and storage costs, and, from the viewpoint of the individual consumer, it would greatly expand the amount of music available to him or her. With the development of personal computers, with multimedia capabilities and the Internet, it has become common for record companies to offer music lovers audio samples of their new products on their home pages. Since 1993, the International Underground Music Archive has been offering on the Internet free music by new and unknown bands. In 1995, David Bowie became the first major artist to release a new single first on the Internet.

Today the quality of the sounds transmitted on the Internet is not much higher than the 78 r.p.m. record. Transmission speed and sound quality would have to be increased considerably. It is not clear how the distribution and billing of recorded music will be organized. Will the buyer be able to keep permanent copies of the music he buys, or pay again each time he wants to hear it? Various systems which are being proposed in 1997 by various companies are usually based on the idea of centralized storage of music in digital form, and a proprietary piece of software which enables the customer to download music via the Internet on his hard disk or a recordable CD-ROM disc. The customer is billed for each piece of music ordered. He can play the recordings as many times as he wants, but only on his personal computer, and it is not possible to make copies (except by using old analog methods). Several major record companies have already indicated their interest in such systems.

It is expected that a fair percentage of homes in industrial countries will have a personal computer and an Internet connection in the near future. But at the moment we do not know how much such services will cost and how wide their selection of music will be. Fans might be willing to pay a premium price to be the first to hear a new release by a favourite performer, but in normal circumstances music on the Internet will have to compete with record shops and the free music available on the airwaves. Over the years, millions of different records have been made by thousands of companies, and unless sound archives also open their collections to the Internet, it is not likely that the full range of recorded music will be available commercially on the Net.

In the long run, this trend might result in bigger changes than are immediately apparent. If it is really successful, it will spell doom for record shops. It might even change the balance between artists and record companies if artists can sell their products direct to the public. If music on the Internet can attract advertisers and sponsors, it might compete successfully with radio stations. However, the history of communications shows that not everything that is technically possible is necessarily economically or artistically sensible. Three-dimensional movies, the RCA VideoDisc and the first LP records in the thirties were inventions ahead of their time which did not survive. Depending on the technology used to record music, we will need producers of the calibre of Fred Gaisberg, John Culshaw and Les Paul, who are prepared to exploit the technical possibilities creatively. We also need far-sighted businessmen like Eldridge Johnson and David Sarnoff, who know how to unite technology and business. And finally we need a public that is prepared to pay for the end result.

CHAPTER NINE

A Hundred Years of Recorded Sound

The Musician Becomes Immortal

Many philosophers have pointed out that the invention of the art of writing – and especially the Greek alphabet – brought about a revolution in human thinking. Thanks to writing it was possible to store knowledge permanently. Human memory expanded enormously. The text took on its own life, which might be longer than the life of the one who wrote it. What is more, writing gave the reader the possibility of returning to the text at any time, reading it again and reacting to it. The art of writing meant a step towards a new kind of society. The invention of printing was a further stride in the same direction, though not such a big one.

Music, too, was first committed to memory using various systems of notation. Notation made the composer immortal. Notation was then put into print. However, notation does not signify the same kind of change for music that writing did for language and thought. Obviously notation has had a fundamental effect on the development of western music. Without notation it would have been impossible for first, polyphonic singing, and then, large-scale orchestral works to evolve. Notation needs alongside it the knowledge of performing practice, however. The recordings of Beethoven's ninth symphony by Furtwängler, Toscanini and Norrington will quickly demonstrate that musical notation does not tell us everything.

The limitations of notation are also demonstrated by the fact that many cultures that have developed their own writing systems do not use notes at all in their music. Indian music makes use of a notation system based on indigenous alphabets (Devanagari, Tamil), which, in principle, is just as exact as western notation, but in practice is restricted to music teaching and theoretical writings. The reason for this is that the musician is expected to perform the work in a different way each time. In fact, the situation was the same in 18th-century Europe: musicians were expected to make their own additions and cadenzas in the score.

It was the recording of sound that became the equivalent of writing for language. It made it possible to store sound permanently, and to copy it. The musician became immortal. At the same time music became a plurality: for the first time in human history it was possible to listen to different musics side by side, independent of time and place. The performance could be arbitrarily curtailed, repeated and renewed.

The invention of recording coincided with a change in approach to concert music. Even in the mid-nineteenth century the bulk of the music performed in concert halls and on the operatic stages of Europe was the work of living composers. By the arrival of sound recording, the situation was already changing. As the twentieth century dawned, the bias was in favour of dead composers. The performance of new music became an exception, and 'modern music' became a separate genre.

This change occurred independently of the advent of the gramophone record. The expanding record industry followed the currents of musical life and, at times, also reinforced them. The gramophone record closely followed Puccini and *verismo*. We can also hear on record all three sopranos who performed in the premiere of Richard Strauss's *Der Rosenkavalier* (1911). On the other hand, the premiere of *The Rite of Spring*, Schoenberg's change of style and the birth of the serial technique happened independently of the gramophone. There was no demand for this music on record. Recordings of concert music, on the other hand, enhanced the art of the soloists and interpreters even more clearly than the concert hall did. The great names in 20th-century music on record are not Stravinsky and Schoenberg, but Caruso and Karajan.

The close connections between records and popular music are not surprising. Music publishers and composers immediately saw in the gramophone a new way of disseminating their hits. Irving Berlin made his first record while he was still a singing waiter at a Manhattan beer garden. Nevertheless, it is interesting to examine how the relationship between records and popular music developed. Until the 1940s other channels were more important than records as disseminators of light music: first, sheet music, then the movies and radio. It is only since the fifties that record sales have been the decisive factor in the success of new compositions. But it was characteristic that records became an essential factor in the development of jazz.

Jazz would certainly have developed and spread outside the United States in any case, but much more slowly. It is both paradoxical and illustrative of the nature of recordings that the gramophone record, which freezes the music played on it for all time, turned out to be of crucial importance as a mediator for improvised music. The record stored and disseminated only one improvised solo at a time, yet it gave the listener the opportunity to repeat that performance, hear the nuances of the playing once more and digest its internal logic. It was through the medium of gramophone records that the improvisational technique associated with jazz spread so quickly to Europe, even to places where no live American music had ever been heard.

In the same way the gramophone record emphasized the role of the performing artist in popular music. As late as the 1920s the composers of hit tunes were better known than their singers. Crosby, Sinatra and Presley created new styles of interpretation whose influence became widespread through the medium of records. We know the tunes by their performers: 'Hound Dog' is Elvis Presley's; only professionals remember its composers, Leiber and Stoller.

Since the 1960s new recording technology has given birth to totally new ways of creating music by storing and assembling sounds together, by 'writing' them into the memory on tape. In this process notation is not necessary at all. Music is born in the studio, layer on layer. After being released, if the record becomes popular, it has been the performers' thankless task to try to reproduce the sound of the record on stage. An ever greater proportion of the music we hear nowadays originates from records.

The average person in industrial countries listens to over an hour of recorded music each day, either directly or on the radio. The record has become the most important factor guiding the development of music. Over the years records have undergone continuous technical development. We can objectively measure the improvement in reproduction of frequency range and dynamics. We can also estimate how faithfully sound equipment reproduces the sound stored on the record. This is, of course, important to the listener who wants to relive, by means of a record, the experience of, say, hearing a great orchestra in a good concert hall.

From another point of view, however, the technical perfection of sound reproduction is of less importance. If we believe that the task of a record is to reproduce music in the same way that the task of the written word is to channel thought, even imperfect technology is good enough. If we get hold of a book from which time has worn away some individual letters and even the corners of some pages, we can still reconstruct the text on the basis of its thought content. In the same way the human brain can reconstruct the message of music stored on a disc, even if the frequencies above 3000 Hz are missing and the scratch of the record is at times as loud as the music. In this sense every historic recording can be of value despite its technical faults. If we could hear Liszt or Bolden playing from wax cylinders, we would be prepared to overlook the absence of the higher frequencies.

The advent of the computer is certainly not as great a revolution as the invention of writing, but in many people's opinion it is a more significant innovation. Printing made possible the multiplication of written texts in their existing form. The computer makes the text constantly changeable, and allows interaction between author, text and reader. This is as true of music transformed into digital form as of text stored in a computer. But this revolution is only beginning, and we cannot yet see where it will lead in the case of music.

The Collective Memory of Music

Tens of thousands of records of various kinds are available in record shops in any big city today. No one knows how many different records and cassettes have been issued in the world, but a cautious estimate would put it somewhere between one and two million. A listener who is interested in the history of recording, however, will, sooner or later, find himself in a situation where the recording he is looking for is not available. Recordings constitute the world's collective memory of music. But compared to the amount of printed matter that has appeared in the world, the number of existing recordings is still modest. It is fairly easy to get hold of almost any publication issued in the world, if one is prepared to go to a bit of trouble. Unfortunately the situation with recordings is much worse. The writing of this book arose from the idea that there are people who are interested in other recordings than those that are available at any time at the local record shop or on the radio. If the enthusiast is mainly interested in new, contemporary recordings, then there is a rich choice available. Many record shops also sell records by mail, and there are those that specialize in mail order sales – some even list their stocks on the Internet. With the growth of free trade, it has become increasingly easy to order records even from foreign sources.

To order records, one must know what records are available. In the United States, England and Germany catalogues regularly appear which include all the records on the market. In the United States, the famous *Schwann* catalogue has now been divided into separate classical and popular editions. In England, concert music is collected in the *Gramophone* catalogue, other music in the *Music Master*. The latest editions of these catalogues together contain details of over 100,000 currently available records. Not all records are available in the shops, however. Reissues do appear fairly frequently, but old records are deleted at the same rate. Many interesting records have never appeared in any other form than 78 r.p.m. The disappearance of the LP caused huge gaps in recording history. Although many LPs will be reissued on CD over the years, a lot of good music will be consigned to oblivion.

The enthusiast who wants to expand his collection backward in time does, however, have many opportunities. Numerous publications appear for various kinds of record collector which contain valuable information and contacts. There are shops specializing in old records from which one can even buy Edison cylinders. Many collectors and specialist shops regularly publish auction lists and mail order catalogues. Appended to this book is a list of collectors' magazines (although it should be remembered that the information rapidly goes out of date).

The historic record enthusiast ought, in the first instance, to learn to use discographies – record catalogues which attempt to list in as much detail as possible all the records by a particular artist, composer or record company, whether or not they are available. Traditionally, the best discographies cover the jazz and blues fields, where the catalogues approach completeness. But discographies have also been published of historic opera records, rock, the output of particular record labels (Sun, Atlantic, Chess, Melodiya, and so on), of Spike Jones's 'music' and even of Italian *zampogna* bagpipes. The most sought-after old records may be very expensive. Nevertheless, there are extremely few really expensive records, if you compare the prices with, say, the market for antiquarian books. On the other hand, a collector will soon find that records are often hard to buy; they can be had more easily through exchanges. In the late 1950s, far-sighted collectors were buying up old stocks of outmoded 78 r.p.m. records cheaply. The disappearance of the LP presents the same kind of opportunities.

Eventually the person interested in old records will turn to sound archives. Most countries today have a national sound archive – sometimes connected to other instutions, such as the national library or a film archive. These archives generally strive to collect as complete a collection of recordings published in their country as possible, as well as international recordings and materials related to music and the recording industry. The National Sound Archive in London, which collects radio programmes, field recordings, wildlife sounds and other types of sound recordings in addition to gramophone records, is one of the best-known institutions in this field, and is frequently visited by researchers from other countries. In the United States, the task of the national sound archive is, in practice, divided between the Library of Congress in Washington and a number of more specialized sound archives in various cities. If major sound archives can ever make at least part of their holdings accessible to researchers on a 'global jukebox', which would soon be technically feasible, this would increase their importance enormously.

Epilogue: Wanda Landowska and the Little White Dog

Wanda Landowska (1879–1959) was a Polish-born harpsichord virtuoso and music scholar who had had a great influence on the growth of interest in performing music on original instruments. She recorded prodigious amounts, particularly the music of Bach, Mozart and Couperin. In the 1950s she wrote the following comment as a note to a record of hers released by RCA, on the significance of the gramophone record:

> Blessed is he who invented recording! But what a pity that he was not born centuries earlier! Think only of all that we would be able to hear and therefore understand better. Oh, the unending research in libraries and museums, the readings and collations of texts, the maddening desire to know the truth! . . . Reading, always reading . . . but how did it sound? What were the tempi, the registration of a fugue on the harpsichord? The ornamentation of a largo? The dynamics of Mozart's and Haydn's pianoforte? Handel's manner of improvising?
>
> Just imagine if, in the midst of these tormenting thoughts, we could place on our phonograph a recording of Scarlatti playing some of his sonatas or of Mozart improvising cadenzas for one of his concertos! Imagine Bach's playing captured on records; his touch, his tempi, his registration, the unexpectedness of his inspiration, the pulsation of his heart . . . I hardly dare to think of it; I stagger at this idea. Little white dog, all ears and so attentive, if only you had been there some two hundred and fifty years ago! Bach, source of miraculous life, kept alive forever! . . .
>
> Yet a recording catches only one moment, one aspect of an interpretation, when there are a thousand and one others, always different.
>
> And here lies the tragedy of recordings!

(From Restout, 1964; 3rd edn 1981, pp. 358–9)

Bibliography

Åhlén, Carl-Gunnar (1984) *Det mesta om tango* ('Everything about the Tango'). Stockholm: Svenska Dagbladet.
— (1987) *Tangon i Europa – en pyrrusseger? Studier kring mottagandet av tangon i Europa och genrens musikaliska omställningsprocess* ('The Tango in Europe – a Pyrrhic Victory? Studies on the Reception of the Tango in Europe and its Musical Adaption Process'). Stockholm: Proprius.

Allen, Daniel (1981) *Bibliography of Discographies. Vol.2: Jazz*. New York: Bowker.

Allen, Walter C. and Rust, Brian (1958) *King Joe Oliver*. London: Sidgwick and Jackson.

Andersson, Muff (1981) *Music in the Mix: The Story of South African Popular Music*. Johannesburg: Ravan Press.

Ardoin, John (1982) *The Callas Legacy*. New York: Scribner's.

Bardong, Matthias, Demmler, Hermann and Pfarr, Christian (1992) *Lexicon des deutschen Schlagers*. Ludwigsburg: Edition Louis.

Batten, Joe (1956) *Joe Batten's Book: The Story of Sound Recording*. London: Rockliff.

Bauer, Roberto (1947) *The New Catalogue of Historical Records, 1898–1908/09*. London: Sidgwick and Jackson.

Baumbach, Robert W. (1981) *Look for the Dog: An Illustrated Guide to Victor Talking Machines*. Woodland Hills: Stationery X-Press.

Beadle, Jeremy (1993) *Will Pop Eat Itself? Pop Music in the Soundbite Era*. London: Faber and Faber.

Beizhuizen, Piet (ed.) (1959) *The Industry of Human Happiness: A Book of Commemoration by the International Federation of the Phonographic Industry*. London: IFPI.

Bennett, John R. (1981) *Melodiya: A Soviet Russian L.P. Discography*. Westport: Greenwood Press.

Bolig, John Richard (1973) *The Recordings of Enrico Caruso: A Discography*. Dover: Eldridge Reevens Johnson Memorial.

Borovsky, Victor (1988) *Chaliapin*. London: Hamish Hamilton.

Borwick, John (ed.) (1983) *The First Fifty Years: Celebrating the Fiftieth Anniversary of IFPI*. London: IFPI Secretariat.

Cable, Michael (1977) *The Pop Industry Inside Out*. London: W.H. Allen.

Canning, Nancy (ed.) (1992) *A Glenn Gould Catalog*. Westport: Greenwood Press.

Chapple, Steve and Garofalo, Reebee (1977) *Rock 'n' Roll is Here to Pay: The History and Politics of the Music Industry*. Chicago: Nelson-Hall.

Charosh, Paul (ed.) (1995) *Berliner Gramophone Records: American Issues, 1892–1900*. Westport: Greenwood Press.

Chew, V. K. (1981) *Talking Machines*. London: Science Museum.

Clough, Francis F. and Cuming, G.J. (1952) *The World's Encyclopaedia of Recorded Music*. London: Sidgwick and Jackson.

Clurman, Richard (1992) *To the End of Time: The Seduction and Conquest of a Media Empire*. New York: Simon and Schuster.

Collier, James Lincoln (1987) *Duke Ellington*. London: Michael Joseph.

Collier, Simon (1986) *The Life, Music, and Times of Carlos Gardel*. Pittsburgh: University of Pittsburgh Press.

Collins, John (1985) *African Pop Roots: The Inside Rhythms of Africa*. London: Foulsham.

Coplan, David (1985) *In Township Tonight: South Africa's Black City Music and Theatre*. London: Longman.

Creighton, James (1974) *Discopaedia of the Violin, 1889–1971*. Toronto: University of Toronto Press.

Culshaw, John (1967) *Ring Resounding: The Recording of Der Ring des Nibelungen*. London: Secker and Warburg.

— (1981) *Putting the Record Straight*. London: Secker and Warburg.

Cunningham, Mark (1996) *Good Vibrations: A History of Record Production*. Chessington: Castle Communication.

Cuscuna, Michael and Ruppli, Michel (1988) *The 'Blue Note' Label: A Discography*. Westport CT: Greenwood Press.

Danielou, Alain (1952) *A Catalogue of Recorded Classical and Traditional Indian Music*. Paris: UNESCO.

Daniels, William R. (1986) *The American 45 and 78 r.p.m. Record Dating Guide, 1940–1959*. Westport CT: Greenwood Press.

Davis, Clive and Willwerth, James (1975) *Clive: Inside the Record Business*. New York: William Morrow.

Davis, Gillian (1981) *Piracy of Phonograms*. Oxford: ESC Publishing.

DeFoe, George and Martha (1982) *International New Wave Discography*. New York: One Ten Records.

Delaunay, Charles (1936) *Hot Discography*. Paris: Jazz Hot.

DeLong, Thomas E. (1980) *The Mighty Music Box: The Golden Age of Musical Radio*. Los Angeles: Amber Crest Books.

Denisoff, R. Serge (1975) *Solid Gold: the Popular Record Industry*. New Brunswick: Transaction Books.

— (1986) *Tarnished Gold: The Record Industry Revisited*. New Brunswick: Transaction Books.

Diaz Ayala, Christobal (1994) *Cuba canta y baila: Discografia de la musica Cubana, 1898–1925*. San Juan: Fundacion Musicalia.

Dixon, R.M.W. and Godrich, John (1970) *Recording the Blues*. London: Studio Vista.

— (1982) *Blues and Gospel Records 1902–1943* (3rd edn). Chigwell: Storyville.

Fagan, Ted and Moran, William R. (1983) *The Encyclopedic Discography of Victor Recordings. Pre-Matrix Series*. Westport: Greenwood Press. (Includes, as an appendix, a history of the Victor company by Benjamin Aldridge.)

Fahey, John (1970) *Charley Patton*. London: Studio Vista.

Farrell, Gerry (1993) 'The early days of the gramophone industry in India: Historical, social and musical perspectives'. *British Journal of Ethnomusicology* 2(2).

Friedwald, Will (1995) *Sinatra! The Song is You: A Singer's Art*. New York: Scribner.

Frith, Simon (ed.) (1993) *Music and Copyright*. Edinburgh: Edinburgh University Press.

Gaines, Steven (1988) *Heroes and Villains: The True Story of the Beach Boys*. London: Grafton.

Gaisberg, Fred (1942) *The Music Goes Around: An Autobiography*. New York: Macmillan.

Gelatt, Roland (1956) *The Fabulous Phonograph*. London: Cassell.

George, Nelson (1986) *Where Did Our Love Go? The Rise and Fall of the Motown Sound*. London: Omnibus Press.

Gillett, Charlie (1970) *The Sound of the City: The Rise of Rock and Roll*. New York: Outerbridge and Dienstfrey.

Gillett, Charlie (1974) *Making Tracks: Atlantic Records and the Growth of a Multi-Billion-Dollar Industry*. New York: Dutton.

Gordon, Robert (1986) *Jazz West Coast: The Los Angeles Jazz Scene of the 1950s*. London: Quartet Books.

Graham, Margaret B.W. (1986) *RCA and the VideoDisc: The Business of Research*. Cambridge: Cambridge University Press.

Gray, Michael (1987) 'Recording Reiner'. *Absolute Sound* 12(49).

Gray, Michael and Gibson, Gerald (1977) *Bibliography of Discographies. Vol. 1: Classical Music, 1925–1975*. New York: Bowker.

Green, Victor (1992) *A Passion for Polka: Old-Time Ethnic Music in America*. Berkeley: University of California Press.

Gronow, Pekka (1975) 'Ethnic music and the Soviet record industry'. *Ethnomusicology* 19(1).

— (1976) 'Recording for the "Foreign" series'. *JEMF Quarterly* 41 (Spring).

— (1979) *The Columbia 33000-F Irish Series: A Numerical Listing*. Los Angeles: John Edwards Memorial Foundation.

— (1982) 'Ethnic recordings: An introduction', in *Ethnic Recordings in America: A Neglected Heritage* (author unknown). Washington: American Folklife Center.

— (1996) *The Recording Industry: An Ethnomusicological Approach*. Tampere: University of Tampere Press.

Grubb, Suvi Raj (1986) *Music Makers on Record*. London: Hamish Hamilton.

Guttmann, Alfred (1929) *25 Jahre Lindström 1904–1929*. Berlin: Carl Lindström AG.

Hall, David (1940) *The Record Book*. New York.

— (1980) 'An era's end'. *ARSC Journal* 12(1,2) (obituaries of Dario Soria and John Culshaw).

Hamilton, David (1982) *The Listener's Guide to Great Instrumentalists*. New York: Quarto.

Hammond, John (1977) *John Hammond on Record*. New York: Summit Books.

Heylin, Clinton (1994) *The Great White Wonders: A History of Rock Bootlegs*. London: Viking.

Hill, Dick (1993) *Sylvester Ahola: The Gloucester Gabriel*. New Jersey: Methuen and London: Scarecrow Press.

Hill, Donald R. (1993) *Calypso Calaloo: Early Carnival Music in Trinidad*. Gainesville: University Press of Florida.

Hirn, Sven (1981) 'Puhekone–fonografi–gramofoni valtaa Suomen'. ('The talking machine–phonograph–gramophone conquers Finland'), in Strömmer, Rainer and Haapanen, Urpo, *Suomalaisten äänilevyjen luettelo 1920–1945*

('Catalogue of Finnish Records'). Helsinki: Suomen äänitearkisto.

Holmes, John L. (1982) *Conductors on Record*. London: Victor Gollancz.

Holmes, Thomas B. (1985) *Electronic and Experimental Music*. New York: Scribner's.

Holst, Gail (1975) *Road to Rembetika: Music of a Greek Sub-culture*. Athens: Denise Harvey.

Horowitz, Joseph (1987) *Understanding Toscanini*. London: Faber and Faber.

Hughes, Patrick (1992) 'Girl you know it's industry: Milli Vanilli and the industrialization of popular music'. *Popular Music and Society* 16(3).

Hunt, John (1987) *From Adam to Webern: The Recordings of von Karajan*. London: Short Run Press.

— (1988) *The Furtwängler Sound*. London: Furtwängler Society.

— (1994) *A Notable Quartet: Janowitz – Ludwig – Gedda – Fischer-Dieskau*. London: John Hunt.

— (1995) *Musical Knights: Wood – Beecham – Boult – Barbirolli – Goodall – Sargent*. London: John Hunt.

Jasen, David A. (1973) *Recorded Ragtime 1897–1958*. Hamden: Archon.

Johnson, E.R. Fenimore (1975) *His Master's Voice was Eldridge R. Johnson*. Milford: State Media.

Jones, Geoffrey (1985) 'The Gramophone Company: An Anglo-American multinational, 1898–1931'. *Business History Review* 59(1).

Jorgensen, Ernst, Ransmussen, Erik and Mikkelsen, Johnny (1986) *Reconsider Baby: The Definitive Elvis Sessionography 1954–1977*. Ann Arbor: Pierian Press.

Joshi, G. N. (1984) *Down Melody Lane*. Bombay: Orient Longman.

Kanahele, George (1979) *Hawaiian Music and Musicians: An Illustrated History*. Honolulu: University of Hawaii Press.

Kaplan, E. Ann (1987) *Rocking Around the Clock: Music Television, Postmodernism and Consumer Culture*. New York: Methuen.

Kawabata, Shigeru (1991) 'The Japanese record industry'. *Popular Music* 10(3).

Kempster, Chris (ed.) (1996) *History of House*. London: Sanctuary.

Kinnear, Michael S. (1985) *A Discography of Hindustani and Karnatic Music*. Westport: Greenwood Press.

— (1994) *The Gramophone Company's First Indian Recordings, 1899–1908*. London: Sangam Books.

Koenigsberg, Allen (1969) *Edison Cylinder Records, 1889–1912. With an Illustrated History of the Phonograph*. New York: Stellar Productions.

Koski, Markku, von Bagh, Peter and Aarnio, Pekka (1977) *Olavi Virta*. Helsinki: WSOY.

Kukkonen, Pirjo (1996) *Tango Nostalgia: The Language of Love and Longing*. Helsinki: Helsinki University Press.

Laing, Dave (1985) *One Chord Wonders: Power and Meaning in Punk*. Milton Keynes: Open University Press.

Laird, Ross (1995) *Tantalizing Tingles: A Discography of Early Ragtime, Jazz, and Novelty Syncopated Piano Recordings, 1889–1934*. Westport: Greenwood Press.

Lambert, Dennis and Zalkind, Ronald (1980) *Producing Hit Records*. New York: Schirmer.

Lammel, Inge (1979) *Diskographie der deutschen proletarischen Schallplatten aus der Zeit vor 1933* ('A Discography of German Proletarian Records from the Time Before 1933'). Leipzig: VEB Deutscher Verlag für Musik.

Lange, Horst H. (1966a) *Jazz in Deutschland*. Berlin: Colloquium.

— (1966b) *Die deutsche '78er' – Discographie der Jazz und Hot-Dance-Musik 1903–1958*. Berlin: Colloqium.

Leadbitter, Mike and Slaven, Neil (1968) *Blues Records 1943–1966*. London: Hanover.

Lebrecht, Norman (1996) *When the Music Stops... Managers, Maestros and the Corporate Murder of Classical Music*. London: Simon and Schuster.

Leimbach, Berthold (1991) *Tondokumente der Kleinkunst und ihre Interpreten 1898–1945*. Göttingen: Author.

Lewisohn, Mark (1988) *The Complete Beatles Recording Sessions: The Official Story of the Abbey Road Years*. London: Hamlyn.

Lotz, Rainer (1991–1997) *Deutsche Discographie: Tanzmusik, Vols. 1–6*. Bonn: Birgit Lotz Verlag.

Lotz, Rainer and Pegg, Ian (eds) (1986) *Under the Imperial Carpet: Essays in Black History 1780–1950*. Crawley: Rabbit Press.

Lowe, David A. (1987) *Callas as They Saw Her*. London: Robson.

Lynge, Birgit (1981) *Rytmisk musik i Grönland* ('Rock in Greenland'). Århus: PubliMus.

Mackenzie, Compton (1955) *My Record of Music*. London: Hutchinson.

Malone, Bill and McCulloh, Judith (eds) (1975) *Stars of Country Music: Uncle Dave Macon to Johnny Rodriguez*. Urbana: University of Illinois Press.

Manuel, Peter (1993) *Cassette Culture: Popular Music and Technology in North India*. Chicago: University of Chicago Press.

Marco, Guy and Andrews, Frank (eds) (1993) *Encyclopedia of Recorded Sound in the United States*. New York: Garland.

Martin, George (1979) *All You Need Is Ears*. New York: St Martin's Press.

Marty, Daniel (1977) *The Illustrated History of the Talking Machines*. Lausanne: Edita.

Methuen-Campbell, James (1984) *Catalogue of Recordings by Classical Pianists. Vol. 1: Pianists Born to 1872*. Chipping Norton: Disco Epsom.

Miller, Russell, Boar, Roger and Lowe, Jacques (1982) *The Incredible Music Machine*. London: Quartet Books.

Mirtle, Jack (1986) *Thank You Music Lovers: A Bio-Discography of Spike Jones and His City Slickers, 1941–1965*. Westport: Greenwood Press.

Moore, Jerrold Northrop (1976) *A Voice in Time: The Gramophone of Fred Gaisberg 1873–1951*. London: Hamish Hamilton.

Muirhead, Bert (1983) *Stiff: The Story of a Record Label*. Dorset: Blandford Press.

Murrells, Joseph (1984) *Million Selling Records from the 1900s to the 1980s*. London: Batsford.

Nettl, Bruno (1985) *The Western Impact on World Music: Change, Adaptation and Survival*. New York: Schirmer.

Niles, Don (1984) *Commercial Recordings of Papua New Guinea Music 1949–1983*. Boroko: Institute of Papua New Guinea Studies.

Noebel, David (1974) *The Marxist Minstrels: A Handbook of Communist*

Subversion of Music. Tulsa: American Christian College Press.

O'Connell, Charles (1947) *The Other Side of the Record*. New York: Alfred Knopf.

Page, Tim (ed.) (1984) *The Glenn Gould Reader*. New York: Alfred Knopf.

Pandit, S. A. (1996) *From Making to Music: The History of Thorn EMI*. London: Hodder and Stoughton.

Pleasants, Henry (1974) *The Great American Popular Singers*. New York: Simon and Schuster.

Pohlman, Ken (1989) *The Compact Disc: A Handbook of Theory and Use*. Oxford: Oxford University Press.

Poyser, Tina (ed.) (1996) *The Recording Industry in Numbers '96*. London: IFPI.

Priestley, Brian (1988) *Jazz on Record*. London: Elm Books.

Read, Oliver and Welch, Walter (1976) *From Tin Foil to Stereo: Evolution of the Phonograph*.

Restout, Denise and Hawkind, Robert (1964) *Landowska on Music*. New York: Scarborough Books.

Riess, Curt (1966) *Knaurs Weltgeschichte der Schallplatte*. Zurich: Droemer Knaur.

Rumsey, Francis (1990) *Tapeless Sound Recording*. Borough Green: Focal Press.

Ruppli, Michel (1980) *The Prestige Label: A Discography*. Westport: Greenwood Press.

— (1983) *The Chess Labels: A Discography*. Westport: Greenwood Press.

— (1994) *Discographies. Vol. 1: Swing*. Paris: AFAS.

Ruppli, Michel and Daniels, Bill (1985) *The King Labels: A Discography*. Westport: Greenwood Press.

Rust, Brian (1978a) *Jazz Records 1898–1942* (4th edn). New Rochelle: Arlington House.

— (1978b) *The American Record Label Book: From the 19th Century Through 1942*. New York: Arlington House.

— (1979) *British Music Hall on Record*. Harrow: Gramophone.

— (1980) *Brian Rust's Guide to Discography*. Westport: Greenwood Press.

Rust, Brian and Debus, Allen (1973) *The Complete Entertainment Discography from the mid-1890s to 1942*. New Rochelle: Arlington House.

Rust, Brian and Walker, Edward S. (1973) *British Dance Bands 1912–1939*. London: Storyville.

Rutz, Hans (ed.) (1963) *65 Jahre Deutsche Grammophon Gesellschaft, 1898–1983* ('65 Years of Deutsche Grammophon Gesellschaft'). Hanover: DGG.

Sanders, Alan (1984) *Walter Legge: A Discography*. Westport: Greenwood Press.

Sanjek, Russell (1988) *American Popular Music and its Business, Vols 1–3*. Oxford: Oxford University Press.

Scholes, Percy A. (1924) *The First Book of the Gramophone Record*. Oxford: Oxford University Press.

Schonberg, Harold C. (1987) *The Great Pianists*. New York: Simon and Schuster.

Schulz-Köhn, Dietrich (1940) *Die Schallplatte auf der Weltmarkt*. Berlin: Reher.

Schwarzkopf, Elisabeth (1982) *On and Off the Record: A Memoir of Walter Legge*. London: Faber and Faber.

Scott, Michael (1977) *The Record of Singing, Volume 1 (to 1914)*. London: Duckworth.

— (1979) *The Record of Singing, Volume 2 (1914–1925)*. London: Duckworth.

— (1988) *The Great Caruso*. London: Hamish Hamilton.

Sears, Richard (1980) *V-Discs: A History and Discography*. Westport: Greenwood Press.

Segel, Harold B. (1987) *Turn-of-the-century Cabaret*. New York: Columbia University Press.

Shaman, William (ed.) (1994) *EJS: Discography of the Edward J. Smith Recordings. 'The Golden Age of Opera', 1956–1971*. Westport: Greenwood Press.

Shaw, Arnold (1968) *Sinatra: Retreat of the Romantic*. London: Allen.

— (1978) *Honkers and Shouters: The Golden Years of Rhythm and Blues*. New York: Collier.

Sherman, Michael W. (1992) *The Collector's Guide to Victor Records*. Dallas: Monarch Record Enterprises.

Solomatin, V.A. (1989) *'Melodia' – Yesterday, Today and Tomorrow*. Moscow, Melodia.

Southall, Brian (1982) *Abbey Road: The Story of the World's Most Famous*

Recording Studios. Cambridge: Patrick Stephens.

Spector, Ronnie and Waldron, Vince (1991) *Be My Baby*. London: Pan Books.

Sperr, Monika (ed.) (1978) *Das Grosse Schlager-Buch: Deutsche Schlager 1800 – Heute*. Munich: Rogner and Bernhard.

Spottswood, Richard K. (1990) *Ethnic Music on Records: A Discography of Ethnic Recordings Produced in the United States, 1893 to 1942*. Urbana: University of Illinois Press.

Stapleton, Chris and May, Chris (1987) *African All Stars: The Pop Music of a Continent*. London: Paladin.

Staubmann, Helmut (1984) *Zur Situation Österreichischer Tonträger/produzenten: Ergebnisse einer Umfrage* ('On the Situation of Austrian Record Producers: The Results of an Inquiry'). Innsbruck: Universität Innsbruck.

Steane, J.B. (1974) *The Grand Tradition: Seventy Years of Singing on Record*. London: Duckworth.

Stewart, Stephen M. (1983) *International Copyright and Neighbouring Rights*. London: Butterworths.

Titon, Jeff Todd (1977) *Early Downhome Blues: A Musical and Cultural Analysis*. Urbana: University of Illinois Press.

Toop, David (1984) *The Rap Attack: African Jive to New York Hip Hop*. London: Pluto.

Tremlett, Georg (1990) *Rock Gold: The Music Millionaires*. Boston: Unwin and Hyman.

Umbach, Klaus (1990) *Goldschein-Sonate: Das Millionenspiel mit der Klassik*. Frankfurt: Ullstein.

U.S. Congress, House of Representatives (1960) Hearings, Subcommittee of the Committee on Interstate and Foreign Commerce. Payola and Other Deceptive Practices in the Broadcasting Field. Washington: Government Printing Office.

Vernon, Paul (1995) *Ethnic and Vernacular Music 1898–1960. A Resource and Guide to Recordings*. Westport: Greenwood Press.

Volkov-Lannit, L.F. (1963) *Iskusstvo zapechatlennovo zvuka* ('The Art of Recorded Sound'). Moscow: Iskusstvo.

Vreede, Max (1971) *Paramount 12000/13000 Series*. London: Storyville.

Wale, Michael (1972) *Vox Pop: Profiles of the Pop Process*. London: Harrap.

Wallis, Roger and Malm, Krister (1984) *Big Sounds from Small Peoples*. London: Constable.

Watson, Eric (1975) *Country Music in Australia*. Kensington: Clarendon Press.

Webb, Michael (1993) *Lokal Musik: Lingua Franca Song and Identity in Papua New Guinea*. Boroko: National Research Institute.

Welch, Walter L. and Burt, Leah Brodbeck Stenzel (1994) *From Tinfoil to Stereo: The Acoustic Years of the Recording Industry, 1877–1929*. Gainsville: University Press of Florida.

Westerberg, Hans (1981) *Boy from New Orleans: Louis 'Satchmo' Armstrong on Records, Films, Radio and Television*. Copenhagen: Jazzmedia.

Williams, Richard (1974) *Out of his Head: The Sound of Phil Spector*. London: Abacus.

Wimbush, Roger (ed.) (1973) *The Gramophone Jubilee Book, 1923–1973*. London: The Gramophone.

Zwerin, Mike (1985) *La Tristesse de Saint Louis: Swing Under the Nazis*. London: Quartet Books.

Periodicals

ARSC Journal (Association for Recorded Sound Collections)

IASA Journal (International Association of Sound Archives)

JEMF Quarterly (John Edwards Memorial Foundation, defunct)

Recorded Sound (British Institute of Recorded Sound, now National Sound Archives; discontinued)

Collectors' magazines

Absolute Sound

Hillandale News

New Amberola Graphic

Record Changer (defunct)

Record Collector (two publications with the same title – one for opera, one for rock)

Record Research (defunct)
78 Quarterly
Storyville
Talking Machine Review

Current trade publications

Billboard
Music and Media

Trade publications no longer appearing

The Columbia Record
Edison Phonograph Monthly
Grammofonnyi mir
IFPI Newsletter
Phonographische Zeitschrift
Talking Machine News
Talking Machine World
Voice of the Victor

(For a more detailed listing of relevant periodicals, see article 'Sound recording periodicals' in Marco and Andrews, 1993.)

Index

Index

Index